CHILD DRAMA

CHILD DRAMA

Peter Slade

Foreword by
DAME SYBIL THORNDIKE

UNIVERSITY OF LONDON PRESS LTD

ISBN 0 340 08598 3

Eighth impression 1971
Copyright © 1954 Peter Slade

All rights reserved. No part of this publication
may be reproduced or transmitted in any form or by
any means, electronic or mechanical, including
photocopy, recording, or any information storage and
retrieval system, without permission in writing from
the publisher

University of London Press Ltd
St Paul's House, Warwick Lane, London EC4

Printed and bound in England by
Hazell Watson and Viney Ltd, Aylesbury, Bucks

375.371/332
DS63

113188

FOREWORD

FOR me this is a very important book because it is about something for which I think Drama—the Theatre—should exist. A playhouse is not only a place where one passes an evening of pleasure with one's friends—a sort of jolly party. It is something far more significant than that. Acting is the art which is common to all of us (everybody can act—more or less !). It is in a way a curative art—also an art which can help to build human beings into something better and more understanding than they are by nature—to build them into sensitive creatures able to feel the sorrows and joys of others as their own. Also by incarnating themselves as actors in other people's lives they can rid themselves of—throw off from themselves—the things they like least in their natures, and so often only recognize in other people. So, by living in the lives of others and with an eye and mind imaginatively tuned and objective, they may effect real cures of their own failings.

Now, Mr. Slade has worked this out in a very able way ; he has discovered how, in children, much may be helped and conquered by the simple performing of a Rite—a Play. He has found in the Play a releasing—a loosening as it were of inhibitions, and many good results have come about with so-called difficult and problem children by the very fact of their being able to "make a play", and work off sometimes excess of high spirits and temper, sometimes excess of shyness and fear of others ; all sorts of inhibited things are brought to light, put into an art form and cast off, or resolved, after which something may be built anew for them—a more free and happy life.

Why this book has excited me so much is because what Peter Slade has done for children I believe the Theatre should be doing for grown-up children —for ordinary human beings. There is profound teaching in this book on the service of the Art of the Play.

This is the first time that anyone has perceived, let alone written on, Play and Drama in so full and all-embracing a manner. Peter Slade has written one of the really important books of our time, and reveals himself as one of the great specialists on children and drama. In addition, his book will have a very real influence on the theatre of the future.

SYBIL THORNDIKE

5

PREFACE

WRITING books is not my *métier*. But wherever I go and speak people ask me whether I have written anything on the subject of Child Drama. When a publisher courageously invited me to do so, it seemed that perhaps the time had come.

Those readers who really know and love Children may understand this book. I beg that lovers of theatre will remember that I am one also, and will not react emotionally without due consideration. My task was to provide notes on the observation of thousands of Children during the last twenty-five years or so, in this country and abroad, and to add some conclusions upon what I saw.

Groups of teachers and individual doctors and specialists in various parts of the world, who are kind enough to keep in touch with me, have advised on what questions, remarks and answers to include, having regard to what in their opinion would clarify the subject.

This rather considerable amount of material has been edited and arranged by Mr. Brian Way, a pioneer with Children and theatre, to whom I am very grateful. For to me the subject is now so familiar that I no longer know what is difficult to understand. To me it all seems eminently lovable and perfectly plain : there exists a Child Drama which is an Art Form in its own right, and that is what this book is about.

PETER SLADE

ACKNOWLEDGMENTS

The author would like to thank all those people, both young and old, who have helped in compiling this information; Mr. Victor Thompson for his patience in obtaining so many of the photographs; and the City of Birmingham Education Committee for giving their kind permission to include some reports on visits to their schools.

Acknowledgment is also due to the following authors and publishers for kind permission to include copyright passages: to Messrs. Faber & Faber Ltd. for a quotation from *The Modern Movement in Art* by R. H. Wilenski; to Dr. W. Viola for three quotations from *Child Art* (University of London Press Ltd.); to Messrs. Denis Dobson Ltd. for two passages from *Dramatic Work with Children* by E. M. Langdon; to Messrs. William Heinemann Ltd. for an extract from *The Prophet* by Kahlil Gibran; to Messrs. E. Arnold & Co. for a quotation from *Education, Its Data and First Principles* by Sir Percy Nunn; and to Messrs. Allen & Unwin Ltd. for two passages from *Authority and the Individual* by Bertrand Russell.

INTRODUCTION

PETER SLADE is the first person to point out that there exists a Child Drama, an Art Form in its own right with its own shape and development, just as Prof. Cizek drew attention to the Child Art of painting.

This book is a comprehensive presentation of the subject of Child Drama. Parts of it were written ten years ago, and the whole completed nearly four years ago ; the interval between writing and publication has been taken up with sifting and compilation of material, and finally with the editing.

Whilst with the West Country Children's Theatre Company, on visits to hundreds of schools of all kinds, and in conversation with Directors of Education, Inspectors, Principals and staffs of Training Colleges, I continually sensed a chasm in educational thought ; that chasm has now been filled by the writing of this book, and my own and the hopes of many have been fulfilled.

Numerous problems besetting my own work were not answered until I met Peter Slade, particularly in relation to the difference between Drama as part of life and Theatre as an Art Form (Slade points out the difference) ; this I soon found was so for many, for his wealth of understanding and knowledge of the subject springs from twenty years devoted to painstaking observation, research and experimentation, backed by a capacity to perceive and document the minutest detail or the broadest concept, so that people from all over the world are now sending their problems to him.

Even before leaving school he had started work with children ; he has pioneered in this and Children's Theatre activities ever since, together with experiments in adult and youth theatre. After training and experience as an actor and producer—including running his own companies and training studio—he turned to teaching and education. He trained and directed experimental Children's Theatre and youth companies in the early 1930s ; at the Midland B.B.C. in 1936 he was the youngest " uncle " on Children's Hour in the country, and in 1937 he was Head of West of England Children's Hour, producing many of the early *Toytown* and *Castles of England* series. He trained and directed the first professional theatre company (the Pear Tree Players) entirely concerned with Education, and was one of the early supporters of drama-therapy in this country. The late Dr. Kitchin, first

Hon. Sec. of the Guild of Pastoral Psychology, said with reference to him : " Psychologists have so far been very concerned with the introvert. One day you will teach us about the extrovert." In his development of Drama as therapy, he began to see more and more that a simple but general prevention was what was necessary.

He has done drama advisory work in almost every county at one time or another, and is now Drama Adviser to the City of Birmingham Education Committee ; in 1948 the Educational Drama Association invited him to be its director. On three occasions he has been invited to tour America, twice in Europe, four times to Africa and farther East, but he considers his most important task to be in Birmingham. His methods, which are now having an influence on modern professional theatre training also—Schools of Drama in both London and Birmingham are now training on his lines—were discussed at the Educational Theatre Conference in the U.S.A., and provided a detailed report to UNESCO. He is now on the Sub-committee on Youth and the Theatre of the British Centre of the International Theatre Institute.

Despite all this, Peter Slade would be the first person to point out the value of experiments undertaken by others. His success, whether as producer or adviser, lies in his acutely sensitive awareness and quickly responding appreciation of the teacher's or actor's capacity, point of view and " where they have got to in themselves ". From perception of these points does his help commence, so that none of his work involves imposition of a new idea but rather organic development from what already exists.

In a similar manner, his book points a way rather than seeks for any dogmatic change, although anything like a complete acceptance of these methods would result in fundamental changes in almost any school. But revolution is not what he seeks.

To my mind, the importance of the book lies in its totality—its carefully unfolded theoretical considerations backed by intricate documentation of practical examples. It considers Drama as an important part of education, linking up with every other subject, and an aid to discipline and the three Rs.

This is not a book to read lightly or even quickly (although there is abundant humour in it) ; it is a text-book which, in spite of every painstaking effort to achieve some simplicity, requires deep study and consideration.

The book has been divided into three parts :

Part I.   Observation and General Theory.

Part II.   How to develop the Theory in practice.

Part III.   Subjects associated with Child Drama—puppetry, masks and make-up, films (and their effect on behaviour), and the vast realms of children's theatre and out-of-school work.

For the most part these considerations are inseparable, and, in order to preserve the link between them, Parts I and II are placed in similar sections and age groups, with Part III following as a logical outcome. The theory is put in detail, as it is doubtful whether people should try to do things without knowing why, but those who are not very good at theory might prefer to spend most time on the practical suggestions first and go back to theory afterwards.

As part of my task of editing, I have given references throughout to help the reader's search for particular points, and I have tried to make the index as comprehensive as possible ; throughout the book, the author had put capitals for special terminology and for things he thought important—I have retained these for the most part, but in some cases they have been dropped when it is thought the reader will be familiar with the term in question. Proper emphasis has been placed on the primary thought of the book— justice for the Child and the beauty of its works—by constant capitalisation of the word " Child ".

Because Peter Slade has worked for so many years in this field, and because in that time he has been asked constantly to lecture and write articles on this subject, the ideas and general approach are already being tried out in various parts of the world, not least in this country. Indeed, as the director of a famous theatrical company said at the beginning of a recent conference, " Mr. Slade is a prophet who, even in his own lifetime, has achieved a considerable following ".

BRIAN WAY,
Editor.

A SHORT LIST OF TERMS USED

ABSORPTION—being completely wrapped up in what is being done or what one is doing, to the exclusion of all other thoughts, including the awareness of or desire for an audience. A strong form of concentration. (See Plate 2 opposite page 49 and Plate 23 between pages 232-233.)

AUDIENCE PARTICIPATION—active participation by some movement, sounds or speech, in addition to emotional participation, by those for some reason constrained to remain outside the full action of play or a play. With Children it normally accompanies the early signs of sincerity and absorption in the Players. Fulfilment of the tendency towards audience participation ends logically in no audience. (See Plate 33 opposite page 296.)

BODY SPEECH—the use of the body rather than the tongue to express ideas, often employed by the young Child before being able, by lack of vocabulary, to develop language flow.

CHILD-TEACHER RELATIONSHIP—that which is purposely built up by trust, through confidence, sympathy, common sense and affection. The only sure basis for learning.

CHILD THEATRE—moments of continuous logical play with some resemblance to theatre, amounting to an overwhelming experience, which stand out from time to time during Child Drama.

DAWN OF SERIOUSNESS—frame of mind becoming apparent at about six years of age, and developing rapidly for the next four years or so, bringing with it ability to discern good and evil, awareness of society and joy in work.

GROUP INTUITION—perception through intuition of the needs or desires of the group, as opposed to oneself alone. Often present before awareness of group sensitivity, but able to be developed further through training in group sensitivity.

GROUP SENSITIVITY—a knowledge of the needs or desires of the group as opposed to oneself alone, arrived at chiefly through the senses after the dawn of seriousness.

HAPPINESS-DEVELOPMENT—a stage in creative expression aimed at by the teacher. First signs of joy dependent on out-flow.

HINTERLAND ACTIVITY—activity going on for love, in an absorbed fashion, generally out of view even when some other players are purposely *in* view. A natural development which takes place from time to time amongst Children. (See Plate 47, top picture, between pages 360–361.)

IN-FLOW—the taking-in of ideas and experiences, which becomes easier after a balance with out-flow has been achieved. At moments when the Child is prepared for or in need of out-flow, or when this amounts to a general condition in the Child, because of lack of opportunity, in-flow to a marked degree is virtually impossible of achievement.

IN-THE-ROUND—acting in a manner which relies on inner creative expression, leading to absorption, which in turn tends to a performance which can only be described as acting from self outwards in all directions and therefore all round the body. It is the quality of this playing which makes it satisfactory when seen from any or all sides, rather than just from the front. Sometimes loosely used as a description of the form in which a play is presented. In any case, acting-in-the-round would be necessary to presentation in a circular form. Acting-in-the-round is necessary for any good presentation in the Arena Theatre Form, and for adults needs a special training. The Child acts naturally in-the-round.

LANGUAGE FLOW—flow of words and imaginative ideas with pronounced philosophic or poetic quality, obtained by carefully providing opportunities for out-flow, through improvisation or creative drama.

OUT-FLOW—the pouring out of creative forms of expression, a tendency which can be regulated and encouraged, and which by frequent opportunity becomes a habit promoting confidence.

RUNNING PLAY—discernible phenomenon of intense and sudden out-flow caused by joy, which finds expression in an abandonment of all else to a form of fleet running, generally with bent knees and arms outstretched. Is in part a measure of the success in achieving out-flow. (See Plate 3 opposite page 64.)

SINCERITY—a complete form of honesty in portraying a part, bringing with it an intense feeling of reality and experience, generally brought about by the complete absence of stage tricks, or at least of discernible tricks, and only fully achieved in the process of acting with absorption.

CONTENTS

Foreword by Dame Sybil Thorndike 5

Preface 7

Introduction 9

Short List of Terms Used 12

PART I OBSERVATION

I The Beginnings of Drama. Birth to Five Years 19

II Dramatic Play. Five to Seven Years 37

III Drama and Play. Seven to Twelve Years 52

IV Twelve to Fifteen Years 69

V Comparisons 84

VI Language Flow (1) 93

VII The Aims and Values of Child Drama 105

VIII What Happens to Child Drama? 123

PART II THE TEACHER

IX Suggestions for Early Drama of Under Five Years 131

X Suggestions for Five- to Seven-Year-Olds 136

XI Suggestions for the Junior School 141

XII Suggestions for Twelve- to Fifteen-Year-Olds 151

XIII Language Flow (2) 163

XIV We Visit Some Schools 176

15

PART III

XV Out of School 242

XVI Children's Theatre 265

XVII Masks and Make-up 305

XVIII Puppets and Marionettes 315

XIX Films 322

XX Questions and Remarks 333

Index 364

PART I

OBSERVATION

Dedicated to
CHILDREN EVERYWHERE
particularly the unhappy ones

CHAPTER I

THE BEGINNINGS OF DRAMA
BIRTH TO FIVE YEARS

" Observation leads not only to aesthetic pleasure
but to a knowing and informed pleasure upon
which true criticism can alone be based."
Sir Francis Meynell

THIS book is about a very wonderful thing which exists in our midst but is as yet hardly noticed. It fails to impress itself upon so many not because it is weak, for it is vital, but because for the most part it is either callously neglected or arrogantly trodden under foot. For those who walk with their eyes open it can be found in any place on earth where there are Children, parched and battered though it may be. It is a creation, a skill. It blossoms where there are patience, understanding, happiness, freedom, observation and humility. It is born of Play and is nurtured, guided and provided for by the wise parent and the able teacher. It can be drawn out, though it may evolve alone to some extent. It can take the form of games, dramatisation, classroom drama, acting exercises, free expression, improvisation, activity method, and creative drama.[1]

We are to consider then a human activity, and a skilled one at that, though this skill is to a large extent unconscious.

In considering any subject it is well to discover first and to make decisions later. In considering a human activity, which is always a complex matter, we must watch first before coming to any constructive conclusions. I have said that we are to consider a skilled human activity. But Eric Gill, the sculptor, reminded us that " art " means " skill ". Is it also true that, in certain circumstances, " skill " of a certain kind might mean " art " ? If so, then we should consider carefully the words of R. H. Wilenski, who says : " The only critic who can tell us anything about a work of art is the man who has discovered the attitude, motives and procedure of the artist. . . ."[2] It is

[1] *Some of these terms have come in for certain abuse in recent years; the good which is shared by these things and which has not been recognised before is the existence of Child Drama, as here outlined by Peter Slade, without the knowledge of which only partial understanding and success are attainable.*—EDITOR.

[2] Preface to the first edition of *The Modern Movement in Art*, published by Faber & Faber.

precisely these three things—attitude, motive and procedure—that we must discover before being able to reach any conclusions concerning Child Drama, and our discoveries will be made only by painstaking observation.

All Child activity is fluid, and, whilst it is not essential to try to tie things down and label them, this has been done because it is a most important part of observation that we do actually discern the conspicuous differences which occur in these activities ; we are also concerned with the powers of recognition in the adult—powers that can be developed.

Much will also be said about the behaviour of the adult, because this has a profound influence not only on the Child, but also on its Drama.

Finally, in order to obtain a general picture of the various manifestations, it will be necessary each time to start at or near the beginning of each phase and to work up a little way, taking rather the stage when certain things tend to become conspicuous, and then to return to or near the beginning again for the next phase.

*   *   *

Because Drama begins so early, our observations start with the baby and the toddler, and, as we shall see, many of the earliest experiments of the baby are embryonic forms of Drama, Art and Music, and so differ from mere copying which also starts with the baby, first in action, then in speech.

When experimenting, the baby is more absorbed than when copying. Early creative speech is a sort of babble, intermixed with outbursts of clearly intentional grunt, cry or scream. All these show signs of experiment and gradual recognition of climax and mood. When a sound is loved it is repeated, sometimes at length, and this may be accompanied or followed by joyous laughter.

Early creative movement is of the hands and feet, kicking, extension of fingers, and later, with hands in front, there appear swift sweeping sideways movements, quicker than we can do it. Later still, these become more controlled and develop into that imperious sweep which clears the table of a meal in one fine moment of time. Adults have cause to dislike and even fear this gesture, which is, however, of supreme importance. It is not only an early expression of judgement, but also of criticism, and, in some cases, of self-protection, as when adults or Children want to pick up the baby (or even a Child of one year or over) when it is absorbed in something else. It is clearly an embryo form of creative attempt, too, accompanied by excitement.

The time beat [1] of the hands is different on all these occasions. But

---

[1] See also the section on the Distinction between Time Beat and Rhythm, on page 27.

careful observation helps us to link the movement, first of the whole arm (baby up till about two years), with the more localised movement, later, of the scribble when the Child begins to draw. Thanks to the light shed upon this subject by the guardians of Child Art, the scribble is now seen as an important stage of development. The sideways thresh is of importance, too.

From the baby stage upwards we notice other interesting things such as delight in nodding and shaking the head, rhythmic jogging up and down, and a steady kicking in certain time beats, first with the heel, later with the toe.

As the baby grows into a Child we see it learning to walk and deigning to notice people around it. By this I mean a clearer acceptance of *persons*, not the open staring of the baby. This stage is when the family atmosphere plays so important a part in the sensitive development of the Child (at least from one year onwards), because the noticing of people later blossoms into the gang stage,[1] apparent from about six years onwards. The gang stage and how it develops will be the test of the Child's social adjustment, and much depends on the earlier " noticing " and the family atmosphere.[2]

As encouragement and confidence come with adventures in walking, talking and gesticulating, we note the new powers being put to constructive uses. This is where the adult and Child may cross swords, for the Child considers crawling or waddling towards, clutching and then tearing a piece of paper to bits, a delightful and absorbing task. Eating the bits is good, too. The adult may hold a quite different opinion, particularly if the piece of paper was valuable. But here we have a clue. The piece of paper was valuable because it had a different value for us. To the Child it was valuable only in so far as it was a satisfactory type of paper for the adventure of tearing.

This puts a strain on all involved and has a consequent result on family atmosphere. Clearly a compromise must be found, and it is according to the wisdom of the adult at such times in finding a legal and reasonable opportunity for (in this case) tearing, that the Child will continue to be happy and not feel guilt, fear or disappointment because of violent handling.

The particular matter for us to note is that there *are* two points of view, and the Child has one, to which, in all justice, it has an equal right. This is very important, for if we are to understand Children we must realise that there is a logic and a reason for everything, which prompt certain actions.

[1] See also page 52 for further information about the gang stage.

[2] The point about family atmosphere was raised under another heading by Dr. Winifred Rushforth, in the Sixth Annual Report of the Davidson Clinic : " Increasingly we become aware that neurosis is a family problem." We are not concerned with neurosis here, except to note, in passing, certain times of importance which influence the Child for good or ill. These " times of importance " we *are* concerned with, because they may be moments of prevention.

It is these actions which confuse and often irritate the adult, and at such times we are apt to think that we alone are right.   If we have the opinion that we are in any way superior to the Child (and, looking round at the world today, that, one might think, is open to argument), we should use that superiority and prove its existence by arranging the type of compromise which is of the best advantage to the Child, and not just the easiest and most comfortable for us.   For this we need patience, understanding and humility.

Does this mean that the Child should never be corrected ?

Certainly not—that is anarchy, not freedom, and does not lead to happiness.   But it does mean that we should really think about what is reasonable and best for the Child, making allowance for its logic, behaviour, wish and adventure within those terms.   For example, continuing with our paper, to give the Child a piece of paper that it *can* tear would be reasonable, rather than smacking it or shouting.   And to salvage the remains of our important piece and to consider whether it was not our fault for leaving it about, would be some sign of mental superiority.

Similarly, we encounter banging and pulling apart.   This, too, we call destruction, but to the Child it is quite clearly something more than that—it is another adventure in investigation.

We are right—it is destruction.   The Child is right—it is investigation.   Who, then, has the greater claim ?   Again, both claims are based on a different set of values.   Both are right.   Pulling apart may have a destructive instinct to start it off, but it is also the result of an inquiring mind.   Who can say where destruction ends and construction begins ?   All we can hope to do is to keep our eyes open, our hearts warm and our heads clear.   We are so wonderfully rewarded for our trouble—but it is a trouble ; it is hard work seeing the other chap's point of view.

In all these cases it is for the older to prove that he is the wiser by finding the correct solution, and, whilst he is finding it, he should bear in mind that this banging develops forms of rhythm and climax.   It is the beginning of appreciation in music and language, and can be used in later years for an approach to literature and the dance.

Following hard on these early experiments by the Child, we come across the first obvious signs of Art Forms.   Little pattern arrangements are made with bits of dirt, matchsticks and fragments.   They are the sweet trail of the very young human, who tells us all day by his " making " and " doing " how far he has got with life.   We call it being untidy.   This is a wild generalisation, again based on a different set of values.   We are really confusing one abandoned and forgotten thing,[1] or something in our way, with a clear pattern formation of objects. How many grown-ups can discern the difference, and how many are aware of the existence of such a difference ? Finally, how many care ? To most of us it is all clutter.

There is an important distinction between the pattern formation and " one abandoned and forgotten thing ", for the former is recognisable for what we call Art, and the latter is a sign of Drama. In a general sense, of course, all is Drama, for Drama means " doing ". But my point here is that the abandoned thing, particularly when in an odd position, is exciting evidence that there has been Play. It is like finding the warm ashes of a camp fire when the dancing is done. And wherever there is Play there is Drama, but Drama of a kind which is not always recognisable to the adult.

It includes somewhere a form of impersonation—and who shall tell what leading roles that " abandoned thing " played ?—or was it the " property ", was it the warm and sticky treasure which helped some panting little ego to experience being king ? (Or as Adler might put it—to experience the Power Instinct—for the one-year Child does not yet know the meaning of king.)

In the tiny Child, who can say when Play ends and work begins, or work ends and Play begins ? All is a trial, all an adventure. Indeed, one may call it Play Trial.

Beginnings of the Game

By one year of age, though, we see distinct signs of the game appearing. This is often accompanied by a developing sense of humour. The game develops into forms of impersonation. All manifestations in which apparently the whole little body and Person are used to portray something, or in which the whole mind is concentrated on a Life situation, as in Play with dolls and toys, I would call Drama of the obvious kind. The quite distinct pattern-making one might call Art. But the boundaries can never be mapped, and, as a form of creative " Doing ", Art is Drama of the less obvious kind.[2]

[1] " Abandoned and forgotten things." These are *treasures after use.* By treasures is meant dolls, bricks, old paper, etc.—in fact, any object upon which love is momentarily poured or upon which affection which is somewhat difficult to understand is lavished for long periods.

[2] Other examples of the embryo art forms are : sucking a finger whilst at table and describing a circle with the wet finger on the table, or "painting" with spittle in the more localised movement of the sideways thresh, already mentioned. This is more obviously Art. Clenching the wet fist and banging the table with meaning (e.g. " more food ") is more obviously Drama, whilst banging the table with a clear interest in the sound value and time beat only, is more obviously Music. Where climax is intentionally brought in and enjoyed, Music might be said to be bordering on Drama. Music gives us considerable experience of mood and

With the appearance of the tiny Person's recognition of the game, and
with the development of humour, we find additions to the ancient joy of
" peep-bo ".   Joy in this curious sport begins before walking.   The loved
one is there—oh joy !   The loved one is hidden—expectant hope, accompanied by quiet.   The loved one is there again—joy, often accompanied by
chuckles or even screams of delight.   It is important to note that if the loved
one is hidden for too long, anxiety sets in.   This is akin to the tears shed
when the loved one goes out of the room.   Sometimes the leaving open of the
door has a certain calming effect.

All this, of course, has good reason.   To the ordinary Child the loved one
is immediately " *in* my life " or " *out* of my life " according to whether the
loved one is seen.   But as the Child gains confidence, it begins to try the
same trick.   This is partly copying, but the emotional experience quite
clearly is a form of creative discovery.   As the Child gets older and first
waddling begins, the trick emerges from primitive present and not-present
(by forms of hiding, perhaps only of the face or eyes), and there is an oozing,
in an interesting way, towards the door.   Peep-bo is tried round the edge of
the door.   As walking improves, we find a little running to the threshold,
followed by expectant pause, and then a dashing away.

All this begins with " in my life " and " out of my life ".   But it is now
the early distinct form of dramatic entrance and exit.   And what entrances !

Never again after that short early period does the same *flood* of Spring
come upon us.   It is accompanied in later years by a tendency to boisterous
excitement—charming, too, in quite another way, but never the same.   It is
important, of course, for the adult to take notice of all this, not by giving too
much attention, nor by laughing *at* the Child, but by taking part in the joy,
without fuss, and laughing *with* the Child.   Thus we *share* the experience,
and this sharing has a marked effect on the Child in its growing period. One
cannot over-stress the importance of this point, because we are concerned
here with the whole future behaviour of the little Person.

It is essential that we should at this time take care not to allow the trick of
showing off to develop.   Even if too much attention has been paid to the
baby earlier, this is our last chance to get things straight, for we are now firmly

dramatic climax, and knowledge of Drama can aid considerably in the interpretation of Music.
Again, the exact borderline cannot be fixed.   Dabbling and smearing fingers in a puddle and in
mud is more obviously Art, as also, at a later stage, is a sideways or forward-and-backward
sloshing of the foot in a puddle.   This is nearly always accompanied by extreme absorption
and quiet.   Stamping in the water, generally accompanied by exhilaration, is more obviously
Drama, and is related to the dance.   I say " *is* " here, instead of " might " or " maybe " because
exactly the same movement appears in genuine Child Dance in the years following.

planted in the relationship between actor and audience. Sharing *with*, in every aspect, is more healthy than acting *at*. The Drama, which some of us do not even notice, can now take a fatal turn and be a cause of great distress not only to the Child in later years, but to those grown-ups who have to live in the same community as the Man. Later we shall see that even the Child's acting, in further stages of what is more obviously Drama, suffers from this showing off. The tendency is always there. The desire to show off is a strong form of emotion, and it needs careful guiding.

The intelligent adult has a fundamental duty and responsibility here, as this sharing of experience breeds in the home an air of community—a tremendous bond in which everyone is involved. It is this which gives the tiny Person deep unconscious roots, and helps to develop the sense of stability. The Person does not know about all this. It only drinks the right emotion or the wrong. The wrong is a potent poison. In some ways this community-sharing spells " home " or " no home ", according to its success. It is an integral part of that family atmosphere of which we spoke before.

Drama means " doing " and " struggling ". It is the great activity ; it never ceases where there is life ; it is eternally bound up with mental health. It is the Art of Living. It works right only when the full healthy emotional side is correctly balanced with the physical. At all other times you get bad Drama, and it is interesting to note that this is not only so of Drama in its widest sense, as it is here used, but also of Drama in its most obvious forms.

Importance of the Circle

Almost as soon as the baby has any confident balance in sitting up (and even more so when sitting down, a little later), we find, together with a banging of heels, a sideways shove with one or both feet. This shove has the effect of turning the Child round, and is the first obvious sign of the circle or ring shape which takes so important a part in all Child activity,[1] and in primitive communities. Here the Child sits and describes a circle with its feet, whilst Self turns on the sitting-down part of the body. We see this happening before and after the Child can walk.

In the sitting-down circle we have a link with the adult actor's task when he attempts to dominate a given circle round his body, and with the teacher or discussion leader who holds together, in a spiritual clinch, a group of

[1] Parallel with this will go circular formations of the " Art " type, described by the index finger in spittle or some other " paint ".

people.   It is easier to do this if the group is in a circle or half-circle than if it is in front, in flat rows.   Flat rows tend to make us act *at* rather than share *with*.   We find the circle particularly referred to in the teachings on Drama of Stanislavsky, who suggests " circles of attention ".   This is the other end of the scale, for it is advanced *adult* artistry of which Stanislavsky speaks. He also says that even the externalising of a role is greatly influenced by the unconscious.

There is indication of a clear progression of behaviour from the earliest years in the Drama seen as a form of Life.   And back at our original end of the scale (the baby) again, it is interesting to note, as Dr. W. Viola [1] informs us, that William Stern, at the third congress for experimental psychology at Frankfurt-on-Main in 1908, commented : " Every man experiences himself as the centre of the space surrounding himself, but this space is only conquered by steps."   In the process of Drama it is conquered not only emotionally but literally " by steps ".   There is then a link, perhaps, between the inner processes of emotional behaviour and the " outward visible sign ".

Dr. Jean Biggar, speaking at Edinburgh in 1947 about the nature of the newborn baby, said : " In a sense he is the whole world.   As he begins to learn to use his own senses, touch, sight, hearing, taste, smell, he begins to distinguish between himself and other people and things.   There is now a *me* and a *not me*.   And that is how the ego is formed."

Here, then, it is suggested that even at the first step of personal growth there comes a consciousness of " me " and " not me ", or " me " and " that which is around me but not of me ".

We need not attempt to delve very far into the matter at this stage, or try to prove anything, except to note, as part of our process of considering and observing, that the circle and its implications are connected with something of inner as well as of external significance.   We should not forget, either, the importance attached to symbols by the Jungian school of psychology, and, related to this, that the circle appears often in primitive art.

To construct our progression, then, we might take Dr. Biggar's statement on the formation of the ego first, William Stern's next; then there is a big gap and we arrive at Stanislavsky.   Meanwhile, observation may help to fill in some of the intermediate stages :

The crawling Child often crawls in a circle.

When the Child can toddle we see, for instance, not only the revolving on

[1] Dr. W. Viola, *Child Art*, page 13.   Published by University of London Press.

one part of the body, but a waddling round in a tiny circle, and also turning round and round on a given spot by means of a dancing step. This is our first clear link with the dance of primitive communities. Exactly the same movement is used by them, but with clapping often added. No doubt Moorish influence brought the stamp to Spain too, and the castanet may be the miniature of other and vaster forms of percussion. A less subtle stamp is also found in the country dancing of most peasant communities as far north as Scandinavia. As the Child gets older, we see that clapping and gesture (starting with the sideways thresh) are slowly added to this circular dance, though spontaneous (unprovoked [1]) outbursts of this appear to occur less often between two years and four.

The Distinction between Time Beat and Rhythm

The late Miss Elsie Fogerty, in her comprehensive study *Rhythm*,[2] points out that there is a distinction between time beat and rhythm, and that although rhythm contains time beat it is not the same thing, but is animated by something else as well, which contains also forms of repetition.

This fact becomes important now in the life of the Child, as any time from one year onwards we find a testing out of the time beat, which increasingly develops into progressive attempts at creative rhythms, containing repetition, which have a quite different quality from those moments when using only the time beat. An indication of these creative moments, which helps one to take notice (if the sound itself is not enough), is the marked joy of accomplishment. Here again we should carefully share the pleasure without becoming an audience.

It is interesting to note that with adults also there is this testing and preparing, as differentiated from intended creation. In the rehearsal of both certain types of adult Drama and of Music, considerable study of " time " goes into rehearsal, but at the actual performance (and at rehearsals growing up to performance) something else creeps in. Time is there, but the whole creation becomes knit together in a recognisable rhythm. I have called this " Symphonic production ", when it is intentional and when it applies to a formally presented play.

The interesting thing is that, certainly after the age of six years or so, this gift of rhythm appears naturally in Child work, but the adult has to toil hard for it and often does not attain it. Those who are most successful in doing

[1] By " provoked " is meant here, for example, reaction to music, or stimulation by objects which inspire joy, when these are allowed purposely to the Child.
[2] Published by Allen & Unwin.

so are, for the most part, those who have actually retained it from Childhood. We call them great artists. The Child is a great artist too, sharing as it does this fine quality with the older great artists. But the art of the Child, for those who have experience of it, is the more lovable [1] because it is unconscious and therefore genuine ; however, it remains so only in so far as we guard it from showing off. When showing off starts, attempts at creation become profoundly conscious, and deterioration sets in. This in some ways appears to be slightly less so in Music, more so in Art, and most of all in obvious Drama.[2]

Although the Child makes increasing investigations into the use of the time beat, which are early advances in Music and Drama, it shows very little recognition of time in the sense of clock time. There is no real reason why it should, because at first the clock is a musical experience and is unreadable. Its dogma, anyway, is quite artificial, and bears only a small relation to the infinitely more important rhythms, tides and seasons of genuine life as we know it on this globe. The Child is closely attached to things genuine, and it is the intrusion of the artificial, through various laws of civilisation, which, coming as they do sometimes too suddenly, cause unbalance, through a quite correct unconscious knowledge that things (real deep-down things) have been changed from what they ought to be. Again one might almost say that civilisation is an imposed time beat, which does not always fit in with, and never equals in excellence or purity, the rhythmic breathing of Mother Earth. That is why we have to put our clocks back. Primitive people live by Mother Earth, who tells them everything. It is interesting, for instance, that they are undisturbed by the civilised tempest of puberty, and that their Art Forms develop without break. In this they are firmly balanced.

The Child in its early stages is much the same. Its only clock is the meal-time clock. That is as near as it can get to our time. Certain regularities it can sometimes manage, but, as it develops powers of concentration, it becomes absorbed in experiences and takes no pleasure in being disturbed. Increasingly after one year until about six, and according to temperament, any interruption in this important " absorption " is a genuine emotional

---

[1] To most adults who have not fully experienced it, this may appear to be somewhat extreme.

[2] There is less showing off when creating *Music* because, as the mind is on the creation of the sounds, there are not so many opportunities (showing off may come later). In *Art*, the time comes when the Child notices other Children or the teacher taking an interest in his creation (and there is usually good opportunity for this) and so begins to paint in an " ungenuine " way to attract attention. In *Drama*, it is obvious that the opportunities to show off are there, and the Child will seize these as coming first, before the creation itself.

torture (sometimes causing hysterical crying and flinging oneself on the floor). This may affect the Child's future ability to learn, for violent reaction gives way to indifference, which is the enemy of health and eager concentration. We must take care not to buy obedience at too high a price.

For almost all clock time, other than the meal time, young Children have something approaching complete indifference and profound contempt. In this they are better artists than we are, for it is right to do a job and finish it. But not all adults are able to perceive that there is a job, nor a finish and a " near-finish ". Interruption at the "near-finish" is not so violent a frustration, so if we watch for this we can thereby keep our own laws and yet give some latitude to the Child on occasions when split-second " time " is not absolutely necessary.

" Absorption " is always a test of the importance of an experience to a Child. We should try not to interrupt when it is absorbed. The arch enemy of absorption is clock time. It's always time : time to get up, time to wash, time for lunch, time for bed—often at the very moment when the greatest experiences and creative work are going on.

But we have to be wise about this, because a life of absolutely no timetable also brings a sense of insecurity. Some daily things which are steady or near steady are essential ; for the rest, as much latitude as is reasonable— non-interruption brings content and confidence. This is true of a baby's sleep and of that magic thing which develops so rapidly after the recognition of " game "—that is Play.

Play

Some Child observers would make a distinction between Realistic Play and Imaginative Play. But, in fact, Play (certainly in the earlier stages) is so fluid, containing at any moment experiences of everyday outward life and of imaginative inner life, that it is debatable whether the one should be judged as a different activity from the other. It is important, of course, that the difference is understood, but the distinction pertains to the intellect rather than to Play itself. The Child develops towards reality as it gains experience of life. This is a process rather than a distinction.

The only true distinction in Play is that of personal Play and projected Play.

Personal Play is obvious Drama ; the whole Person or Self is used. It is typified by movement and characterisation. We note the dance entering and the experience of being things or people.

Projected Play is Drama, too ; the whole mind is used, but the body not

so fully.   Treasures [1] are used which either take on characters of the mind
or become part of the place (" stage ", in a theatre sense) where Drama takes
place.   During moments of typical projected Play we do not see the whole
body being used.   The Child stands still, sits, lies prone, or squats, and may
use chiefly the hands.   The main action takes place outside the body, and
the whole is characterised by extreme mental absorption.   Strong mental
projection is taking place.

Playing with things starts with the baby, but it is more accurate to call
this " elementary testing experience ".   It is often a grim business, though
sometimes it brings laughter.   When the rudiments of this testing are
mastered, life affords opportunities for Play.   It is rather like learning to
skate.   Whilst in the falling-over stage we wear skates but cannot be said to
skate.   When we master, through testing, we gain an experience which
enables us to begin to receive the joys of skating itself.   This brings a flood
of new tests, but now they have joy and a new interest in them.

To my mind, Play in its full, wonderful sense, begins in this way.   It is a
definite stage arrived at, in which one can detect a new life experience starting.
It may begin early or late.

In this process of skating on the great Lake of Life, the Healthy Child,
except for unfortunate moments, is now able to remain standing or to proceed (literally) forwards and backwards.   It is a state of great satisfaction,
bringing with it a feeling of accomplishment.   This feeling, however, is only
complete in so far as emotional experience balances with exterior experience.
The link between the imaginative dream life and reality is becoming of increasing importance.   The most obvious exterior form of mastery is that of
walking.

Walking brings with it new possibilities of Play.   It is this that makes
(for most Children) the years between the ages of one and five a period of
rapidly increasing dramatic experience, during which personal characterisation, using the whole body and soul, is closely bound up with the power of
walking and running.   This desire in Man to travel has, in modern times, led
to a quite extraordinary craze for speed.   We have to guard the Child against
this as far as is possible, for it may be the cause of inner emotional hurry
which brings anxiety and tiredness.   The best form of guarding is a full
appreciation of the Child's *Play*, and the arranged allowance for it.

*Through Play, experiences and rhythms are discovered by each Child in so
far as it is able to absorb them at the time.*

[1] See footnote 1 on page 23.

The Child's own pace is very important, though it may be maddeningly slow for the adult. If slow Children have to be hurried at certain times they should be allowed to be slow at others. They may have a slow personal rhythm and/or be " slow developers " (i.e. a Child whose mind or personality is developing slowly, not necessarily a backward Child). They will be slower if continually bullied over their slowness, as this makes it more difficult for them to concentrate on their natural growing pace. Stammering and other ailments can sometimes be traced to speed anxieties started early in life. An occasional exhortation to speed at certain times is another thing altogether, and may be necessary for most Children.

As Play is the chief method of finding personal rhythm, we should consider it as very important. We, the wonderful adults, have even shifted the emphasis from Child's *Play* to *Child's* Play, as if this were an unimportant, easy, even silly thing, and as if we could do better. We have " put away childish things " no doubt we think. But most of us have not. There is a great difference between " Childlike " and " childish ". It requires little experience of human nature to perceive that in fact we retain, for the most part, what is childish—the passions—and tend to lose far too soon what is Childlike—that is what is good in the Child, such as simplicity (until spoiled), faith (until broken), imagination (until ridiculed), hope (until soured) and charity (until hardened).

Play is one of the best means of balancing the passions with the virtues in the Child. This is also true of the adult. We talk of " fair play " and " sportmanship ", which infer that the apparently aimless pursuits of leisure allow time in us for considerations of justice. No one who has watched a losing team pull round and win, or who has felt personal determination strengthen in adversity, can doubt that Play calls forth courage, both moral and physical. And out of this particular form of activity arises the term " team-spirit ".

Team-spirit is connected with a social consciousness. It is the development of Self outwards, towards a consideration of others. This binding together by consideration (conscious and unconscious in its effect) produces a form of group dynamic that is not at all unlike that intended " symphonic production " mentioned earlier. Indeed, one might feel that a first-class cricket or football team, working as one, is a perfect " production " in the sense both of aesthetic joy and as a mirror of Man's Activity (Drama). And, in that it is often produced conspicuously (production) for a body of attenders (audience), it is in fact Theatre. We should note, though, that it is by *personal* experience of Play that the adult obtains social standards, and that when large crowds (many members of which do not play) continually watch a few specialist players, the passions tend to predominate. " Do it yourself " is a healthy corrective.

Social Awareness through Play

It is not surprising to find, then, that Children, by personal Play, discover and evolve social obligations and graces. This is particularly true in the early stages of Drama when treasures [1] are employed. It is the terrible test of sharing what is loved, between the ages of one and five years, that builds a sense of co-operation ; and whether the gang stage,[2] which appears later (*circa* six years upwards), will be healthy or unhealthy, depends largely on the success of this process. Sharing, between one and five years of age,[3] is largely concerned with treasures, but not only is the emotion of love involved, but also the instincts of maternity and paternity, also self-defence and defence of *creations*. *Monuments*, I feel, is the right name for these creations. In the Old Testament we meet references to the strong urge to " build a tabernacle " (of stones). The Child's monument is of bricks, stones or anything to hand. Monuments are " anything by which the memory of a person or an event is preserved ", the dictionary tells us. This is why the Play test is so valuable for personal development, for interference with one's Monument by another person is an attack on preservation, and, perhaps, even on the dream perception of Home and Country.

As to the Drama, life situations are evolved round and projected on to these monuments from now on. How often one sees a screwed-up bit of old paper or an old match living between, say, two bricks and a piece of string (one-to two-year-old Drama) ; this develops into a doll living in a quite luxury flat of, say, a chair roof with brick walls round (five-year-old). The

---

[1] See footnote [1] on page 23.   [2] See page 52.

[3] Although there is not space here to go deeply into the very urgent problem of the only Child, we should not forget that the full sharing and balancing process is impossible for it, as a rule, unless other Children are in the same house—or street. This makes its entry into society so much more difficult, an inner loneliness remaining often throughout the whole of life. The only Child often has to remain a spectator by reason of its backwardness in social practice. It is an audience to the activities of others. This tends to stir the passions, and resentment easily turns now to introspection and recluse tendencies. The opposite of this is bursting out into uncomfortable and flashy leadership. The attendant troubles, which come with this, cause a frequent return to introspection. The more normal companions come to be suspicious and lose trust in such a leader. The position for the only Child is then worse. All this can be seen to start between two and five years, though from six onwards it is more apparent, particularly in gang activities.

Even first-born suffer to some extent, depending on how soon the next Child arrives.

life experience or " what might happen to the person living there " is now involved—in fact, study of civilisation.

For these reasons much agony is caused if the Monument is assailed. Both the creation itself and the Person in it may be involved, as well as all the instincts and emotions connected with them. The Person living there is part of Self, anyway. Because of this, and because of the " preservation " quality of Monuments, it is important for us to *try* to arrange for obvious creations to be left untouched. Automatic, unthoughtful clearing-up does not necessarily teach tidiness. It may teach " don't care ", by shrivelling of the young heart's affection. It is love for things and people which ultimately develops *care*, which leads to tidiness.

Drama, and Play tendencies involving intense story situation built around, with and as an integral part of Monuments, are quite obviously enriched if they can be continued from where they were left off. This can be *seen*. What is suffered cannot always be seen. So important is all this that the value of one room set aside for Children cannot be overstressed. Housing difficulties and social conditions make things very difficult for the Child, as well as the parent, but fortunately the need is being recognised.

Knocking down what appears to be one's *own* Monument is anything from quite fun to exquisite thrill. Thrill appears to enter into it exactly in proportion to musical appreciation of the sound involved, or to the violence of the Dramatic climax. In this last we have the link between personal action and projected Drama situations, because " I, the conqueror " personally knock down that which *was* a place for Drama to happen in. One can even invite or allow others to take their turn at this " destruction " after a time. Why ? Because at that moment it is not necessarily destruction in the full sense. It is certainly not destruction of the Monument (with all implications). The (mental) Monument no longer exists. What can be seen at this moment is chiefly an instrument for personal joy in Musical or Dramatic Activity, and can therefore be shared. In this moment, the Monument is an " abandoned thing " of the mind ; the treasure that is left (it looks the same to us) is now something else—an instrument or a property.

This sharing is part of the team dynamic, and it is this sort of manifestation, together with the many others, which leads one to urge the importance of Play as a particularly valuable human activity, shared by young and old alike. Mrs. E. M. Langdon, Department of Child Development, London University, in her *Dramatic Work with Children*,[1] says, for instance : " Social

---

[1] Published by Dennis Dobson, Ltd.

living is learnt by taking part in social situations, and the natural occasion for much of the young Child's social learning is through Play."

We do not like it when Children take our tennis balls and hurry off with them ; worse it is should they move a golf ball.   So, too, we should consider *their* view and *their* rules.   As we have discussed earlier, there are two points of view.   The Child's is as important as our own, and its needs are probably more important.   Our difficulty in assessing Children's needs are twofold. First, they have their point of view ; second, everything is so fluid that it is not always easy to recognise the various parts of Drama (doing) as they occur.

The moment of time when a Monument ceases to be a Monument and becomes, as it were, an abandoned thing—not necessarily in the physical sense (the physical is only the outward sign) but in the mind ; and the moment when this abandoned thing in turn becomes a treasure in use as a Dramatic " property " or Musical " instrument "—by which conquering (knocking down) may be enjoyed—such moments are certainly elusive, as, indeed, is the whole process.   But we can understand it the more easily if we will abandon clock " time " in our sense, and think in terms fluid.   We shall then be more able to follow the rapid mental changes and characterisations that often take place.   For instance, it is possible for a Child to be several people at once ; it can also be several things at once, or even several things *and* people.   Character may be changed in the middle of a sentence, and the people or things may be such as we have never considered.   Examples are : " a three-headed bicycle " (which I have been taught to ride), and " the String Man who has a knot in his tummy ", " the Worm Car " and " the Flying Pipe ".   I defy any adult to improve on these creations for sheer poetic imagination.   They would make good titles for plays, too, and the only well-known examples of our thought which appear to approach such quality are to be found amongst the old names we have given our public-houses ; next to this come local place-names.

In the Child's knocking-down process, the first movement employed is generally the sideways thresh, with the familiar difference in time beat and energy, according to whether the Child is listening (Music) or conquering (Drama).   This develops into occasional trials of forward-and-backward movements, interspersed with a knocking downwards, like hammering. The last does not always knock over.   Hammering for sheer delight in the *volume* of sound appears to come about the same time as the sideways thresh movement (*circa* one and a half years upwards).

Language develops through Play by stages, from squeaking and muttering to speaking. Singing, whistling and shouting also occur from time to time. We find here our first indication (from before one year of age, and rapidly developing from then on) of the great importance that accompanying sound (Music) has in Play.

Developments from Personal and Projected Play

Out of *personal* Play we may expect to develop later : running, ball games, athletics, dance, riding, cycling, swimming, fighting, hiking. These are forms of acting. To these should be added Acting in the full sense. Child Acting contains these things too, sometimes before the actor knows how to do them. Imagination and copying are mixed. Leadership and personal control are developed. Speech and Music are employed.

Out of *projected* Play we may expect to develop later : Art, playing instruments, love of freshwater fishing, non-violent games (from snakes and ladders to chess), reading, writing ; observation, patience, concentration, organisation and wise government. To these should be added interest in puppets and model theatres, and, in the full sense, Play Production. Speech and Music are employed, sometimes intermittently, sometimes as a running commentary.

In personal Play the tendency is towards noise and physical exertion on the part of the person involved ; and if noise is not employed, exertion is. In projected Play the tendency is towards quietness and physical stillness ; and if there is not quiet some physical stillness is there.

Throughout the whole of life, Man is happy or unhappy in so far as he discovers the right admixture for his life of these quite distinct manners of using energy. Both the type of person and the life occupation are connected with the balance of Self and projection. These two early types of Play have an important part in the building of Man, his whole behaviour, and his ability to fit in with society. And, though they are easily recognisable, they too overlap to some extent, and more so as we get older. Play opportunity, therefore, means development and gain. Lack of Play may mean a permanent lost part of ourselves. It is this unknown, uncreated part of ourselves, this missing link, which may be a cause of difficulty and uncertainty in later years. Backward Children often respond to further opportunities for Play, for this and other reasons. They build or rebuild Self by Play, doing when they can what should have been done before.

The Child who has the right opportunities will try out in personal and projected play many pieces of thought and experience between the ages of one and five years. Projected Play is more evident in the early stages, but, as mastery of the body comes, personal Play is more frequent and easier to distinguish. Thus Drama, always there, always vital, always beautiful, proceeds slowly from the less obvious to the more obvious, and thence to the unmistakable, though certain characteristics are recognisable throughout.

The two main forms of Play add qualities to each other, and also to the Person who plays. Thus projected Play is mainly responsible for the growing quality of *Absorption*, and, by absolute faith in the part portrayed, personal Play develops the quality of *Sincerity*. From now on the Child will show us these two wonderful qualities according to the richness of its early opportunities. By five years of age personal Play should at times be quite apparent, and, although Absorption will be far ahead of Sincerity still, the two qualities combined, together with a certain mastery of the body, should be strong enough for even the somewhat unobservant to perceive moments of unmistakable acting.

This now becomes, in its various forms, so established a part of young life, and is so easily recognisable, that it has come to be known as Dramatic Play. From this point onwards we shall be chiefly concerned with obvious Dramatic Play, because it too is a stage of development following hard on the heels of Play.

We have considered general activities of the young Child, many of which have clear or less-clear Dramatic qualities, and which, in turn, are undoubtedly related to the inner Self and to the past and the future ; and we have observed two main forms of Play. Throughout all this, one external sign and shape appears again and again. It is the circle or ring. This occurs in both personal and projected Play, and, even when the Child first draws a Man, that Man is round—nearly all head, like a great sun with tiny legs ; when hands appear, they are round, and so too are fingers ; even the hair is sometimes composed of shy half-circles growing out of the face of the sun. We shall continue to find the circle. We follow it into Dramatic Play. Play with intense dramatic quality should be firmly established by five years of age. What is known as *Dramatic Play* (an even further stage) is generally at least precariously established by five years of age, and should be firmly established by seven.

CHAPTER II

DRAMATIC PLAY. FIVE TO SEVEN YEARS

WE have spent some time observing the baby and the toddler, and we have also considered the adult's behaviour because of its profound influence on both the Child and its Drama.

What the Child does *itself* is intimately connected with the state of the Child, and this doing—Drama in the wide sense—has a close connexion with special forms of doing, or obvious Drama.   In the young Child most of the guidance may fall on the parent, directly or indirectly, but at the age of five the question of school enters, if Child centres of one kind or another have not entered before.   Increasingly, therefore, our observation takes place outside the home, and, though much of importance takes place outside of school too,[1] we shall here consider some aspects of Drama *at* school.

The Child of five years is still in urgent need of considerable time for Play.   In the preceding years the obvious dramatic quality of Play has been developing [2] towards a conscious recognition of Drama and its possibilities. This development takes place within the Child, but, though the Drama accords somewhat with our adult views, it is still far from the traditional adult notion and should remain so for some years if it is to be something which is genuinely of the Child.   *The Child's fully conscious recognition of Play as Drama should not be rushed*—a mistake often made by adults with Children of from five to seven years.

The slow dawning of the uses to which Drama may be put appears now in the form of clearly intended impersonations ; much outside experience is brought in ; there is more copying ; situations (more obvious) are used for playing out personal experiences ; treasures are used for working off emotions.   We note a good deal of loving and/or hating of dolls.   Great delight is taken in sheer noise such as banging and shouting.

Sometimes an inanimate object may be used for working off hate.   For example, a remark, typical of many I have heard, was : " That brick is very

---

[1] See Part III, Chapter XV.

[2] I intentionally avoid the use of the word " improving ", for that is a judgement by adult standards and does not allow of a standard according to Child values ; these are very beautiful and important in themselves, and it is for us to recognise them.

wicked. I'll 'ave to smack 'im. And if 'e's not good then, I'll stand on 'im. 'E's very rude. Keep 'im in prison ". There are many things involved here, but we might take a special note of the fact that the brick is *kept* in prison. It is kept for hating. Better that the brick be hated than a person. Too sudden a disappearance of things or dolls that are hated sometimes gives rise to a strong animosity towards some person ; or sulky behaviour may start. Likewise, the whole Play urge itself, containing love, hate and all experience, if not allowed and fully provided for, will have repercussions in other ways. Even adults talk of " taking it out of so-and-so ", and " don't take it out of me, just because——".

From earlier times we have another example of played-out hate (though here it was generally consciously linked with an individual) in the realm of witchcraft, when wax images were stuck with pins, with the intention that evil happenings might occur to the hated one. The Child is not usually so conscious as this. It is, however, aware of the pleasures of hating things, and realises that Drama adds to the joys of persecution, without necessarily recognising any person or circumstance that may, in some cases, have been the original cause of displeasure.

Amongst primitive people, images and hate spells continue to this day, together with legends of changing from animals to humans, and vice versa. The Child can be, or turn things into, anything at any time, and to this extent the process is the same. The Child is a *great* artist in witchcraft of every kind, though white wizardry is usually the power employed.

Sometimes adults are worried by the remarks and behaviour of the Child in its Play, as they often give us stark pictures of its own life-background, and we tend to recoil at what we see and hear. Are we, the intelligent adults, unable to face what the Child has to face ? We must allow a certain amount of playing out, for not only is this a relief to the Child, but it is a considerable confidence given us. We are sharing an important personal secret. We should not shut it up, nor rebuff it in any way. But it *is* possible to lead, by a word sometimes, to happier and richer things, and the Child will take the hint when ready.

As it has only just come through the chief years of Play trials and projected Play, the five-year-old still shows a strong tendency towards the use of treasures in Dramatic Play. It is apt to become over-greedy about these, and we do not always help it by giving it too much. Marked improvement in happiness and creation often comes with a certain austerity over treasures, whereas overloading beyond a certain point brings laziness, chiefly through mental indigestion. In haste and eagerness to stimulate, the adult often spoils the Child at this age. Too many toys are a cruelty. The treasures themselves are often too " real " ; it is the slightly unreal treasure which is the best friend at this age. For example, a paper crown may be kept for a long time, whereas one of wire and stones will be picked to pieces. Why ? Because the paper crown is " real " to the Child, and the real crown (real to us) is much better for a picking adventure than for wearing.

To understand this fully we have to be aware of something that pertains to all Play in the young Child, namely that our unreality is to the Child more like reality, since the greater part of its life so far has been of a drifting-mist consistency, with sudden vivid visions of fact and truth. And our reality is a perplexing unreality, conforming to which is the somewhat unpleasant task of all Childhood. Sometimes the lesson is never learnt.

So, then, the Child starts at a disadvantage and so do we, for the Child and adult look at life differently. The Child has got to come to a grown-up point of view in time, but we, on our side, should not hurry the process. Nor should we expect the Child to hold our own point of view even when it does become grown up. If a real Person has developed, there may be a new view.

Action and Words

Whilst young, however, the Person has ideas already. The ideas are shown to us both by words and action. Action tends to be used rather more by the five-year-old, no doubt because of its growing mastery over some forms of movement. We notice a tendency to stride about ; the sideways thresh has given way, via the sweep, to quite lordly gesture with clearly intended mastery of certain simple interpretation of mood, accompanied by some grace. Absorption keeps these movements graceful, but if too much attention is given to the Child then the whole turns to a showing off, and, at once, the stride becomes a strut, facial expression changes, and we note a glowing grin, with rolling eyes constantly heaving away from important things towards us. Concentration breaks down. We are outside this whole experience, though we may become a fatal instrument, and if we cannot do the right thing by our presence we are almost certain to ruin Dramatic Play.

Just because movement plays a greater part in the Drama at this time, speech is left a little to itself. Speech is by no means yet mastered, and will not be for some years, but now the Child increasingly recognises that movement is a language in itself. This can be, however, an obstacle to the development of actual speech, and when too many properties for acting are provided there is an even greater stress laid on movement, by concentration on exterior things—in short, on materialism.   Speech is of the inner Self and can be choked at this age.

Some observers feel that speech is only that which arises out of Play. This is certainly true of Play accompanied by too many properties, because the overloading stimulates too much, and the action relies heavily on the stimulation.   This type of action is easily recognisable by its lack of " speech " in the movement—that is movement used in itself as a beautiful form for conveying meaning.   In its own turn, therefore, it is not surprising that *actual* speech becomes very poor under these circumstances.   If less properties are provided, then there is more speech-by-movement, and more hope for real speech, which comes as an outburst, well timed, well planned, and with economy and conciseness.

Frequent periods of Play with no properties whatever, with stimulation relying entirely on sounds such as knocking, tapping of feet, gongs and drums, and music, brings concentration, and is an important reminder of the use of the ear as against the limbs.   It is this that begins to develop love of sound, which leads to speech.   There are indications that these experiences help to balance the capabilities of the Child, and that the flow of language released by them is strong enough on its own to stimulate moments of Dramatic Play.

The real and intense desire to communicate strengthens the quality of Sincerity.   This communication is lifted entirely out of the spheres of mere idle and pleasant enjoyment, which the use of too many properties indulges. And the concentration needed for the communication strengthens the quality of Absorption which, in its turn, wars against the evil of showing off.

Where the right conditions prevail we begin to see the now unmistakable signs of an *intended* Art Form, though at the age of five great moments occur only occasionally, increasing nearer six, and occurring *very often between six and seven*.   At seven one expects Dramatic Play to be firmly established, and, when carefully nurtured, it can be Play of a high quality.

Just as it has been suggested that too many properties may hamper natural speech and movement, so also too much dressing up hampers them— movement particularly.   The laws of economy and simplicity (as with the paper crown) hold good for the best expression in movement and speech.

The evil effect of too many clothes used too often can most easily be seen in types of movement associated with dance.   Not only does the Child find difficulty with its legs, but its gesture is greatly impeded, and the language which should be beginning to travel up the arm into the hands and eventually right off the finger-tips is gagged.

Imagination and creative energy can also suffer by too easy a passage at this age. " Too much too often " may even block the passage altogether. Man in his natural state uses what is nearest, and if there is nothing near does without. The Child is the same.

All this is associated with the two basic forms of Play, for, just at the time when (because of the strides forward in mastery of the body) it is the Person who needs developing through personal Play, too many material aids lead the mind away from Self and back to material investigation, and therefore to projected Play. The mental hesitation, which results in lack of Absorption (and a tendency to need more and more comforting and interest from others to make up for this), is a direct outcome of becoming wedged between personal and projected Play.

" Too much too often " does not lead, therefore, to full personal development ; it only seems to do so because stimulation has lately become the fashion, and has taken the place of utter lack of it ; this has suggested further stimulation. But we must be careful not to place *all* faith in objects. It is the human which matters, and it is the presence of older and wiser humans who know what is needed that helps to create an atmosphere of happiness and energy of a kind which surpasses that arising out of objects.

The materialist exterior influence of lighting and stages in infant schools can also act detrimentally to personal development and the Drama. So does the script play. These are out of the personal rhythm and context of the Child of five to seven years old. They bring the Child far too rapidly to the adult view, very often entirely cutting out vast realms of development and complete experiences which occur in the next ten years. These developments and experiences, some of which we may now pass on to observe, are the Child's natural heritage—and ours ; ours because most adults can now begin to enjoy the creations of the young to some extent, and, when we judge them in the way we set out to do, and when the right environment and the correct amount of aid are given to them, they proceed to acquire an intense beauty both of essence and of outward form.

Perhaps we have seen enough of Play now to realise that it is an inborn and vital part of young life. It is not even confined to humans, as animals also show us advanced examples. In the human, Play is not an activity of idleness, though it is often mistaken for such because the Child needs it so badly that it is preferred to our idea of work, particularly when the conditions of work are unhappy and when not enough Play is experienced. But it has not occurred to all adults that healthy Play, by its intense effort and constant discovery, is in itself a form of work—indeed one of the most strenuous and creative forms of work. Further to this, because of its qualities of constant discovery and its dependence on personal rhythm, it is the ideal form of education for each Person, according to his unhurried ability to absorb, remember and re-use knowledge.

So the Child at Play is not necessarily escaping a duty, of the kind we imagine, though it may be temporarily escaping, by an entirely natural and unconscious process, the full brunt of a particular worldly experience which it is not yet ready to face. When it is nearly ready to face it, it tells us so by what I have called the " near-finish " (of a particular piece of Play), and, as Absorption decreases and it nears our reality, it is the more likely to obey, in sweet reasonableness, the apparently mad demands of the uncomfortable dream world which the adult calls reality.

Play is the Child's way of thinking, proving, relaxing, working, remembering, daring, testing, creating and absorbing. Except for the actual physical processes, it is life. It may well prove in future years that if Play is the actual manner of a Child's way of life, then Play may be the correct approach to all forms of education. There are signs that many experienced persons already believe this, but the subject is beyond the scope of this book.

Discovery and Use of Space

Before the age of five, many experiments in the use of space have been made. Apart from the outstanding ones already remarked upon, we find the moving of objects from one place to another. These are systematically replaced by other objects. After walking is mastered, a small journey is often included. There is much repetition of movement, and a fairly steady time beat turns to a rhythm as the Child gets older. In this type of action can be traced not only Art pattern, but a form of sorting out and an early approach to exchange (money and barter consciousness), a certain feeling for the elements of mathematics.

But these actions are important to Dramatic Play because, whilst being primarily connected with projected Play, the inclusion of the journey and the careful placing of the objects concerns itself with space, and links it with personal Play through movement (i.e. the journey). It is part of the process towards Dramatic Play, one of the noticeable features of which is that, after preliminary testing, objects often end by being placed equidistantly from each other. We shall notice this equidistance more and more as time goes on, for it is the basis of that symphonic production which we considered earlier. (See Plate 2, opposite page 49, and Plate 40 in End Section.)

The little journey, too, is, after all, the most primitive form of " a move " (in the Dramatic sense). The Person moves from point A to point B, returns rhythmically, and is concerned with an intended arrangement of objects in an equidistant pattern. These inanimate objects of the one-to five-year-olds have, for most children of five years, become the *living* companions of school, and it is one of the most touching characteristics of Dramatic Play amongst infants that they try so hard to master equidistance, and attempt not to bump into one another. They are not always very successful in this, though, and perhaps one might be forgiven for suggesting that during a period of Dramatic Play in the average infant school (certainly in the younger classes of it) one has the impression of viewing a number of cheerful letter-boxes waddling, still with traces of uncertainty, and not minding too much if they bump into each other, but on the whole trying not to.

After the years of fruitful and often solitary projected Play, and with further certainties about Self, comes the need for more personal Play with others. It is now that the only Child comes in for special difficulties. Those used to some companionship find things easier, even if they have been overcrowded at home. Companionship is eternally bound up with space. My world may have been, up to now, largely Mine. Now it must be shared. Is there room for so many other people ? If so, how do they fit :

1. into my life ?
2. into the room I am in ?
3. into my Play ?

The answer is *always by sharing*.

They fit :

1. into my life by allowing others to share my emotions, property and rights.
2. into the room I am in by sharing my desk, table or floor space.
3. into my Play by sharing experiences, and by participating in what I do.

The most obvious forms of sharing [1] (and the successful or unsuccessful attempts at it) are connected with properties and space ; the rest are not easy

---

[1] Cf. page 32.

to see because they go on inside the Child, but their effects can be both observed and felt in subsequent behaviour. *Because of these sharing processes the right place for Dramatic Play is an open flat floor space.* The best Play takes place here.

As to Play itself, it is certainly not only a necessity for the Child but is the creation of the Child ; however, it is quite inaccurate to think that it springs entirely from the Child, because all sorts of experiences are drawn into it, generally with success. The little Artist uses everything it can lay its hands upon, and what the teacher or school can supply by way of friendship and atmosphere it lays its heart upon and uses too.

Three factors contrive against the Child's Dramatic Play :
    1. Too much help, either by word or use of objects.
    2. Adult " time ".
    3. *The wrong experiences of shape and space.*
Of these factors the third, as we shall see, is the most harmful.

If too much help is given too often, this can be equally dangerous, and, whilst there are ways of counteracting the effect of adult " time ", or even of carefully utilising it, this too can do great harm. But nothing can be done to mitigate the harmfulness of the wrong experiences of shape and space ; they destroy utterly the full glory of the Child's Dramatic Play. The Child will never be the same, and only the Child expert will be able to recover enough of the real Child to aid in any way the future crippled attempts at Dramatic Play. These are likely to be of an ordinary, vulgarised. stereotyped or even quite uncertain kind, and will never again compare with the original.

The main form of " wrong shape " experience is that of the proscenium theatre. It is often introduced, with the very *best* of intentions, far too early —even by those adults who love Children greatly, and who only wish for Children to have knowledge of what they (the adults) love.

At the risk of offending many well-disposed and genuine Child lovers, it is, however, necessary to state that the proscenium form of theatre has disastrous effects on the genuine Drama of the Child. All the slow and delicate natural processes of shape, space, sharing, mastery of the area round the body, depth discovery,[1] and integration of Self with others, to say nothing of personal creation, are shattered ; and the new blinding experience, not yet genuinely and *personally* arrived at,[2] is something to be tried and copied.

---

[1] See also pages 50, 58 and 66.
[2] The experience is not personally arrived at until *circa* thirteen years. See pages 70–73.

In this process the young Child loses confidence in its own work. This change is not so noticeable in schools where Dramatic Play of only a moderate standard is to be found ; indeed, the untutored adult eye may even feel that, for a time, certain " new ideas " entering Play are of benefit, and that experience of the proscenium show should therefore be encouraged. It is only when full appreciation of the Child's actual state of space discovery is realised, when the Child's own chosen and repetitive shapes in Play are fully recognised, when speech and movement, Absorption and Sincerity are carefully nurtured, and when the delicate beauties of the Child's own work are joyfully understood—only then is the full shattering effect of the proscenium show seen for what it is. The Child seizes on what it can—thus its own Drama needs guarding in some respects.

Because the Child seizes on everything to help it, it seizes also on adult friendship to aid it in inspiration. Play and games do arise spontaneously amongst happy Children, and at certain ages they have Dramatic quality, but *a very careful and discreet sharing in discovery with an adult* brings to Child Dramatic Play a geniune and fruitful experience.

The adult is vital to the best in this form of activity, which should be nurtured and cared for much as a gardener cultivates a flower. Like the flower, if it is left untended, it goes back to a wild state, and the weeds that come—fighting, getting hurt, cruelty, rudeness—will promote unhappiness and lack of confidence. These weeds are found often in the streets and playground, whereas in the happy school and fortunate home they can be plucked out.

In the right atmosphere, Child Dramatic Play develops slowly into story form from five years to seven, though there is still a lot of unlinked Play with hardly visible connexion.

We find, also, a curious coma-acting which is the later stage of the staring baby ; apparently nothing is happening, but a great deal really is. The Child is experiencing. It may break off in the middle of Play to consider its experiences, and, when the consideration or less conscious sinking-in has taken place, action and/or words start again. If Dramatic Play does not start, the Child often breaks into a run. This is possibly with the charming intention of trying to meet the adult half-way and make up for lost time, or it may be in order to dash after new experiences mentally, which brings a physical reaction. If less sense of hurry is experienced, a good deal of Absorption remains, and movement is then a leisurely skip which gives way to a gallop (at the " near finish " ?), and then perhaps the run.

Does the run come with the full finish of the experience ? We cannot quite know, but it appears like that.

These are all minor forms of Running Play.

Running Play

Running Play has special qualities. It appears to develop out of that early entry and exit, the running peep-bo, the dashing to the threshold and dashing away. The older Child now dashes to the threshold of new experiences, and away. But it dashes *into* rooms, as the material threshold now holds less awe.

There is also a Running Play of the street, which is often observed as a Play trial in the sphere of Music and Drama. This is concerned with time beat and a higher level. One foot runs in the gutter, the other on the kerb ; after a time the Child stops, turns round and the other foot takes the higher level. Very occasionally, creative rhythms are tried out. More satisfactory, as rhythm, is a slow, calm running of the rather older Child, with heavy footfall on the full pavement changed to a different sound when *down* and crossing the road, *up* and on along the pavement, *down* and across the road. Both these, whilst clearly wonderful to experience and exquisite to watch, are intensely dangerous for both the Child and the motorist, as movements are unpredictable and Absorption is terrific, to the exclusion of traffic-consciousness.

Hardly less dangerous is the instance of the circle, which appears occasionally, particularly near right-angle road junctions. The Child runs from one pavement with noisy steps, *down* on to the road, describing part of an arc, *up* on to the opposite pavement, round a bit and *down* again on to the road, forming three parts of the circle, and *up* on to the original pavement to complete the circle. Generally, at this time, the Child seems to be fairly wide awake (in our sense) and chiefly enjoying the circle, so approaching cars are more easily noticed. But if Absorption should set in, the circle might widen and the Child would run out past the right-angle junction into the main road. (See diagram.)

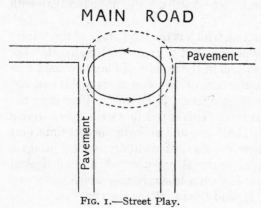

MAIN ROAD

Pavement

Pavement

FIG. 1.—Street Play.

These forms of Play are no doubt one cause of accidents. They pertain rather to personal Play, and owe their beauty to the fact that they are bound closely to a Self experience. They are nearly always played alone, though sometimes our first runner is accompanied by another ; but the other does not go through the same experience, as is clear from the lack of both interest and rhythm. This Child (generally younger) is running merely to keep up with the first.

The Running Play of the street, which also includes mixed walking and rhythmic skips or hops, so delicate and lovely to behold, is quite different from the careless running out after a ball or away from a companion, or the foolish adventure thrill of purposely running across a road as near the front of a car as possible. Running Play of the street has recognisable Music and Drama qualities, and in itself can be a first-class theatrical experience. It is clearly a tremendous personal experience, too.

I have mentioned Running Play [1] now, particularly of the street, because it seems to appear as a Form at about five years of age, although it does not attain its full beauty until the runner is nearly as much a master of running as of walking (*circa* seven years upwards).

There is also a cultivated flower of the Child's Running Play, which begins as a particular form of entry into a room. It has a shape of its own, and I have called it " cultivated " because it only appears, even as a bud, where certain happy conditions prevail. It can be found in the infant school, but, as we do not meet it in full bloom until after seven years of age, I will speak of it later.[2]

Shape of Acting

In conditions where the Child is happy enough to evolve Dramatic Play, aided or unaided, we see the simple elements of Life appearing in that Play. They appear so regularly and automatically that one cannot escape noticing

[1] The nearest adult approach to this experience (other than doing it oneself) is to hear, see or experience a good long jump when the " take off " is planned and accomplished as a climax to perfect mathematical striding down the short track ; also, the loveliest of all experiences— the full flight of hurdles perfectly flown in threes without a touch by a single member of the heat ; also the extraordinary ritual and Drama of the change of baton in a relay race. In general, all athletics arise, perhaps, out of personal Play, and have their direct link with Running Play.

[2] Through roller-skating there can also be discovered a substantial kingdom of Drama and Music, together with many mood and sense experiences. There is not enough room to observe it fully here, but it lies half-way between personal and projected Play and is associated with Running Play. The same basic shapes are to be found in it as those which occur in Child Play and Dance. It is important to note that it exists.

the continuing general pattern of personal development which exists, nor the fact that it is, in broad terms, the same for each Child.   This is not at all the same as saying that Children are all alike—they are quite different, each with its own individuality, a different rate of progress and a personal rhythm.

The constant repetitions and use of symbols in the realm of Child behaviour, also the acting out of situations sometimes before they can have been experienced, is entirely in line with the Jungian conception of the collective unconscious.   We find story themes concerned with birth, marriage, parenthood, death and resurrection.   All dolls and treasures are, in a manner, babies ; weddings always come into Dramatic Play, as do mothers and fathers, and people who are killed but often get up again (resurrection).   We also hear references to the hereafter and to eternity, and at five years there is already apparent a certain recognition of good and evil, or at least of opposing forces.

As we have seen, Dramatic Play is constantly fluid, and is quite unlike our conception of theatre.   Indeed, where our theatre is introduced too early (apart from the other things already considered [1]), the Child does not at first even connect the joys of its own form of Drama with what it attempts to do to please us.   To begin with, the Child is still greatly concerned with Self, and has been from babyhood.   But because of the expanding recognition of things and persons around it (the " me " and " not me " as earlier mentioned), gradual domination of ever-widening circles of attention begins to take place.   It is not surprising that this general attitude of the Child is continued in Dramatic Play.   Given a flat floor space and a happy atmosphere, there is, with each Child, the tendency to Absorption which marks genuine creation ; and, whilst absorbed, they are not conscious of being watched.   They act outwards from Self all round the body.

I have called this " acting-in-the-round ", and it is as near a description as one can find of what happens when Children act in their own way.   It is a description of a *form of acting*, but it is concerned only incidentally with the circle shape or playing or " *performing* in-the-round ".

Performing " in-the-round " is something quite different, though it is found that what the Child teaches us in qualities about acting-in-the-round is absolutely necessary to good arena theatre (of the adult kind).   It is vitally important that we fully appreciate what acting-in-the-round is, or we may never really understand or appreciate the genuine Drama of the Child.

When the Child is absorbed, it neither needs nor wants an audience, and,

[1] See page 44.

PLATE I

INFANTS. The Spiral at the " happy entrance." (*See* p. 49.)

JUNIOR MIXED. " The school uses sound a lot, and I counted twenty-one spirals being painted in the same room." This is one of them. Example chosen for clarity, though the opposite way round to usual " happy entry." (*See* p. 49.)

INFANTS. Close-up details of "happy entry" into a classroom.

Photos by Victor Thompson

PLATE 2

INFANTS. " Because the movement of this story is a slow and steady one when played, it is less impeded by dressing up than any other." (*See* p. 50.)

By courtesy of the " Birmingham Gazette"

Example of *equi-distance* used in patterns during play, as mentioned again and again. (*See* p. 43.) This is the Queen looking at her dishful. Is chess a development of this form of projected Play ?

SENIOR GIRL. Study of **Absorption**. (*See* p. 12.)

Photos by Victor Thompson

because it needs no audience, it faces in any direction and moves where it will. It is during this movement-at-will that the Child begins to cover the actual floor space in so interesting and beautiful a manner, filling the space as if it were a picture.   For this reason, if we are interested and can keep quiet, it is better to see genuine Dramatic Play looking down on it from above.   But an audience on the ground is a dangerous thing—it tempts the Child to show off, Absorption is shallower and Play deteriorates.   The joy of Dramatic Play is that it is the creation of the moment.   The energy and imagination *can* be interrupted, and then the " moment " is gone for ever.   Audience is often the enemy of the " moment ".

As with personal movement, the movement over the floor space deteriorates if too much costume or too many properties are used.   It is still an adventure for the five-year-old to move across a big space, and it does so less easily when hampered in movement.   Where this is fully understood and where sounds are used (as previously described for personal and speech development [1]), considerably more use is made of floor space.   Equidistance and avoidance of bumping comes quicker.

Recurring Symbols

There are two main shapes which occur all the time—one is the circle, the other is the spiral, which is always the shape of happy entry.   Where sounds are used, Children run joyfully into the hall (this is the bud of Running Play) and, running or dancing round, they form a spiral shape.   This changes to a circle (filled in), Children being more or less equidistant over the floor space.   When intended sound stops and story Play begins, the ring shape is seen again.   The ring in infant schools is generally a large one including nearly everyone, but it breaks into group rings from time to time.   In the spiral entry the little People nearly always run to the left with hearts to the centre [2] of the room ; this may be because their right legs are rather stronger. (See Plate I, opposite page 48.)

Painting and drawing are closely associated with Drama from now on, and there is a direct relationship between filling the floor space and filling the page.[3]   Not only are stories or characters painted after Play, but the composition of pictures improves in direct relationship to grouping and the

---

[1] See page 40.   [2] The adult athlete runs round the track this way.
[3] Once when visiting slightly older but backward Children (who would therefore be, in some ways, similar to infant mental standard) I came upon them painting.   The school uses sound a lot and I counted twenty-one spirals being painted in the same room (see Plate I). The backward Child tends to bring out clearly on paper the shapes that are connected with important experiences.

use of space during Play. (See Plate 15, between pages 184 and 185, and Plates 39 and 42, between pages 360 and 361.)

Dr. Viola, who tells us so much about the Child in his book *Child Art*,[1] says of Kerchensteiner, who examined 300,000 drawings and pictures by Children in Munich, that he found : " the Child cannot represent space, the third dimension." [2] I believe that the Child's own Drama, particularly the type of Drama that arises out of recommended sound-experiences, supplies a missing link here. Although Children cannot *represent* space, in the sense of the third dimension (i.e. " depth experience ", as Oswald Spengler calls it [3]) in their early pictures, they *experience* space by Drama. *And perhaps their first appreciation of the third dimension comes through the slow process of the integration of Self into the society of others whilst acting-in-the-round.* The first experience is clearly unconscious, but later on (nearer ten years) we see Children beginning to look across the hall full of companions, and clearly taking in " depth "—taking in not only their immediate neighbour but the companion beyond and beyond that one—and it is after this that perspective of a simple kind may begin to creep into their pictures. At a slightly later stage of their development we shall see that this creeps into their Drama even more obviously.[4] It all comes slowly, and whilst we should observe it we should not hurry it.

But for the moment we are still with the infants, and we already note that *both in their pictures and their Play the same shapes and signs occur.* These are the circle, the spiral, the cross, the square, the S shape, the triangle and the zigzag.

Shapes, as life-experience is incorporated, are : ships, water, cats, men, houses, children, women, stars, the moon, trees and fish. The Jungian would not be surprised, therefore, to find in Dramatic Play at this age the frequent appearance of the characters and situations as mentioned earlier,[5] nor to notice that an ever-popular story for playing is the Christmas story with its Father, Mother, Baby, journey and the star. Christianity is symbolised by the fish. Because the movement of this story is a slow and steady one, when played out, it is less impeded by dressing up than any other. (See Plate 2, opposite page 49.)

But these are not the only reasons for the Christmas story. The spiritual quality of Child Play no doubt moves many teachers to suggest the acting of this theme. However, apart from anything the adult may do, something happens

---

[1] Published by University of London Press.   [2] *Child Art*, page 14.
[3] *Ibid.*, pages 20–21.   [4] See page 66.   [5] See page 48.

to the Child round about six or seven.   It is the dawn of a certain seriousness.

This dawn of seriousness generally occurs before the Child leaves the infant school, and it brings with it not only a marked step forward in application to lessons, but a certain judgement and a finer sense of right and wrong. Sometimes it comes quite suddenly.   Serious questions are asked, and a moral responsibility begins to show itself.   The grinning and bumping of the average infant tends now to give way to more serious consideration for neighbours.   Those who have had their dawn of seriousness tend to become leaders in Dramatic Play.   Their language contains moral and philosophic references, a new poetic flow and views which often surprise.   They can link pieces of Play together better and help their companions to taste further of the joys of Drama.   The Child who has not had the dawn of seriousness by seven years of age is a slow developer.

The period is one of increasing skill, of great enchantment, and the extra sensitivity that is developed brings the Child to the threshold of the most wonderful years of Dramatic fulfilment.   We find exquisite moments in their new Drama creations from now on, in which deep soul-experiences and ice-cold logic walk hand in hand.   It is not for nothing that the ancient Christian Church chose seven years as " the age of reason ".

CHAPTER III

DRAMA AND PLAY. SEVEN TO TWELVE YEARS

IT should be clear by now that the adult's part in the Drama of the Child is a very special though not a dominating one.[1] The adult's attitude has a considerable influence at all ages, not least at this wonderful period of from seven years onwards. Our task now might almost be looked on as that of ensuring that the Child is going to *trust* adults. With its new interest in serious things, it is through the adult that the Child satisfies its desire for deeper knowledge, and, from the frank and trusting confidences exchanged, there arises a tremendous bond of friendship. Civilised life needs this bridge between youth and age, and unless it is satisfactorily established the Child tends to become suspicious and then rude and disobedient. This cuts the adult off from the latest news of the growing generation, and for the Child it often means the loss of a treasure casket of intellectual, emotional and aesthetic joys.

From the Child's point of view, this is a period of rapid further development from Self outwards, which takes the form of a further sharing of life-experiences with its companions. These experiences often become, and should remain, a realm of mystic secrecy, from which arise the wonderful creative forms of group decision which not only help the confident personal development of the Child, but enrich with such splendour its genuine Art and Drama.

Any break of trust with adults now, or removal of a loved one, may drive the Child into an unbalanced form of life in which the realm of mystic secrecy is over-enlarged. This may be a solitary affair, or there may be a feeling that there is only one camp, and a sort of sullen secret rebellion is started of the younger set against the older generation. Even one unhappy Child can cause a good deal of trouble now, and it often needs great patience, understanding and courageous action to get things right again.

Just as unhappy can be the condition where too great a reliance is placed on the adult, bringing contempt of companions, and suspicion on their part. Companions are an important part of normal life now, which is why we see the gang stage developing.

[1] Because of its importance this will be considered more fully in Part II.

The gang develops round a leader with a strong Self, not yet quite ready to integrate too far with the group. This strong Self is an intermediate personality between Child and adult for the other members of the gang. It thereby becomes a living symbol of the needs of that age, and, embracing as it does something of the strength and decision to be found in the adult and also the vivacity and actual youngness of the Child, it often wields tremendous power. For this reason the group dynamic of a gang can have tremendous energy for good or for ill. In the Drama it emerges, partially, as Group Sensitivity.

Group Sensitivity

At a time when this group feeling is growing we notice a great development in community efforts. There is the straightforward group creation, where stories and ideas are built up by several Children and acted out, but there is also the new feeling, both conscious and unconscious, for the place of others. Where properties are used, a Child who is not certain in choice will be aided by others ; a friend will rush up and thrust forward the right thing. There is also a much clearer conscious attitude about the need of space for others, though this is not yet fully conscious. There is far less bumping than with infants. Equidistance between each Person becomes more rigid, and one may frequently see a Child automatically moving out of another's way if the balance of equidistance is upset by any sudden unexpected happening. This is the outward sign of social awareness. It is part of the integration of Self with society. We see, also, particular movements taken up by several or all members of a group at once. This is further evidence of the growing one-mind, the shared intent. Seeing, hearing, feeling, noticing, all come into this. It is a sensitive business, and it pertains not only to each little Self but to the group. It can only be called Group Sensitivity.

With these developing senses come other things : from seeing—greater powers of observation ; from hearing—greater joy in time beat, rhythm and climax ; from feeling—more intense joys in materials, such as clothes, colours, wood and clay. One often sees Children of this age fully appreciating the *particular qualities* of materials, in a quite different manner from the earlier sense and Play trials.

With all this developing interest comes ability to concentrate, which the adult can aid by recognising, and by allowing frequent periods of uninterrupted Play. We can destroy it by over-rigid timetable or by the type of shyness and fear which causes us to impose an iron-like discipline.

The further powers of observation bring the full flood of questions which we *must* treat with patience and answer fully and seriously. This is where the adult may escape into lie-legends and do great harm, or answer impatiently and even angrily, thus blocking the in-flow of knowledge.

In-flow and Out-flow

In-flow and out-flow both have their place in developing Persons. Both are necessary and both are generally, to some extent, blocked. They balance each other when natural development is allowed. In creating, the Child has natural out-flow and begins to feel its way towards in-flow by using experiences of life and/or Self in its creations. It thus begins to " draw in " and use things. This has been going on to a lesser degree steadily up to six or seven years of age, but, at the dawn of seriousness, the process comes to something of a climax in the fuller, more conscious desire to draw in knowledge. If the right knowledge is available at the right time the Child is satisfied to some extent ; a digestion process takes place and, because of the actual strengthening by the nourishment in energy, joy, confidence and desire for more, *it becomes absolutely necessary for immediate new creations*. Here the Child's Drama is most essential because it is the chief medium for out-flow and it provides the actual proof trials of experiences. What is learnt is tried out. It is not far from the truth to say that without frequent opportunities for Creative Play what is learnt is never proved, since it is never physically and emotionally *experienced*. For this reason much knowledge is either rejected or forgotten, because it makes only half an impression instead of a whole one. The tragedy of so much of our education is that it appears not to appreciate fully the existence of an in-flow and an out-flow, and, instead of harnessing nature to the teacher's difficult task, insists quite often in blocking in-flow *and* out-flow, and relies on the physical effort of bashing things home. This method is a great strain on the teacher, particularly with large classes, and holds no guarantee that knowledge is actually forced in, or that it is retained.

Any one-way feeding-pipe to a small Person is a slender thing and easily gets choked. Then nothing much happens—the Child and teacher eye each other across a fixed chasm like Dives and Lazarus ; but if the teacher be Dives, his wealth is squandered. Thus it is that, despite the fears of those who dare not try out these things, or will not persevere with them, or else stubbornly reject them, Children who have frequent opportunities for Drama and creating of their own kind, not only equal the success of other Children, but frequently surpass them—even in scholastic attainment. And as to happiness, good manners and obedience, there can be no comparison.[1]

Group Creations

With all these developments taking place in the Children, it is not surprising that the outward form of their Drama is affected. Where floor space is properly used, we see a change in the appearance of the circle. What in the infant class tended to be a big circle, splitting occasionally into other shapes, develops into a more frequent appearance of small circles. These circles in the junior class are the outward sign of the gang stage. Anything from about three to seven members is common, though they are sometimes larger when special imaginative creations call for more Persons, e.g. human cars, trains or lakes. These circles, besides being an outward sign of an inner condition, often even comprise members of a gang, for, whenever Play takes place, the gang members tend to join up, and confidences are exchanged which grow into group creations either of acted scenes or of dance.

These group Drama creations tend to be made up increasingly by the Children themselves now, often without any help at all. Sometimes they are made up after swift or lengthy whispered conversations, sometimes prepared for several days. Occasionally all will be done in secret, and the teacher will be asked, as a surprise, if they may " act it ". These are improvisations, and the flow of dialogue is often amazing for its wit, charm, and mixture of naïvety and deep philosophical content.

At the best moments of playing they are still unconcerned with audience ; they are far away in " the Land ". But sometimes a petering out gives indication of the " near finish ", and we can clearly see or feel them coming back to earth. Nevertheless, if they are not entirely convinced that any adults present understand that Play is temporarily finished (or if they have never met an adult who knows " finish "), they will often turn and say " that's all ", just to make quite sure. Sometimes the end is so abrupt that it is very

---

[1] The following remarks from head teachers are chosen from many I have received ; they all tend towards the one conclusion that teachers who generally try to understand and to give some rein to the Child's real nature reap a harvest for themselves as well as the Child :
" This is a very happy school, we don't get fighting here."
" Doing Drama the way you suggest makes them try out things they learn, and then they seem to remember them."
" Since giving them more time for their own acting and painting they seem to be more obedient somehow."
" I rather funked giving more time to acting—I mean *their* kind of acting—at first, what with exams and things. But I've never regretted it, it has made such a difference, and (with a smile) they still pass their tests." (Grammar School.)

difficult to be sure of its arrival, particularly as under these conditions the Players often stay absorbed in " the Land " and remain coma-acting for a minute or two. Adults here often mistake the end of " theatre " for the end of Play, whereas the two may be quite separate. Signs of theatre may or may not be present, but, if there are Children not actually in the creation they always know when it has finished ; they move, and that generally breaks the spell. These improvisations, if loved, may be repeated, but details are generally different. A polished improvisation is often better understood by the adult, but it is not necessarily as important as the original creation.

Dance is also made up by the Children, but they often wish to build together with the teacher, and this communal building brings its own rewards and promotes confidence between Child and teacher. It also helps to break up the gang, for which these little groups are sometimes quite pleased, for, though they are bound by fierce and voluntary loyalties, there is a certain involuntary tyranny about them which each Child both loves and fears. It appears to be a relief, therefore, to have the gang split up sometimes by an outside agency, though much Play will take place in, with and through these gang groups.

Too much repetition of a particular dance or improvisation brings laziness ; some repetition, combined with fresh creations, brings the happiest results.

It is particularly important that the little groups on the floor space, whether manifestations of the gang state or actual gangs, should have opportunity for Play in the presence of a sympathetic adult and in a *legal* surrounding. In this way the gang dynamic is influenced for good by frequent constructive group adventures, when just one word from the adult is often enough to tip the scale of behaviour in the young gang leader or potential leader, who is ever ready to become dare-devil and lead others the wrong way. This is what is meant by saying that Drama of this kind can be a cultivated flower.

The flower of the street is wild and often thorny. It is no good pretending that it doesn't exist, because it does and has great vitality ; indeed, it has such beauties that it pays us to cultivate what nature provides.

Where the teacher is consciously aiming at happiness-development we still find, of course, the spiral form of happy entry into a room at this age ; this immediately turns into a circle, which quickly evolves into the filled-in circle or disc, and then as rapidly again splits into personal activity—and then the gangs join up. That is the general pattern of behaviour. It happens *always* where the right happy background exists.   It is as dependable as day and night.   One could almost say with truth that the outward sign is proof of the right conditions, so marked and regular is the Form of the Child's own Drama.

Because the Child has more inner clarity about life, we see clearer outlines in every way between seven years and twelve.   Footsteps are more certain, thinking is sharper, and so is decision.   Personal viewpoints are expressed.   Hand and arm movements give clearer messages of intent in portrayal ; eyes, face and speech take on more vital forms of expression. Painting, drawing and modelling have fuller design.   All this can be noticed where Drama created by the Child and nurtured by the teacher is allowed to take place.   Where it does not take place there is hardly any way of noticing or finding out anything about the Child because (1) the Child cannot tell us anything ; (2) we cannot therefore observe it or know it, and (3) the Child does not develop properly.   We thus never see the *real* Child, and if it dared to speak at all it would tell us, in a roundabout way, only about what it lacked (this it does to some degree by its markedly more difficult behaviour).

Children may be hesitant in portrayal, but they are only waiting for a mental door to open.   Again, sometimes their Play dies out.   In either case the teacher can help—even by one word.   At this age the Children, in places where companionship is encouraged, help one another too.[1]

Actor—But No Audience

Care must still be taken to guard against showing off.   The usual fatal mistake at this age, or even earlier, is to introduce a conscious differentiation between actor and audience, which is the realm of the generally understood adult theatre.   It cannot be stressed too often that the Child's Drama in its early (and in many later) stages has very little to do with this.   There is not the same artificial differentiation between actor and audience (unless we make it), and so there is no need for the audience to face one way only and the actors the other.   There is a general tendency for everyone to act, and they face any way they like.   Drama is all about us—it is much more exciting —and not at all necessarily in front of us.   Everyone participates, everyone is creating.

Left to itself and unspoiled by adult notions of theatre, the Child develops

---

[1] This is also true of painting.   During the gang stage, group feeling is so strong that a number of Children can work in harmony on a big project, or paint a mural as one Person.

a deep sense of constructive criticism about Play in others—it knows who does well, and often how a thing can be improved. This, of course, implies moments of temporary observation on the part of the Child, and these moments are often mistaken for audience in our full sense of the word. But they are just the first-fruits of the dawn of seriousness, and the Child will quickly want to start to Play again. Nothing is more cruel than to force Children to sit as audience when others are playing. If they *want* to, then things have gone very far wrong—we have already suppressed them.

The Child is actor *and* audience in one because of its delicate balance of out-flow and in-flow in the realm of experience and knowledge. This balance is violently upset by any sudden differentiation between actor and audience, and showing off immediately begins.

The surest way of developing showing off is to put the Child on a stage at one end of the room. This raised-up position, arranged for observation, is diametrically opposed to Sincerity and Absorption. These two qualities die, and with them the Child's own Drama. But there are many other things involved here. The Child cannot move freely, nor can it move in its own way. Worst of all, as we have already seen,[1] it is being introduced to an important experience before it is ready for it. In Drama of the Child's own kind it is slowly finding out the truth about depth experience. At the ages of seven, eight, nine, or even ten, it has not arrived at a full knowledge of perspective. In painting, many pictures show no sign of it. But the proscenium theatre is designed and built up upon notions of depth, lines of sight, and, above all, *perspective*. For this reason it is a tremendous upheaval to experience it too early in any way whatever. Great lack of confidence is the immediate effect both inwardly (more hidden) and outwardly (always seen and always unmistakeable) on the Child's own Drama creations. Laziness follows. I have always found that those who dispute this point are talking about something different. They are not speaking of the Child's own Drama—they are often not fully aware of its existence—but are thinking of some part of " adult theatre ", picked up and copied by Children, or imposed upon them. The latter is the more usual, and is a very dreary affair compared with either nurtured or un-nurtured Child creation. Those who see no evil effect of the proscenium upon the Child's work are not fully considering Child Drama for what it is.

Where this *is* seen and understood, if only in part, one finds full-hearted attempts to make use of the school hall, or, if overcrowding makes this im-

---

[1] See page 44.

possible, some freedom is given in a classroom where much good work can be done. If desks are moved, the circle appears at once, but, even so, we cannot as a rule provide enough space and freedom. If there is only a limited space, with desks all facing towards the teacher, it is practically the same as a proscenium theatre and is likely to hurry consciousness of this somewhat unduly. The unwise teacher will, in such conditions, treat the acting as of the proscenium type, and one may hear such remarks as : " We want to see you " ; " don't hide, so-and-so " ; " face front ". When left alone the Child does *not* always face front. In fact, if Absorption develops to any extent in Play, backs are solidly turned on the " audience " (i.e. the unfortunate ones forced to remain seated, who, if not yet repressed, will show clear signs of wanting to be " in it " rather than where they are) and a half- or three-quarter circle is often formed by the Players against the wall at teacher's end of the classroom.[1] This is because the Children are trying to act-in-the-round, and also because they take up a circular position when doing their own work. There is not enough room for the whole circle, but we see their courageous and heart-rending attempts to make the best of miserable conditions.

The actual bulge or half-circle is, in a way, a lesson for the adult in the next shape that is going to arise in the Drama. It has arrived too early and almost, as it were, by chance or mistake, because it is the outcome of proscenium conditions. But it is not surprising to find, therefore, that when the proscenium *is* accepted by the Child we meet this bulge again, in a slightly extended form.[2]

Audience Participation

In the meantime, though, Play is going on, and the impatience or boredom of the enforced watchers can be relieved to some extent by *Audience Participation*. Where it is realised that the healthy Child prefers to act rather than to watch (because at this age personal Play is so important), the tension may be relieved by encouraging the enforced watchers to join in Play with noises of all kinds—even with remarks. Actors may move happily off our mistaken conception of the " stage ", and will approach the wrongly termed " audience " as if they were other actors and sell them something, or perhaps bite off their noses. Participation then takes place and builds towards that wonderful atmosphere which is only experienced where the right attitude encourages Children's real Drama.

[1] See Part II, Chapter XIV. We visit some Schools.   [2] See pages 70–73.

This joining-in happens to a large extent, anyway, as when any enforced watching takes place, violent facial movements, biting of nails, waving of hands, stamping and jumping up and down will be noted on all occasions when the thing watched appeals. Where joining-in has been accepted or nurtured to the point where it becomes an important part of Play itself, I have called it Audience Participation. It has qualities of its own, both relieving and artistic ; it can be a happy step towards the right conditions, and I hope it will be used a great deal in the future, particularly when adults play to Children. One should not think that Audience Participation encourages rowdiness [1]—it encourages *life*, and helps an artificial situation to be less harmful. (See Plate 33, opposite page 296.)

Rostrum Blocks

Walking in and out of desks, with everyone joining in, sometimes brings the next natural step in the Drama—the finding of a *higher level*, and its attendant joys. The higher level may be found by stepping on to teacher's rostrum or climbing on to a desk or chair. It will have been found earlier, of course, as a general experience and in such games as " King of the Castle ". But levels may begin to be introduced after seven years of age as an integral and harmonious part of Play, and this will be helped by having rostrum blocks and shaped and coloured blocks in the school hall. These can be built into large Monuments which form a shape in harmony with and accurate for the scene in which the Child wants to Play. To the Child it is necessary to build a scene. Most of it is in the mind, but the newer masteries of the body and of skills make further use of material substance valuable at the age we are discussing, whereas it would not necessarily have been so at an earlier age. (See Plate 4, opposite page 65, and Plate 18, opposite page 193.)

We note, in all this slow development, how closely Children follow the general trend of the history of Drama. We have arrived now at something like the mediaeval central stage—a higher level in the middle of the playing space. We must not expect to stay there, though ; all is floating, all is fluid. Presently the lumps will be pulled away and shunted off to different parts of the room where Play with a journey, localities, centres of interest, equidistance, and gang domination of an area of floor (mentally pegged out like the claim of any gold rush) will occur again. Is this wearisome, or untidy, or even boring to the adult mind, or are we just admitting, perhaps for the

---

[1] For those with doubts, it should be said that the Child's own reserve, which develops in later years, will help it to " behave " in our own theatres.

first time, that we cannot keep up with the wonderful rapid flow of creation and the vivacious flexibility of art-forms which are beyond us ?

Improvised Dance

By eight years or nine we find tremendous advances in improvised dance. This can be done with or without music, or to noises. The sounds and the music have their own function. If the Child needs aiding to freedom and personal expression, improvised music is of value. This *accompanies* the Child creations. Music on a gramophone record adds a certain discipline— it cannot alter, and the Child conforms somewhat to it. This brings out obedience and docility. It also promotes confidence and stimulates Dramatic mood. " It helps with ideas," as a little boy once put it. (See Plate 15, between pages 184 and 185.)

An interesting thing here is that the mood is often heard and reacted to, even though time beat may be slightly out, and reaction to a change in the music may come after a while and not necessarily at once. A further sign of that group sensitivity of which we spoke before, but of a higher kind, is that Children up at the far end of the room will, so to speak, " catch " time beat and mood from the group, when only the few Children at the near end of the room can hear a soft record or weak gramophone. Those nearest catch the message, which is passed on through the various gang groups dotted about the hall. This helps in establishing the next stage of personal and group integration which usually comes after ten years of age and any time up to twelve, though in first-class conditions it may appear earlier. It is the stage when not only the Person integrates with the gang, but *gang integrates with gang*. Thus, slowly, we see the full group functioning as one, and, from the social point of view, this is a complete harmonious society. It is a vital experience which only takes place where Children do this work ; all others leave school without the experience, and society loses greatly thereby.

The experience begins as something unconscious through the dream state of the dance itself, but it is clear that the Children do in fact recognise the quality of it in time, and rejoice in the harmony and unity of it. From our dramatic point of view they are tasting something which only the greatest stage artists know—Group Intuition.

Group Intuition is the furthest limit of group sensitivity, and is a rhythm of wisdom shared by a group, the members of which know intuitively what is needed, what should be done and what others are going to do.[1] It is one

[1] For example, see Chapter XIV, page 195 (8).

of the great perfections of the age we are discussing, arising out of the spiritual awareness after the dawn of seriousness. It is often lost at puberty when realism and competition threaten all.

The dance itself can become extremely well developed between seven and twelve years of age, where opportunity is given for it. By nine or ten we may expect to see intense imaginative work of either a flowing or a stylised kind. It can be ethereal or broadly comic. It can be of the gang (a few Children dancing together) or of the whole community (all the class). Dances, as with Plays, may be creations partly of the Child, partly of the teacher ; often the Children make the whole thing themselves. Great attention is paid to the sound of feet and to space relationships.

The intense beauty of the work is in the shapes drawn, as it were, by the path of movement over the floor space, and in the ever-changing groups. Absorption and Sincerity are the core of this work, and its outer mastery is in the use of space. When Mr. Martin Browne, Director of the British Drama League, saw some of this work, he said : " I have only seen space used so perfectly before by first-class ballerinas." But an interesting point is that, given equal opportunity, boys of this age on the whole outshine girls. They are naturally more virile, and become more inventive. The girls, though, equal them in grace.

A delightful development of the early noise experiences provided by the teacher from the beginning of the infant school is the use of sounds introduced by the Children themselves. It is not really the function of this book to speak much on Music, but one cannot escape its importance, and I feel I must say here that far more could be done in the encouragement of Child-made instruments and Music. I have known Children make up the most intricate rhythms and interesting sounds, and introduce them to their Dance and Drama in a fascinating and most subtle manner, very much as the Spanish do. The dancers make their own sounds.

Group Sensitivity and this instrument and music creation is also instanced in a story related by Dr. Edmunds, late of the Birmingham Midland Institute, and originally told by Sir Granville Bantock. He was in Africa, and a group of boys said they wanted to play to him. They rushed off and returned with instruments made from oil drums with bits of wood of different sizes placed across them ; the size affected the note, as with the xylophone. Suddenly they started to play. The astonishing thing was that there appeared to be no conductor and no sign given, yet everyone started at once, and as one (Group Intuition). There followed, for a considerable period, an infinite variety of subtle and interesting rhythms extemporised. The boys appeared to be very absorbed, and then, suddenly, it all stopped.

Group Intuition is no wild, unusual magic, but the adult reaches it only by discipline, the Child only through freedom. This is the measure of difference between youth and age, this the chasm that has to be crossed. By facing the differences honestly and bravely, we may learn to understand each other better.

Beginnings of Language Flow [1]

Not only is mood stimulated by music, but we note that Children will also speak while the music is going on. They listen in a different way from us— not intellectually, but emotionally. They then speak words during Play that fit the music. It brings beauty of thought and sound, furthering their first interest aroused by sounds from the infant school upwards. They can learn to listen more as we do by tiresome forms of concentration, but they often listen very hard when speaking through music. This is quite clear, even if they do not tell us about it.

Language Flow comes from this process, as from the confidence developed by frequent opportunities for improvised Drama. Speaking is, after all, arrived at by practice. Many schools still think only in terms of " Keep quiet ". How can they expect good speech ? Well, of course, they don't get it, except that which is drilled. Children who have been helped to practice develop remarkable gifts from five years upwards, but if they are not showing signs of poetic and philosophic creation by the middle of the junior school it is clear they are being badly frustrated.

In its early state, Language Flow is halting and often peters out. It includes rough expressions, and cannot be heard. It improves if time is given to it. Time makes the habit ; uninterrupted habit brings confidence ; confidence brings the flow.

Running Play (Later Stage)

Allied to music and happiness is another phenomenon which we have met before—Running Play. This running Play of the eight- or nine-year-olds in the hall is a cultivated flower. At sudden and special moments a Child will

---

[1] Under the separate heading of Language Flow I have collected various examples and have tried to show a few ways of recognising, developing and encouraging it. See Chapters VI and XIII.

break for sheer joy into a run, whether acting or dancing. It may not happen very often, but is like a flash of lightning when at its best. Knees are always bent, and arms are generally held out like wings. These actions are accompanied by great Absorption and an ecstatic expression. (See Plate 28.)

The cultivated qualities of this flower are that it is very rhythmic, the design is snakewise or figure of eight, there is hardly any knocking into anything, profound attention is paid to the sound of the feet and it always contains some intended climax. Climax is encouraged by the presence of a low rostrum lying about—just as in street Play, one or both feet pass on to the higher planes, and a very clear, exceedingly moving and beautiful piece of theatre is acted out before our eyes. The climax, so beautifully timed, is of high realms of Drama and Music. It is great artistry. (See Plate 3.)

This Running Play, so vast an experience both for those who see it and for those who do it, does not take place to perfection where there are no rostrum blocks, and it can only take place at all where there has been conscious happiness-development by the teacher, and where there is space. *I have never seen it take place in any school where young Children are made to work on a stage.* For this reason alone, were there not so many others, one might consider stages as quite unsuitable for junior schools.

Costume and Make-up

Though Children of this age take great delight in dressing up, their grace and beauty of movement are still somewhat hindered by clothes. Where the work and conditions as described do not obtain, more use is made of clothes, but where the Child's own Drama is allowed and understood we find more pleasure in the actual Drama itself, and Children by their own wish may use only very little clothing, or discard it altogether. The adult should take care not to burden the Child with dress, for this bewilders it. From the creative point of view, pieces of attractive stuff are better than ready-made garments, as Children can continue to create with these, building up a true character with costume to match. An over-elaborate costume often overbalances the creation, and true characterisation decreases because of interest in parading up and down. This, in turn, tends to more showing off, and eventual deterioration in perhaps a whole period of work.

The creative use of bits and pieces also has valuable lessons in the sphere of choice and taste, with a whole range of most interesting creative needlework ; bits of paper or objects may be sewn or stuck on to coloured stuffs.

PLATE 3

RUNNING PLAY. Arrested by camera at top speed. "Climax is encouraged by the presence of a low rostrum lying about. Just as in Street Play, one or both feet pass on to the higher plane." (*See* p. 64.)

Photo by Victor Thompson

PLATE 4

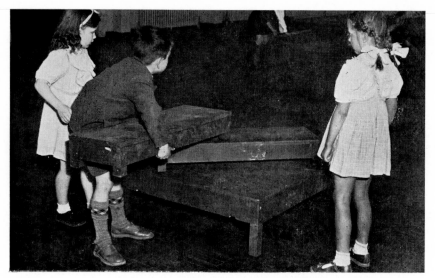

INFANTS. The blocks are easy to lift. They are being used like large bricks and are built into a scene. This is a development of the early Monuments of projected Play, which can become linked to personal Play by this process. It provides a happy balance. Even more useful between seven and twelve years. (*See* p. 60.)

JUNIOR MIXED. Discovered in progress whilst crossing a quadrangle. The witch rides her horse. I don't know where to. It's a secret. They were preparing this to do in a classroom, I was told.

Photos by Victor Thompson

But the fuller version of this task is in itself so absorbing that it is best done separately.   Again, the final costume (which is better than that of " uncreated " garments) is often too greatly loved, admired and cared for to be a useful aid to good Drama.   It is used for a careful absorbed parading, which is rather more a personal fulfilment of the process of Art creation, and is only Drama of the less obvious kind.   On the other hand, the quicker simple creation is definitely intended as an aid to Drama.   The wearing of " uncreated " garments is seldom Art or Drama ; there is usually a motive behind it, often linked with the adult, and generally bad.

Another interesting point about costume is that when Children are allowed to choose and create their own, they often use the materials in such a way that the final creation is a manifestation of their own character.   We are used to this now in Child Art, but costume-making, being essentially external, often gives an even more obviously readable statement about Self. One remark by a Headmaster is typical of this : " I was amazed," he said, " to see a number of my class dressed somehow as their own character, and others as I know they will be twenty or thirty years hence."   I myself have always found this form of prophecy very startling.   It may be partly conscious, partly unconscious, partly accident—but it is also due to the increasing perception of deep truth, which is soon to give way to intense reality about details.

Make-up is not often found by or offered to the Child of this age, but, where it is, most interesting things take place.   These will be dealt with separately,[1] so for the moment let it suffice to say that, for the Child, make-up is an extension of Art, and we should not enforce the adult photographic conception of it.   The average adult has certain ideas (borrowed from the proscenium stage) about make-up, whereas Child make-up is more of a pattern mask having certain characteristics that are reminiscent of the high cultures of other lands and past ages, and is not primarily intended as make-up to be seen on a stage.

Beginnings of Play-writing

Play-writing may begin now, but early attempts are often disappointing ; they are really symptoms of the desire to write, the form chosen being pressed forward by the wealth of experience in Play.   Being allowed to act these first attempts is often a shattering experience to a Child, at an age when its improvisations are so much better.   A young Child is quite incapable of the

[1] See Chapter XVII.

mastery of body and mind necessary in order to write down the flow of language and ideas found in its normal extempore work.[1] Added to this difficulty is the mental agitation of trying to hurry through the writing of the play in order to act it. This does not improve the play as a work of Art, and, even if great freedom is allowed over the difficulties of grammar, spelling, punctuation and the actual mechanics of writing, the business is still not easy.[2]

However, without in any way pouring cold water on these early attempts, the adult can aid the Child by leading it to write straight descriptions of Drama experiences, for when the Child either paints or writes about these there is not the same uncomfortable reason for haste, and the work is consequently of a much higher quality. Practice at this simple assessing of ideas and of scene adds tremendously to the ability to write actual plays later on (between the ages of twelve and fifteen) when situations are better understood, length of scene is appreciated and vocabulary is larger. But of even greater importance than this necessary practice is the love of language itself, which is stimulated both by the early actions to sounds and by the nurturing of Language Flow.

The development towards play-writing is something like this : Play ; Dramatic Play ; improvisations ; polished improvisations ; some words written down ; stories and dialogues copied from films, radio and life experiences ; improved expression (coming from Language Flow) and improved writing ability mix with improvisation and begin to equal it. Out of this last stage comes a tolerably good written play. The age—*not in the junior school*, but *circa* thirteen years upwards.

Approach to Proscenium Theatre

Towards the end of the junior school we find, in the painting, tendencies towards perspective. Parallel with this, and maybe before it, we see Children noticing depth when acting on the floor. Drama is an important link in the recognition of depth and space relationships, and, where little opportunity is given for this Drama, the Child undoubtedly loses much intermediate experience. *I think their own Drama supplies us with a lot of hitherto unknown information about space and the Child, and helps us to see better the slow development towards the understanding of depth.* About this

---

[1] It is almosti mpossible for an adult expert in shorthand to catch the flow of a Child, let alone a Child itself.
[2] Nor is it as successful as, for instance, the quick costume creations already mentioned, which can be swiftly and beautifully achieved. They have a spontaneity that the written play cannot have.

time we occasionally see the proscenium arch appearing unconsciously in the painting and drawing. One rather expects this, as in the pre-puberty era appreciation of perspective is beginning to seep through. Thus we find the first signs of approach to the perspective theatre which may become more important after puberty.

And then, at this very sensitive period, comes the terrible break from junior to senior school. I headed this chapter " Seven to twelve years " because in the Child's own Drama the flow up to puberty is steady, and that is how it should be. I have put puberty even somewhat early, at *circa* twelve, because that is a bit nearer the break in school (or was at eleven) ; for both the Drama and the Child many a tragedy takes place now, as eleven plus to twelve is generally a peak of the flowering period under good conditions. However, the attitude of education is as yet so indifferent to the young Child entering secondary modern schools (particularly for boys) that the peak is often ignored or relentlessly crushed. And now that Children change schools even earlier, the difficulties of safeguarding their creations are so much the greater, though this, of course, may change.

But let us look on the bright side for the moment, and take stock of the position as far as we have gone.

From the earliest years upward we see the Child developing, ever finding and adding to Self, ever attempting and often being successful in mastering new skills. The manner of this mastering is eternally connected with Play. Both the inner Self and the outer Self of the Person develops, and the two forms of Play—personal and projected—are connected with this development, in that the flow between them makes possible, in part, the ultimate process of ideas becoming conscious.

By building outside itself, the Child learns to see itself and others. Personal Play is rather to do with inner Self and personal mastery, though outward material things may be used. Projected Play is rather to do with outward material things and their organisation, though it draws on the inner Self. From these come the harmony and the intense beauties of the growing Child.

Acting and painting go hand in hand, because acting is personal Play and painting is projected Play.

Material shape, then, being part outer and part inner Self right from the time of the early obvious Monuments, is of supreme importance, and it is natural, therefore, that in healthy conditions we see skills and shapes going together in personal development. The shapes are repeated. Running through everything we find the circle or ring formation which appears whenever the Child is allowed to build and create in its own way ; whenever, in fact, the work is genuinely of the Child. Even in the gang's Dramatic Play of pirates, gangsters, wizards and elementals we see defined shapes and forms. (See Plate 17, opposite page 192.)

Between the years of seven and twelve we find extreme spiritual beauties and intense sensitivity, at times equalling in skill the talents of supreme artists—the adventures, attempts and creations have *their* forms of skill (many of them now conscious) and all *their* beauty. And yet they have what Clive Bell has called " significant form "—and it has been suggested that that which has significant form is Art ; we have also considered that Art means skill. The Child brings skill to its Drama, through the "doing" of which it not only learns how to live, but to love living.

There does, then, exist a Child Drama, which is of exquisite beauty and is a high Art Form in its own right. It should be recognised, respected and protected.

CHAPTER IV

TWELVE TO FIFTEEN YEARS

MOST children of twelve years or thereabouts have had a change of school, and one often hears teachers affirm that they become difficult and shy about this time. It is true that there is such a tendency, and it is partly caused by too sudden a change of work and atmosphere, particularly in the manner of handling the Child ; this is certainly so of Drama, and there are indications that the same applies to other subjects.

In a number of ways this change of school can place a sudden, unexpected and even frightening strain on many Children, and even if they appear to surmount the main difficulties it sometimes affects their ability to create. There are, however, many schools that now seem to realise this, and are doing what they can to remedy the matter. Sometimes it may only be one brave teacher who is trying out things, but one teacher can make a world of difference. If the handling of the younger Child is not too different from the junior school, pleasure in the new fuller prospect of schooling may result.

Drama at this age is too often associated in people's minds entirely with the script play. Certainly script plays may be of value sometime between twelve years and fifteen, and the older Child comes to like them, but they are not by any means the only thing, for the strange and wonderful truth is that, if Child Drama is not now forgotten or squashed, it continues on, and even adds to its beauties. For this reason we shall not be much concerned in this book with other forms of Drama.

We have already considered, to some extent, the Child's slow appreciation of space and depth through Drama, and I have suggested that there is an unconscious tendency towards the proscenium stage now, as manifested, for instance, in the occasional appearance of the proscenium arch in the painting. In schools where Drama is virtually dropped from the Child's life, or where only a few occasionally take part in formal productions, one can of course see nothing. But in schools and clubs where a certain freedom is given (and when one observes Children of this age acting in the holidays), it is quite clear that the Child can continue to develop perfectly normally at its own rate.

69

Under such conditions we find, at twelve years and at thirteen, similar work to that of the junior school (acting-in-the-round and on the floor space), though movement becomes more sure and vocabulary is increased. There is action still in gangs, but the tyranny of this self-imposed society group does not seem to be quite so strong during Play. (This is so of the cultured Child Drama, not of the Drama of the street.) There is a further tendency to realism in detail, and although fantasy of a peculiarly lovely kind is often to be found amongst girls, it is true of both sexes that they are increasingly occupied with playing out life experiences, and in drawing on cinema, radio and worldly knowledge for these creations. We find comedy, horror and frank adventure all mixed up together, and we meet fewer imaginative creatures and people.

The physical shape in the Drama is still, at first, the ring or part ring formation, but when left to themselves the Children often begin to move towards one end of the room ; this happens sometime between twelve and fifteen, and is caused partially by strong unconscious tradition, partially by exterior influences. (See Plate 45, between pages 360 and 361.)

This is the position *now*, in the year 1952, but I do not say it will always be so. For instance, I know of a teacher who had town Children (up to fifteen years) in a country area during the war ; they were cut off, and consequently the community was somewhat like a primitive tribe, without much contact with modern life. The Children showed depth in their painting to some extent, but continued to act quite naturally in-the-round, and the main formation was circular. I know of country Children in some out-of-the-way country districts who act like this, too ; and lads in a town school who do the same without any question of proscenium entering their Play. But for most Children it does enter, and, as a rule, more obviously with those that have closer links with civilisation, where their whole process of growing up is hurried, anyway. However, the natural tendency toward proscenium is a slow process, and even when the joys of using a higher level at one end of a room are found, the Child in its own creations does not remain there. All is fluid, and strong-minded decisions are made about when and where a stage is or is not of value to the production.

First Use of Stages

Actors flow up on to the stage and back on to the floor space they love, when they judge it to be right. This happy flowing to and from a higher level is extremely lovely to watch, and the intense unconscious wisdom of the Child here creates exactly the right conditions for it to test out depth experience (and the higher levels) in so far as it wants to, for the right length of time and at the right moment, by playing on a stage. For the rest, it seeks comfort and stability from space relationships on the floor as before ; the senior Child still has its roots in the past, and the future is all uncertainty.

This flowing backward and forward takes place in two ways : there is the manifestation of Children, in a perfectly plain hall, using rostrum blocks to build an open stage up one end of the room. This would seem to show conscious or unconscious influence of our traditional stage. The urge and flow is rather *to* the stage and away. Then, where a full proscenium stage exists, there is the flowing out from behind a proscenium arch, down steps or other device, on to the floor. The urge and flow is here rather *away from* the stage and back. (See Plates 25 and 26, opposite page 240.)

The general outline of movement, in both instances, is exactly the same. The shape is that of a long tongue coming straight out from the stage, and rounded at the end farthest from the proscenium. This is, as one might expect, because the floor end is influenced by the circle and is associated with acting-in-the-round, and it goes rather into the straighter lines of sight as it approaches the stage, which is primarily concerned with perspective. Just as in junior Child Drama the spiral and circle are as certain as night and day, so, when a stage at one end of the room is used and when *genuine* Child Drama takes place, the tongue shape is certain and regular also.

How is it, then, that, under certain conditions, there can be this acting entirely in circular form, even with older Children ?

Many factors have a bearing on this : Child nature develops at varying paces, the tempest of puberty may come early or late, or the inner Self may be more or less advanced than the outer Self. Environment and background also play an important part in determining how far each Person is generally balanced, which is shown to some extent by the exterior form of the Drama.

So then, those rather out of the world, uninfluenced and unhurried, arrive at proscenium consciousness more slowly. Children develop more evenly in their whole Self if they are not hurried.

Would they, perhaps, under certain circumstances never ueed the proscenium, and never the full use of perspective for their various Art creations ? And how far would a protected white race community resemble, in other ways of calm development, the primitive tribe ? And would it be that the proscenium stage (in a society that never considered it) was never fully approached unconsciously and consciously, or would it be that it was by-passed altogether in favour of the modern arena theatre, arrived at unconsciously ?   Perhaps we can never know.   And perhaps it does not matter, for the circle is a symbol of deep inner instinct in Man and belongs as securely to the Drama of the past and its whole history as it undoubtedly will to the future.   It seems likely, though, that in our present civilisation the proscenium stage will be arrived at and experienced at one period in the Child's life, though it may be discarded later.

If, then, the age is reached when a stage at one end of the room becomes exciting and is voluntarily employed, the general process at this era, when the proscenium strongly influences our adult life, is for the tongue to get slowly smaller as the Child gets older, until it is rather more like a half-circle out from the proscenium stage.

We considered the history of the Drama, and the similarity between junior Child Drama and the mediaeval theatre.   We have now arrived, with the senior Child, at something like the Elizabethan theatre, with its area of projection from the stage into the audience.

The shape of the tongue only *half* out, or the part circle or bulge, also appears where there is lack of space, as for instance in the classroom ; but now the older Child sometimes faces the so-called " audience ", being more conscious of perspective and that whole type of theatre.   We had a preview of the bulge in the classroom of the junior school, though there nearly all the Children faced away from those not fully participating.

Some psychologists suggest that " time ", as the adult understands it— i.e. clock time—is appreciated only by those who have reached a certain maturity.   There is some suggestion, too, that understanding of depth and finality are also connected with time.   Puberty, in a way, is a period of growing up and of maturity ; we possess at last that which will pass with us into adulthood.   Thus it is interesting that, at this period and soon afterwards, if the Child is *left to itself* it often gropes towards the form of theatre which above all else is concerned with depth, perspective, screening, intense light, intense shadow, and that this theatre's technique, largely because of its extreme conspicuousness, demands accurate " timing ".   And if contrast in mood, and in every way, is the life breath of this theatre,[1] it is also the life pattern of behaviour under the trials of puberty.

In any flow to and from the stage we may see a stress one way or the other.   Predominant flow *to* may be a symptom of eagerness to explore, find

---

[1] See *The Play Produced*, John Fernald, published by Deane & Sons.

and use the stage as an extra to the floor space. It is also a sign of confidence. Predominant flow *from* the stage is quite clearly a symptom of eagerness to escape, either from an enclosed space, a conspicuous place, too high a level or from the wrong type of theatre. (The Child makes this quite obvious.) It can also be a sign of lack of confidence, or of too dominating a place of the stage in the general work : (1) as being used too often ; (2) as being too important by its very (inspiring) existence in the hall.

Happy and general equal flow either way, as obviously connected with the needs of a creation, is the sign that the stage is having a not undue influence, and is subservient to and mastered by the Child in its need.

I have said that this movement may come any time between twelve and fifteen. If unhurried, it comes generally after thirteen. (See Plates 5 and 6, opposite page 80, and Plate 45, between pages 360 and 361.)

Emotional Training

The young adolescent commands our urgent attention and respect because of being at one moment grown up and at another a Child, and lost again. We find energy, lack of energy, happiness, sadness, confidence, shyness, curiosity, boredom, turned on like taps at any moment. The Persons of this age do not know yet who they are, and they need our help tremendously.

Their own Drama is a great safety-valve now. It offers continual opportunities for playing out evil in a legal framework, and for trying out who you are and what you are going to be. The emotions can be somewhat turbulent at this age, and it is very important that there should be training in the emotions as in other subjects. In fact, looking at our world today, you might say that training in the emotions is one thing that has been lacking above all else.

At puberty and after, each Child goes through a second testing period. It is their second dawn of seriousness. They face great trials now, and must decide whether they will stick to the values which came to them as perceptions of right and wrong at the first dawn of seriousness (*circa* six years).

The Drama is often used, therefore, for playing out situations in which the individual has to make decisions about morals. By making situations conscious, the Child is able to look at life as an observer and make slow inward decisions. It is greatly to the credit of young People that when they have to face truth in this way, as long as they are unhurried and undominated, they nearly always choose the right set of values and behave accordingly. Sometimes they enlist the confidence and friendship of an adult, but this is generally to bolster up their own views. In most instances they have decided already. On the other hand, in all of us there is a certain joy in doing what we know to be wrong. The " legal framework " mentioned just now is very helpful here. Girls will often act brassy, flashy or tomboy characters—be women, in fact, that a yearning part of them would like to be. It is far better that they should work off this yearning in a legal framework than *be* the character in real life. Similarly, with boys we see great violence and roguery being worked off ; gangsters and spivs would appear to be the symbols of this age's evil. The eternal nightmare character of both sexes is the dentist.

With both boys and girls it is most marked that continued opportunity for playing out brings its own release, and girls ultimately turn their Play to smart women rather than flashy ones, comedy girls rather than crooks, and with lads we see an eventual movement away from " wide-boys " to adventure characters like Holmes, Robin Hood and Christopher Columbus. The good story of any period may now be seized upon by Children of this age, and the adult, judging the right moment very carefully, by one right word may successfully lead Play out of eternal blood to hope and constructive adventure.

There is often a remarkable capacity for learning at this age, and there is a certain danger that too much may be forced upon the Child. It is very important that out-flow should balance with in-flow. It will not be found that time taken away from learning is a loss, as out-flow will aid the process of digestion. It must happen, and it should be regular. This is one function of Child Drama.

Because of the delight in learning, Children may often incorporate into their own Drama things they have learnt, such as country dances, long speeches or poems that have nothing to do with the piece. Songs may be incorporated that may seem out of place ; I remember a very holy band of monks, for instance, who would keep bursting out suddenly into *Roll out the barrel*. But there is a certain logic about this, after all. Most of what seems out of place to us is the result of using our own set of values again, as we did over the toddler and the piece of paper. We associate intellectual ideas and situations together. The Child associates *joys* together. Loved learnt things, together with loved improvised things, may be inserted in Play at any age, but it happens more often with older Children.

Most Children act grown-up parts. This fact should make us seriously consider our own behaviour, for a general assessment of what Children act, as a part result of what they see, is indeed a shattering indictment of human nature. Above all, the Child's interpretation of the way most teachers behave gives much food for thought.

At an age when the body, exterior things, materialism, practical details, economic factors, further understanding about discipline and clock time come into the picture, we notice, somewhat naturally, that there is not quite such suffering at being interrupted. Life is slightly less of a dream, though dream moments are still of value. The Child is more prepared to have life ordered into a timetable ; there is a certain delight even in personal organising, though this might turn to bossiness and superiority if not carefully watched. There is joy also in being tidy and " on time ", and some Children show a genuine irritation at slackness and lateness, and will persecute persistent offenders with their increasing vocabulary and sharpened wit.

In their Drama, these things are evidenced by a much greater regard for and need of correct properties. Details must be absolutely right. Much time often goes into preparation. I have seen a table moved fifteen times before a piece of Child Drama commenced, and it had to be right to the inch. Nevertheless there is still the danger of overloading, though as a rule the Child is now old enough to sense this danger to creation for itself, and often discards what would hamper it. This is excellent training in common sense and thrift. Child Drama owes much of its beauty always to its concern with economy. Its finest examples have a true simplicity about them, even an asceticism. What is left is utterly *necessary*, and for this reason it shines like a jewel. The late Egerton Clarke once said to me : " Good poetry has a stone-like quality," and on another occasion : " That poem is well cut." Child Drama is like that.

Language Flow (*Later Stage*)

The increased vocabulary brings with it further developments in Language Flow, but these will be moving rather away from deep unconscious philosophy towards the amusing phrase and quick wit of a cultured society. This is all part of the increased consciousness of things material. The flow itself, though, may now become phenomenal. I have known Children speak clearly for over an hour, and so rapidly, and with such full dialogue, that it seemed almost impossible to believe that one was not listening to a first-class company performing a play by some new Oscar Wilde. (In a way, of course, it was a first-class company, for they were practised in Child Drama, and may or may not be writers of the future, though that is not the point at issue.) The dialogue was of course improvised. Sometimes when using a story the same sort of thing will happen. Very little of the original dialogue where such exists may be used ; the plot will be taken, the rest will be created. The gang and its leader will still be apparent, but often the Language Flow is common to the group, and not just carried on chiefly by one or two persons.

Projects

Projects can play an important part at this age. The detail is enjoyed. Gangs are employed. Leaders have opportunity, but gang may integrate with gang. The particular form of this creative study is unequalled in its natural balance of in-flow and out-flow, and this is probably one of the secrets of the remarkable results of this method upon learning and general behaviour. Child Drama enters into projects a great deal, particularly in the impersonation of peoples of other races and other times. Projects can also actually *aid* Child Drama for the above reasons.

It will be noted, too, that there is also opportunity for a balance between projected Play and personal Play. In preparation, or in making things, there is projected Play, and any final impersonation is personal Play.[1] By attaining this balance (and remember that the Child never works harder than when at Play) it is astonishing the amount of knowledge that can be gained ; it is the way in which a Child can immerse itself in a subject, as a university professor will do by other means ; and common to both is extreme pleasure in learning, tremendous use of the imagination, and intense joy at the process. It is one way, at least, of making school a happy place—and why shouldn't it be happy ?

How many Children are made to suffer from the stormcloud of the exam, hanging there dark and sinister, night and day, till the only thing that one has room for in one's brain is the sheer *worry* of the cloud ? And, where this does not actually happen, how many schools centre all life round tests, and leave no time at all for personal development, leisure-time interests, emotional training, and training in loyalty and good manners ? Can such schools be said to be turning out even good citizens, let alone human beings? Would not more training in shape, beauty and personal relationships be equally important to society as well as to design, craftsmanship and team spirit in our business houses, professions and factories ? Child Drama provides great opportunities here, and can do so, if need be, in periods of only twenty minutes at a time.

---

[1] For an excellent example of this, see the description of a visit to a senior girls' school. Chapter XIV, pages 226–230 (24).

Preparation for Life after School

The tendency to draw on and notice outside things, and, above all, people, brings about a certain emulation.   Adolescents will try to be like people they have seen.   There is something of the gang leader in this, something of hero worship, and also a quite frank Life-trial not unlike the early Play-trials ; for the strange thing is that there will now appear not only a copying of people admired, but even at times of people definitely disliked or despised. This is a further form of Drama and characterisation.   Who am I ?   I must try to see.   Could I be her ?   I will try for a bit.   I do not think I am him, but I will try it for a time and see.   Or even there may be : " I could never really be so-and-so, but I must be them for a while."   Film stars, television stars and " pop " singers are associated with : " if only I were her " in girls, or when it has sunk deep, " I am her ".   This last is not a very satisfactory state, and needs watching carefully.

Playing out and trying out follows naturally on all this, and, with girls, hair may go into funny shapes now, and faces a funny colour.   Much Drama, particularly outside school, is associated with hair styles amongst girls, until they have decided that they are *not* a certain film star, and a period of comparative calm sets in again.   It is of the utmost importance that none of these manifestations should receive undue ridicule from adults, as this will come from companions, particularly of the opposite sex, and is enough to stand.   There should be the same sharing in trials, mastery and joys at all times, and often one word of personal opinion (not obvious advice, unless asked for) will ease the situation.

With lads, we enter upon a full spate of hair oil and coloured ties.   Odd things may go on in the area of side whiskers, with the older ones, should any question of shaving begin before leaving school.   They will often become clumsy and pretend to be over-masculine and lout-like, even rude in a pathetic sort of way, to cover this up.   It becomes more apparent in feminine company, though it then takes on a cloak of jocularity.

Both sexes can work happily together at this age, when necessary, although much good work is done apart, but there is a difficulty of the girls developing faster in some ways and becoming more interested in older boys, so that younger boys are discountenanced.

Many adolescents are violently disturbed by blemishes, and the pain and loathsomeness of this scourge, bringing with it continual taunts and questions, may affect behaviour much more than is generally understood.   Shyness, moroseness, effeminacy in boys, masculinity in girls, bad temper, dislike of opposite sex, distrust in companions, lack of concentration in study are among the things that can be traced to this cause. While it is true that many Children pass fairly smoothly through puberty, and that sentimentalising does not help the situation, it is also true that many agonies are entirely overlooked, even exacerbated by adult unthoughtfulness. Child Drama will aid what in many ways is a difficult period. Make-up and masks both offer temporary relief from a face which the owner may hate.

There may be a strong desire for dressing up as the opposite sex, and, although this should not be crushed, care should be taken, and further opportunity for meeting the opposite sex provided. It is a form of personal identification not too much to be encouraged, for should it in any way become arrested, difficulties will without doubt arise. Great harm may be done by the continued forcing of one Child into playing parts of the opposite sex because of looks or behaviour. This is, of course, less likely to happen in Child Drama, which only exists where the circumstances are propitious. But it is a menace of the script play.

Script Plays

We are not really concerned in this book with script plays as generally conceived, because they are not Child Drama. If during rehearsal, however, the characterisation is bad, if reading becomes a difficulty, if a scene becomes somewhat dead, and if Children are losing initiative by being ordered about, Child Drama can even help with these. It may be employed by breaking up the scene and saying, in effect : " All right, come down off the stage. Now forget all about your books, the words, the moves. Just think of the story and who you are. Now, if you were really that person and that was happening, what do you think you'd do and what would you say ? " When they have been somewhat coaxed, Children will often begin to forget about lines of sight, and start to act-in-the-round on the floor space. They become released by this process, and encouragement may help them to build a really life-like scene in their own words. When returned to the stage, the script rehearsal is generally very much improved, though that which chains the Child will still remain to some extent.

By this method it is often possible to obtain alarming revelations about how little the average Child does really understand a play written by an adult. When asked to say what they would say in their own words, they often admit to not understanding in the least what the script words mean or what the situation is supposed to be. When this is re-explained to them they then start to create with that indomitable courage with which they face everything when given a fair chance.

With or without script plays, though, it is not good to give too many suggestions, for this makes them give up trying, and everything goes dead. The adult's difficulty is that the Child's interest in all Dramatic work, even that which strangles its own expression, makes it chary of admitting what it does not understand. But many far older actors and actresses attempt to get away with this half-understanding. Only the deepest, most penetrating understanding is of any use in the study and portrayal of a part, and that is why the Child's own Drama is so infinitely better, because what is played is fully understood, in so far as personal development allows. The stage script play, though attaining a certain standard at this age, cannot compare with Child Drama in the realm of electric atmosphere and emotional shared experience. The Child's own work often gives us a vital theatre experience, whereas in the script play we too often see little actors merely acting at being actors.

I do not say this because I want to malign in any way the courageous attempts of the young people themselves when acting adult plays, but I do seriously question seeing so much second-rate work (and if it is not seen for second-rate, things are worse than I thought), and I question, too, the vulgarity of creative artists being made to do the work of other people when their own is so much better, not only in its effect but also in its suitability. Let those of us who delight in literature and intellect take a joy in it. Let those who are unsurpassed in creating mood, exhibiting grace, dominating space, working together, and creating a modern form of the old Italian theatre be allowed to do so. And let us older ones open our eyes and try to recognise beauty when it comes our way. Literature is only digested when people are ready for it. Some Children are ready at this age. Some are not.

Dance

The Dance is again an important factor between twelve years and fifteen. It can become a thing of great wonder and fantastic charm with girls, and it is not entirely unknown amongst boys either. In both sexes it nurtures grace, confidence and virility. There can be wonderful moments of sincerity and absorption, and, despite the realism of the age, occasional flights into the world of fantasy. We notice again, as in their speech, the influence of more formal training, particularly of modern dance, country dancing and Greek dance. Complete sections of this work may be inserted from time to time. At others, the technique, steps or general movement may be partly drawn upon. At others we discern only the accumulated wisdom which has arisen as an aroma from any or all of these experiences, the dance itself being Child-created. The worst dance is the frank imitation, whether of ballet or anything else. The attitude of the dancers is generally different on these occasions, and there is an unsatisfactory atmosphere. The process might be described as dancing at being dancers dancing a dance, for it is the same as the un-genuine acting.

Modern Dance (Laban) can produce a certain widening of the mind to envisage the use of space and imaginary characterisation, where previous opportunity for the use of space has not been adequate. Much technical excellence can be achieved at this age. Too much dressing up destroys the dance, but fortunately the practice costume for most formal dance is sensible and free for girls nowadays, and they often take some of this asceticism voluntarily into their own creations. The best dance I have seen amongst girls has been in tunics and headdress, and amongst boys with ordinary shirt and trousers. (See Plate 6, opposite page 81.)

Boys are not always easy to handle at this age and there may be some noise at times. There are moments when firm handling is needed. But one cannot always have climax without noise any more than a workshop without banging. The tendency towards realism often makes fight scenes somewhat tough. There comes a time, though, when they themselves realise that too much noise and reality make things uncomfortable for everybody. In the first fight scenes of older boys, who have not had free work earlier, there is always a sort of rugby football scrum. The shape is always circular, and filled in—very filled in. It is like a toadstool. It ultimately collapses. In order to get away from the extreme desire for handling one's opponent it may be found appropriate to suggest fighting with various imagined weapons. There can even be a forfeit for anyone who actually touches another person, until moral responsibility is fully accepted and recognised. Further freedom can then be allowed. (See Plate 26, opposite page 241.)

It is possible to achieve high forms of beauty in stylised fighting to a music or percussion background ; and this may be a lead into dance. I am inclined to think that a much wider study of Greek dance for boys would be of great benefit. There are many movements associated with athletics and field events, and the link between extreme physical hardiness and other forms of beauty would do much to overcome any natural shyness of culture,

PLATE 5

SENIOR GIRLS in improvised play, semi-stylised dumb show.
Note the spill-over from stage.   (*See* pp. 70-73.)

SENIOR GIRLS.   Imaginative dance taking place at the far end of hall
nowhere near the stage.   (*See* p. 79 and p. 217.)

Photos by Taylor's Press Service

PLATE 6

SENIOR GIRLS.   Flowing up to the stage.   Note influence of Modern Dance, particularly in group on right.   (*See* p. 8o.)

SENIOR GIRLS.   Dance of the trees.   Imaginative improvisation.

Photos by Taylor's Press Service

which may arise at this age—partly born out of fear of being clumsy at an age when the opposite sex is less clumsy. Any boy who is less clumsy, becomes, therefore, somewhat more like the opposite sex and thus open to ridicule. The whole attitude wars continually against Art, literature, cleanliness and good manners. We could help all of them here a good deal more than we do, though physical education has done a lot, for this pose about toughness has its dangers, and if allowed to continue is not altogether unconnected with the more violent street-gang outbursts, which, under certain circumstances, lead to crime.

The general attitude also succumbs, without any real relinquishment of true manly qualities, to social training in Drama—as scenes in a drawing-room, how to behave in the office of the boss—and both sexes derive much benefit from group documentary-play creations built around personal and social problems.

Polished Improvisations and Play-writing

The polished improvisation is very popular at this age. An improvisation is worked upon and polished until the older Child's concern for detail is satisfied. They may want to show this to their companions, but the general feeling running right through the best Child Drama is : " I am creating this here and now because I want to, and because I find it joyous and beautiful." The extreme concentration arising out of this virile and remarkably healthy attitude does not leave much room for audiences as the adult understands them. (See Plates 23 and 24, between pages 232 and 233.)

As has been described earlier, we find the best attempts at the written play arising out of these improvisations. Loved sentences or moves are kept and sometimes noted down. The wealth of experience from these, and the greater ability of the older, more meticulous mind to arrange facts, together with the further practice in writing and speaking which have now been had, all bring to these later attempts at play-writing something which makes them at once more actable and more acceptable. Furthermore, these plays belong more nearly to the type of theatre which is being arrived at in the organic development of the Child and, because they are a truer expression of the age, they are altogether more genuine. They compare as Art reasonably well with other Art processes, whilst the earlier attempts at play-writing, save for very rare examples, cannot compare with anything else that the Child does at that time because they have not grown truly out of the Child. But these plays of the thirteen-, fourteen- or fifteen-year-olds may have quite worthy qualities. Their dialogue is often good and they offer more action to the Players. They are not so disappointing to act. They often contain lovely moments, if earlier attempts have been somewhat restrained, and if some preparatory groundwork has been envisaged and employed.

To some extent in their written play attempts, Children maintain an element of secrecy. They may keep very quiet about their work, then suddenly disclose it. In group play creation with the teacher there is a good deal of sharing, and further advance may come from this, but much is done entirely by them. There appears to be a real need for moments of privacy at this age. Groups will go right away, if they can, and thrash out a story and rehearse it in a room or place unseen.

Associated with this, there is also a most interesting phenomenon of a sort of Hinterland Activity. The simple form of this is that, where a stage and curtains exist, the stage will be " borrowed " by a group (not necessarily for performance), the curtains will be firmly closed and creation and discussion take place behind their warm privacy. This is particularly true of girls. Sometimes there will even be further secret activity going on behind a shown piece. There may be Play on view on the stage whilst other Play is going on behind a back drop or in a room behind.[1] There is always a feeling of something " going on behind the scenes " in this activity. It is a hinterland activity, not on view at the coastline ; it is deeper in the Child's nature, inland and nearer the actual " land " that they go to during high moments of creation. (See Plate 47, between pages 360 and 361.)

The older Child may begin to approach adult plays on occasions, but they will not always do the ones we would like. Care must be taken in any introduction to our world that there is no forcing, and often plays will be seized upon which offer further opportunities for playing out characters rather than for literary study. Occasionally laying good literature in the path of the questing adolescent may be useful with the fourteen-and-a-half- to fifteen-year-old. (Good books should be always available.) Good literature may be accepted. If not, the time is not ripe. In most instances their own group creations are still better material for them to act, and may remain so for some adolescents even after leaving school. In both sexes, drawing near to, and even accepting our Drama in some cases, brings with it a natural flood of interest in lighting, scene painting and construction. Much good genuine Child painting is obtainable at this age.

We still find many intelligent people bemoaning the fact that great artists

---

[1] See example on page 215 (*19b*).

do not yet write plays for Children to act. This is to misunderstand completely, and to underestimate considerably, the Children's own creative ability. No one can write for them. There is no need. There is complete acceptance of adult standards when the time is ripe. But those not ready, in their own way, and under the right conditions (which show signs of being widely extended) are of themselves supreme. They have their own Art. Ours pales before it.

Kahlil Gibran, writing about Children in *The Prophet*,[1] says :

" You may give them your love but not your thoughts,
For they have their own thoughts.
You may house their bodies but not their souls,
For their souls dwell in the house of tomorrow, which you cannot visit not even in your dreams.
You may strive to be like them, but seek not to make them like you."

Although this is less true of the adolescent than of the young Child (only because, in growing up, there is an approach towards our mentality and way of life), it remains fundamentally sound advice on the Child in general. Any bond built between youth and age is a tender, breakable thing. We are allowed to share more if we do not expect too much. But what we can do is pause to sympathise and admire.

[1] Published by Messrs. William Heinemann, Ltd.

CHAPTER V

COMPARISONS

PERHAPS one of the reasons for our difficulty in appreciating Child Drama at first is that we tend to compare it too rapidly with what we know. Most people know the type of theatre where you merely sit and watch; when curtains open you are expected to look, when they shut you stop looking. But this is by no means the only type of theatre, and even within the framework of this theatre we find examples of attempted rebellion.

But let us take a quick glance at the general field of Drama and its history.

One of the chief characteristics of Child Play is the Journey; there is no permanent place of rest, all is fluid; but as the Child grows older it slowly imposes upon itself a more rigid and static form. The Dream World of the young Child needs the space of the Journey. Later, acceptance of our reality fines things down to a particular place, at first temporarily used, and finally mainly used.

We have a very close comparison with Child Drama in the ancient Egyptian Passion Play of Osiris,[1] which was performed at *and in the neighbourhood of Abydos*. Its date is thought to be some 3,000 years before Christ. We have an account of it by its producer I-kher-nefert, who speaks and behaves just like a young gang leader. He organises everything, and chooses and plays the best parts himself. He performs, for instance, the great Coming Forth, follows the God in his footsteps, makes his boat to move. After other adventures he arranges the overthrow of all the God's enemies on the dyke of Netit. Compare this with the chapters on Language Flow and the examples given.[2]

The Osiris play lasted three days and the procession *moved from place to place*. Drama is all about us. We find in it pomp, enemies, journey, marriage, death, vengeance and resurrection. All are typical of Child Play, even to the body of Osiris which was found cut in fourteen pieces. There

[1] See *Osiris and the Egyptian Resurrection*, by Sir E. A. W. Budge (published by the Medici Society). "*Adonis, Attis, Osiris*", from *The Golden Bough*, by Sir James Frazer (published by Macmillan & Co.). For short reference account: *Dramatic Criticism*, by S. R. Littlewood (published by Pitman).
[2] See Chapter XIII, page 174.

were fights at various places (repetition of particularly loved improvised action), and we even find *Audience Participation* when the vast crowds, which had gathered to watch, joined in, and uttered piercing shrieks, the women beating their breasts, at the entry of the body into the temple.

The description itself, as we have it from I-kher-nefert, is so uninhibited, is such pure Language Flow, is so *good*, that it might have been declaimed by a six-year-old. In fact, the only thing about the Osiris Play which differs from Child Drama in general terms is that it seems likely that actual death of animals, and probably people, was associated with it. Thus, although highly organised in some ways, it was rather what we have called the wild Drama of the streets, ending perhaps in what modern civilised society, with its different values, calls juvenile delinquency. It is this ending to wild Play that Child Drama under supervision in school, home or club, tries to avoid.

Another characteristic of Child Play is the circle, and we find it appearing in many old traditional dances of this and other lands. Often it is associated with hunting and the chase, and we even find it in the rings of the target in archery and modern shooting, thus associating it with the very weapons of the chase.

In the African tribal dances you find stamping, clapping, the circle, the journey and also considerable Audience Participation ; smear and pattern make-up too, as well as masks. All pertain to Child Drama.

In this country an interesting example of tradition is the Abbots Bromley Horn Dance, Staffordshire. By kind permission of *Staffordshire Life* I include part of M. M. B. Higham's description of it :

" . . . this is a place which is *held* by its past, however much its younger citizens may elect to work in Uttoxeter or Burton. It has no railway station and men who live there today can trace their family name back for centuries.

" I met such a man there the other day, when visiting the little township to see the Horn Dance. He was the leader of this ancient dance, which has made the place famous. Dressed in the quaint, traditional coloured breeches and jacket of the team of local dancing men, he was standing, resting a few minutes under the 'Butter Market', before starting the Dance again, while the rest of the men and lads sat at their ease on a strip of grass before the inn. I could not help watching him, for his face entranced me—lean, parchment coloured, as some old manuscript, immobile. . . . Tomorrow he would be at work again, a twentieth-century workman, but today he had the absorbed look of some Renaissance scholar. All at once, I realized why he had that look of culture and reserve. It was because he was guarding something he values. He was guarding the Horn Dance ! . . . This was his great day. He must protect it, preserving for all time the Horn Dance, and his eyes looked almost jealously over the old-world properties ; the hobby horse, the triangle, the great spans of antlers. . . . At a swift signal from the man, the dancers rose to their feet and once again, as they had done at intervals throughout the day, went through the movements of the Dance. First they moved slowly in a circle, holding their heavy reindeer horns, then they wound in and out as in an old Morris Dance. Next they formed themselves in two lines and proceeded to mime the pageantry of the hunt, to the accompaniment of triangle and modern concertina, with almost fanatic sincerity, as if taking part in some rite. I watched them with sympathy and respect as they stepped slowly, heavily, in time to the simple little air, repeating the movements again and again—the circle, the weaving, the long lines to and fro, while the crossbow clicked and the hobby horse clacked and Maid Marion, crowned and in a long white gown, once again made her annual obeisance to her lord and master Robin Hood !

" No one knows for certain the origin of the Dance, though there are several theories, all of them likely. Does it celebrate the winning of forest rights from some hard-hearted feudal Lord Paget, Welles or Bagot ? Is it of greater antiquity, celebrating some pagan idea of animal power, as men danced in antler and hides ? Is it a Moorish dance introduced by John of Gaunt ? Are the reindeer horns pre-Norman ? Such questions may never be answered for certain, but this we do know, that the Dance is really ancient, that the horns are kept for safety in the church and that, by unwritten law, it may never be performed outside the Parish boundary."

One cannot help being struck by the extraordinary similarity of this to Child Play, and the amount we can learn from it.

The author of this account even starts by speaking of humility and of " walking delicately, like Agag " before launching into his description. This is the right attitude in which to approach Child Drama.

We find that the leader of the Dance had an " absorbed " look ; later we find mention of " fanatic sincerity ". These are the qualities of the best

Child Drama.   There is the man himself "guarding something ".   The Child, too, guards its creations, but the creation is easily shattered, and we have to help in the guarding.   This man was old enough to guard it himself.   The sounds and percussion are common to the Horn Dance and to Child Drama, also the weaving, pageantry and circle.

This intelligent watcher looked on with " sympathy and respect ".   That again is exactly the attitude with which we should watch Child Drama, if we come upon it.

We note antlers are worn.   There is a little dressing up (the main costume appears to be a period costume almost, so that it would have been, perhaps, practically everyday clothes at one time).   The concertina is somewhat modern, having been added.   Thus time adds, and period is mixed.   Such anachronisms often appear in Child Drama.

Finally, there is considerable latitude for dancing in different places, except outside the Parish boundary.   This might almost be likened to the classroom walls or those of the school hall.   (See Plate 7, opposite page 88.)

We have already mentioned the mediaeval central stage and the some-what circular audience, so like the shape found in some infant and junior schools, where rostrum blocks rather than a formal stage are used.

In the chapter on Children's Theatre,[1] some mention is made of the gallery and of the importance of looking down on Child work.   It is thus that we see the beauties of the movement and the use of floor space.   A modern comparison with this is the spectacular film.   We often see a dancing scene photographed from above ; sometimes there is even recognition of the beauties of the circle, when dancers join in a ring and sit or slowly lie down, forming, as it were, with hands and leg movements, swift-growing flower petals, which blossom before our eyes.   This we find in Child Drama in a simpler form.[2]

For high levels, low levels, different localities, entrances by different doors, comedy and surprise, we have our fill in the joyous antics of the Palladium Theatre Crazy Gang.   They also use " flow on and off " the stage, though prolonged periods of acting, including slap-stick, take place *on* the stage.   The first part of this paragraph is similar to junior school Child Drama, where rostrum blocks are used, the second to the evolution in the secondary school (*circa* thirteen years upwards).   The jumping up out of the audience is not unlike Child Drama in the crowded classroom, where some have to sit but join in as and when they can.

[1] See Chapter XVI.   [2] See Chapter XIV : Improvised dance at a senior girls school, page 233.

Modern floor shows share some things with the Child, particularly flowing off the stage, or sometimes by putting the band *on* the stage and letting action take place on the floor. The adagio dance is often an example of dancing amongst and surrounded by people. And in the wandering singer we find the Journey, and Drama, as it were, all about us, sometimes far, sometimes near.

Passing through the audience does not occur only in the West—it is to be found in the East also. The masks of the East have many things in common with Child Art, and the Japanese theatre with its charming toylike quality and sensitivity is worth study. The Chinese theatre, too, has much to teach about the incorporation of sound and sound effects. It is worth our notice, in passing, that a certain " spiritual " quality has been extolled in Japanese theatre, and that, this apart, there exist the Nō plays—" Plays of accomplishment ". It is accomplishment that is the essence of Child Drama.

In China, it was the Emperor Ming Huang, as long ago as the eighth century, who founded the Pear Garden, a mixed Youth School of 300 persons, to study a new Art-Drama. It seems that he got the idea from a profound mystic adventure into the Dream World, on his return from which he knew about Drama, in which he included much emotional sound training. The use of sound occurs in Africa also. In China, Africa and Japan there is a strong traditional link with the past. Children incorporate sound in like manner.

The toylike charm of Child Play and its simple outward expression of vast, inward vision is to be found also in the American Negro Play *Green Pastures*. The Negro spirituals are also full of the Journey, as is that considerable bulk of musical expression lumped together under the title of "the Blues ". It is interesting that the Negro music of modern times arose out of improvisation ; there is intense interest in time beat and percussion, and the blossoming of the sound arose around marching festivals (the Journey). The Drama did not stay in one place, and that is why we find the names of different streets entering, e.g. the old classic *Basin Street Blues*. Whatever we think of Jazz, it has lessons to teach, and we could approach it with humility, for it offers us such things as the " jam session ". In the 1920s musicians would gather together for evenings of music, not for an audience, but in order to create. Chamber music is the same idea. Children create their Drama in this way.

The manner of the Jazz creation was improvisation, and its quality was spontaneity. This spontaneity is prized above all things, and, though it is clearly and rightly pointed out that an improvisation was a description only

PLATE 7

Rough Circle. The Horn Dance, Abbot's Bromley. (*See* p. 85.)

By courtesy of "Staffordshire Life"

The Horn Dance, Abbot's Bromley. (*See* p. 85.)

By courtesy of "Staffordshire Life"

Older actors, and some young, playing in tongue shape flowing on and off stage. A scene from the Wanstead and Woodford Road Safety Pageant.

By courtesy of the "Amateur Stage"

PLATE 8

Intimate Arena Theatre.   The Apex Theatre, Birmingham.

Intimate Theatre Group.   Arena Theatre, August 1948.   *The Little Foxes*—Lillian Hellman.
(*See* p. 92.)

By kind permission of " Birmingham Post and Mail " and Intimate Theatre Group

fitting the first creation, repetition could be tolerated and approved if it contained at least an illusion of spontaneity. In other words, it must have *life*. This is exactly the same as Child Drama, and the Negro rule about repetition applies also. We have called repetition a "polished improvisation"; it should, however, be repeated only in so far as it continues to contain "spontaneity", as when this dies so do Sincerity and Absorption—but it is spontaneity above all else that practice in Child Drama ultimately brings to adult theatre.

Paul Edouard Miller has drawn our attention to the fact that appreciation of jazz is dependent upon the listener's comprehension of spontaneity, to which he adds sincerity.[1] He also points to its emotional intensity. In its technique he values not complexity but *facility*, and in its organisation—clarity. These are wise and excellent yardsticks, not only for measuring the fascinating romantic phenomenon that arose out of New Orleans, but also because they tell what to seek in good Child Drama. Those who cannot feel the emotional spell of spontaneity will never understand the beauties of the Child. But if you can feel it to any degree, it can be developed.

Spontaneity, of course, is not by any means confined only to modern times ; it has always existed as a quality, but it came very much to the fore in Italy about the same time that the Renaissance was influencing the building of theatres for spectacular productions.

The now famous Commedia dell'Arte was a separate development, it was simpler, more part of the people. The dialogue of their plays was improvised, and to this extent it was exactly like Child Drama, though they rather confined their activities by developing set characters—rather like our "type casting". An actor would become this character, so to speak, and by eternally being that person, began in time to turn on the sort of speech that that person would use. (We have here the exact interpretation of the more modern Russian training, e.g. Stanislavsky's "if "—*If* you were that person under those circumstances, what would you say and what would you do ?)

The Child can type-cast itself, too, but its best work is done by being many different characters. Nevertheless it uses the chief weapon of the Commedia dell'Arte—improvisation. A great many teachers still feel that improvisation is unimportant. For those that have doubts, not only did the Commedia dell'Arte win tremendous popular favour in face of terrific competition and alternative propaganda, but had a strong influence on

---

[1] "Analysis of the Art of Jazz", included in *Esquire's Jazz Book*, published Peter Davies Ltd. (London).

Europe for nigh on 200 years, particularly in France. Perhaps we might say with more truth that it has influenced the world ever since, for many a play-wright short of characters or plot has fallen back on the commedia stock characters, and mime and improvisations are still appreciated in France. We have, in modern times, the interesting experiments of M. Chancerel in Paris with his Youth Groups, Mr. Robert Newton with the unemployed in the early 1930s in this country, and many others who have found the approach invaluable for starting things off. It is only recently, though, that it has again been possible to obtain any serious consideration for this form of playing, which could have done so much for our theatre.

The Pear Tree Players,[1] with which I had the honour to be associated, were among those who began to consider this work seriously. In the early 1940s they started training on improvised dance, and ended by being able to make up a play anywhere, any time, producing a remarkable flow of language. Sometimes stock characters were used, sometimes a few stock sentences, at other times completely new characters and scenes were devised. Even amongst their more formal programmes they would include a mime (without properties) to sound effects. Others group in this country that I know of who have carried the art at all far in modern times, are amateur ones—the Phoenix Players of Birmingham, comprised almost entirely of teachers, the Birmingham Children's Theatre Players and others.

The noses found on the masks of the Commedia dell' Arte appear fre-quently in Child Art to this day, and probably always will, because the type of joyful outlook which created the masks is shared by Children everywhere.

A very remarkable theatre opened in 1926 under the name of the Cam-bridge Festival Theatre. Its director was Terence Gray. The policy of this theatre was quite frankly one of rebellion—to wage war on illusion and glamour. Regarding properties, Gray felt that more message lay in depict-ing what was not there than in using the thing itself. This is the same as the Child, and is the basis of the asceticism we have already observed. Also at the Festival Theatre, Drama was all about you. Different levels were used ; the wings of the theatre were removed at one time, so that stage hands could be seen. This would be a very good excuse for forcing an audience to understand " Absorption " in one particular scene or place and learn not to notice what didn't matter. But various explanations are given as Gray's reason for doing it. Amongst other things, he held that the picture stage of the West End was two-dimensional. This is a point worth consider-

---

[1] For further details about these players, see Chapter XVI, page 291.

ing, for it is undoubted that a good deal of trickery has to be used in order to provide an interesting picture. Perspective of any kind is a trick. The young Child has not learned the trick, nor does it see things in that way. It therefore indulges naturally in three-dimensional Drama, and only becomes fully interested in theatre later, as audiences and trickery fit in with its mental development. By that time perspective and " reality " are appearing in its paintings and drawings also.

An excellent short account of the Festival Theatre appears in Norman Marshall's *The Other Theatre*,[1] but no description can do justice to the impact of the directness of presentation received at that place. Apart from the insistence on the use of imagination, and the use of interesting groups and shapes, it is a particular form of impact that the work of this theatre shared with Child Drama. It can occasionally be perceived now in the work of a good junior school.

The ascetic tendency of arranging for a view of the actors waiting to come on, and the scene-shifters, is to be found also in the work of Thornton Wilder. The sparseness of furniture used in his plays is very akin to using a plain rostrum as a mountain, a seat, or upside down as a ship. A great load is put on the imagination. What is to be our attitude ? Are we to confess that we are too comfort-loving and we cannot accept the load, or do we prove ourselves as virile as the Child and join in, saying "We can take it"? The Child goes further, of course, with " I really prefer it ".

When we come to the flow *towards* the stage, normally arising after twelve years of age in Child Play, we must consider such productions as *The Marvellous History of St. Bernard*, at Birmingham Repertory and at Malvern Festival. The Devils and the Pilgrims entered from the audience, and flowed up on to the stage. It was utterly right and necessary to allow for this flow and for this Journey. Likewise, the entry of the Airman down the aisle of Lichfield Cathedral, in the 1946 production of Dorothy Sayer's *The Just Vengeance*, was a tremendous addition to the emotional atmosphere. I have never experienced such a moment anywhere else except in Child Drama, when the same sort of movement takes place. The unexpected rush, and the gentle flow of the Pilgrims' entrance mentioned above, are both discovered by the Child in the happy secondary school, or even earlier, without perhaps ever going to the theatre.

In the Shakespearean theatre we find projection out into the audience, and in the Greek theatre we find the part-circle. Both these are similar to

[1] Published by John Lehmann.

the " bulge " in Child work, which happens in cramped classrooms and with older groups in the senior school hall.

In modern times the Intimate Theatre Group, under John English, has presented the public with its horseshoe arena productions with the intention of " bringing the intimacy of the film to modern audiences ", and placing their faith in " sharing *with* rather than acting *at* ". This is exactly the attitude of Child Drama. (See Plate 8, opposite page 89.)

At the Little Theatre conference at Highbury, which took place before this experimental group was launched, Prof. Allardyce Nicoll put forward the idea that, even from the literary point of view, the theatre would not obtain any more great writers until it changed its outward from, as form affected the playwright. Be this as it may, form affects the Child, and it is interesting that the general trend is now coming more into line with what Children have been showing us or could have shown us all along. Some adult groups go even further than the bulge, and have been playing in a full circle[1] for years, particularly in America. It is a most exciting way of playing, and if you know nothing of it, it is a delight to come.[2]

These then are but a few examples out of the multitude which history provides. From these alone, though, it may be seen that a wide view of Drama and Life is valuable in assessing Children's work. Some indication is also given in these examples of certain lines of further study for those interested. Our lesson from all this is perhaps that, far from producing an inferior Art Form, the Child creates for itself something which draws upon all the beauties known to Man from the beginning of time, upon the history of the theatre and upon Life. It uses what has been found to have integrity, and therefore what is best. It has its temptations, but we can help in this. Child Drama draws unconsciously upon the wisdom of the world.

[1] *In late years we have seen the development of Theatre-in-the-Round under Dr. Stephen Joseph and numbers of Theatre for Children Groups.*—AUTHOR.

[2] *Since this was written, the author has drawn my attention to the tremendous increase in ice pantomime-carnivals which, according to statistics, are rapidly exceeding in popularity the normal proscenium Christmas productions. He feels that in this entertainment his remarks about the shape of the journey taken by the actor will prove even more forcible. He has already mentioned this as imagery (see page 30) : here it is becoming fact.*—EDITOR.

CHAPTER VI

LANGUAGE FLOW (1)

DURING the trials leading to Play, and through Play proper, we hear the growing creation of speech and perceive its processes.

In the first stages of the baby's vocal sound attempts, experiments in time, rhythm and climax can be heard. Loved sounds, or sounds of sudden created pleasure, are repeated, sometimes very often. Attempts at message begin. We now have the embryo mixture of sounds and ideas. As soon as we perceive this meaning entering, we may greatly encourage further effort by taking the first efforts seriously and by answering the baby in jibberish of made-up sound. Care should be taken to use intended climax and vary vowel sounds and musical intonation. At the same time there should be clarity of diction and stress laid on consonants; no sentimentalising. Sometimes this may all be begun by our copying, as nearly as we can, the attempted sounds of the baby.

I have many times been struck by the ability of babies to recognise a repetition of their own attempt. I would put this at *circa* one year. The recognition is a wonderful experience for both adult and Child. A look of radiant joy passes over the baby's face; there is generally a pause, taking in the experience (" in-flow "), then a burst of laughter or shriek of delight. Creation then starts afresh with renewed vigour and joy (" out-flow "). Meanwhile, a special bond has been established between two persons, and I have often taken joy in quite long conversations of this kind which have been eminently satisfactory to both parties. What was the satisfaction ?

I think it is in every such case the shared emotional experience (later in adult life we call this experience " good theatre "), and the delight of using music as an interpretation of ideas. For music has a language of ideas. Words no doubt grew out of sounds, and therefore out of music, and in their preciseness of meaning they are only *sometimes* more accurate than music ; they are perhaps easier and may be less emotional, but this first conversation bond with a baby is an emotional affair and is not primarily of the intellect, largely to satisfy which words were invented. This musical approach furthers *joy in sound*, which is the Child's first approach to all language. Thus may

93

come the first flash that emitted sound can form communication, other than the instinctive howl for mother, which is not yet consciously perceived as language in the same way.

The next step one might suggest is to continue with created sound language of this kind, but to put in an occasional word (of our adult language) which should be repeated often over several days. Then the early babble and cry, with its experiments in time and rhythm, and its attempts at inclusion of ideas, slowly gives place to some imitation. Some sounds are mastered. Words are not always quite mastered, but they will be in time.

As the Child grows older there is a great charm in solemn inexactitudes, and here again we should be careful not to laugh, but to share the pleasures of attainment, and, occasionally, gently correct, though *not* until speaking has ceased. Interruption causes confusion.

There are two developments in speech, apart from the actual physical mastery. They are of sound and of meaning. On the whole, too much stress is laid on meaning, and too little on sound. Meaning is of the realm of intellect, sound is of the realm of emotion, and it is because most adults cannot stand much of what we call " noise " that we tend to stifle a great deal of experiment in sound ; this prevents emotional and aesthetic development to some extent, and hinders the growth of love of sound. A genuine critical faculty based on a true love of sound leads to real appreciation of both speech and literature, as well as of Music. And it is this genuine love which is often lacking, not only in later years during school, but long after leaving, if indeed it is ever attained.

The intellectual side of speech dawns slowly on the Child, and if it is over-stressed we get from *early years* a lack-lustre form of speaking and a distressing habit of saying things without thought—saying things to please us, not because these things are loved. Real outbursts are what we should encourage and seek to develop. The early outbursts may be partly filled with unintelligible sounds, to fill up a sentence and make rhythm, where words are unknown. This is not talking nonsense; it is very sensible, and is the only thing to do under the circumstances. It is often jumped on, and the first unrecognised poetic attempts are thus stifled. These are not the same as baby-talk. Examples of similar expression are to be found in early English songs.

Baby-talk grows out of a sentimental adult attitude of intentionally using the wrong word. We should use the right words, once the Child can understand. However, a few specially invented descriptive names or words are valuable family symbols if accepted judicially. These can be easily distinguished from lazy-talk and baby-talk.

Occasional adult " jabber-talk " with Children who don't know a great many words yet (two–three years) sometimes brings a flush of joy and confidence, a memory of the past. But, when grown-up language begins to be understood and appreciated, we shall be informed fearlessly and peremptorily about the undesirability of jabber-talk if we use it at the wrong moments. It is only on very few carefully chosen occasions that it can now be used with value.

Jabber-talk names stay on, and sometimes become used by the family. They often lead the Child to imaginary, descriptive and musical words, nearer our language, but still not to be found in our dictionary. Here again care should be taken to differentiate between baby-talk (adult idiocy which associates Child noises arbitrarily with things or people) and musical or descriptive language. A cow should be called a cow, a spade a spade. There is no good reason for calling a horse a " gee-gee ", and it is only delaying growth to call a dog a " bow-wow ". Saying " there's Mike, bow-wow " may be a different matter and is only used to connect Mike and the other sound together. If the Child says " bow-wow " on seeing Mike after this, one's obvious answer is " Yes, that's Mike ". " Mike " is the operative word and should be used.

But when a Child says " that's a so dilanguinry cow ", that is sheer musical beauty and joy in creative language. The word cow is kept sanely for what it is, but the adjective adds greatly to our picture of a tired, strolling, dilatory cow ready for milking.

One might feel, then, that actual names of people and animals or in rare cases things (as when we name a car or boat) may be of value if imagination and creative joy are given full rein, but that otherwise, as a healthy safeguard, imaginary words might rather be associated with adjectives than substantives. It seems that substantives are so often the cause of downfall. Baby-talk slips in so easily. Verbs and adverbs have their dangers, too, though occasional genuine creation occurs with them.

" Bow-wow " and " gee-gee " are typical of the unuseful substantive (the real word has to be learnt later), whereas a " dilanguinry " cow, a " blobby " pen, a " swimmery " (hot) day, a " swordy " knife, a " pudgy " horse, a dog " all dragon's breathy " (panting) show real signs of creation and in each case add description besides having sound value. Such words may even remain in the vocabulary if they stand the test of use and time.

An example of a created name is the word " Beeze ". Beeze was a cat. The cat was not called " pussy " or anything else. The original Pussy may have been a genuine name too, but it is now used much more as an unuseful sentimental substantive, and the capital letter has been practically dropped because the word is hackneyed. Beeze, however, was a big cat. He was big and lovable, and he had a curious liking for a squeeze. The sense and logic therefore of " big " and " squeeze " becoming Beeze cannot escape one's attention. The name fitted the personality ; it was accurate and correct. For many cats, the lazy sentimental generalisation of " pussy " is a complete lie. " Spike " would be more true. So would " yap-yap " for many " bow-wows ". But even in print the words make one squirm.

The word Beeze is musical, and also conveys a certain meaning by the actual sound itself. This is what is meant by the language of music. It stirs the emotion too (the Child's approach to language and music). The word is short and easy to say and, being accurate and accepted immediately by the cat, might also be said to be functional ; it was invented by a five-year-old girl.

Of family place-names the "Slub" is an example. The "Slub" was where one family I knew deposited their weeds and garbage and made a manure heap at the bottom of the garden. Interestingly enough the word " Slub " is also an East Anglian dialect word for mud. In dialects and in local usage we find similar Child-like unlazy creations, but here substantives take their stand with place-names.

It is when the adult is dealing with Children that substantives seem to go wrong. The example of mangled meaning and sentimental lazy ugliness may be summed up in the ousting of Father Christmas by " Da-dah Exmerse ". This, I submit, is baby-talk at its most ugly and unuseful worst.

Even in slang, it is the adjectives which often have most meaning. But in slang there is always an element of intellectual showing off, and its use is commonly associated with winning a cheap victory or laugh. The Child's approach to language, musically and emotionally descriptive, is much more healthy. Perhaps our nearest approach to Child language creation, in modern times, apart from local terms, was the so-called R.A.F. slang of the Second World War. This was really a language of its own, and it is doubtful whether slang is the right term for it ; only later did it become slang in the real sense, when comedians took it up and prolonged its life artificially, slanging their audiences with it long after the worthier associations had faded. This is not unlike a polished improvisation of Dramatic Play being repeated too often ; it goes stale.

The judicial use of some family terms has a certain importance. They are often the shared creation of both adult and Child, and go far to make " family atmosphere " and give a feeling of stability. They tend to go wrong when intentionally or unthoughtfully or too often used so as to exclude or embarrass friends and guests. They are in a sense Monuments, but of the mind. They are certainly symbols of home and preservation. They preserve attitudes, youthfulmindedness, shared experiences and the " home atmosphere " itself. They may be shared with others, and one may knock them down (mentally) by laughing at them. But woe betide any outsider who tries to knock them down uninvited.

As an example of a local place-name, not unlike the family place-name of " the Slub ", I would give " the Stretters ", a place in Staffordshire, though I would not vouch for the spelling. Long before knowing its local name the place had struck me for its unusual little walks, and glades like tiny streets. One strutted down them as if in a kingdom, unseen, alone ; and everywhere were sticks. Sticks, streets and strutting. Imagine my delight on hearing that its name was " the Stretters ". Had others felt the same ? Was this a similar logical creation to the word Beeze ? Coincidence or intention—no matter, the name was right.

So, then, my point is that lying deep in the bosom of language is a curled-up, intuitive, embryo dream. It is both music and poetry. It is the emotional essence of language, which brings Joy. With this Joy would seem to come preciseness, economy and beauty.

Language is destroyed by sentimentalism and an unemotional materialist outlook ; the outward sign of the first is baby-talk, and of the second journalese and the modern bureaucratic jargon. We learn in time to understand and laugh at journalese, but one sometimes wonders whether it will ever be possible to learn bureaucratic slang, which only swells in volume and in vocabulary as it avoids saying anything precise, whilst spreading the disease of its insulting and arrogant ugliness to eat up not only the paper of our mills but the soul of mankind.

Outbursts of speech of any kind, whether obviously creative or otherwise, are greatly to be encouraged, for like other parts of the Doing of Man, it is important first that there should be practice, which can so easily be interfered with by the adult ; such interference brings great disappointment and shaking of confidence to the Child.

Just as the adult often squashes sound trials by being unable to stand noise, so also we too often squash outbursts of any kind, and are quick to take offence at what we fear is impudence. Frank and open Children are not on the whole impudent, and by winning their friendship and trust one is ultimately rewarded by their trying to be pleasant and helpful. But this entirely depends on whether the adult honestly treats the Child as a decent human being or as something inferior. If we think them inferior we eternally have to prove ourselves superior, and this lays us open to easy vexation over imagined impudence.

The sense of inferiority imparts itself very rapidly to the Child, too, and at once has an effect on joyous outburst. If outburst is blocked, there naturally follows an impeding of Language Flow. A shy and less creative Child is the certain result ; a somewhat difficult Child is the probable result.

" Children should be seen and not heard " is an old saying, and, although it is not a view commonly held today, there is a sort of hereditary hangover which unconsciously prompts many adults to think of quelling before anything else. Here we might again remember that the Child also has a point of view. Quelling has a great effect upon the Child, for all Children are by nature extremely sensitive to tone of voice. It is, however, possible for a hard skin to grow over this sensitivity by reason of many an emotional beating received from the birch rod of a rough tongue and a harsh voice. Once this skin has formed, the harsh tongue can only get a hearing, or any obedience whatsoever, by continued use of its birch-rod qualities. The adult is thus in a self-imposed difficulty, for the very part of the Child ever open and ready to respond to instruction and friendly direction is hardened away. That part is its natural Joy in and sensitivity to *sound*. Nearly all this pertains to out-flow.

Now let us consider in-flow.

We have seen in Play how the Child both expresses itself and sucks in knowledge and experience. So also in speech, for, just as violent speech directed at the Child for a prolonged period will hinder its creative expression, so too does it begin to affect the musical ear of the Child. Because copying is part of the sucking-in process of in-flow, before the next reaction to out-flow, it is not unnatural that an unpleasant noise emitted eternally by a larger creature than oneself presents itself ultimately, consciously or unconsciously, as something to be copied. So when the Child does speak, it tends to shriek or speak in a harsh chiding manner, even when making the simplest of observations. This, added to by the necessity of often calling down a street or across a playground and being heard amongst other similar voices, makes for a most offensive and objectionable manner and tone, which is completely alien to the real nature of the Child and ultimately has an effect upon both outlook and behaviour.   There grows up in the young heart a strange habit of competition and hostility to all, and obedience tends to be a thing too ridiculous to contemplate.

Speech has been likened to the message of the soul.   Let us beware of the message then, for in its changing music we learn much about the Person.   To put it quite bluntly, many Children speak rudely and roughly entirely because their parents speak threateningly to them.   Some teachers, too, fall into the habit, without knowing it, of eternal strident command, which takes friendship out of the voice and out of the soul, and limits the musical experiences of those hearing.   This commanding often goes with the bashing-in method of teaching.   Both nurture a conscious or unconscious reluctance to co-operate. It is virtually impossible to create the right atmosphere either for Language Flow, Child Drama or any other subject unless the voice and attitude of the adult is worthy of its task.   The harsh remark conveys meaning as much by the language of music as by words.

Laughter and ridicule play an important part in both out-flow and inflow.   Laughing at a Child may either make it bashful, or ultimately desire to show off.   Showing off leads to insincere and self-conscious creation in both Play and language, whilst bashfulness leads eventually to a state of utter non-creation.

I knew of a father who was stupid enough to make fun of a Child that spelt out letters as sounds to help itself to read.   The Child eventually stopped trying to read, and it was only when it began to cease speaking also that it was noticed that something was wrong. It was in this state that I found the Child, and getting it to speak again to *anyone* was one of the hardest tasks I ever had.

As for in-flow, the disgusting experience of ignorant adult laughter is one of the ugliest sounds in the world.   The Child suffers greatly from this.   It is wounded and offended by the evil of this music.

As another example of unthoughtfulness I overheard this the other day : A father had used the word " inscrutable " in a sentence, and a Child on hearing the word began a sequence of sound trials to help it learn and master the word, no doubt as much out of interest as in order to seek its meaning later.   The Child said: " K, skr, in-k, skr, koo, scroo, in-koot, in-skroot." An old lady then laughed, and interrupted with " What are you talking about?   You don't know what you are saying."   The Child flushed at first, looked glum, then suddenly changed and began to laugh uncertainly.   It then pretended that it had been trying to be funny, as if covering up a guilty secret.   Such is the effect of laughter used the wrong way.   Speaking to itself out loud or under the breath is the young Child's manner of speech trial.

Akin to this is the vexed question of dialect.   Dialect is primarily a question of music, and the ear becoming used to certain sounds.   Though we may love good speech, it is very important not to make Children feel ashamed of the music of their home background.   To force an artificial change of personal music may sever many ties and produce a fish out of water.   Artificial half-improved speech is a joy to no one.   It is much better to let the dialect remain, but encourage some habits of clarity.   At the same time it is perfectly possible to give the Child the idea of turning on the tap of another kind of speech, which should not be presented as *better*, but different.   Most Children are very adaptable in this way and can turn on the tap quite easily, and, if encouraged in the right manner, are quick to discover the occasions when the different types of language are appropriate.   For instance, it is common for Children to speak reasonably well and quietly in school and to be loud and unintelligible in the street.   But it is interesting to note that where good opportunity for Language Flow is given *in* school, rowdiness outside diminishes.   This does not happen if formal training is the only training received, for one of the causes of stridency is lack of opportunity for outburst.   There *will* be outbursts somewhere and somehow ; we might just as well en- sure that they are legal, intended, creative and beautiful.[1]

EXAMPLES

In order to show what is meant by " Language Flow", I include here a few examples.   They all come from Children who have had some adult encouragement in Play and speech.

Self : " How's that porridge, is it nice ? "
Child (7 years) : " It's full of smiles crushed up, thank you."

Child (7½ years) : "Mummy dear, I don't think that workman is a funny man, he hasn't got wit in his face."

[1] Further details and suggestions for this appear under " Language Flow ", Part II, Chapter XIII.

Litany

"... Get off there or you'll be prosecuted.
Grown-ups taking things from Children will-be-prosecuted.
All Children taking things from Children will-be-prosecuted.
All people trespassing on my land will-be-prosecuted.
No grown-up can come on this place or they'll be prosecuted.
All Children—if they're good shouldn't be prosecuted.
Out of the way of my bicycle or you'll be prosecuted.
All grown-ups ... if ... who ... are unkind to Children ought-will-be
prosecuted.
Ow, I bumped my knee."

The above was chanted by a girl of seven and a half years whilst pedal-
ling one wheel's turn to and fro on a tricycle.   I did not hear the early part,
only the sound of chanting.   I have written down what I heard at the end.
We notice the intense joy in the repeated sound, and intellect (i.e. meaning
of a new word) being incorporated at this age.   Intellect enters more after
the dawn of seriousness.   But the repetition, which occurs like this with all
Children, first gave me the idea of adding one word at a time and repeating it
often, together with some jabber-talk, for the first step of intended vocabulary extension with babies.   It would seem to be one of the Child's ways of
learning, and is not unlike an actor covering up lines, repeating them in
jabber, and learning a new sentence or so at a time.

We hear, too, the old familiar break with the dream world.   The Child is
coming back from the Land on the word " if—who ".   The Language Flow
is stuttering.   Things are becoming more conscious.   It is the " near finish "
that I have mentioned earlier.   The last word " prosecuted " was rather
self-conscious.   The bump on the knee brought back full reality—that is our
reality.   It was the complete finish, and the flow ceased.

Child (6½ *years*) : " Do you think their gods would be pleased if I took
my soldiers away ?   I could, you know.   For I am the General of Generals.
I am the strongest in the world."

Child (7 *years*) : " In the night you know I had a bad throat.   Well,
I opened my mouth when the baby was crying to deafen the naughty germs
so they wouldn't hear the good germs coming, and my good germs pushed at
those bad germs, away and away, and now they are gone."

Child (7 *years*) : " If *only* we lived in a star, it would be wonderful. The world's gone mad. I shall write to the King."

Child (7½ *years*): " The world is in danger, the world is in danger, the world is in danger. Soldiers of the King, go in! All come to the play, or I shall bomb the King. Why ? Because a motor car flew very high in the sky and hit a mountain top. This made the cloud men angry. I am a cloud man. So come in—or I shall bomb the King."

We note here a certain similarity to the style of the Psalms.

Child (7½ *years*) : " To cure spins and needles, you spit on the place and rub hard. You rub and rub and all the pain goes—all away and away."

Adult : " Come on, a minute's up."

Child (5 *years*) : " Oh no, a minute isn't up till the apples are ripe on the tree."

Conversation on a short walk.

Child (7 *years*) : " We are the posting men. We post the letters of the staying-at-home ones. I am the light carrier. I shine my light up and out into the air. . . ."

Self (*rapidly interjecting*) : " But not at those who pass by, for they are the driving ones, who must have no dazzling. . . ."

Child : " Yes, they are the driving ones. For them I shine my light on the ground. That driving one has two large lights. One shines to heaven, the other . . . spits in a puddle. Oh, this is where we stop a moment."

Self : " Looking right and looking left and . . . " (Simple Road Safety Instruction).

Child : " Yes, we are the searchers, we are the posting men. We take the letters which will make happy the readers over the sea. The sea is bright blue with white spots, for it is snowing. You can go in the shop now and buy a stamp. I stand here, for I am the guarding man. I guard the large mouth in this letter-box. It is red."

Note.—By keeping more or less to the rhythm it was possible to give an urgent order without breaking the flow. The order about the light was infiltrated into the game and obeyed at once, whereas a sudden stern command would have caused a break as well as resentment. The road safety instruction also considered the Child's rhythm with some sympathy ; though looking now at my own words, as they flowed then, they appear to be palely imitative of T. S. Eliot, whereas the Child's are a reactive and unconscious approach to Arthur O'Shaughnessy's *The Music Makers*.

There are two widely different minds here. Nevertheless the purpose of the attempt was successful (i.e. not to shatter the Child's joy in creation, nor the creation itself, since there was no need), and the walk was a very happy one for both of us.

Child (7 *years*) : " Here is the Station of Birmingham. This is the train from Africa. In a minute there will be a little silver stream for a rocket, for going through the air."

Child (6 *years*) : " The rain is like dragonflies flying backwards down. Stripes of them."

Child (7 *years*) : " I am a big boat, with a hundred funnels, dancing through the waves. Over the sea I go to the far far lands, and that little island is *England*."

Girl (9 *years*) : " Where is my bird, my dove ? Where is my messenger ? Call for him, call for him with a loud noise, use your highest voice and tell him The ON-DRAGON is coming."

Spoken by a girl 7½ years whilst ironing clothes, and after creative play :
Star is world,
World is star.
Star is gold.
Gold is star.
Sad and cold,
Where is the mole ?
Sailor gone with me,
Sailor.
Souls will go to all Good Places,
Heaven for me is all good sense.
Ha the gold.
Gold is the soul.
Adam and Eve wore gold.
Heaven is very old.

Oh !
Pinch, pinch, pinch, pinch,
pinch, pinch, pinch me.

Note.—The above may no doubt be of interest to psychologists of the Jungian school, containing as it does so many important symbols.   We have also the process of coming back to earth after being away in " the Land ", by the repetition of " pinch ", which may well have been an association of ideas after Adam and Eve.   The everyday association, perhaps, brought on the swifter speech and swifter ironing, which had happened till now, when all ceased abruptly.   The Child then cried, " Mummy, I've finished ".

There are indications that the speeding up of words at the end of a line of *learnt* verse, as differentiated from Language Flow, is connected with this coming back to earth.   But in that case it is the returning to reality and hurrying to get a task (generally unchosen) done, together with lack of breath control, whereas in Language Flow there is generally a calm control of breath, even in swift dialogue, which becomes slightly gasping only on moments of return to what the adult would term " reality ".   It is interesting that the Child, in this " reality ", is as a fish out of water in *real* life.   It gasps then.   It is calm in the Land of Dreams.

Regular breathing is noted in happy sleep, too.   When fully awake the human is beset by the varying tensions of life, and breathing changes quite a lot.   During bad dreams (relating to the unpleasant times of being awake) breathing ceases to be calm.   It is only slowly that Man learns how to face and deal with life.   Therefore it is not unnatural that Children should spend a considerable time in the Land before they have learned how to face life.   This does not teach the Child to be a dreamer.   Being in the Land is natural and necessary for the Child, and it may well prove that a repressed determination to obtain enough moments in the Land, where opportunity is not achieved, is as real a cause of the unbalanced dreamer as over-indulgence in sentimental mental laziness.

Certain it is that calm is something increasingly difficult to obtain whilst awake, as the tempo of a life aided by science increases, and as world anxieties lie deep in the unknown.   The Arts are increasingly employed as therapy.   But nature provides the simple preventive.   It is for us to provide the opportunity.

CHAPTER VII

THE AIMS AND VALUES OF CHILD DRAMA

MANY people ask what are the aims of Child Drama. Probably the shortest answer is : a happy and balanced individual. But this is only a partial answer, for although we find therein some suggested accomplishment in the realms of education, and even partly of health, it does not entirely cover the effect of the individual upon society, the fullness of personality developed, nor take into account the quality of the activity itself, and finally what effect that activity has on any like activity of an older age group. Nearly all these things are bound up in each other, and, apart from the fact that Child Drama is of itself fluid and therefore difficult of analysis, it would need a far greater scholar and observer than myself to give adequate answer to our question. I shall therefore not attempt to answer it by myself, but shall make full use of the services of a number of kind and experienced minds who have come to my rescue, some unwittingly. To all of these I am most grateful, for what they say helps also in substantiating some claims for the value of Child Drama.

First, though, one must reiterate that *Child Drama is an Art in itself, and would stand by that alone as being of importance.* But it is interesting and perhaps fortunate that there are other things about it which gain for it valuable allies.

The Adult

Child Drama tells the teacher who and what the Child is and where it has got to in life. It helps the teacher to become a friendly and sensitive person, enriching both the mind and personality enormously. It may provide the teacher with amusement, it can move him emotionally, and provides important aesthetic experiences. For even the moderately wise it can teach the history of Drama.

Not less valuable is its effect upon the art of the adult theatre, which it enlarges and enriches an hundredfold, both in acting ability and in imaginative approach to production. Finally, it tends to imbue with a wider philosophy of life those who become acquainted with it.

For the Child

It provides within it the two forms of Play. From projected Play the Child gains, to an extent, emotional and physical control, confidence, ability to observe, tolerate and consider others. There is also a process of blowing off steam, and a great realm of adventure and discovery is encountered.

In balancing these things Man finds happiness and health. These, in turn, not only put the young Person into the best frame of mind for learning at school, but provide thereby a future adult who may be of value to himself and to society.

By Child Drama :

Love and hate can be worked off by use of treasures.
Sound can be slowly appreciated and finally loved.
Trial and adventure can become joyous.
Confidence is gained by practice.
Practice improves movement and speech.
Resourcefulness is developed.
A bond of friendship and trust is built with adults. This aids all learning, and civilisation needs this trust.
The gang finds a legal outlet ; so do violent emotions.
Secrecy and rhythmic development are provided for.
Personal rhythm of development is provided for.
Obedience comes from lack of unnecessary frustration.
The natural process of in-flow after out-flow aids this too, and also adds to general scholastic attainment.
Memory is aided by trying things out and repeating them.
Understanding is aided by clarification in story form.
Sympathy is developed by personal experience, through acting, of other persons and conditions.
Faith is strengthened by personal experience.
Spiritual experiences take place because of emotional training and aesthetic encounter.
Command of others and obedience to companions is learned.
Discovery may be made of who you really are.
A concern for economy in words, action, property and dress is engendered.
It is possible to develop taste, common sense and thrift.
Adequate use of imagination takes place.

Good manners are discovered.

A desire for dance is developed which provides further outlet for joy.

Many new and happy approaches to other subjects are found.

Grace and virility are nurtured.

At all ages the Child takes over slowly the moral responsibility of good behaviour.

Pre-experience of possible later Life experience is encountered and dealt with.   This brings a steadfast wisdom and courage in adversity.

Sincerity is developed and aids concentration on values.

Writing is developed.   Painting is aided.

" Depth experience " is more easily absorbed.

Let us add some Dramatic values too :

The sincere form of playing helps the Child to get into the skin of a part.

An enormous number of characters is experienced in a short time.   Footwork, handwork, body work are all learned, loved, and slowly mastered, instead of taught and not mastered.

Group, pattern and team work are studied.

Rhythm and timing become second nature.

Immense love of Drama is nurtured.

Unconscious absorption of the whole wisdom of historical theatre takes place.

The writing of plays is properly founded and encouraged at the right time —not forced.

Symphonic production is experienced early.

Imaginative interpretation of a part is expanded, as also presentation and production.

Good literature is slowly approached and more genuinely accepted.

Sincerity and Absorption become habits, bringing to acting a particular quality which is rare and arresting.

Spontaneity continues on into adult artistry.

Unbalanced, romantic, emotional characters discover other ways of life than that of cluttering up the professional stage.

A slow genuine approach to technique is evolved, *and craftsmanship is attended to when artistry is certain to stand the strain.*

Every Child has an *equal* chance, over a *long* period of regular work, of showing ability, so that genuine talent can be noticed and aided where thought fit.

The Child, through Child Drama, avoids the imposition of well-intentioned, ill-informed adult plans ; the dilettante type of producers who thrive on sentimentalism and will not learn their craft ; and the flinty-hearted slavedriver who is out for personal credit.   Both the theatre and the Child prosper by such avoidance.

But what do other people say about these things ?

First, let us turn to Child Art, for it is so akin to Child Drama.   Indeed, if all teachers interested in Drama, but not yet ready to accept the value of Child Play, could spend two or three years on studying Child Art, they would discover an enormous amount about Drama in general.

Dr. W. Viola always says of Child Art that the main purpose is " the development of a full personality ".   It is a very good way of putting it. The same might be said of Child Drama.

Prof. Cizek, so Dr. Viola tells us in his *Child Art*,[1] said : " The principal aim is that the creative power develops and influences right through life."

Miss Marion Richardson said there was no more certain way of understanding painting than trying to paint sincerely.   I would say also that there is no more certain way of understanding Drama than to act sincerely. Drama means " doing ".   And sincere " doing " is the Child's way of acting.

Dr. Viola is also always pointing out that Children who have the opportunities for Child Art are, as a rule, better in other subjects because of an added ease of expression.   They are not afraid of speaking out.   Without in the least detracting from what Dr. Viola says, how much more true must this be of Child Drama, which uses the *whole Person* in its expression, and actually employs " speaking out " as a natural part of itself.

Regarding Play in general, we find considerable support for the views already expressed, and particular mention of the Child's own rate of development, in a letter to the *Times Educational Supplement* of March 19th, 1949, from Miss Barbara Rapaport of the Department of Education, University of Bristol.   By kind permission of the Editor, and of Miss Rapaport, I include the following extract :

> Children must be encouraged to work with their maximum effort
> but at their own rate, so that each may have opportunities to dis-

---

[1] *Child Art*, by Dr. W. Viola, published by University of London Press Ltd., p. 60.

cover his own best method of learning and raising his own standard of achievement.

Intelligence should also prompt us to use the natural resources of our human material. Children of about eleven years of age abound in mental energy and their interests are many and varied ; their curiosity, their love of collecting and making are at no other time so marked, so that learning through purposeful activity might not seem so poor an approach. We might do well to remember that Froebel found that " play is not trivial but highly serious and of deep significance ", that Sir Percy Nunn asserts in his brilliant Chapter on play, in *Education, its Data and First Principles*,[1] that at their highest level work and play become indistinguishable.[2]

In this we begin to find ourselves on the verge of wider social and moral questions, for work assumes its full dignity only when it is indeed considered as playing before the Lord. In this way it becomes a prayer, after the manner of the *Jongleur*. It might be said also that in this Play-Prayer (which the mystics urge should be continuous) we find a manner of guarding our Doing. For Doing, in the moment that it becomes wrong, becomes also less dignified, and therefore, according to our definition, second rate.

But in considering this high level, which few of us attain consciously or for long, we must be very humble in admitting that the Child (on good authority) reaches such peaks, unconsciously at least. The Divine Word goes even further and urges us consciously to try to be like that. Any attempt of Man towards such ideals has some social effect, and in the process is concerned with a standard, and with authority.

Here we might well turn to the philosopher, and in Bertrand Russell's *Authority and the Individual*,[3] we find a number of suggestions about behaviour, dependent upon the Nature of Man. Those who wish to understand the reasons for developing Child Drama could do no better than read every word of this book as a starting-point for further thought. Child Drama and its nurturing tries to carry out many things mentioned therein.

It has been suggested that Child Drama provides an opportunity for blowing-off steam and acting out evil. Bertrand Russell suggests that " innocent outlets " will have to be found if we are to circumvent " our

[1] Published by E. Arnold and Co.
[2] See also Child's answer to my question on this in section on questions. Part III, Chapter XVI, page 299.
[3] Published by Messrs. George Allen & Unwin, Ltd., by whose kind permission I include these extracts.

largely primitive ferocity ",[1] which is necessary for the unification of mankind.

On page 21 of *Authority and the Individual* we find these words :

> Any one who hopes that in time it may be possible to abolish war should give serious thought to the problem of satisfying harmlessly the instincts that we inherit from long generations of savages. For my part I find a sufficient outlet in detective stories, where I alternatively identify myself with the murderer and the huntsman-detective, but I know there are those to whom this vicarious outlet is too mild, and for them something stronger should be provided.

With the warring instincts of adults we may not be able to cope, but for those of the young we can.   Detective stories are acted out vividly in Child Drama, and often turn later to adventures of history.

There is great adventure in Child Drama, and surely we would not have it crushed ?   On this Bertrand Russell says :

> A life without adventure is likely to be unsatisfying, but a life in which adventure is allowed whatever form it will is sure to be short.[2]

With the Child, we find adventure by Drama satisfies, and improves behaviour if conducted in school.   Life can be long and wonderful that way, but the Drama of the street often ends in delinquency, and to that extent freedom at least, if not life, is " sure to be short ".

Child Drama takes a significant step towards reality and practicality, in a controlled form, though it may originate in the realm of fantasy.   Even adults seek some dramatic form of behaviour, particularly at times when their instincts get the better of them, and more particularly in the unbalanced type of leader.

We have already mentioned the spontaneity of Child Drama, which is perhaps its greatest gift to us.   On page 49 in the lecture on " The Role of Individuality ", we find Bertrand Russell saying :

> The decay of art in our time is not only due to the fact that the social function of the artist is not as important as in former days ; it is due also to the fact that spontaneous delight is no longer felt as something which it is important to be able to enjoy.

---

[1] Reith Lecture on " Social Cohesion and Human Nature".
[2] *Authority and the Individual.*   Page 25.

And again :

> ... as men grow more industrialized and regimented, the kind of delight that is common in children becomes impossible to adults, because they are always thinking of the next thing, and cannot let themselves be absorbed in the moment. This habit of thinking of the " next thing " is more fatal to any kind of aesthetic excellence than any other habit of mind that can be imagined, and if art, in any important sense, is to survive, it will not be by the foundation of solemn academies, but by recapturing the capacity for whole-hearted joys and sorrows which prudence and foresight have all but destroyed.

The avoidance of the " next thing " in Child Drama comes about partly by the Child's natural absorption ; by our intelligent non-interruption ; and appreciation of the " near finish " curbs our somewhat unbending prudence.

In *Individual and Social Ethics*, we find these words on the subject of facing what is in us—our desire for fighting and hunting :

> We must not ignore these instincts, and we need not regret them, they are the source not only of what is bad, but what is best in human achievement,

and, finally, on the last page :

> We shall not create a good world by trying to make men tame and timid, but by encouraging them to be bold and adventurous and fearless except in inflicting injuries upon their fellow men.

In these last words of Bertrand Russell it might almost be said that we have a reason both for our hard work in balancing the intensely beautiful stylised fighting of would-be aggressive senior Boys, and also for the new approach to Physical Education with younger Children, which offers them the full scope of apparatus and urges them to dare what they will. A report on this work informs us that the Children demand a higher standard from themselves as their balance and poise improves, that nervous Children begin to emulate more daring classmates, and that enthusiasm brings together teacher and Child in further co-operative endeavour.

As an indication of what those who train teachers may feel about Drama in general, we might recall the set of principles prepared by Miss M. B.

Gwynne of the Institute of Education, University of London, for the Advisory Committee on Drama in Education of *Theatre News Service*.[1]

Drama in Education Principles

Dramatic Work (both classroom Dramatics and play production) is of value because :

(*a*) The special combination of mental, emotional and physical activities which acting demands absorbs the whole energy of the person. This co-ordination vitalises activity and heightens individual out-put, in itself a beneficial and satisfying experience.

(*b*) It is a natural opportunity for practice in purposive speech, as an instrument of expression and also in its technical aspects involving good diction (confidence, audibility and clarity). It provides the real situation which stimulates expressive speech.

(*c*) It is an occasion in which the necessity for co-operation and teamwork arises naturally.

(*d*) The need to adapt oneself to the art form which drama dictates is at once an experience and a discipline. As an experience it promotes emotional reaction impelled by art : as a discipline it imposes a particular pattern or shape on these responses.

(*e*) The drama, dealing as it does with immediate situations in daily life, enlarges concepts of character and action and so deepens perception and increases sensitivity. The individual, seeking to identify himself with another person, is released from self-centred preoccupations. Drama may, in this way, relieve repressions and inhibitions.

In addition, dramatic work in school provides opportunity for a happy teacher-pupil relationship in that the success of the pupils' effort is inherent in the handling of material and does not depend on the teacher's superior knowledge.

This conference was remarkable for the intense sincerity and earnest conviction with which all shades of opinion were put forward. These differed at times considerably, but in bringing together those concerned chiefly with

[1] This short document formed the basis of discussion at the London Conference on Drama in Education, held at the Bonnington Hotel, on January 5th and 6th, 1948. It was, of course, not only concerned with Child Play, but Play was taken seriously into consideration.

education, and others whose chief love is the theatre, it was possible to achieve an important exchange of views. As a purely personal opinion, I believe that this conference, organised by *Theatre News Service*, will one day be seen as a turning-point in views about Drama and its possibilities, for there, perhaps for the first time, the full impact of the Child's own Dramatic endeavour and its implications was faced by a widely representative gathering. Those of us who are ardently concerned with the Child's own endeavour notice a considerable and generous change of attitude towards such things, dating from that time. For this reason the conference was a milestone in educational and Dramatic history.

And now, having considered certain opinions, and related them to our subject, let us see what the schools consider are the aims of Child Drama.

Here is the *Plan of Education* of a primary school, which bases almost all its work on genuine Child Drama and Child Art :

The aim, which is guiding the experimental course of education of each Child at this school, is to assist the child to improve the quality of his living, and therefore :

(a) To present to the child Christian standards, moral and spiritual, as criteria by which the child may judge his thoughts and actions and deepen his religious sense.

(b) To condition the child, so that he becomes emotionally balanced, and is therefore ready to receive education.

(c) To introduce the child to activities which are closely connected with his inherent natural senses, so that progress is stimulated without artificial effort.

(d) To develop the child's confidence and initiative through an arranged series of experiences.

(e) To encourage mental liveliness through stimulation of the imagination.

(f) To provide media through which the imagination and desire for experiment are maintained, and through which the desire for information and research can be usefully assisted.

(g) To foster the resulting desire for information and research by the provision of media through which the imagination and desire for experiment may get information to assist a further stage of inquiry.

The place of Drama in the school experiment :

Drama can lend itself to the aims of the school to a greater degree than any other activity, in the following ways :

(a) It can be the natural outcome, and a continuation of the child's games of " make believe ", which begin very soon after a child can move from one place to another.

(b) It can, together with the use of music, stimulate a child to movements which can be individually controlled and disciplined as an outcome of the use of imagination.

(c) When allied to music, movement in drama can be the highest form of aesthetic movement, and is so natural for a child that his psychological balance is aided.

(d) Through freedom, after interest is captured and self-consciousness banished, comes inspiration for imaginative expression through movement and speech.

(e) Through drama, the child can be introduced to the richest material in literature, history and human experience throughout the world ; and share the depth and colour embodied in the creative genius of music.

(f) If drama is guided sympathetically and with understanding of the age of the child concerned, while divorced from superimposition, it can stimulate in the child, as few other media will, creative speaking, creative writing of literature, rhythm and music.

I have visited this school very often, and personally I would ascribe the happiness of its Children to the sensibly controlled manner of arranging " liberty, equality, fraternity ".

Now for a senior school.

Here is a short article, which I include by kind permission of the editor of *Creative Drama*, the magazine of the Educational Drama Association [1] :

" An Experiment in Drama ", by K. Wheeler

Nine years ago, when attendance at school was voluntary and an air-raid shelter often became the bedroom of a child, it was felt that war-time stresses, added to the usual problems of adolescence, were

[1] The Drama organisation which deals specifically with Drama as Education.

causing powers of relaxation and concentration to deteriorate. The times demanded experiments being undertaken to find a remedy.

In a girls' school with an age range of eleven to fourteen years, Dance which provided a means of relaxing taut muscles and minds, and Drama demanding concentration and healthy imagination were taken separately, but as time went on, projects were introduced in which Dance, Drama, Music and Art all had their place.

The only way to use every girl of a group of forty-odd seemed to be to choose well-known stories such as Grimm's *Twelve Dancing Princesses*, *Hansel and Gretel*, *Pandora's Box*, *Alice through the Looking-Glass*, to add to the principal characters as many minor parts as there were girls to play them, and use the whole floor space. Some stories were used once, others offered further possibilities, and a script was evolved by the girls and the teacher. At times there was no costume, sometimes suitable headdress for characters was worn with dance tunics, and, in the Autumn term, suitable costumes were designed and worn, and characters were interchanged, so that girls played several parts in turn. They used the stage and floor space and moved freely between stage and floor.

It was noticed that highly strung, physically ungainly and particularly mentally retarded girls, gained much benefit from this activity, which engrossed them and made them use every part of their being. Their self-confidence developed, and consequently their attitude to work and play became happier and less apathetic, so that the result of the experiment called for a continuance of the scheme.

Now the eleven-year-old girls choose and act topics and stories which satisfy them, but which, to adults, seem to be without shape and to end abruptly. The characters speak their own language as it comes to them, and only rarely is a story repeated. The older girls have varied success with improvisations, and the fourth-year girls prefer to work on a semi-polished improvisation, gradually building up a script for themselves, using stage and floor, and combining Dance, Drama and Music.

What is here described contains this school's discovery of the natural Child Drama outward form at this age, and it shares with the junior school a belief in the value of Drama as a balancing factor and as an instrument of personal development.

This, of course, continues after the senior school too, as can be seen from this extract from a report on *Youth and Young Adult Work* :

> The produced play is not the ultimate aim of this section of study. The aim is the education and personal development of the individual. The play is merely the result, and should in no circumstances be unduly hurried on to the stage for publicity or any other purpose. Time has not been wasted if the play is never produced, although as a general rule the ultimate production tends to bring its own success.

Medical Support

Drama can, of course, be used as an intentional form of therapy, though this is going rather further than merely aiding the backward Child or providing an adequate balance. It is here used as an important part of diagnosis through observation of behaviour, and also as a constructive manner of cure by suggested action. The action is generally accompanied by extreme emotion, often presenting an example of mental block. When the block bursts out, certain relief may be obtained. Stammers and bad dreams may be aided by playing out semi-directed scenes. Emotions and difficulties are faced, and in a manner also confessed by " playing out ". I remember a very nervous adolescent playing out a simple mime one day ; suddenly she cried out " There, now I've *said* it ". She had not actually said anything or acted very much, but, in beginning to act her problem, she had faced it strongly within, and even the determination to start to act at all had aided the process of release. This case was particularly interesting, as at that time no one had asked her to say anything ; she had merely joined a group of others who were finding some relief in simple Drama processes.

A certain amount of psycho-drama is now used in this country, and apart from its more obvious associations I would like to add my own humble suggestion that Drama used in short improvised scenes can be of value to a patient, particularly after physical treatment, when he has been brought back to normality, and, in a manner, down to bedrock. He is now somewhat like a Child. He can think again and remember. But his memory of the time when he was confident to walk alone, or to buy things in shops, is somewhat slender. As in facing nightmares and in acting them until you prove that there is no fear in them, so buying things and asking the way a number of times, the little everyday things of ordinary life, practiced enough, instil a confidence which may be of considerable comfort. To me it appears to be, in a way, a form of simple justice that we have sympathy enough to ensure that the re-facing of life is done in a state which starts by at least being strong enough to avoid, on release, the immediate emotional tension which, in many instances, may have been a part cause of the original illness.

For Special schools and other types of Home school, Drama in its various forms may prove of value.

In connexion with therapy, here is an additional note which Dr. W. P. Kraemer kindly wrote in support of a short talk [1] of mine published some years ago by the Institute of Pastoral Psychology :

" The Use of Drama in Psychology ", by W. P. Kraemer, M.D. (Siena)

There is hardly any psychotherapist or educational psychologist who is not aware of the great value of the several arts to the practice of modern psychology. In the wide field of occupational therapy the arts hold the second important place, the most important being held by the crafts. The advantage of using the artistic capacities of the patient instead of the merely mechanical ones of pure craftsmanship are obvious in all those individual cases in which the relationship to the world is primarily aesthetic.

The arts cannot be replaced by any craftsmanship in the more active stages of therapy and occupation. Whereas in occupational therapy the accent lies on the importance of occupying energy by giving a certain task to the patient or student, in active development of the personality the Arts render the most effective service in the explanation of the case to the medical as well as to the educational psychologist. The phrase " show me how to paint and I shall tell you who you are " has found a wide application in psychological practice and experiments. Painting and drawing have a favourite position amongst all arts used in that direction. Many modern teachers and physicians think that colour and form as symbols of the unconscious could not find a more ideal expression than in the patient's artistic productions. Many, however, have recognised the equal or even superior value of arts which are not limited to two dimensions.

Without trying to exclude these branches of art, it is necessary to emphasise the enormous importance which we attach to the use of Drama. Drama is, so to speak, the art of all dimensions, of which life itself consists. Drama covers all the possibilities of expression of

[1] *The Value of Drama in Religion, Education and Therapy.* Guild Lecture No. 8.

which we can think. It should even include the other arts if and when occasion arises. Drama can be used in psychology and psychotherapy in the following ways :

(a) Within the framework of the reductive techniques as introduced by Freud, Drama could be a valuable complementary method. The value of catharsis (in which the patient was led to a revival of any cause which might have produced psychic trauma) was later denied by Freud himself, as he found that the treatment of the unconscious or semiconscious personality can never have a permanent result. Drama is connected with consciousness. The revival of causes of psychic traumas either after or without catharctic treatment might prove to be effective in the course of, or after, reductive analysis.

(b) Manifold are the possibilities of Drama in Jung's system of analytical psychology. In " active imagination " the attention is concentrated upon " the phenomena of the psychical background ", and it is in itself " an effort to formulate and express them adequately in words, colour or plastic form ".

(Toni Wolff.)

Drama is the late-comer amongst the arts recognised as a means of expression in active imagination. Perhaps it will soon gain first-class importance.

(c) Occupational Therapy. Drama, more than anything else, will counterbalance the egotism of the neurotic—the archetype picture, at first produced quite pure and raw, can be used for further shaping and forming expression. I see a great possibility of balancing the extremes in us by the proper use in Drama of pictures from the unconscious. As an educational instrument the importance of Drama has been emphasised by various psychologists. The Adlerian school, with its emphasis on power instincts, could use Drama effectively in harmonising the relationship between individual surroundings. I have actually seen cases in which children who previously have been labelled " difficult " become docile and free through Drama.

Drama plays an important part in religion. The physician and educationalist are about to awake to the fact that their profession is partly a religious one. Drama is the bridge.

Though these are highly specialised fields, they are not unconnected with ordinary schools and schooling, for it is often the type of upbringing which is in part responsible for mental ill-health. For this reason the question of prevention is being more widely considered, and I would go so far as to say that one of the most important reasons for developing Child Drama in schools generally is not actually a therapeutic one, *but the even more constructive one of prevention.* Prevention of many things is provided by the general balancing process, discovery of personal rhythm, and by " playing out".

I am glad to say that this view, in general, is shared by others : At the 1949 two-day conference organised by the National Association for Mental Health at Seymour Hall, Professor MacCalman, Professor of Psychiatry at the University of Leeds, put forward the thought that those charged with the responsibility of providing care and treatment of mental illness and defect had come to feel that the official attitude was still over-anxious about care and control ; Child guidance was too frequently concerned with behaviour problems, many of which could have been prevented by good upbringing and enlightened education.

In recent correspondence with Professor Sir Cyril Burt of the Department of Psychology, University of London, I was interested in a reference to an article of his which appeared in *School Hygiene* as long ago as 1916. Here he was suggesting that amongst other things the education of the emotions might include " dramatic exercises to be treated primarily as an active means of emotional training rather than a form of mere recreation, accomplishment, or pedagogical device ".

He also mentioned that he had suggested it (amongst other proposals) as a useful adjunct to the treatment of the backward.

Some people are a little worried at the idea of " acting out ", but it is difficult to see how Child Play can take place at all without it. It happens naturally, and can be guided to new forms of expression. In her short *Introduction to Dramatic Work with Children*,[1] Mrs. E. M. Langdon, of the Department of Child Development of the Institute of Education, University of London, says, of the young Child :

> The playing out of things which frighten, confuse or puzzle him is in itself both a form of comfort and reassurance, and a way of moving on towards new attitudes about these things.

[1] Published by Dennis Dobson, Ltd.

During correspondence, a number of people have added their support, and by their kind permission I reprint their views :

Miss Margery Fry (on the value of " playing out " both in and out of school) :

> I quite understand its being extremely useful in helping children to realise the reactions of society to anti-social behaviour. Might not some of these school plays, whether spontaneous or acted from script, serve as basis for discussions on the rationale of social ethics ? I think that older children would be helped by thinking out the wider bearings of the questions which the plays present.[1]

Professor Morris W. Travers, F.R.S. (on the general approach to Play) :

> It seems to me that there is too much stress laid on giving boys and girls better opportunity for getting on in the world, and, to do this, training has been substituted for Education. For the average boy or girl I look upon organised games as of equal importance to anything else in school life. They learn that all activities must be conducted in accordance with rules, and that these rules have in them an element of common sense. Because the type of Drama you describe is based upon Play, in which children find their obligation towards other people and society, I entirely agree that it would be of great importance to the personal development of the individual.

Professor Sir Cyril Burt, of the Department of Psychology, University of London (mainly about play and playing out) :

> Your suggestions undoubtedly have my fullest sympathy. I very much enjoyed reading your broadcast talk. So far as I have any right to a view on the matter, I should certainly agree that what dramatic work the child is likely to do would be different from that of the adult.

Dr. G. Scott Williams, of the Pioneer Health Centre, Peckham, London :

> I am very interested in the whole of this problem, particularly in the drama as a means of education. I think children are quite natur-ally interested in acting, and will, if given the opportunity, make use

[1] This is exactly the process outlined in the section dealing with older age groups and the use of plays for stimulating discussion. See Chapter XII, page 156.

of drama. I am entirely in favour of children's spontaneous play as a means of personal development.

Dr. C. L. C. Burns, Director of the Child Guidance Clinic, Birmingham (with particular reference to " those spontaneous productions which involve violent action, murderous deeds and somewhat strong language ") :

I do not think there need be any fear that this kind of representation is going to do harm, or negatively, that it is rather useless. Boys have always played out in make-belief such themes as hunting and killing, victory and defeat. It is in a way a form of the drama which, we are told, purges the emotions. The expression of these emotions is of greater value when it is cast into an art-form, however simple and spontaneous, and when it is witnessed as well as performed, i.e. when players and audience alternate. It is possible to suppose that in a community which has not lost its traditional folk-lore, ritual and drama, mental health is more likely than in one where life is mechanised, and practically everybody is nothing but audience. Many years ago I realised the importance of mime and movement in treating nervous and maladjusted children, and had groups of them doing Margaret Morris movement. I published these observations in *Psyche*, 1930, and prefaced my remarks with a quotation from Plato :

" Rhythm . . . is the expression of order and symmetry, penetrating by way of the body into the soul and into the entire man ; revealing to him the harmony of his whole personality."

It is important to realise that " Rhythm "—whereby Plato means what we include under the Arts—is something which must be re-created or reintroduced consciously, in our educational system, if we are to escape from the mechanisation of life today. This is what you and others are trying to do, and there are already signs here and there that you are succeeding.

Art is not something which is to be grudgingly added to a " curriculum ", but it is an integral part of man's mental health, of his religion, of his happiness—and we have to start them young !

Dr. William Kraemer, Hon. Deputy Medical Director, The Davidson Clinic, Edinburgh (on playing out and the value of Drama) :

We all use it, of course. Every analytical hour is Drama, and in the playroom every play hour too. You see, we act these things out constantly. We are doing it all the time. I am quite sure you are right when you say you want to see it established as a preventive.

By January, 1949, Dr. Kraemer felt able to go even further than this :

I find myself in complete agreement with Peter Slade's ideas on Drama. I have heard a good deal of his work and seen some, and I feel sure that Drama as conceived by him will prove of great value in education and therapy of society and the individual. Slade rightly emphasizes the role Drama should play in the prevention of neurosis. I fully agree. There have been many cases under my observation in which Drama has had a curative effect in neurotic illnesses, and sometimes it has been of the greatest importance. There is hardly a patient who does not in one way or other find in his artistic expression the highroad to health. It may be drawing or painting, music or poetry . . . it is always a creative activity, it is always Drama in Slade's definition of it as creative " doing ".

Summary

It should not be thought that all this is a complicated, difficult process. As far as ordinary schools are concerned, prevention, at least, is somewhat eased for us by the attitude of the Children. So much is done by them, of themselves, for themselves. We only offer opportunity, by sympathy and common sense. Thus do we nurture. It is all much simpler than it sounds, but it is necessary to give reasons for doing it.

In attempting to draw attention to the fact that the Child's Drama is an Art as well as valuable education, it is necessary to stress again that the Art itself is a simple thing and stands alone, though its repercussions are more complex. I do not feel that I can do better therefore than to end this chapter with a strong simple statement sent to me, in approval of these ideas, by a person who is well known for his knowledge of Children and particularly their drawing and painting :

Drama is absolutely essential in all stages of education. Indeed I regard it as that form of activity which best co-ordinates all other forms of education through art. Since, in my view, education through art should be the basic method in all education whatsoever, it will be seen that too high a value cannot be placed upon Child Drama.

Herbert Read, 31st March, 1949,

CHAPTER VIII

WHAT HAPPENS TO CHILD DRAMA?

WE have now seen how Child creation can develop in its own way, and how at a certain age our own more familiar adult Drama is approached, until finally the script play is reached. But it may be wondered what influence all the years of training, or lack of them, have on the Child. Enough is known to tell something of this with certainty.

It was suggested in the section dealing with the twelve- to fifteen-year-old that right up to the school-leaving age there is evidence of Child Drama, and that part of the processes can even be associated with the early script-play trials to improve the acting and vitalise the scene.

The truth will no doubt have been guessed before now. The organic development of Child drama does not stop. It goes on well into the youth-club age and can have a strong influence even on the adult work that follows. This is all to the good, and is as might be expected, for, if it is in any way right to develop the Child's creative ability, one would hope that this might have fortunate results on the grown person.

The girl who has not had much Drama experience in school tends to enter the youth club as emotionally unstable, often unreliable, giggly, and often addicted to an inhibited form of jive, bebop or the current craze in hot dancing. This is a perfectly natural and pathetic attempt to get at some form of personal expression, whilst bringing closer contact with the opposite sex. What is pathetic about it is that it is often suppressed by unsympathetic club leaders, and is lamentably poor of its kind, often only one or two vulgarised movements being employed. If accepted, however, with sympathy, this urge can be gently led away towards an interest in good ballroom dancing, country dance, improvised dance, modern dance, mime, keep fit and social graces. It is a step back towards the primitive in the search for truth and what has been lost. Jiving, jitterbugging and " bop " activities are forms of improvisation. All young people are, deep down, interested in improvisation, and unless they get enough of it " bop " is their way out.

The girl who has suffered over-dominated school production in script plays, tends to enter the youth club as a mouse-like, somewhat nervous creature, bursting out at times, but retiring again at others. She relies on adult direction for all activities and all Art processes. She knows nothing of creative adventure, will lead in nothing, and when invited to join in Dramatic work becomes like a block of wood, puzzled, even faintly on the defensive.

The lad who has had little Drama at school is, quite frankly, in many instances a lout. He cannot move, and does not want to. He also is searching, and tends to find his only hope in hot swing. In this sound he hears, somehow, through the steady time beat and the wailing cry for liberation born of the slave in captivity, some far sympathetic note from the " house of tomorrow ". All that has been lost to the Child is forced to the surface at the unsteady approach to manhood. Hot Swing and the like become in this way a deep symbol for safety, and at the same time an echo of hope. Its primitive origins make the message of a lost Land easier to understand for those who are often not far removed emotionally from a simple questing people.

The *blues*, too, is in itself an eternal lament for a lost Land, lost freedom. That is why we find frequent allusions therein to the longed-for journey and the train. Youths addicted to this music will hang around the gramophone in the club, and it is exceedingly difficult to get them to do anything else. I always think it ironic that the shape they form is the circle, and, with hopeless hands hidden in pockets because they have never been taught to "speak" in gesture, with backs bent by boredom, and chests that may never have been happily and freely thrown out in joyful creation and in throwing off personality, they tap their untiring feet over the miles and through the hours to make up for fifteen years' lack of training to a background of sound and musical accompaniment. As they cannot speak, they smoke. One way to free them is for a sympathetic adult with firm ideas to enter the club, and either to ban the music temporarily, and start improvisation without it, or use swing, and improvise *to* it.

It is necessary to start with simple things such as lads of twelve would do, and, perhaps, work up to the fighting with imaginary weapons. Hot swing rather than " bop "[1] goes well as a background, and later other music can be introduced ; the gradual loosening of both body and soul brings a confidence, which may in time enable pleasure to be derived even from asking a young lady in a decent manner whether she would be kind enough to dance. Swing is better than " bop " for these first attempts, because it is more open and understandable, and has in it the potential of wider gesture

---

[1] These days one can say the same of "twist" and a lot of "Mersey beat". They induce rather static end repetitive movement, whereas Dave Brubeck inspires action — AUTHOR.

and movement—more journey. The little journey of the partner in actual jitterbugging is very much the same movement as that of the baby in its regular journey to and fro arranging treasures in equidistance. The other main movement is a frenzied form of turkey step round in a circle, over a small locality, ending logically in the lady being turned turtle (in really warm examples not seen in clubs !) by the male at the centre of the circle.

" Bop " has been described as a form of surrealism, and it is true certainly that it shares that very personal quality of kaleidoscopic dream interpretation that makes the actual message difficult for others to follow. The fast, uncatchable treble " chasing " does not release movement widely, so we find more dancing on the spot induced by this music, and again we see the baby stamping round in one place. For this reason general swing is more suitable for primitive " remedial " Drama. " Sweet " jazz does not have the same results. It is not dramatic and it is not genuine. Its sentimental hypocrisy can be discovered by youth, through movement, and may henceforth be relegated to certain uses only. Thus from the simple we proceed to the potential in Drama, Art and Music. But what a task ! What an unnecessary, disgraceful burden on overworked club leaders and helpers ! I would add to this the fact that often less than a year after leaving school many boys and girls of this category appear to be almost totally unable to read. It gives one profound food for thought. What has happened to the years of formal teaching—without Drama ? Was there an utter and complete lack of success in bashing *anything* in ? One hesitates to answer.

The lad who has been bullied in over-dominated Drama at school, often turns sullen at the suggestion of a play, or any form of Drama. As far as he is concerned, Art died a blessed death the day he got his first job.

The adolescent of either sex who has had a sensible training in Drama at school can be recognised almost at once. In watching thousands of young people in different parts of the country, and in being privileged to create things with them, and to share confidences about their earlier years, I would say without hesitation that cleanliness, tidiness, gracefulness, politeness, cheerfulness, confidence, ability to mix, thoughtfulness for others, discrimination, moral discernment, honesty and loyalty, ability to lead companions, reliability, and a readiness to remain steadfast under difficulties, appear to be the result of correct and prolonged Drama training. For this reason, those who have had good Drama training are easily noticed. To a lesser degree it is possible to develop these things in the club itself, but results may not be permanent, as they have not the same roots.

As for acting, the results of good opportunity at school, with wide and free experience, bring to it a continued infusion of brightness and zest, and ability to get into the skin of the part, a quicker understanding of character and situation, quicker and better speech and reading.   Created group plays continue, and can be excellent, particularly documentaries around such problems as " my job and what it means to me ", " the vote ", " the latch key ".   As the age increases we find intellect creeping in to balance emotion. Documentaries then get even better.   Script plays, when used, have greater vitality, words are understood more easily and so is situation.   The many earlier imaginative adventures develop a wider taste in literature.   There is construction and trial in experimental stages and lighting.   Heavier script plays will be tackled, even musical shows, but there may be continued imaginative creations through improvisation, mixed programmes and the dance.

It is not surprising that the early joy in acting-in-the-round and in circular form is not forgotten.   This develops a healthy and natural approach both to historical study of the Drama and to the arena theatre presentation. The truthful, concerned portrayal, and the intimacy, which this latter type of presentation often requires, has no better training than can be found through Child Drama.   The space relationship, group sensitivity and joy in shape all belong here. Indeed, adults who wish to play adequately in this form will have to learn from Children, for the only adequate form of training is along similar lines to those hinted at in this book.

Where Child Drama has been a constant forerunner to youth club activity we find a complete release from any actual domination of the proscenium form, which will only be used when desired and *when it best fits the production*. At other times there will be constant use of various shapes in presentation, adding to the interests of production and affording many deeper and more delightful experiences to actor and audience alike.   Audience, in our sense, is at times accepted in full, but there is no showing off, because the players are ready for audience and know how to behave with one.   However, they often create things with no audience.   I have used, or been asked to use, the ring, the extended tongue, the bulge, a square projection, an L-shaped stage, an oblong central stage, the whole room as stage with various rostrum levels, the square floor, the central mediaeval stage and the oval arena, as well as the proscenium, for those intelligent adolescents (as well as adults) who shared my own joy in a wide range of imaginative theatre.   At all times there has been reason and taste in their use of a particular shape.   In general club work where there has been slightly less pre-training the two most common shapes would appear to be the two extremes : the proscenium and the circle.

Round about eighteen, but nearly always between seventeen and twenty-one, there comes what I describe as " the night ".   As the result of some last straw, some joy, some disappointment, some love agony, a person suddenly grows up.   After a week-end, maybe, Jack or Jill will walk into the club, and behold !—an adult.   There is a gravity, a quiet realisation of life.   Some laughter has gone, but with it comes *dependability*, and a new flood of intellectual interest.   Now the full stream of technical knowledge in Drama, particularly of the proscenium and arena theatre, may be thirstily desired.   The great wealth can now really be understood in all its immensity, and properly discussed and digested.   I am inclined to think that too much tuition (overloaded, mistimed, and therefore misguided) takes place in early years, and that explained and detailed training in technique should perhaps be left till after " the night ".   You then have something new to work with, in a different way.   You may then be a teacher of another adult.   Before this the wise teacher has been the eternal pupil of the *Child*.   " The night " is less obvious, of course, in some cases than in others, but I have never known it not happen, except in extreme cases of arrested development.

By increasing interest in the method and general outlook which provides the right environment for Child Drama, it is not impossible for a new Folk Drama amongst adults to arise.   Those who have worked amongst country people, or with those who think they " can't act ", know full well that they will often act simple created scenes in-the-round with great sincerity, whereas nothing would induce them to go up on a stage.   Great poetic flow and imaginative creation can sometimes be obtained by this method, and, just as Child Drama offers equal opportunity to *every Child*, so, by being unafraid and able to join in, simple improvisations by grown-ups can be an expression of a genuine Art of the People.

Adults who have anything like a full Child Drama experience behind them are fortunate indeed.   They may be excellent actors and producers and carry their knowledge with them.   They will generally be released enough and have a full enough life not to want to go on the professional stage.   They may not even want to act.   It may have been worked off.   But the important thing is they are likely to be balanced, happy people.   But if they do act, whatever the form of presentation may be, they will bring to it, amongst many other things, the two great qualities of the Child—Sincerity and Absorption, the two qualities so lacking in our grown-up theatre of to-day, and yet without which no theatre of any value or interest can exist.

AN INDICATION OF NATURAL DRAMA DEVELOPMENT

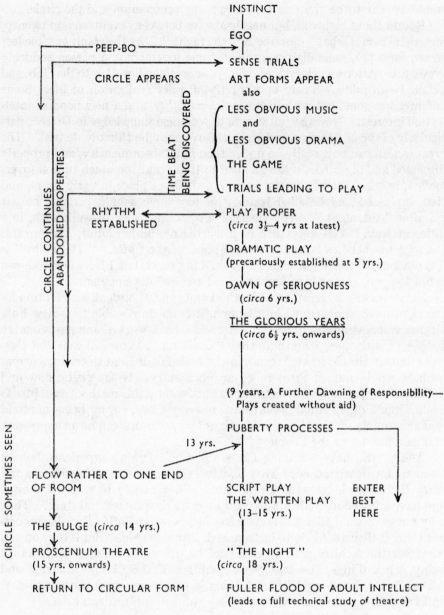

INSTINCT

EGO

PEEP-BO

SENSE TRIALS

CIRCLE APPEARS   ART FORMS APPEAR
                 also

LESS OBVIOUS MUSIC
and

LESS OBVIOUS DRAMA

THE GAME

TRIALS LEADING TO PLAY

TIME BEAT BEING DISCOVERED

CIRCLE CONTINUES   ABANDONED PROPERTIES

RHYTHM   PLAY PROPER
ESTABLISHED   (*circa* 3½–4 yrs. at latest)

DRAMATIC PLAY
(precariously established at 5 yrs.)

DAWN OF SERIOUSNESS
(*circa* 6 yrs.)

THE GLORIOUS YEARS
(*circa* 6½ yrs. onwards)

(9 years. A Further Dawning of Responsibility—
Plays created without aid)

PUBERTY PROCESSES

13 yrs.

CIRCLE SOMETIMES SEEN

FLOW RATHER TO ONE END
OF ROOM

SCRIPT PLAY   ENTER
THE WRITTEN PLAY   BEST
(13–15 yrs.)   HERE

THE BULGE (*circa* 14 yrs.)

PROSCENIUM THEATRE   " THE NIGHT "
(15 yrs. onwards)   (*circa* 18 yrs.)

RETURN TO CIRCULAR FORM   FULLER FLOOD OF ADULT INTELLECT
                           (leads to full technical study of theatre)

PART II

THE TEACHER

Dedicated with profound respect
TO ALL TEACHERS
even those who may disagree

CHAPTER IX

SUGGESTIONS FOR
EARLY DRAMA OF UNDER FIVE YEARS

... And then the whining school-boy, with his satchel,
And shining morning face, creeping like snail
Unwillingly to school. ...

William Shakespeare

Why should he ?   School should be a happy place.

Peter Slade

IT would be a difficult and responsible task to advise exactly what any teacher ought to do, and, if one did, it would defeat its own purpose, for in developing Child Drama the teacher must be an artist, and create also. Each school is slightly different, but there are certain things common to all groups and thus to all teachers.

First, it should be said that the teacher must really love Child Drama and believe in it, and must learn about the Child and the school.   Observation and trial enter here, though these may indeed have been the cause of the first love.   Finally, the teacher must recognise when the Child is doing well and the Drama is flowing on.   If this is not recognised there will be too many fussy, unnecessary suggestions, and creation may die.

The following are suggestions, therefore, about a manner of approach. They may not fit everything.   They are primarily intended to help the development of Child Drama, but it may be perceived that this in turn considerably affects the child in other ways.

If these suggestions sound dogmatic, they are not intended to be so. The headline method has been used for brevity, and I would only say that the suggestions themselves are concerned with methods which have been found, over a fair period of time, to nurture the Child Drama we have now observed.

*   *   *

With the baby, think often of its different state, its strength, its handicaps. Notice its attempts.   Share its joys.   Recognise its successes.   Do not

always look at it when it is engrossed.   This breeds self-consciousness.
Learn to recognise, perhaps even delight in, its simple Art and Drama processes.   See how Drama is the whole Doing of Life.   Notice trial and repetition, notice pattern.

Watch for the " sideways thresh ".   Know it may come.   Arrange
crockery on the table to suit, when you see the mood of energetic agitation
starting.   Follow with sympathy the progress of the " thresh " into the imperious sweep (basis of gesture).   Do not take it out of the Child if you have
not recognised this and something is broken.   Chiding at moments of light
disaster, resulting from the sweep, merely puzzles.   The Child wonders why
we are annoyed—it was Drama, that sweep.   It is obvious and different.
See it.   Do not be too violent if you see messing with spilt food.   It may be
painting.   Watch for expression, and watch for pattern in mess.

Be careful of the family atmosphere.   This is attained by a sharing of
Joys.   It is not always obtained by constant and conscious looking *at*.   This
last is actor and audience, and breeds an artificial form of " theatre ".   Sharing *with* breeds a wide attitude of Drama, the Doing of Life.   It is valuable
to note the difference in the earliest years.

Over-attention to frustration can bring on a sentimental attitude of too
much guarding, which may end in weakness, or, at the other extreme, violent
licence.   Sensible remembrance that such a thing as frustration exists is a
different matter.   Recognition of the early trials and creative efforts is of
considerable help in judging necessary moments of freedom and opportunity.
These necessary moments are the " times of importance " mentioned in
Chapter I which may act as prevention of neurosis.

Remember the Child's point of view and that it has its own values.
There is a reason and logic for everything.   Arrange compromises accordingly.   Your tone of voice is very important.   It affects reaction, relationship (particularly affection) and ultimately the Child's own speech and attitude to others.   Those who lament that Children make ugly sounds should
start with training the adults who live near or with the Children.   Listen for
climax and rhythm in speech trials.   Take up the baby's first attempts at
talk, and converse, occasionally, quite seriously in jibberish.   It is the
musical tones and sympathy (music language) that it catches first, not word
meaning.   Add an occasional *word* into the jibberish.   Repeat often.   Note
what words you use to the baby and try to discover why it remembers and
uses certain words earlier than others.

As the baby gets older, don't take too much notice of showing off.   Don't be over kind about picking up every time it falls down. It cannot find its feet that way (inwardly or outwardly). Finding feet, stumbling and noting the rhythm of movement is very important. Note how after a stumble (not quite a fall) the tiny Child will often stand still and consider the experience before going on.

If not actually doing harm, allow kicking and drumming of feet (Drama and Music).

Do not be amazed at " destruction ". Give things that *can* be picked to pieces. Distinguish between angry bashing and investigation. Do not be over-ready to clear up treasures placed in odd positions. They are sometimes less important if only one or very few together (" abandoned things "), but a lot together means Art pattern or maybe a Drama " set ". It may be re-turned to. Only disturb if absolutely necessary. Note the pattern and equidistance. It will help you to understand the later developments of Child Drama, and, if you learn to find these patterns beautiful, your life will be greatly enriched.

As far as possible, provide right clothing for wet days or Play with water. Do not be angry at puddle-sloshing. It is either Art (creating mud models) or may be the beginning of Dance. Allow getting dirty and playing with mud. Wash after. Try not to interfere *during* creation. It will be easier to recognise high moments of Child Drama later if you study the more obvious simple movements of the tiny Child.

Watch for the " near " finish and the actual finish. Try to recognise when each starts. Actual finish is quite often crowned with " Dere ! ", meaning " there ", accompanied by beaming face, or squeaks and agitation of the hands. This is the crowning of achievement. It invites sharing *with* and does not demand looking *at*.

Use peep-bo in one form or another. Encourage the Child to do it too. This is a very early example of how the adult may stimulate Play. Do not push your large face too close. It is very large. Notice the Child when it does peep-bo round the door. It is early entry and exit. Share the experi-ence. Do not run away and hide from tiny Children for too long. It is a terrible anxiety to impose and is not the least bit amusing to the Child. Above all, never run away round a corner (even with older Children) when out in the street. It upsets the whole balance of trust in personal relation-ships, and can affect absorption in Play. Many Children suffer nightmares for years after from this experience.

Do not laugh at the Child's achievements. Laughing *with* is quite different.   The Child is often offended by being laughed *at*, and that may start shyness and resentment of other people.   This is very obvious in early speech trials.   Do not build up " seen and not heard " atmosphere.   Do not shut doors abruptly in the face of a tiny Child.   This is an agony.   Think of the size of the door.   If doors have to be shut, try to shut in time, when the Child is a little way off.   This is less of a rebuff to the adventure of walking in that direction; a direction walked by choice is part of creation. Guard it.

If the Child is continually looking round or sideways to see if it is watched, don't look.   It is showing off to an audience.   If encouraged, this works against absorption, which in turn affects both later Play as well as study at school.   If the Child looks up suddenly and beams, *share* the experience quietly without fuss.

If adult timetable interferes with Play, watch for the " near finish ", particularly if there is any sign of the circle ; it is something fundamental. Try to wait a moment or two.   Do not snatch things away.   They are treasures.   Coax away, or offer something else.   Gentle tapping noises may also be effective in turning the attention away from valuable or dangerous clutched objects.

In general terms, appreciate the importance of Play.   Allow for it.   If possible, arrange a special room for it, so that adults, other than those wishing to be with the Child, can live a separate life.   Periods entirely apart from any adult are important too.   Confidence, concentration, having to overcome difficulties are learnt about when alone, and above all, undisturbed periods of creation.

If there is only one Child, try occasionally to provide companions in Play of like age.   Do not arbitrate too often over squabbles about property, i.e. over the use of toys and treasures.   Part of the Child's opportunity for social adjustment is then lost.   Rather interfere only for safety or rank injustice.

As children approach five years, large coloured bricks are useful for building scenes to act with.   They are the forerunners of rostrum blocks.   1 ft. to 1 ft. 6 ins. square is the best size.   If a rather young Child plays in the same room as an older one, it may be better to keep them slightly apart in their play by some sort of compartment barrier.   They can then share each other's company in the room but they are less likely to be quite un-understanding and assail each other's Monuments.   There is a social gulf in ages.

As the Child learns to walk and talk, watch for the circle, note obvious Drama.   Allow free speech and do not laugh at creative attempts.

The above section is for early Child Drama, pertaining perhaps to the home, but this is also the age of " sitters-in ", day nurseries and nursery schools.

CHAPTER X

SUGGESTIONS FOR FIVE- TO SEVEN-YEAR-OLDS

WHEN you see attempts at Play which you may feel are more obviously linked with Drama, take care not to rush any notion or conception of adult Drama.

Situations will be used more for personal experience now. Expect treasures to be used for working off love and hate. Do not be sentimental about this. Provide time for it.

If a Child shocks you by a glimpse of home background, do not shut it up and make it feel ashamed. Allow use of own words and choice of own subject in Play if such appear. This leads slowly to the beginning of Language Flow. The Child can be led away gently to other and lovelier themes. Be sympathetic but not sentimental.

When personal Play starts (obvious acting), do not give too many treasures in the way of acting properties, as they tend to hinder both gesture and speech, and take away from imaginative creation. Much harm is caused to Child Drama at this age. There should be absolutely no mention or consideration of the words "theatre" or "audience", and one strange adult watching is too many. If he or others *must* be there, place them in an unobtrusive position and do not bring Children's attention to them, otherwise Play and atmosphere will be destroyed. They are difficult enough to obtain in any strength of absorption at this age.

Try to understand that simple things are loved, e.g. a paper crown.

Do not press for too much reality in detail.

Allow for and expect occasional unusual creations either of words or animals. Accept them seriously, even if offered you with a giggle.

Do not pay too much attention to individual Children when acting. They will begin to show off. Be aware of sincerity and absorption and do everything your intuition prompts you in order to build up an atmosphere where these qualities may begin to appear.

Do not despair of the eternal grinning and bumping. They have their charm, too, but they will slowly disappear.

Do not force speech. Not too much formal training of speech at this age,

PLATE 9

YOUNG INFANTS. Stimulating dramatic action by sound effects. " What does this remind you of ? " Early steps in learning to love sound. (*See* Chapter X.)

INFANTS. The spiral beginning to form. (*See* Chapter X.)

Photos by Victor Thompson

PLATE 10

INFANTS.   The spiral disintegrating into the large circle.   (*See* Chapter X.)

INFANTS.   Happy entry.   They run in.   Here the spiral has just wound itself to the centre and is about to break up into the big circle.   They run with hearts to the centre of the room. More difficult to discern than when seen from above.   (*See* Chapter X.)

Photos by Victor Thompson

if any.   Formal training *can* run parallel to, but should not supplant, emotional sound training.   Many sentences and thoughts are spoken entirely through the body at this age.   Try to arrange for this by allowing space for movement.   There should be frequent periods of movement and Play *with no " helpful " properties whatever*.   This makes the body language of movement necessary, and prepares the way for speech.   These are the periods when the teacher can use gongs, drums, whistles and every sort of noise for stimulating Play.[1]   Whilst the body is " speaking " silent *messages*, the ear is becoming accustomed to interesting *sounds*, sympathetic to the movement. It is reminded of sound as against limb.   The sounds are often nicer than the Child can make with its own mouth.   Give lots of this at the age in question. This is how the Child learns to love sound.   Mix moods, arrange climaxes and contrasts.   Make long sounds and short sounds obvious.   These are introductions to the vowel and consonant.   Do not try to explain the process to the Children ; many intelligent adults would not understand it. See that you are not amongst them.   The Child accepts the situation, always with Joy and nearly always without question.   Enlighten simply if asked.

Look out for enjoyment of, and accuracy of movement to, time beat. Movement will be late.   Do not correct this.   Let the Child find the experience and master the art of it alone.   Perhaps once in two or three weeks some suggestion might be made about " being in time ".   Judge for yourself.   Do not be impatient, you are dealing with the foundation of a whole life's understanding.   You may find your suggestion brings a certain drilled deadness.   If so, do not repeat your suggestion—things will get better again in time.   Reserve such suggestions for older ones in your school.

Use noise of feet.

This treatment brings the " happy entry " mentioned in Chapter II. Watch for the spiral (see Plates 9 and 10).   Try to appreciate the rush in (dramatic entry), and when the spiral turns to a circle.   Be able to say "now it is happening."

This all aids you in observing Child Play and in being accurate as well as understanding about its beauty and procedure.

Where possible allow space for the spiral to appear.   The best work can only be done in the hall, but *something* can be done in the classroom, though we cannot see the spiral there.   Watch for space relationship.   How soon does less bumping appear ?

[1] See Chapter II, page 40.

Watch for coma-acting, when a Child stands still and stares. Do not interrupt.

If you tell stories for acting, make them short and simple.   Put in noises, and invite Children to do the actions.   Do not cast characters all the time, but, as in this example, sometimes let everyone be everything :

Teacher : " Once upon a time there was a king . . ."

If there is no piano you might say : " And you are the king ".

If there is a piano, royal marching music might start.   The Children begin to march.   If some do not join in, do not make them.

Teacher : " One day when he was out riding he met a bird . . ."

All Children become birds.   (You might get a primitive attempt at running Play.)

Teacher : " And this bird said : ' Look out, Your Majesty, there's an ogre round the corner ' . . ."

Everyone becomes an ogre, and so on.

In this way every Child has an equal chance to be the leading character. (Method discovered by observing that Children would rather act than watch. Know *why* you do things.)

This may be followed by : " What does this noise remind you of ? " The Children then begin to use their own mind instead of yours, and start to be things *they* think of.   Then try stopping your story and asking them to finish it in action or with words.   Generally they cannot, but there does come the day when they can, particularly near the top of the school.   Vary the above with occasional picked characters for improvised stories to be done again.   Do not do this often with the young Child, and do not correct or polish detail.   The beauty of Child Drama now lies not in precision, but in the first buds of group creation, and the grinning Joy of uncertain little people.   You will feel moments of shared thrill when a Child is successful in something it attempts, and out of clumsiness there appears a certain grace.

Watch for moments of absorption.   Above all note the shape of the journeying figure over the floor space, and see in your mind's eye what lovely shapes would have been drawn if it had been a skater on virgin ice.

Compare at this time with the Art.   If you are doing work regularly along these lines you will notice symbolism common to Art and Drama, and also that space and composition begin to improve.   There are less-muddled lines and objects running into each other.   (This last is the bumping on the floor appearing on paper.   As the Children bump into each other less, we expect composition to improve, first by equidistance and later by more subtle relationship of weight and colour—not depth.)   As far as genuine Child Drama is concerned, a stage in your infant school can be a menace. It is too high, but not wide enough as a rule.   It is in the wrong place too, but is useful for taking no notice of whatever.   Seat observers on it—higher and farther off the Children.

On no account use script plays.

Do not polish improvisations too much.   Do not repeat them more than three or four times.   Use the shapes of grouping that the Children use, if you make up a play.   Encourage both speech and movement.   Incorporate interesting sounds in everything.

A few rostrum blocks can be of value.   Allow them to be built up as the Children like.   Interfere for safety reasons only.

Notice how much space the Children can conveniently use without getting lost.

Never put on a show for an audience at this age.   You will shatter Child Drama.   Recognise that with Children, Drama is all about them.   That is why they face in all directions.   For " theatre " experiences, if you must allow them, encourage only those few bands of players who come to school and act in and amongst the Children and *with* them, not *at* them, i.e. who present Child Drama shapes.

In all, encourage rather *what* to do, not *how* to do it.   No direct showing " Do it like this ".

Be content with small beginnings in the infant school, for the small things are really great.

If you and the Child discover the full significance of " time beat " and " rhythm " and their differences, if the older Children do not bump into each other, if they have learned to love sound, if they can act a polished improvisation without going dead, if you occasionally get good contrasts and climaxes, if the flow of language is confident (apart from being clear), if reaction to sound is swift, if exits are quiet or noisy as you intend, if you have got " hear a pin drop " control, and have developed sincerity and absorption a *little* by six and a half years, and have avoided ever having an audience, you have done a magnificent job.   Don't expect or try to do any more.   If you understand what has been written here (and if it all happens in your school), you will already have discovered in your Children and school, and in their work and behaviour, a vision of a new world that you hardly thought existed.   This is not exaggerated, it is what successful teachers find. Incidentally, you have laid the foundations for a first-class actor, if that is considered of importance, and in the history of Drama you have covered the period beginning with the earliest tribal dance, via the " journey " pageants, arriving at the mediaeval central stage, if you allow the use of rostrum blocks.

The Second Best

You cannot use the hall. You have to do it in a classroom. Move the desks. If this is not possible, do what you can and *use* the desks. Turn them into mountains, ships, horses or cowsheds. A certain amount of movement can take place amongst them. Use noises here also. (See Plates 13 and 14, between pages 184 and 185.)

If only a few can act at a time, encourage audience participation.[1] I remember a wonderful football match in a school that had never tried these methods before. Only two commentators stood up. Everyone in the desks registered excitement or despair. The roar of delight on the winning goal, depending entirely on the energy of the improvised commentary, and the shared emotional experience were very considerable. It was a great match. All was imagined. No movement took place except rising out of seats.

But movement is better, for it provides a journey. In accepting the principles we can only do what is possible under bad conditions. Fight against the shape of the rigid theatre with actors' end (teacher's end) and audience end (pupils' end). If actors turn their backs on the other actors who sit and participate in the desks, do not on any account correct this. The actors who have more movement than the others are merely forming part of the circle, normal to this age, which we would see in entirety under better conditions. Remember, in Child Drama there is no real audience, and take comfort in the fact that, by your kindly sympathy, Children will get much more than you think out of the worst possible conditions, because of their wonderful imagination. They need opportunity, that is all.

Common to both the best conditions and the less good is the task of the teacher in acting as a kindly and gentle guide. Encouragement is needed at this age, and some stimulation. If speech or Play fails at a certain moment, learn to be sensitive about when to make a suggestion and what suggestion, and learn when *not* to. This is the art of nurturing.

[1] See Chapter III, page 59, and Plates 13 and 14, between pages 184 and 185.

CHAPTER XI

SUGGESTIONS FOR THE JUNIOR SCHOOL

THE task at this age is to build a strong bond of trust and friendship. If the Child does not learn what is good in adults now, life will be much more difficult. It is the bond of friendship which promotes learning for pleasure ; it is Child Drama that promotes pleasure.

As there are still junior schools that are uncertain about developing further the work of infant schools, these first suggestions pertain rather to starting things up.

You will need firmness at times, for Children will " try it on " occasionally. Show that you *can* be firm as a rock. Understand, though, that the " try on " is a logical life trial. Some freedom has been offered, and the gay and adventurous souls will see how far this freedom extends. Be sure that they know for certain beyond which point it does *not* extend. This will give them confidence, just as it will give you confidence. It is the understanding of reasonable liberty as against licence. Licence enters when you do not make the frontier line plain. Do not, however, perplex by allowing freedom on some days and by being abrupt and difficult on others. Know yourself ; discover the honest limits of your patience, and try to create an even regular atmosphere, which the Children can feel, and which contains the same level of freedom on each occasion—as much as you can grant on your most tired or irritated day. This is the safest way, as you are then less likely to react in a violent surprising manner. It is the shock of sudden change in adult attitude which breaks a Child's trust—and in many instances a Child's respect.

When introducing rather more free methods, go very carefully. You are not helping the Children, the school or the Drama if you let the lid blow off too far or too often. There will, however, be moments when the lid *will* blow off, particularly if the tradition has been very disciplined. It is the pent-up imprisonment of years bursting forth. Dramatically, it is the emotional climax. Your job is to harness and guide it. It is yours, and given freely to you. It is never to be found in the ordinary produced script play at this age. But you must harness it early or it will get out of hand.

Know this well ; it is your greatest treasure if you know how to handle it, for it is this that makes real live Drama.

Head Teachers: Understand what is happening if you enter a classroom (or hall) of more noise than you are used to. Climax is as necessary to good Drama as banging is to the workshop. But it will only be a *period* of discomfort. Encouragement and understanding from you will hasten the teacher's orderly task of finding the level of freedom and restraint necessary for good work. In some cases this is very much more difficult to find than in others. Each group of Children is different. Understand, too, that the way you run your school, or have run it, affects this. Be comforted, though, that many teachers are clever enough to find the level of freedom almost at once.

For Control

When starting free work, if you are worried by noise, have play without words, and start by the Children being quiet and acting while *you* talk. The simple story is useful for this. Quite soon you will find it possible to inform them of the story first, and they may want to act it after.

Do not force any Child to act who does not want to. It is very rare that they do not join in in time. With younger Children, use periods of all being all characters, but cast occasionally.

Encourage them early in this process to make suggestions about the story, as this makes them feel it is part of their creation. Gradually they will take over from you the task of inventing the story. This is important. You are smoothing over on to them further responsibility for creation, giving them more freedom, and thereby testing their sense of personal responsibility in behaviour. Our ultimate aim is to give *almost full responsibility of behaviour,* which is achieved when they want to create enough, and when they feel *free* enough to create. It is your job to build this atmosphere slowly. A trust and wisdom is built between you and the Children. No good Child Drama can take place without this, and it is this that makes Child Drama such a good influence on general behaviour and other subjects. It prepares the Child for co-operative in-flow of knowledge, and further experience. At the moment that the Child wants to create and, above all, wants to create what *it* wants to create (not what *you* want it to create) you can be sure of good behaviour, and good behaviour becomes more solid and utterly dependable from then on. So the earlier you make the Child see that you invite it to be the original artist that it is (though may not know it), the easier is the task for both you and the Child. Much of our difficulty lies in the fact that not until recently has it been at all generally perceived that the Child could be an original artist in its Drama as in its Art.

As you feel confidence of control building in both you and the Children, allow speech to enter by such suggestions as : " Speak if you want to this time." You may get a burst of speech at one place only. Interestingly enough, you often obtain exactly the right remark for the moment, and often an intuitive group agreement, when all burst out and say the same thing. At other times one Child will start to say two or three words and others will take up the cry.

Sounds and music can enter at any time ; you will find them an immense aid to control, because of the power of the emotional language of sound. It will often tell a Child what to do, and obedience will be more ready than to the spoken word. Children are quickly accustomed to reacting, for instance, to a bang on a tambourine or cymbal, and will become quiet. You then speak to them. Creation starts then from silence. This aids concentration.

Piano spread chords, too, have an effect. Even putting on a gramophone may stop any tendency to noise. Quick suggested alternations between loudness and quietness, and between energy and relaxed movements, bring control also.

After " speak if you want to " comes such occasional encouragement as " let's have talking this time ", slowly building towards the free flow of language. Ultimately, plays put on by the Children (i.e. created by them without aid from you) will begin to occur, and they will find ways of acting them. Encourage Dance, too, either to piano or gramophone. Polish an improvisation occasionally to give experience of more finished work. Vary this with invitations to act a story you choose or one built by them and you (as against entirely their own work). But once they *can* build creations of their own, allow a great deal of it. Whereas you use many people or all in your productions, note that they will not necessarily do so ; they may prefer to work in gangs. (See Plate 16, opposite page 185, and Plate 17, opposite page 192.)

Though much has been suggested about using space and numbers of people, if you are worried in any way about control, use smaller numbers at first and less space. Enlarge each according to the successful results of granting of freedom, bringing with it creation.

Watch for : absorption, sincerity, interesting groups, imaginative ideas, grace of movement, covering of the floor space, equidistance, the circle (smaller and more of them than in infant schools), and the spiral if you achieve happy entry, which by some such methods as these you will.

Do not introduce proscenium theatre in any way.   The Child chooses to act-in-the-round at this age, if not imposed upon.   Note that this does not mean acting in a circle, though this is a common outward form.   Be sure that you understand that acting-in-the-round is a process of acting outwards from Self all round the body, as opposed to acting out in one direction (as towards an audience through the proscenium arch [1]).   Avoid audiences if you can and never use the word " audience ".

When you speak to Children, remember the tone of your voice.   Music language is stronger than the meaning of words.   You create atmosphere by not shouting.   Work for conditions of quietness.   This aids absorption.

The Ideas Game

A game which I have often used may be found useful for starting things going.   I include, therefore, an excerpt from the script of a gramophone record : [2]

> " Now you may say—' Yes, that's all very well, but my mind just doesn't work that way.   I can't make up stories.'   All right—try the Ideas Game.   It is one that I made up and have used with all ages from infants to adults.   Ask one or two people (or Children) to give you an idea in one or a few words—' What's in your mind ? '—sometimes they can't think of anything—' Well, did you come here on a bus—did you notice anything, anyone *on* the bus ?' "
>
> *Child :* " Blue hat."
>
> *Self :* " All right, thank you—blue hat.   Now someone else—you ? "
>
> *Child :* " Please, sir, food."
>
> *Another Child :* " Umbrella."
>
> *Self :* " Yes.   All right, thank you.   Now we have three ideas ; blue hat, food, umbrella.   Will you help me to remember them ? " (Child-teacher relationship.)
>
> " Once upon a time there was a funny old man and he lived in a funny old house, over there *in that corner*, and there were two things which he wanted very much in the shops—*over there* (in another corner), but he was very poor and he couldn't afford them.   But they

---

[1] See Chapter II.   If you do not understand this, you will not fundamentally grasp the basis of Child Drama.

[2] By kind permission of Messrs. Hollick & Taylor, Sound Recordists, 16 Grosvenor Road, Handsworth, Birmingham.

were : (1) food ; (2) a blue hat. And he didn't know which to get. But he shuffled out of his little house, down the winding road (all over in the middle of the floor space, *there* you see), and by the road were *trees*, which bent towards him as he passed, saying, each in turn, ' Good morning, old man, good morning '. But when he got to the shops it began to rain, and he *did* want a blue hat and he *did* want some food, but suddenly he saw—what ? "

Everyone : " An umbrella."

Self : " Yes, he saw a wonderful umbrella, and he went in and bought it with his last penny. But he didn't know it was a magic one, and he *couldn't* help wishing he had his blue hat too, and he was very hungry. But what do you think happened when he got home (the house can be made of twenty or thirty human bricks if necessary)—he found that by wishing with the umbrella in his hand his friends the trees had brought him two presents. What were they ? "

All : " Food—blue hat."

Self : " Yes, and he put the hat straight on although he was in the house ; not very polite, but the trees said he might just for once. And they all leaned over him and filled him and filled him with so much food that he slowly went,—to—sleep, and all the trees passed quietly out of the house and rustled back to their places. There you are, you made it all up, didn't you—just from three ideas ? (They didn't, of course—you did. But they helped, and the ideas stimulate one's imagination.) Now let's act it, and you shall add some more ideas. (Improvisation then starts, mimed or with their words.)"

It should be understood that this game, as outlined above, is only useful in that form for *beginning* things. It starts a regular friendship feeling and begins to offer freedom. Many teachers question the value of straight-forward dramatisation, because it may impose upon the Child a story it does not want to play at that moment. The Ideas Game improves upon the imposed story, as it invites co-operation, and by that shared creation one finds a tendency to eager participation.[1] The Ideas Game can be developed into other things. The most obvious first development is to get not only the

---

[1] It was once suggested to me that if a Child says " Sir " or " Miss ", the work was not being done properly. One can only say that most Children *do* address teachers thus, if speaking to them directly. During Play " Sir " or " Miss " may be dropped, though. You may be honoured with a special name. This is different. No wise teacher would take offence at this if it is within decent bounds. Watch for difference between created names and intended impertinence. This last is *very* rare in a Drama period.

ideas from the Children, but the story also. When you have built up a bond with the Children, the story will come from them, and soon they won't need the Ideas Game at all, but will make up their own stories entirely alone. So where Play is well established the Ideas Game is redundant.

Developments from the Infant School

Thus far we have been concerned with the beginning of things in the junior school, but now we have arrived at the point of considering conditions where Play is somewhat established, or at least used and understood.

The next suggestions, therefore, are for developing Child Drama itself, as if there had been no break, or at least a smooth passing over into the junior school.

With bottom classes, continue with Play to sounds, as in infant schools. Lengthen stories a little. Cast more often. Answer questions more fully. Do not escape into lie-legends.

When you judge the right moment, mention that the sounds you use as part of Play are like speaking. Typical of a discovery of this, which eventually happens, though less consciously as a rule, was this : A little girl of seven and a half ran up to me and said : " Ooo, joo *know*, what you just said is the same tune we played this morning." She had heard the same time beat or rhythm in my words. It is exactly this recognition which leads on to appreciation of speech itself, and later to the love of literature. It is an emotional experience. It is Joy.

When Play is established and language is beginning to flow, show sympathy and arrange a legal surrounding for " acting out ". The themes may not please you, but be patient. Lead away gently. The acting out is valuable.

When speech is beginning it will be poor. Show sympathy and encourage. The words may not please you, but be patient. It will improve in time. *It will not improve if you shirk the issue now.* If you do, you have cheated the Child and broken faith. There will have been simple attempts at speech in the infant school. Be careful to ensure that the Child thinks this school is as good as the last, and do your best to develop language further.

Do not interrupt Play. Only make a suggestion if Play or speech goes dead.

Learn to hear when " the scene is going down ". That, with Children, often coincides with the " near-finish " of an episode. You will note more moments of more obvious theatre at this age, but do not make any suggestions of actor, audience or stage, as we understand them. If there is a stage, use it only as a place, such as a palace or high ground, and do this only if you are sure that it is not being thought of as *the* stage. All the room is the world in which to act. Use more rostrum blocks, if you can get them, for a slow finding of the higher level. This is the right approach to the stage.

Notice the smaller circles appearing during Play. Know that they are the outward sign of the embryo gang stage. Split them up occasionally by doing suggested group work on a theme *you* choose, or one created between you and them. A word to gang leaders if they boss *too* much, but don't destroy leadership. Use piano and gramophone music more. Do not hurry them into accurate reaction to time beat of gramophone. Recognise difference of " accompanying " piano music and " directing " of the set gramophone record. The last contains useful disciplines not to be over-looked. Allow speech during music.

Help with improvised dance creations. Watch for a development of grace and the way floor space is covered.

Take note of the Child's behaviour during Play. It tells you much about the Child and its home. This may help you with its other studies and ex-plain puzzling things. You can learn some things only through Play.

Foster Sincerity and Absorption. See them grow. Notice the building of Group Sensitivity.[1]

Watch for and recognise bursts of running Play.

Be ready to recognise a mistake in handling. For instance, a teacher lately suggested " lions ". There was music going on. She suggested " fiercer lions ". Music started again. But it was *the wrong music*. The lions were puzzled and ended by being less fierce. The teacher recognised her mistake and said afterwards : " I should have had *silence* then." That would have offered better opportunity for thought and further creation. The first creation had been stimulated by suggestion and music. Her next suggestion was an attempt at polishing. Silence was needed for the best result in the next step. After that perhaps music—but the *right* music.

Suggest occasional writing of stories centred on Play. Stop Play occa-sionally in middle, if near end of period, and suggest Children write the finish of the story. Do not seek good spelling and grammar in this, as it is ideas and joyful flow that you are seeking to develop in these moments. Walking round, correcting, will kill everything. That is for the more formal lesson

See Chapter III, page 53

(which can go parallel). We are encouraging them to *want* to write. It is the basis of essays and good plays later and just as important as spelling.

Link Art all the time—occasionally let them paint what they act, or " finish a story ". Note masks and near-mask faces.[1] Note composition, and its relation to use of floor space.

Allow occasional polished improvisations, and improvisations prepared by Children in their own time.

Try a little make-up work,[1] but not formal. Relate it to, and see it primarily as, Child Art. Do not feel that it has to be used for acting ; it may be painting faces merely as painting pictures. Be ready, though, in case there is stimulation for acting. Allow for this if at all possible.

If properties are used, do not push too many on the Children. Suggest use of half-masks. Show some—not realistic. Let them create their own. Note when dress or masks hinder movement.

Encourage some dress creation out of bits and pieces. If sewing takes place, do not insist on too much clever stitching. This will ruin the creation. But often sewing does not take place—pieces are wound on, or draped. Do not overload with ready-made dresses. Note when " parading " takes place. Do not try to stimulate Drama while this is in full spate. It won't work, as a different process is going on.

As Children near the top of your school, watch for moments of coma-acting, when space and depth are being noticed during Play on the floor space. *On no account interrupt at these moments.* Do no mistake them for mere non-participation. Very still standing, and great mental absorption, often with mouth open, give a clue.

Watch for proscenium shape, which may appear in Art about this time as an edging on the sides and top of the paper.

Expect questions on grouping fairly soon after this. They may come, and so may some first true, unhurried audience consciousness.

You expect to obtain great control in the seven–eleven age group and a steady development of the Child's own Drama. Use the shapes you find in the Child's own work, if you produce a polished improvisation on a suggested theme. There should be tremendous contrast between extreme controlled quiet and strong outburst. Equidistance during dance attains perfection, during the integration of Self with society. Co-operation and obedience should be very good. Use of space excellent. Very graceful movement develops. It is *improvised* Dance of which we speak.

See Chapter XVII.

Try to think of this work continuing in beauty until at least twelve, and avoid giving any notion of the end of a period, although the Child will leave your school.   In junior clubs, play centres, out-of-school groups, there is already some direct organic development without a break in the Child's Drama, and no doubt this will be more so in future, e.g.—in Children's Theatres, perhaps.[1]   If you have a chance, co-operate with teachers in senior schools as well as infants, so that what is done in your school links at both ends and aids a smooth development.

If you have been privileged to share and understand the extreme beauties of Child Drama at its best in the junior school, try to interest teachers in secondary schools in what has been done.   It will help them also to guard the peak of a period (up to *circa* twelve years), which under the present school system becomes their responsibility.   They may not know about it.

Second Best

If you have to use classrooms, move the desks.   If there are sufficient reasons for not doing that, consider complete and permanent change of shape so as to allow more space in centre.   It will aid all teaching.   The same number of desks may fit on three sides or in a semi-circle.

If not, use the desks themselves, as you would for occasional finding of a higher level with rostrum pieces.   (See Plates 14 and 15, between pages 184 and 185.)

Do everything you can to avoid suggesting actor and audience as different.

Do not encourage a narrator who breaks up the scenes and talks as to an audience.

Encourage audience participation, if some have to sit in desks.

Do not stop actors turning their backs.   We are not in the theatre.   What is taking place is much more important.   It is Life in the making.   There may be small circles in a cramped space, or a half-circle against the back wall.

Encourage Play between the desks also, if in rows with aisles.

The existence of the gang makes splitting up into smaller playing groups a fairly natural process in the junior school, but do not yet encourage actor and audience differences, or you will get showing-off.   The classroom is a perfectly reasonable place, though, for short playlets created by Children and acted in succession.   Though space is lacking, much else is gained.

Encourage Language Flow.   If it has had a fair chance and a clear run from the infant school up, it will be good by now.

[1] See Chapters XV and XVI.

The more *you* use stories the more difficult it will be for Language Flow. Don't stop improvised speech because you can't put up with it, or don't see the point of it.   You don't stop practice in writing because you are bored with Children's essays.   Do not stop practice in speech.

Use good story themes occasionally and let Children use their own words, particularly in top classes.

It is possible to introduce Drama as History, Geography and Scripture in the junior school.

Do not write Plays for them, and do not see the end of this work as training for the professional stage.   Make sure you are not doing this unconsciously. Think out honestly why you do this work.

Common to both the best conditions and the less good is the task of the teacher in acting as a kindly, gentle guide.   But in the junior school there is occasionally more polish needed, when you do enter into things.   However, responsibility for good creation should be handed more and more to the Child, until with the older ones it is almost entirely handed over ; together with this goes responsibility for good behaviour.   This is the way to help parents and in part avoid delinquency.   Successful Child Drama in the junior school is not only education at its highest, but prevention also.   It provides a legal out-let for the atom-bomb energy of that social group we call the gang.

CHAPTER XII

SUGGESTIONS FOR
TWELVE- TO FIFTEEN-YEAR-OLDS

REMEMBER that for many Children the peak period of acting in a manner which does not include the proscenium stage continues after eleven years old, and that the consciousness and understanding of depth may not have any pronounced manifestation in outward forms of Play until about thirteen years.

The " shape " of behaviour on the floor space often holds on to the past after shape in painting has begun to grope towards the future. Not all the Self is ready to take a full step forward.

Because of the above, discover and understand what can and often does take place in the junior school. The compartments of school life may be necessary, but they are to some extent artificial. The Person needs to develop smoothly. Do not think that the earlier schooling is not your affair. In Drama it is.

For at least the first year allow, encourage and expect Play on the floor just as in the junior school. Themes will be fuller and accomplishment more polished, but outward shape will often be the same.

Have in mind that there may be a gradual advance over the floor space towards the stage, or at least to Play up one end of a room.[1]

With first-year Children, keep the curtains of the stage (if you have any) shut. This reduces the overwhelming influence of the stage upon their work. Any move towards using it is then likely to become a genuine inner urge towards new forms of expression and sensual discovery.

Do not expect the Players to remain on the stage even if they do begin to use it. They may flow off. This shows their inherent artistry. There is not enough room for what they want to express. They do not merely wish to focus the intellect on some abstruse psychological or social problem, or tickle the senses as adult theatre does, confining action to a small area. They are discovering Life, and the canvas needs to be larger. They are young and *alive*. Do not treat them like " tired business men ".

[1] See Chapter IV.

Note how the tongue shape, out from the proscenium, begins to appear, and how the floor end is rather rounded, and the lines of movement nearer the stage and on the stage more straight. Consider how brilliant a method this is of keeping one foot wisely in the past (acting-in-the-round) whilst testing perspective theatre for moments at a time.

Note, too, how this method offers much more scope for dance, pageantry and imaginative forms of production. (See Plates 45 to 49.)

Watch for and hope for flow *to* the stage rather than flow from it at this age. The current in the general movement is fairly clear.

If the Children seize at once upon the stage, but spend nearly all the time flowing off it, allow to a degree, but suggest frequent Play periods without use of stage. Then allow it for short times at the end of the Drama period. This often promotes a gradual change, and a constructive advance to the stage and sensible use of it is more likely to take place.

Allow certain periods of blowing off steam in Play themes you do not care for very much. They work off a good deal of outside influence that way. But watch for the wise moment to lead away. It is often possible to change a gangster story into a thrilling and absorbing episode in history, and thence to a consideration of period etiquette and social behaviour.

Because of the somewhat remarkable capacity for absorbing knowledge in many Children of this age, do not hurry the use of the script play and add to the memory a quite unnecessary burden. This may start a certain dislike for formal theatre, which continues right into the youth club, where we often suffer the full reaction of what Children have had to put up with at school.

Allow and encourage preparation of Children's own plays. There will be a continuation of imaginative creation and spontaneous speech, if not squashed, and this helps the young adolescent over a tendency to self-consciousness, largely caused by the break in schooling and method. Smooth development of the Drama process is very helpful here. Remember that out-flow of energy and expression is as necessary as in-flow. In-flow (study and learning) will come easier if there is not too much pent-up steam trying to burst out. It is the balance of energy that is needed. The Child's own Drama provides for this in a natural manner.

If formal dance training takes place in the school, allow incorporation of pieces during Play. Allow, also, movement of the Child's own making, if utterly different from formal dance. This is their way of finding mental relaxation and of devising their own creation from what has been absorbed.

Or there may be a temporary complete and intended rejection of " stuff they don't like ".

Formal training in dance has its value at this age, though, and often leads to wider mental vision ; but it may stereotype expression, despite the fact that it is intended to enlarge it.

Avoid interruption during Child-created Play. Make suggestions afterwards, if you feel them necessary. Play should run on its own very healthily by now, if the Child's school life has been anything like a happy one dramatically.

But in general matters, Children are less anguished by the idea of detailed timetable and period. They will stand more interruption now, though they do not like it. You need not watch for the near-finish so carefully.

See that leaders do not become too bossy over tiny details. Be ready with advice if asked.

Consider the use of Drama projects. They can be very valuable. Be sure to encourage complete impersonation, though, of all Children in characters (personal Play) after prolonged immersion in " period " of construction (projected Play).

As thirteen years approaches there may be more use of the stage. Allow it.

Use more polished improvisations ; there is a need for the experience of a good "finish" to craftsmanship. Constructive, critical faculty may be developed strongly.

Still do not hurry on the script Play for literary or any other reasons. Use if reading is very good or if strong wish has been expressed.

Discourage one person from taking too many parts of the opposite sex.

If script plays are begun, do not force what *you* want. It may still be necessary for life trials to take place in certain characters. Second-rate funny plays may be chosen first. Allow this. Leading to better appreciation can come from occasional choice by you of improvised Play themes. First script plays must be enjoyable and easy. They can be, and generally are, a shattering bore, when compared with the delights of genuine Child creations. Nor do they approach anywhere near the dramatic achievement of, say, exercises in stylised fighting with imagined period weapons by boys, executed to music, noise background, percussion bands or the stamping of feet.

With girls, try to lay a firm foundation of charm, joy, co-operation and graceful movement. With boys try to lay a firm foundation of gaiety, joy, co-operation, sensible understanding of aesthetic values, and good manners ; abolish contentment or satisfaction at being clumsy.

In both sexes, develop intentionally in some periods speed in creation, and in preparation during Play. Try the Ideas Game. Create and Play out in a few minutes. Get *them* to create and play out swiftly, too ; not *always* swiftly but sometimes. This aids them in general efficiency for modern life lived at a very fast rate. Take care not to fuss them, though. " Let's see if we can—in so many minutes " is better than " get it done by —— or else." Dramatically you are laying the foundation for good and swift scene changing, and good stage management.

If the hall cannot be used, consider what has been said about classrooms in the junior school section under " second best ".[1] The half-circle and/or full circles may still appear at this age, though there will be more conscious- ness of audience. Do not yet correct for sight-angles and backs being turned ; this will change as more audience consciousness enters.

Despite the emergence of more audience consciousness, do not forget that moments of privacy are very important at this age (still speaking of thirteen years). A curtain on the stage, to play behind or for times of secrecy, is necessary to Child Play, particularly for girls. Apart from new factors entering their life (which may be partly the cause of the Hinterland Play), is there still perhaps a link here with the utter non-necessity of audience for the best Child Drama of earlier years ? [2]

About fourteen, and even earlier, there may be sudden changes in hair style and the wearing of clothing out of school. Hair may become of great interest to both sexes. Boys may collect hair oils and squirt or plaster water on. Be careful to treat all personal manifestations of oddity with sympathy. Do not laugh at trials of this kind. An occasional tactful remark about the picture of someone in the paper, or a fashion plate, will often have more effect than direct criticism. Boys get much out of wearing a hat in odd ways, and if you don't like their ties, remember that male clothing is incredibly boring, and ties are about the only splash of colour allowed. Even that causes comment in the dreary world we have built about us. Do not upbraid girls for their make-up trials.

Use stage make-up at school. Do not interfere. Give advice if asked.

---

[1] See Chapter XI, page 149.

[2] In connexion with this, whilst in correspondence recently with Professor Sir Cyril Burt of London University, he mentioned that when he was still in his 'teens he, his sister and their school friends used to act plays in a loft, but that the peculiar feature of it was that they never thought of inviting an audience. My wife also recently discovered such a " theatre " in a North Country village, and I know of adults who remember years of joyful Drama behind a curtain. These are interesting additions to the numerous other instances of personal discovery and observation.

Much taste is learned this way, legally and in the open, shared with a friendly adult. It is happier than the secret plastering and the screwed-up courage to face the world (by girls uncertain of their artifice) which is needed out of school, where trials are often a complex problem. Its use in school may even satisfy the desire for make-up in younger girls, or for a moustache in a boy.

From fourteen years onwards the script play may become valuable. Judge the time to introduce it. The playing shape may have changed from the tongue to a bulge out from the proscenium, or only the proscenium may be used by choice. If script plays are asked for, still take care not to force your choice too much. Be patient. Real deep down appreciation and literary choice may not come for some years yet. Occasionally, though, do something *you* like, and get their agreement in trying it. If the scene is dull or lifeless, break it up and employ Child Drama methods of improvising the same situation off the stage in their own words.

If you find ignorance or lack of understanding of the situation, be patient ; perhaps it is your fault for misjudging the time for script plays. In any case, early attempts at really getting into the skin of a play are somewhat disappointing. Expect this. *But do not put up with it.* Work harder for absorption with more improvisation, and balance with more play-reading.

Do not make too many suggestions, but if asked, answer fully. Technical advice may be sought. Be ready for a sudden hunger for knowledge about lights, scenery and all the trappings of the theatre. Begin to satisfy this in small doses, gradually giving over full responsiblity for organising, directing and running the business side of theatre as well as the plays.

Be ready for sudden re-emergence of improvisation on or off the stage. Allow it. Always let Children feel that their work is valuable and worthy of consideration. Do not stop improvisation because script plays have started.

Do not encourage bogus copies of ballet. It will ruin their own Art. If they wish to progress further, they can now be taught properly. The quite few outstanding Children will have been picked out earlier, perhaps, or will have expressed a determined desire to dance. Judge *very* carefully. This is a great step towards professionalism. Tragically, it is often judged wrongly, and does not pertain to normal educational processes. Ballet, modern dance and country dance are all special delights and specialisations. Of these, modern dance is of a wider general value. But the Child's *own* Dance is a thing apart ; do not undervalue it. It contains the very spirit of the dance, without which, Arnold Haskell suggests, technical excellence has little point.

One word about control. If you are worried, and you and they are not used to space, use a little at a time and enlarge. Do not let your fear confine Children to the stage. Better to confine them to a floor area first, then expand, then advance to the stage and broaden out generally. They are quick to see, though, that no good work can be done in a scrimmage. This will aid you.

Suggestions on improvement such as " Speak a bit louder, I like to hear what you say wherever I am in the room," not during, but before and after play, induce in time a habit of attack on words during their acting. With a script play you can suggest it in the middle ; there will be numerous pauses and cessations—use one of these.

Occasionally share in creations by adding polish if you feel it is needed, or if they ask you. Audiences are less dangerous now. If pre-training has been right, Absorption and Sincerity will be deeper, less easy to break.

The fifteen-year-olds may still want to create their own beauties, but will normally have an interest in script plays.

Drama as a Means of Study

These older ones (and somewhat younger ones, too, according to your judgement), can use Drama as a general means of study. This can even be done with the aid of the script play.

Though the method was carried out originally with older people, I include here extracts from a report I was invited to prepare on factory work some years ago. The method has since been applied to youth groups and older school Children :

> To begin with it was decided to concentrate on one particular Girls' Hostel. The problem was to rouse interest in the girls themselves so that they could learn some of the content of Drama from the academic point of view—such as literature, history and costume—and at the same time provide practical opportunity for acting, for improvement in speech and movement, and engendering of community spirit by working in a team under difficult conditions. It seemed desirable, so far as possible, to provide the environment of particular types of " world " for the development of various sides of the personality.
>
> The method adopted was at once practical, and three one-act plays went into production, during the course of which the attention of stu-

dents was continually drawn to matters relating to, but wider than, the actual scope of the play. In this way the production process became, in fact, an educational class on a wide variety of subjects, without students necessarily being conscious of their study. Production could break off at any time for a short discussion on a topic arrived at in the story of the play, or by success or failure in presenting the stage characters. Such discussion, with suggestions by the trainer, would vary from practical matters (such as tactful instruction in good manners and self-control) to more abstruse psychological, artistic or social observations, the field being allowed to expand or contract according to the ability of students to follow.

It was found that, after factory hours, concentration on one subject appeared difficult for more than a limited period, and for this reason it is held that the approach to education by discussion and suggestion, stimulated by dramatic production, which offers an almost inexhaustible field for various imaginary environments, is one of the best for this type of worker, *and could be adapted to many groups of various ages*. . . . Yet the process offers scope, also, for prolonging concentration if necessary, and provides, therefore, to some extent, that very training which is essential to serious study.

The results of the training on the first three plays are encouraging. Not only did the girls show ability to absorb and use knowledge of dramatic art *per se*, but they showed also, in some cases to a marked extent, improvement in personal physical control of limbs, in speech and particularly in self-confidence. It must be stressed that the self-confidence thus gained, and traced in some degree to practice in adaptation to new environments and working with others under emotional strain, is thought to be perhaps the most valuable part of the training, both from the personal and the social point of view, not to speak of the potential results to the management for which students may work.

I think that this sort of training can be valuable, too, for young people of fourteen and fifteen years and over, *before* they leave school, as well as after they have entered a job. At school it would be a sort of pre-leaving training, and might prove invaluable at County Colleges.

The report goes on to mention standard of playing and, incidentally, the success of performances, but stresses :

It should not be forgotten that the purely technical side of the Drama training aims also at economy of movement and consequent saving of energy for the individual. . . . But the type of education described, when applied fully, has even wider possibilities, as it develops not only the body and its control, but also the faculties of perception, memory and self-confidence as well as community spirit and interest in life. And, by its wide opportunity for association of ideas, [it] prepares the way for study in many other directions, the most common of which are : languages, practical crafts and carpentry, literature, the arts generally, science and social studies.

If you use this or a similar method, handle it carefully and lightly with fifteen-year-olds. Do not prolong discussion too far unless *certain* of interest. A few moments may be enough. They may want to get on with the play. Judge carefully. At other times, particularly over a point of social or moral values, older Children will discuss at length with a friendly adult, and the play (used only as the instrument) will be forgotten.

With some Children you can call it " play reading ", and intentionally direct the process so that they understand what is happening. With others, the full production method is better, breaking off only at places of interest. They are then largely unconscious of the mechanics of the process. They study, as it were, by accident. But to you alone it is no accident.

A further development of this is the group building of documentary and special subject plays, centring round social or moral subjects, or points of general interest which have attracted the older Child's attention.[1] Here again the wide study has its value, although the play may prove meritorious. Theatre lovers stress the absolute necessity of preparing a piece of theatre, keeping *that* firmly in mind. As teachers, do not be jockeyed into this shallow view ; plays developed by such methods, specifically with theatre in mind, as yet show no proof of being better, even as plays, than those arrived at by primarily concerning oneself with creating built situations, true in themselves, to the study of a certain problem, i.e. Drama, the Doing of Life. There is a different set of values here. The Child adds its immense wealth of creation, and often the result is incidentally good theatre, but with added depth of reasoning. If it does not happen to be good theatre it can be made so, if necessary. But understand, as in all Child creation, there may or may

[1] The subject of a television programme with the author and based on his personality courses in industry.

not be adult " theatre " in it.   A piece of group reasoning written down in dramatic vein may of itself be intensely lovely, and artistically unalterable merely to fit it for vulgar show.   It is in this case rather pertaining to projected Play, and not so much an instrument for personal Play (acting). Understand the difference ; you will be challenged.[1]

Preparation for Life after School

The technique of the proscenium theatre, being concerned with lines of sight and curtained space, is a very precise one.   Use its processes for attaining neatness in disposing of the body, particularly in footwork.   This will help to prevent Children leaving school as oafs, particularly the boys.   See that they understand that there is nothing manly or creditable in being an oaf, but do not tease about clumsiness.   Aid it by occasional exercises valuable both to life and stage : Examples :

1. Precision is needed for a stage entry.   Precision is needed for entering the office of the boss and the head teacher's room.   Without precision there may be a knock, trip or kick, which would cause irritation.

2. Very few amateur actors can open and shut a door well on the stage. Practice.   Much of real life also consists of opening and shutting important doors.   Sometimes doors alter one's whole career.

3. Avoiding knocking into furniture and people is another important thing (though this will have been learnt by unconscious equidistance processes on the floor space in early Child Drama, for those who have experienced it).

4. Getting up and sitting down gracefully.

5. Eating decently, and handing cups round.

6. Learning how different types of people behave, and how different races behave.   Broaden the Children's mind and their judgement of people and regulations by such considerations.

All these and many more Life experiences can be pre-experienced as part of personal preparation for Life, by simple improvised scenes.   But once proscenium stage work is in full swing, and if you know enough of the theatre, you can use the precision of technique which is necessary to the stage.   In this way you can aid older Children tremendously in becoming more cultured and likeable beings.   All earlier observations about not showing off will lead to an understanding that this precise knowledge can be used *naturally* in daily life, and not theatrically, which is most unpleasant.

[1] See Chapter IV.

THE SHAPES WHICH CONSTANTLY OCCUR IN CHILD DRAMA.

· Self

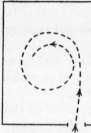

Area round self explored.

The Area widens is slowly dominated

Running in a circle

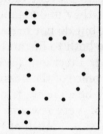

Meeting companions three "selfs" each with an area round

The three run in a circle equi-distance is achieved.

INFANT SCHOOL

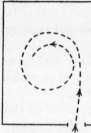

Happy entry. The spiral.

After spiral, the ragged circle.

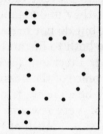

Typical big circle of infants, some smaller ones beginning.

JUNIOR SCHOOL

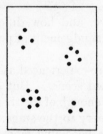

Small circles appear more frequently (7 yrs. on)

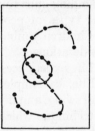

Medium circle and S-shape, which is half of figure eight common in running play.

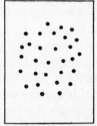

Very common Good filled-in circle with equi-distance Age 9-11. Here whole class feels group entity.

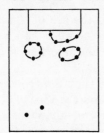

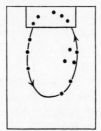

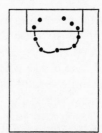

c. 12 years - 13 plus
Circles appear but
nearer stage.

c. 13 plus. Stage is
used sometimes, but
there is strong flow
on or off   This is
the Tongue Shape.

c. 14 years
Proscenium stage
influencing more .
Less flow. We see
the Bulge in front
of stage.

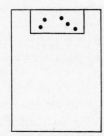

Where proscenium
is finally chosen lines
become straighter.

Where· work has to be done in cramped
classrooms, we still see small circles and
the bulge. Some movements between desks.

Also, according to your knowledge of theatre, develop domination of an area or a crowd by aiding Children to learn about projecting personality out from the stage, and to cause " atmosphere " by means of the voice (easier after Child Drama emotional " sound " training).   This will help them in becoming natural leaders.

Again, take care that it is natural and not " show off ".   This last makes for antagonism.   Often, feeling it once may be enough to make a young mind alert and aware.

These are some ways of using the content of theatre itself as education, according to Child values and as the growing person becomes increasingly interested in adult life.

And now, in arriving finally at the script play and the use of the proscenium theatre by the age of *circa* fifteen years, we come at last to actual intended and prepared stage presentations.   They are an important though small part of the whole of Drama.

Handle so that as much polish goes into a presented show as is consistent with sustaining life.   If you kill that life, all your efforts are wasted.   The production will just be boring, a dead drill.   But do not allow the older Children to skimp all detail.   Make them understand that to put on a show less good than they *can* do, and ask people to watch, is an insult to their audience and to their own dignity.   If you handle them so that they are keen they will work very hard, but do not overstep the mark.

Use Child-painted scenery, if any.

See and recognise how the vital characteristics of Child Drama, particularly Sincerity and Absorption, blossom on and on with the right handling. They are wonderful qualities, laboriously built up and nurtured into good habits, and should be jealously guarded.   If preserved they present to *all acting* from now on a gift of supreme excellence, which lifts it above other acting.

This then is your last task, apart from all the personal development of the Child.   By your care you must keep alive the fragrance of that other Land, so that Child Drama, so carefully nurtured, now full grown and firmly established, provides a permanent feature which distinguishes certain actors for the rest of their lives.   This is done by continuing improvisation. Imaginative creation should never stop.   It can go parallel with the formal script play, which is only one small part of the great world of Drama.

CHAPTER XIII

LANGUAGE FLOW (2)

FOLLOWING on what has already been suggested in Chapter VI, each teacher must find his own method. I do not pretend that the suggestions already made, and those which follow, present the only ways of releasing speech, nor that they are necessarily the best. All I would say is that their use has had a marked effect upon many Children's apparent happiness, upon their behaviour and above all else upon their speech. It is in the emotional realm that I would develop speech further, where, in fact, the energy for speech should come, and I have found that this produces what I have called *Language Flow*.

This chapter, then, contains suggestions for aiding the development of Language Flow, which I hold to be both important and a phenomenal part of Child Drama.

There is always present in Children a desire for histrionic declamation, and it is this as much as anything that we nurture and bring to the state of real Language Flow.

Enough has already been said, perhaps, for it to be clear that opportunity for musical and joyous experiences is the chief need. And when we come to look more closely at the manifestation of histrionic declamation we may come to the conclusion that it indeed grows out of the baby's first joy in sound and that it is primarily a musical form of expression. But as experience of the Doing of Life (Drama) is slowly incorporated, we hear the fuller and more intellectual expression, which may ultimately become not only the added jewel to Dramatic Play, but, at times, the very core of creation which leads to Play.

In both the home and the nursery school there is an important task to be done in providing for musical experience, but, before considering what we ourselves might do to help, there is one point I should like to stress. *If there is any uncertainty about what to do, it is important to remember that much is achieved by merely understanding and recognising what the Child does for itself, and in offering sympathy and the right atmosphere for further creation and discovery.* So much is stifled, so much goes unloved.

163

Because there is a personal rhythm in each Child, we shall hear from time to time that rhythm being squeaked, banged, stamped, spoken, shouted, sung or tapped out. The average mean of the expressed time beat and rhythm will be found, in nearly every case, to approximate to the speed of personal rhythm. This helps us to know the Child and its need, and aids us in our dealings with it. These emitted sounds are the ways in which the Child eventually discovers at what speed it will speak in future years. Here is the swamp where some stammers may start, for lack of opportunity to discover personal rhythm, or rhythm hurried out of itself, causes the speed anxiety mentioned earlier,[1] which can develop into a neurosis. It is also possible that, in some cases, damage to the actual flow of language may be one of the elusive causes of later cases of mental " blocking ", as well as of sudden distaste for study.

If the Child takes joy in these sounds, and if we can share joys—the basis of the adult's attitude in all Child Drama—we can share the sounds also, and just as it is possible to enter into jabber-talk and converse with the baby, so it is possible to enter into all sound-talk and converse also. Thus we may gently take up the same tapping as a baby is making, and meet with exactly the same delight as in shared jabber-talk. Very often there will follow on both sides renewed effort at creation. Just as we put in one extra " real " word in jabber-talk for the baby to experience and perhaps learn, so we may put in a new sound or a change of rhythm, which the baby may try out or even incorporate in its own vocabulary. An example of this is, say, a baby tapping a table over and over again, ending on a strong note at the end of a " sentence " of tap. We join in, but end our sentence by tapping a different material. The sound changes. The baby will often try it out too, and find new delight.

We should not enter into noise conversation at once, but only after some personal trial has taken place. The moment may be judged, for one can detect something similar to the " near finish ", when a tapped experience is fading or running out of purpose. If we interfere we cause laziness or a break in effort, but occasional joining in is of advantage. We share the Joy.

From the adult's point of view, dramatically we are laying the foundation for a firm appreciation of rhythm, which will give future actors that calm gliding grace which is needed for the stage and for appreciation of symphonic production, though not this but the development of the Child is the main point of the work.

See page 31.

We find some recognition of and sympathy for this vast realm of sound in the toys that are now made specially for banging, whereas the rattle, drum, flute and trumpet have been favourites down the ages (though I note the modern flute is a plastic clarionet). However, as with all other toys, if the modern marvel is not provided, the Child will manage perfectly well without. It will find its own treasures and often love them better.

The early love of sound continues, if it is allowed, and I would suggest that we foster it in the home, throughout the nursery school, and particularly in the infant and junior schools.

Sound is divided into roughly two parts : long sounds that are drawn out or remain ringing, and short sounds which may be sharp and sudden, or merely unsustained and flat or dead. Almost everything we touch or bang comes to the ear as pertaining to one or the other of these two types of sound. In language we also find the two main sounds : the vowel and the consonant.

Musical instruments provide in their own sphere for the vowel and the consonant too, as, for instance, the violin and bell (mainly vowel) as opposed to the drum (consonant). Some instruments are arranged to provide for both. The violin is, of course, one, but usually it acts in the same way as the vowel in speech, for the vowel provides the tone, resonance and notation of speech, and the consonant provides the time beat and rhythm, dividing up the long sounds. We find a musical-bar system in formal poetry, but in less formal poetry and prose a certain division is brought about by meaning and pause, and the consonant helps with this. Punctuation has been invented to help this process also.

One of the early things we learn about speech in the theatre is that by pronouncing the consonants clearly, even banging them on occasions, we are more likely to attract and keep the attention of the audience. This is particularly true of consonants at the beginning of words and at the beginning of important syllables. It is part of what is called " attack ".

The drum, from earliest times, has also excited the ear and forced attention. The consonant is the same thing, though more subtle. Furthermore, in learning a part, it is a distinct aid to memory to learn the time beat and the tune of sentences as well as their meaning. Actors who learn their lines this way produce a very different final performance from those who do not. It is of considerable value in choral speech. In association with these ideas, and apart from Music itself, it has been found that percussion bands act also as a subtle influence on speech, if properly directed.

For all these reasons it is not surprising to find that a baby's typical early speech trial contains the easy consonants which are used as time beat, and the easy vowels which are used as essays in a tune. Example : " bàh-ba-ba-ba " interchanged with " ba-ba-ba-bàh ". Many may be the variations of the first and last drawn-out " bàh ", and it is after several such attempts that the adult may judge it useful to join in jabber-talk. To understand what is happening, to know and love what you are doing, goes far to avoid any embarrassment the adult might feel. Indeed, if there is proper understanding and sharing of the joy, there can be no room for self-consciousness. This is true of both Child and adult, but the very young Child is not an entirely different Person from the baby ; it is growing slowly, so we find ways of keeping sound alive in the age groups mentioned above.

Some consideration has already taken place of the part that properties and costume play in Child Drama. What is far more important is a box full of noises—but for the adult at first rather than the Children. I would recommend a drum, tambour, tambourine, various bells, gongs, a hooter, whistle and any other interesting and less usual sounds that ingenuity can devise. A piano and a gramophone are also useful, but not essential. If none of these things is to hand, then the human voice has to make the long sounds, hands and feet may make the drums.

For early stages of Joy in sound, everybody clapping and using feet together in certain time beat is valuable. Little climaxes cause great delight and laughter. Sometimes association by the teacher of " running after " may add something. The climax is useful for Music and Drama, and will aid in time interest in the spoken word.

But the Child does not always speak with its mouth, particularly when with a number of others. This is natural, as the Child does not speak very well yet. But it does speak with its body and will move and speak in dumb crambo fashion saying similar things to what it would say if talking. We see facial expressions too, which are and will be used during speech. Sound, at these moments, is supplied by the adult as stimulus. There may be much movement-speech of this kind ; integration of sound and body is taking place.

Here is an example of movement being like speech ; when actual speech does begin to flow it often starts with a long-drawn-out sound, as " Ōoh, that is the bad cat that has been stealing my pollidge ", or " ĪĪĪ am the royal one who comes walking like a camel ", or " Yōu shall go to be cut up for lunch with pins in you ". This is the same way as the baby which sometimes starts with, say, " bàh-ba-ba-ba ". Later on the slightly older Child comes to moments of swifter entry into speech, a shorter vowel starting the sentence, such as, " Get out of the way, *you*", which is similar to " ba-ba-ba-bàh ", where the stress is at the end of the sentence. In movement-language (first used in personal Play with Dramatic flavour), a sweeping gesture is often the beginning (bàh-ba-ba-ba). It is the expression of a long-drawn-out sound, just as in the spoken declamation. Later, smaller movements begin Play, which may end with a sweeping gesture (ba-ba-ba-bàh). This, in both cases, besides being language of the body, is a development of the sideways thresh—sometimes the actual thresh itself. But, as we have seen earlier, the thresh always carries a message, as do most movements.

Nursery and Infant Schools

The actual use of sounds delights the Child and catches its attention, so that we find interest, obedience and pleasure in classrooms (or preferably halls) where this method is used. When obedience is growing, gesture from the teacher can take the place of vocal command. A firm bond of sensitive understanding and friendship is built. Again, just as the audience's attention is caught by the consonant stressed by an actor, so a teacher beating a drum or a tambour becomes the cause of Children running joyfully into a hall, where the emotional sound language they love is going to take place. This is the cause of the happy entry, and it is as they run in that the spiral is formed. This is followed by the circle, which in turn splits up as the sound stops.

I often ask Children what a certain noise reminds them of. Then, having used about three different sounds, these can be pieced together as a little story if desired.

EXAMPLE

Teacher : " What does this sound remind you of ? " (Makes a noise with tambourine.) (See Plate 9, opposite page 136.)

A Child : " Ponies."

Teacher : " Yes, Ponies." (Makes noise again.)

Many of the Children will begin to gallop. Teacher makes a decisive bang and stops. The Children will stop running—such is the command that sound has on the attention.

Teacher : " What's this ? " (Blows hooter.)

Children : " Motor. Motor-bike. Bus."

Teacher : " Yes." (Hoots afresh.)

Bikes, motors and buses will whizz by. More Children will join in.

Teacher : " And this ? " (Clangs a big bell.)

Children : " School time. Fire Engine."

Teacher : " Ooh, yes. What colour is the fire engine ? "

Nearly all the Children, delighted : " Red."

Teacher : " Good. We're in the street. Be careful of the traffic, won't you ? Mind all the buses." (Starts to hoot.)

Buses and cars begin to whizz by, and other hoots (vocal) and peeps will be heard, perhaps, together with grinding gears and acceleration. This is creation beginning.

(Teacher stops hooting.) Traffic will die down a bit. " Near-finish " is coming, attention is going back to the teacher. (Teacher times it well, then clangs bell violently).

Teacher : " Look out ! "

One or two, or dozens of fire engines may start careering round. (Noise ceases as before, then changes to slower clanging).

Teacher : " Listen, there's the bell for school. Don't be late."

Walking takes place. Slow drumbeat getting faster might be added, then stopped without a bang. Feet will continue in the same beat for a time, before getting ragged.

Teacher : "Oh dear, I'm sure its getting late. But what's this ? Well, if it isn't your little pony that's followed you all the way." (After some weeks at similar work one might drop the word pony, and merely make the noise. It would then read : " Well, if it isn't your little (tambourine noise) that's followed you. . . ." An inquiring look will produce cries of " Pony ".)

Teacher : " You jump on his back and away you go to school."

Ponies gallop madly round—in roughly a large circle, partially filled in. Hearts will nearly always be to the centre. There will be neighs and shrieks of delight. A big bang, and silence, however, will bring the ponies to a standstill.

Teacher : " Are we in time ? " (Clangs bell.) " Yes, we are." (Bell stops.) " But only just. Tie up your pony (mimed) and tiptoe into your places." (Soft taps on tambour.)

If the period is ending, the real classroom may be intimated and Children will tiptoe out of the hall right to their desks if the spell of the sound is unbroken. (Training by noises brings quiet as well as speech.)

If there is a different answer to the question " Are we in time ? " arrange the story accordingly. With older Children of the infant school a march on the gramophone or piano might be added. But the younger Child needs *short* stories, and by this method the Children and teacher have created a story together. This adds to the interest.

It is not possible to elaborate in detail the many different ways of using sound, nor would it be wise to do so, for every teacher must be a creative artist in this work. It is not difficult, but requires thought and care. This simple glimpse may suggest many better things.

The next stage is creating a story and saying : " Speak if you wish to." Very few words may come at first, but encouragement should always be there. Music and sounds should be administered where the teacher thinks fit, or Children be allowed to make their own noise. So, slowly, sound and speech grow up together.

After this, piano or gramophone music may be used to build atmosphere. This will often aid the flow of speech [1] as young Children speak through the music, which often " tells them what to say ". They listen to it emotionally. It is not, as with older people, unheeded background.

It is important to bear in mind the two different functions of :

(1) Improvised piano-music accompanying, and therefore offering freedom of expression ;

(2) Gramophone music, rigid and therefore disciplinary as well as stimulating.

Once any flow of words is attained by these or similar methods, we may begin to hear home truths and home expressions coming out. We should not check these. The story will lead away in time and the subject of speech will improve.

When tiny story improvisations are developed, always encourage the use of sound. And if you decide to polish an improvisation of the Children's making, sounds should be included, as in the Chinese theatre. This adds greatly to the Drama itself, and has a marked effect upon the flow of words. Children will want to make their own sounds as they get older, and this is particularly valuable where only a few can take part at one time, because of too many desks or lack of space. Audience Participation [2] will have to be arranged, and the noise education can then continue. Tapping of pencils for rain and hail; whistling, sighing for wind; desk lids for explosions. Fists make interesting sounds. A fish shop I once saw (and heard) was

[1] See " Out of School," Chapter XV.   [2] See Chapter III, page 59.

delightfully created by different fist smacks representing fish on the counter. Many unexpected sounds will bring delight.

If answering a Child who addresses you in Language Flow, pay attention to its rhythm whilst answering. You may judge it wise to use a similar rhythm to keep the flow. Adult ideas of contrast in character often wreck speech in this way. A sudden new time beat or a new rhythm tends to cause surprise, and a certain disharmony is felt. Why? Because the Child does *not* listen intellectually. *It hears emotionally* and therefore the younger Child is quite right in thinking that a sudden contrast is untidy and out of harmony. Only later it learns to appreciate sudden change.

Language Flow may start very early—at two years or three, can be commonly developed at five, and should flower between six and seven onwards.

Junior Schools

Sounds should continue, but the Child is by now being weaned (after the dawn of seriousness) and should be on to fairly extensive spontaneous outbursts of language. The flowering time is between seven and twelve years, when the flow can be so great that it is almost impossible to take notes of the words. If improvised speech has been allowed only periodically, or late in the Child's life, it will be poor at first. Do not stop because of this or because the Child " plays out " situations you don't like. Lead it away slowly to better things. Outburst is necessary. Be grateful for what you learn about the Child's life in this way, and what it has to face. Do not interrupt whilst Language Flow is in progress. Answer questions properly. Do the work regularly, and encourage regular improvisation.

Working on these lines one finds that Children say imaginary, beautiful, creative, religious and even philosophical things, particularly from five to nine years. After that the wit gets quicker, and is incorporated more and more. But our whole attitude should be based on understanding of the Child's musical and emotional approach to language. It takes joy in speech. Our task is to nurture that Joy.

All children say lovely things from time to time, but we may help them to say even lovelier things. The use of sound helps here, and not only does the creative release make the Child happier and more obedient, but the habit of listening to sound aids concentration. Finally, after it can read, it is the distant beat of sound that the Child hears and recognises whenever it meets good literature. This is how taste is born. Beautiful language is *heard*, it does not glow in the heart because of the name of its author. Personal recognition of that which is beautiful arises directly out of the musical approach to words, and it is my own personal opinion that without some such approach a lasting love of what is good is mostly a matter of chance. *It may or may not come.* And if it comes it may or may not stay. It is often imposed, and is sometimes a pose. So, then, Children should be seen *and* heard in our homes and schools. They should hear, too. Our motto should be " Let language flow on ".

EXAMPLES

Seventh Birthday

Child : " My face was covered with water and you couldn't see it and they opened me up and took *everything* away and then they put seven years inside and closed me again and a block on my head. And when it was lifted it was *all new*. Isn't it lovely ? But I am still me."

Age 6 years. Child : " Oh look, there's the first dear star of evening, my friend. Look, shining there ! If it comes over the roof I'll climb out of the window and catch it in my hand."

Age 6 years

A Child went behind the wireless and without turning it on started to announce : " Now we are going to the Zoo." There followed a great variety of noises, including bow-wows, meows, cock-a-doodle-doos, sheep bleats and cow moos. These were very loud and rather trying, and an adult (not being able to stand it any more) stepped to the set and clicked an imaginary button, saying : " I think we will just see if there is anything on the other programme." A long pause, then Child announcing : " All stations are Zoo today, as it happens." The noises were then redoubled. Clever indeed is the adult who can outwit the Child in its own sphere of imagination.

Age 6 years plus. Child : " Oh, I'm unhappy. I've got a very hot ear."

Adult : " Oh, that means a friend is thinking well of you. Which of your friends do you think it is ? "

Child : " Well, you are my friend."

Adult : " Oh yes.   I was thinking well of you."
Child : " Well, *do* stop."

Examples of " poetic language flow " stimulated by Dramatic Play.

Age 6–7 years

" Now you will hear the moon coming up and the sun going down, and now it is all dark and dark and the next day is North Wind and the next day is Spring Day and the next day is Autumn and the next day is Friday and the next day is Saturday and the next day is Sunday and the next day is Monday and the *next* day will not . . . *will* not be told."

Note the Child's mind returning from the dream world to reality as it falls into reciting the days of the week.   But even though it has forgotten the name of the next day, which brings it finally to earth, it sustains something of the rhythm of the piece and finishes the oratory with a good climax.   The forgetfulness has been surmounted and we are left with a feeling of something profound.   This is extremely important and part of what is brought about by Dramatic Play.   There is achievement here and no sense of failure, *because it succeeded dramatically and poetically*, which is of the Child's world, and was not overcome by the detail (which it will remember later), which is of our grown-up world.

Age 6–7 years

(Example expressing knowledge of right and wrong.   This should be showing in their Play by this age.   If not, one should begin to wonder a bit and watch and listen carefully.)

" Once upon a time there was a naughty little dog and he did such a naughty thing one day.   And he did this.   He told a little boy to not do what his mother said and to do what the devil said.   And then he started to make the whole world to do what the devil said.   And God was very sad and fighted very hard with the devil.   And even *harder* than he used to do."

Boy, age 8 years

" Once upon a time there was a little boy and he did all what his mother said.   And he sent all kinds of his food, and God sent an Angel to make him do some big fighting against the devil."

Child, 7 years (in a very difficult state)

Child : " Did you know —— was a naughty man ? "

Mother : " No, what did he do ? "

Child : " He hit a woman."

Mother : " Oh, he must have been drunk. But very few men are like that."

Child : " It broke my heart. *Down the lane it was, near the Church, so I thought of God.*"

Mother : " Yes, darling."

Child : "Why didn't you know he was naughty? Miss —— knows. I went into her house and she took me across the fields to the post office, and I lay on the sofa."

Mother : " Did you cry ? "

Child : " No, but I wished I was with you. Why did you leave me ? I'm never going to leave *you* again."

The terrible thing is that the Child had made great friends of the man, and the man assaulted a woman in front of the Child. It broke down her confidence in human beings and made her frightened and obstinate at the least command or suggestion. This was, perhaps, a sort of continued bravery, a kind of bravado. She met the man in the post office later, and said : " I'm not afraid of you." She is none-the-less afraid of everything and everyone now, but covers it up.

When the story came out, Language Flow helped her to express it. She then wept and has been better for it.

An illustration of the wealth of imaginative notions in spontaneous drama

Child, 6 years : (Towards the end of a very long play, the setting of which changed from room to room and up and down stairs like a pageant of ancient Egypt.)

(In declamatory style) " Come we will down the passage go and fry the noses of those thieves. Do not be frightened because I am the King's own royal royalist soldier and I have two guns, a sponge and a tooth brush with —Mind the stairs which are there for falling down into hell. Adam was a naughty man. (Confidentially) : Do you think he tried not to sin ? "

Self : " Oh yes, I think he tried *hard*, like we do."

Child : " Well, I'm not sure. (Back to declamatory style) : This is where

we shave our face (striding into bathroom).   I will stand a little in the sea
so that I may think better with my cold toes.   (Turns on tap and stands in
bath.)   Thy will not stand in my sea will thou ?   It is too large (laughter)—
I mean too *small*.   (Coming out of character) :   What a silly thing to say
wasn't it ?   *Too large*.   (Back in character) : We will take their babies and
boil their eyes and thou will borrow my Mother's nail file and file their teeth
away.   (Breaking into Staffordshire dialect) : Oh, Oi trod on the Caledonion
fish.   'E's very round, int'ee ?   But 'e's so flutt too (stamps on flannel).
Stick 'em on the wall, luv.   (Moulds flannel like fish, carefully, and sticks it
against tiles.)   There's our breakus.   Now we needn't 'urry, luv, need wa ?
(Slight pause, then changing voice to ordinary) : Now speak properly, Petie,
you shouldn't *talk* Staffordshire."

Self (unmindful of this gross injustice) :   " All right.   Here's a towel.
I'm going downstairs to see your mother.   Come down as soon as you're
ready."

Child : "Yes.   Good-bye."

The play had clearly ended on the logic that a flannel fish to eat on the
spot, in the bathroom, removed the necessity for going down to afternoon
tea.   Immediately that point had been made and accepted, however, and
objection to authority registered, the dream world began to fade, there even
being some doubt about who had been talking all this time.   A new set of
values took shape when we came back to reality, and the Child was then
quite ready to understand and to obey the different set of rules.   For my
part I regretted this return to the mundane.   It had been a *great* journey,
and there are many treasures to be found in Dreamland.

Note : The style of this declamation is similar to that of I-kher-nefert in
his description of the Passion Play of Osiris performed at and around Abydos
over 3,000 years before Christ.[1]

Age 6 years

Child (to Mother) :   " When I saw that your breakfast was smaller than
mine, I cried in my mind and tears fell on my heart."

Age 6½ years

Child (declaiming) : "I'm the wickedest one.   I whip all the people in
pink (noticing her baby sister, and then hurriedly)—except babies.   (Self-

---

[1] See description in Chapter V, page 84.

defence coming in) : I am wearing pink and red, but that is a uniform."
(So *obviously* that is quite different.)   She was wearing her Mother's dressing-
gown.

Adult (bringing the Child's attention to breakfast) : " Will you have some
royal treacle on your porridge ? "

Child (not wanting to stop acting yet) : " That is not royal treacle."

Adult (far too wary to be caught up in *this* argument, in which she would
undoubtedly be outwitted, tries another tack.   There is something green
behind the treacle and this shows through the treacle, changing its colour) :
" It's green treacle."

Child (not going to give in just yet, but beginning to smile) : " No, it is
shamrock colour.   It comes from a speshull island, the island is called . . .
(remembering) Doblin."

Having, as it thought, proved its point, the Child felt more confident.   It
then sat down at once and ate up its porridge quite happily.

Note : It may be wondered why the Child was not told to sit down
straight away.   That is one method.   But this Child, anyway, is a particular
case.   She had had certain experiences whilst away from home which were
very unfortunate, and these, together with too much scolding and a slight
backwardness in simple school work, have tended to make her lose confidence
in herself.   By allowing her full advantages of Play and opportunities for
Language Flow, she is becoming happy and balanced again.   Obedience is
slowly returning by avoiding wherever possible a direct command which
might arouse a defensive opposition.   The example is included because it
shows that by the intelligent use and recognition of real Child Drama, much
can be accomplished ; and the actual words used, though interesting in
themselves, often reveal a great deal about general background.   If we never
encourage Language Flow, there is much that we shall never know about the
Child.   In the realms of education this lack makes the friendly bond between
Child and teacher very difficult to build.   Without this bond there is much
that can never be accomplished, and, on the even more practical side, it
makes the control of large classes very much more difficult.

CHAPTER XIV

WE VISIT SOME SCHOOLS

TEACHERS often ask how this work can be seen or introduced. In this chapter a number of reports have been collected together ; they are of actual work seen and of conditions that exist. Where possible, exact detail of movements appear in diagram form. Remarks are introduced, and conversations have been noted down. The reports have been carefully graded, in age, and in approach to and development of the subject. It will be understood that few of these reports are connected with routine visits to schools for the purpose of helping productions as usually understood ; all are primarily concerned with the development of Child Drama.

INFANTS

(1*a*) *Discovery by Play*

The Headmistress is interested ; she " prefers to leave Children alone as much as possible ".

First I saw some rather over-dominated improvisation.

Then one little boy came out and walked round inside a ring of watchers.
Another Child (getting up) : " Are you Johnny Snowball ? "
First Child : " Yes."
Second Child : " May I be your good companion ? "
First Child : " Yes."
They linked arms and walked round.
Another Child got up and said to the second Child : " Who are you ? "
Second Child : " I am Johnny Snowball's good companion."
Third Child : " May I be your good companion, too ? "
First Child : " Yes, you may."
The third Child linked arms with the second, and they all walked round inside the circle. Other Children added themselves to the first three in the same way, after the necessary password had been given. Eventually there was a long line, too long to swing round in the same way, inside so small a circle.

PLATE II

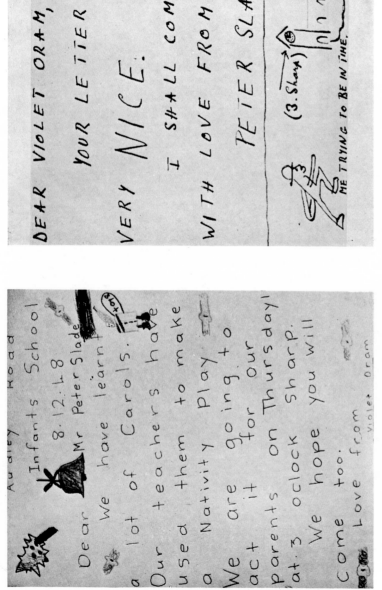

Important correspondence.
Photos by Victor Thompson

PLATE 12

INFANTS. Look out, the tigers are coming.

INFANTS. Gun duel. The bullets give out.

Photos by Victor Thompson

Then an important thing happened in the physical experience of those "companions". They veered to the centre more, and became strung out right across the centre of the circle. A Child in the middle then started to turn round where he stood. Those on his left went forwards and those on his right backwards. This appeared to them to be a completely new experience.

Those watching began to clap, and the little companions flushed with enthusiasm.

Thus are the great secrets discovered.

I have seldom seen so sweet a finding of what we know as a pivot.

(1b) *Not quite the right way*

Later we saw a scene about robbers—very much teacher dominated. It had been intended that a little girl should speak to the king in the corner of the room, but some jolly robbers were eating porcupines somewhere else. With shining eyes and hungry looks, she changed course and went over to the robbers.

The teacher shouted "No;—to the king, Eileen. Over here, dear". The light died from the Child's face. The vision of eating porcupines faded. The robbers became subdued. The jolliness subsided. Eileen appeared confused, shook her head a little and waited for orders.

"Eileen, did you hear me? Over here to the king." Eileen went towards the king, whose royalty had somehow slipped from him. She had to be prompted for the rest of the scene.

We have our choice. Either the Children do what *we* want and die, or what *they* want and live in their part.

The good teacher *suggests* only, and knows when something new is being added. If this something is different from our own conception, leave it alone. In that moment the Child is beginning to use its own imagination and is successfully stimulated by the subject. Any interruption at this point will kill the flow of confidence and ideas, and educationally we have crushed one of the most difficult things to bring out of the Child : interest in a thing, because it *likes* it, which is the foundation of sure learning.

The teacher was most ready to listen to the suggestion of more freedom and promised to note results.

(2) *How not to do it*

The Head is prepared to think of improvisation, and a few of the staff have done some.

The Head suggested that one of the younger masters should show me some of his experimental work. This man appeared to be untrained, and was to go to a Teachers' Training College in the near future. He appeared very unsure about the value of his work, but had, nevertheless, felt it necessary to try what he felt was the right thing.

So often teachers, left to themselves, find the right way eventually ; Children left to themselves find it, and when both teachers and Children are left to themselves, they both begin to find it. Only the experienced specialist without quite enough knowledge impedes this development, by inducing worn-out traditional methods which bring only stagnation.

A Play started about a girl who didn't want to wash her hands. There was a certain amount of talk, of which I could hear very little. The master and several Children shouted " speak oop ", and the Child playing the daughter began to speak louder.

Another, playing mother, gave her daughter a sudden healthy bang, and the daughter began to mime washing her hands.

A Child watching : " What about washing her head ? "

No one took any notice of this remark.

Teacher : " I can't hear you ; speak up." Pause.

Teacher : " Don't turn your backs. No, you stand that way because you're on the stage, you see. You others aren't on the stage. Yes, you stay where you are."

The next five minutes were spent trying to get the Children to understand where to go. This, of course, was entirely unimportant and the confusion was immense ; hardly anyone understood which was supposed to be the stage and which the audience, and by bringing in the necessity to decide which was which the play was killed. When the master saw that no headway was being made he picked up a school bell and rang it. The Children, remembering this noise from former attempts at the playlet, were pulled back into their parts and hurried to their desks. The play restarted.

A Child entered as teacher, but the master in charge began to speak.

Master : " Can you remember what to say ? Do you remember the names of the class ? " The little teacher thought and began to speak.

Master (interrupting) *:* " Go on, scowl." He added a number of other suggestions.

The little teacher became confused and ceased trying to speak. A number of attempts were made by other Children to pick up the thread of the play, but after the first eight minutes of my watching they all began to give up trying to act and relied on the many suggestions given by the master. Had these been fewer they might have been helpful (though this is doubtful), but as they were many, the Children were becoming increasingly confused.

It is no good offering them mental freedom by improvisation and then immediately pulling them back into reality.

The teacher changed from strong suggestions to commands, saying such things as : " John, you go there ; Mary, over there," or " You must ask someone with a nice clean dress or jersey to get up." The Children were not a bit absorbed.

Most of the audience were frankly bored and became increasingly interested in me. This appeared to be because I had said no word, and because they wondered what I was thinking about it all.

A Child picked up some paper flowers and placed them, together with some pencils, into rather a nice bouquet.

Master : " No, don't use those silly paper flowers, just pretend."

The Child, rebuffed, flushed slightly and put down the flowers, folded her hands in her lap, and awaited orders.

Master : " Come in, princess." The princess entered and waited for orders.

Master : " Say ' Good afternoon '."

Princess : " Good afternoon, Children."

All Children in desks : " Good afternoon."

Only about four Children were by now trying to act at all, and these four stood up at the entrance of the princess.

Master : " Come on, come on. I said 'Shall we sing a song to the princess '."

Some Children : " Yes." They started to sing a song, but the pitch was too high. They had begun to act now, but the teacher stopped them. " Oh, I can't hear the words," he said, " and it's rather too high for you, isn't it ? Start off a little lower."

They started again (the young are full of courage), but it was ragged, so the master had to start conducting.

The atmosphere changed at once from play to class control.

In the last scene of this play we met again the mother and her daughter. They talked for a little time.

Mother : " So yer see, yer must alwis 'ave clean 'ands."

Master : " Hands, hands, where's those h's ? "

Child : " So yer see, yer must alwis 'ave clean hands."

Master : " That's better ; now do it again."

Child : " So yer see, yer must alwis 'ave clean 'ands."

All in the audience : " Hands."

Child (in a whisper) : " Hands."

Master : " Yes.   Just let's take it once more."

Child was now very embarrassed and quite unable to speak.

Master : " What's the matter?   We're all waiting."

Child : " It's difficult when you're acting."

Master : " What is ? "

Child : " To remember."

Master : " I know it is, but you must."

There was a pause, and then the Child ran through similar words including the word after H but with no life whatever.

If it remembers anything of this afternoon it will have little to do with English pronunciation ; it will only remember the acute unhappiness which it suffered in company with myself.

Master (to another Child) : " Well, that wasn't too bad, but there is one thing ; don't say ' my goodness ' twice over, think of something better than that."   There was a little more talk, and the play fizzled out.

Master (to me) : " Would you like to say anything to them ? "

But I was too sad to speak to them, so I said, " No thank you, not at this stage ".

The Children were then told to start painting.

A great deal of chattering followed and the master had great difficulty in keeping them quiet, clearly wondering why they were so noisy.

They had, of course, been stimulated by their attempt to play, but had been unable to speak freely during it because of the constant interruption, so that in the following period all that remained of their experience was the stimulation.   And, because no suggestions were made during the painting period, the speech which should have taken place in the performance now flowed freely, and control was more difficult.

If the improvisation had gone well, the Children would have said in their own manner : " That's all, sir," or the play would have clearly come to an end, whereupon they would have settled quietly to their next task.

Master : " They're not up to much, are they ? "

Self : " They show promise, but it would be better to allow them more freedom."

Master : " Freedom ! They'd tear the place down."

Fear of what *may* happen is often the reason for over-domination. But no student-teacher relationship can be built for this work by fear on either side. Confidence and friendship bring the ultimate calm, though there may be some noisy times before this arrives.

(3) *Promising beginnings*

The Head was grateful to hear that improvisation was of use, but has a regard for speech and play books.

A lady teacher had been sure improvisation was important, and decided to go her own way.

We saw a beginning of a play by infants. All Children came in and sat by a wall. Groups of them were placed in various parts of the hall as flowers, fairies, hobyahs, a dog, gnomes and rabbits.

There was a good deal of interplay and chasing between good and bad characters.

The dog rhythmically bit the hobyahs as they came near him. The hobyahs cut up the dog and threw the bits away, retiring into a corner much pleased. The flowers trembled and the fairies flew, dancing all over the hall, but not very free.

The beginning of pattern was there—but no real interpretation. The play fizzled out.

Self : " There were some promising things in that. Have you tried freeing them more ? What would happen if you asked them all to be hobyahs and move about while you played hobyah music ? "

Teacher : " Oh, they'd do it all right."

We tried. Considerable freedom and joy were expressed.

Self (to children) *:* " Now just listen to the music carefully and when it changes you change too. If it reminds you of being a rabbit, be a rabbit, if it reminds you of fairies, gnomes or birds, be that or be just what you like." The piano started again.

Change of characters came slowly and late on the change of music. The music only sets the mood and they become only half-conscious of it when thinking of their dance. The space began to even out, rhythm of a group nature showed occasionally, and the floor was well covered. The teacher promised to develop this regularly, and appeared delighted with the encouragement given to her ideas.

Note that the young Child cannot sustain a long complicated story. Simple things are best until they are free and " out-flow " has arrived.

(4) *More than promising beginnings* (*Five and a half years*)

The teacher, from the centre, was conducting a class of dramatised movement to music. All was being taken at a very animated pace, almost like a P.T. class. Some of it was rather too fast, though the Children had a good relationship with the teacher.

Teacher : " Grow into trees."

The Children fell on the floor and slowly got up, growing as they did so.

Teacher : " Chop the trees."

The Children jumped out of that character and became woodsmen, chopping down what had been themselves. (It is quite usual for very swift change of character to take place in very young Children, so it was no surprise to them. Indeed, concentration for too long on one thing at this age often brings a certain deadness or even inattention.)

Teacher : " Pull the trees to one end of the room."

They all pulled. Piano music accompanied all of this, building up mood successfully and helping the Children to feel dramatic climax.

Teacher : " Gallop."

The piano started off again swiftly, and the ponies careered round the room. The teacher joined in, but soon knocked over a Child. (It is not easy, nor always an advantage, for an adult to join in ; we do not often fit. Here it had been clear that group sensitivity was developing in the Children —they did not bump into each other—but the teacher was not " of the group " and had not the same sensitivity. Size, experience, and many things make it difficult for us to be much more than suggester-guide, or a stage property.) The Child was comforted. The teacher picked up a tambourine and shook it and banged it in a steady beat.

The ponies shrieked with joy, galloping delightedly. This was splendid " out-flow " and happiness-development.

Teacher : " Lie down."

A spread chord on the piano ; all ponies relaxed and lay down, breathing heavily. When they were rested in silence the teacher nodded to the pianist. A spread chord was played and the Children got up. A sudden " jangle " on the piano, and they fell down. Such opportunities for tenseness and relaxation were repeated several times.

Teacher (when Children were on feet) : " Parties."

Circles of three or four Children formed all over the room (no music). They were left entirely alone and began to eat or pour out tea. Some unwrapped parcels. One little girl tidied her friend's hair, another smoothed her frock and danced to the others in her little group.

Teacher (timing it carefully) : " A postman brings toys. Would that be nice ? "

All the Children : " Yes."

Two or three boys became postmen. The teacher saw that she had created the right atmosphere for Child Drama, and ceased to guide the class. She backed quietly into a corner. The boys moved to one side of the room and suddenly turned themselves into lorries. (Taking letters ? Probably. They may have been post vans by mental association, but their noise was that of a heavy lorry. Note the Child experience not fully developed, perhaps. Something to watch. When will they give us post vans that sound like vans ? Or do letters go by lorry in their " land " ? The teacher might suggest " vans " in the weeks ahead, without any suggestion that lorries are wrong, and see whether the noise changes.) Some of the lorries (and/or vans) changed into trains and then *a* train. Others became aeroplanes.

This was the supreme moment of real Child Theatre. Five excellently placed rings of little girls remained absorbedly eating and pouring out tea. The four postmen were in one corner, on an imaginary platform. The train had formed on the other side of the room, preparatory to running round the whole playing space in one large circle.

Lorries were driving towards the train between the tea-parties and behind the postmen ; inter-crossing waves of six and six aeroplanes were weaving a snakewise dance in the only space left, their arms outstretched and banking as they ran. (Excellent example of " running play ".)

I longed for a gallery to see from. This is what we should realise. The Child creates theatre in its own way, own form, own kind. It is original art of high creative quality. Most adults are stubbornly blind to the loveliness they will not see.

Children create theatre in small groups which build to a large group, and often offer moments of complete symphonic production, which the advanced adult tries to obtain by intellectual processes—and generally fails miserably.

This wonderful pageant continued for seven minutes, then came to an

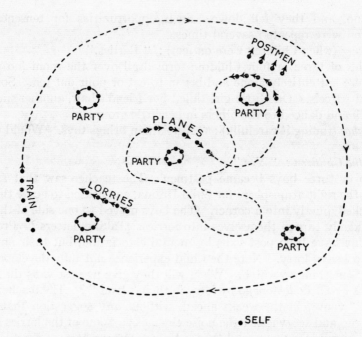

FIG. 4.—Example of a moment of Child Theatre : Five rings of children eating and drinking. Aeroplanes (six and six) weaving between " parties " during excellent example of " running play." Lorries with letters were speeding to catch train. Train ran in large circle round room and finally stopped near postmen.

end. It just fizzled out.

Teacher (immediately, waiting and ready, knowing she has probably had all for today, but not meaning any sense of anti-climax to be felt) : " Skip."

All the Children skipped. They were now right out of the play.

Teacher (offering new idea) : " Let's play marbles."

Music started. The Children mimed marble playing. Music changed.

Teacher : " On your toes."

They marched round lightly. Music changed. They marched heavily, like giants.

Teacher : " Snowballs ? "

All the Children : " Oo, yes."

Note : Through having done it before, and because of good Child-teacher relationship, quick response is developed. Only one word was needed.

PLATE 13

Driving a horse down the street under difficult conditions. (*See* p. 140.)

Letting a bird fly free from the top of a mountain. Height is being discovered. First steps towards the stage. (*See* p. 140.)

INFANTS. The King and Queen receive a message. His Majesty is pensive. Note how they have built up the blocks. Other blocks form a stage at the back. But it is not used as such. The units comprising it may be pulled out and used as the period goes on. (*See* p. 60.)

Photos by Victor Thompson

PLATE 14

Working under difficulties.   Having to work with desks.   This is a circus parading down a narrow village.   One animal has escaped, and the keepers are looking for him.   See how they use a higher level on the desk, just as they would if working with rostrum blocks in the hall.   (*See* p. 140.)

JUNIOR MIXED.   Working under difficulties.   The circle appearing even in a cramped space.   On the left, dinner in Mexico, on the right, breakfast somewhere else.   (*See* p. 149.)

Photos by Victor Thompson

PLATE 15

JUNIORS.　Picture of a Shipwreck as resulting from Dramatic Play.　(*See* p. 49.)

Photo by Victor Thompson

JUNIORS.　" Oo something behind me."　Acting exercises to music.　(*See* p. 61.)

By courtesy of the " Birmingham Post and Birmingham Mail"

PLATE 16

OLDER JUNIOR MIXED. Rhythmic throwing to sound effects, encouraging wide gestures. Later incorporated into polished improvisation about Noah.

OLDER JUNIOR MIXED. Rhythmic exercise of preceding picture becomes rhythmic stoning of Noah by the neighbours, to the sound of a tambourine. Photo taken as semi-stylised movement is held for a second during the play. Note the circle. (*See* p. 143.)

Photos by Victor Thompson

Teacher : " Nice and round."

They all made big snowballs and threw them at each other. A few began to collect snowballs to make a snowman. (Child creation starting again. Teacher did not suggest it.) But this fizzled out soon.

Teacher (alive to it at once) : " Let's skip round the snowman."

All joined hands and skipped round.

Teacher : " On the floor. Rest."

All lay down. There was complete silence.

Teacher (having established the correct bond of trust and sensitivity with the Children) made a hand movement : They all got up, and calm, but flushed and happy, tiptoed out to another class.

Teacher (to me) : " You are absolutely right ; I find it easy to get them to create this way and they are much easier to handle afterwards."

Self : " It was grand theatre in the middle, wasn't it ? You have built a lovely bond of teaching-friendship with them. How long has it taken ? "

Teacher : " About seven weeks."

JUNIORS

(5) *Junior Mixed* (*Eight years old*)

I asked to see some improvisation and was taken into a classroom. The teacher was beginning this work.

We saw a shopping scene, which was not very good. The Children were conscious of me all the time—because they were asked to do it *for* me.

The teacher kept interrupting.

There was some absorption after eight minutes.

The desks were set straight and there was little room for action. The usual formations took place none the less (see Fig. 5), and, as Play developed, two actors visited a desk and asked for books. Those sitting there " sold " books to them.

There was a good train which went round and in between the desks, and a criminal was chased there, too.

The work was poor, though the Children enjoyed it. The chief trouble was that the staff had not decided yet that it was important and the Children were not getting their proper opportunities.

The Head and the form teacher chatted most of the time, and did not

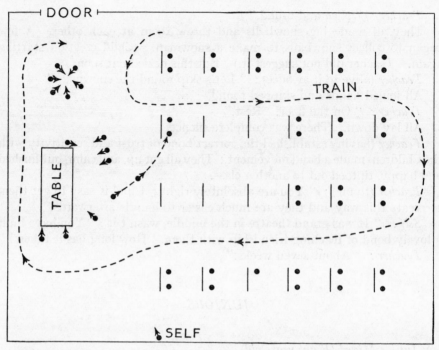

Fig. 5.—Chart showing positions at one period or another. Backs turned to class. A ring formation near door. Path of train and criminal traced. Two actors sold books at front desk.

notice this was a considerable disturbance to the Children. It would have been almost impossible for anyone to concentrate. We expect quiet in our libraries. Should we not extend elementary courtesy to Children if we wish them to behave, let alone produce Art ?

Later there were questions from the Head.

Self : " Do teach them that they do not do this work for me, you or anyone else. They do it because they love to do a thing well. It is theirs, the thing which they make.

" They need more space, less interruption and more quiet. Please forgive me for not answering your question in the room. It is necessary to be silent if watching, otherwise the Children cannot become absorbed." I was invited to come and talk to the staff. In this way schools often co-operate most kindly and it is possible to go further into why we do this work and how to develop it.

(6a) *Junior Mixed (Nine years old)*

The Head had invited me to see some particular work which he was not sure about.

At this school they do a lot of free dance to music. Generally the Children do not dress up or use properties, but today they had seized rags and scarves and brought things to school to wear.

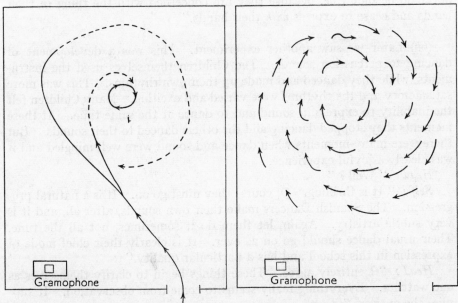

Fig. 6.—*The Scarf Dance*, at start. Children poured in and then burst into two streams, the inner ones to form a small ring and the others to form a bigger ring, moving in direction of arrows.

Fig. 7.—*The Scarf Dance*, at finish. Typical filled-in circle of movement ; but movement is generally the other way round.

Music started. Many Children threw pieces of coloured material into the air in delight. This was lovely to see, but they were not so free in their movement. They tended to use one kind of move with their arms and found difficulty in moving their bodies. As is nearly *always* the case, the dress hampered their true expression. Some Children clutched their dress with both hands. This made the upper part of their body stiff. Group work deteriorated and the Children were not in the part as usual.

Head : " It's not so good, is it ? "

Self : " No, it seldom is with costume. Certainly not with full costume. A few bits sometimes help."

Head : " Should we go on with it ? "

Self : " By all means. But allow it occasionally, not all the time. Watch carefully; it would be of great interest to discover how long it takes them to get their hands anything like free with the scarves. Generally they never do become free, because they are concerned with the thing *in* their hands and cease to express *with* their hands."

(*6b*) Later we saw another experiment. This was a development of dancing to percussion sounds. The Children themselves used the instruments, while they danced and made up their own rhythms. This was more satisfactory and the rhythms were varied and exciting. Many Children felt the inability to express in sound and to dance at the same time. At these moments they stopped dancing and the others danced to their sounds. But there were many moments when dance and sound were well mingled and it was clearly a joyful experience.

Head : " Well ? "

Self : " It is thrilling. Of course they must go on. It is a natural progression. The Spanish Dancers make their own sounds, after all, and it is very subtle artistry. Again, let them do it sometimes, not all the time. Their usual dance should go on as ever. It is clearly their chief mode of expression in this school and has a particular quality."

Head : " I entirely agree. These things begin to clarify themselves as one watches. Everything really seems to come from observation. It supplies the answers."

This is the key to all Children's work. We must observe. Only by prolonged observation do we learn about Child need. Perhaps all the best teachers hit upon this truth in time, but it is a fundamental weakness in the adult to rush in and direct things in a far more reckless manner than we would tolerate if the Children tried to help us.

(*7a*) *Junior Mixed. Ten years (plus). (A class of forty-eight.)*

The Drama here is taken by a pupil of mine who has worked with me for some years. He has evolved a fast form of what is almost Dramatic P.T.

Teacher : " Face the wall." All the Children turn outwards to the wall in a circle round the room.

Teacher: "Listen to the music." They listen to improvised piano music.

Teacher : " Burglars walking on tiptoe." They become burglars. (Music stealthy.)

Teacher : " Carrying heavy bags." (Sudden change to slow music, with pronounced beat.)

Teacher : " Now you are a forest, all standing about." (Music stops abruptly.) They take up an attitude of trees, quite still with arms and hands in weird positions.

Teacher : " Wind starts blowing. Here it comes." (Dramatic scale from base on piano ending in sudden climax chord.) All fall down and remain quiet and relaxed. The teacher runs round lifting limbs here and there to see whether they are quite loose enough.

Then, whilst the Children are still on the floor, the teacher starts an adaptation of the " Ideas game ".[1]

Teacher: " Ideas, please! " No explanation needed—he has a bond with the Children, so they understand.

He runs amongst them, kneeling near them, so they remain quiet and relaxed. They whisper in his ear and he repeats so all can hear : " Trains, animals, fairies, ghosts ".

Teacher : " Thank you. All ready ? "

All (eagerly waiting) : " *Yes.*"

Teacher : " In a wood (all jump up and become trees again) were some boy *fairies* (piano music starts. The boys start leaping about violently like gnomes) and girl fairies. (The girls start to dance. Several examples of ' running play ' occur. Then the chromatic scale comes again, like a huge gust of wind. The climax chord is played and all fall down.) They dreamed they were human and they liked *trains*, so they had a train ride. (Train music. All get up, form a train and chuff round the room.) They met three ghosts. (Two boys and one girl break away from the train and make ' woo ' noises. All join in. Then the train full of people disintegrates through ' fear ' of the ghosts.) A good fairy came (a tall girl assumes leadership and all recognise her at once for the part) and changed them first into animals (animal noises ; many pigs, one monkey, two cows, nine horses, one elephant I noticed ; the rest were new to me) then back into fairies."

(Very gay music starts. The Children dance vigorously and with great grace, for one and a half minutes. Then comes the chromatic scale and the sudden chord and they all fall down and lie panting on the floor.)

[1] See Chapter XI, page 144.

Only their breathing breaks the silence.

When the teacher judges that they are rested, he asks : " Which did you like best ? "

Nearly all : " The animals."

Teacher (nods quietly) : " Horses ! "

All gallop round to exciting music.

Teacher : " Circus ! "

Music changes and they become clowns and performing animals.

Teacher : " Speedway ! "

A few girls and all the boys become cars and motorcycles and rush round. All make the noises.

Teacher (knowing what they like and returning occasionally to it) : " Circus ring ! "

A number of Children form a ring quickly, and inside it a circus begins. Two boys become clowns and mime funny actions to music.

This was quite a new approach for the Children, and although their control and sensitivity are developing rapidly, as well as the loss of self-consciousness, they still take time to become fully absorbed. They were fairly well absorbed now, but they had been at it for just over half an hour. They will take less time to become absorbed each time they experience the work.

Teacher : " Can you do this ?—elephants ! "

Heavy music. All dance round heavily.

Teacher gives look at pianist. Music stops abruptly. All the Children stand still. Only one is taken quite unawares and overbalances a bit. They all laugh. The unready one is quite happy, though. He knows there will be no scolding. But he will be ready next time.

Teacher : " Knights putting on heavy armour ! "

All struggle into unseen armour. Several girls place helmets carefully on the boys and buckle them into breastplates ; one smoothes a plume with great care.

Teacher : " Good. Now, a man went for a walk to the zoo. What did he see ? "

A Child : " Elephants."

Teacher : " Right—elephants."

All become elephants.

Teacher : " What next ? "

A Child : " Pythons."

Teacher : " Right—pythons ! "

All become pythons, wriggling on the floor. Then they are tigers, monkeys and bears, at their own suggestions.

Teacher : " Bears, you are very tired now. Over there in the corner is where you sleep." (Note " is where ". Everything is real while it lasts.) The bears amble over and relax.

Teacher : " All asleep." (Then, clapping his hands sharply) : " Do what the music says."

The Children march about, some with hunched shoulders. The music changes and they march normally. The marching is in any direction, but nobody bumps into another person. They then pull ropes and dance. One Child balances on one leg with arms outstretched as if on a tight rope.

A Child (in delight) : " I'm a wasp." He spreads his wings, bends his knees and is off in a wonderful burst of running play, winding in and out of the others at incredible speed, leaping at times into the air. It is more like a dragonfly in the sun. Several other Children become infected with his joy and spread their wings also. Their running play is not quite so full blooded, though, nor their climaxes so neat. They finish earlier. But the first one keeps this up for one and a half minutes. He is bursting with joy.

This was one of the best examples of this phenomenon that I had seen for a long time.

During the latter part of this, two girls started to waltz together in wide, sweeping movements. The running play ceased.

Teacher : " Skaters ! " All begin to roller-skate.

Teacher : " Telegraph pole ! "

All stand still and stretch up as tall as they can.

Teacher : " Take a sweet apple and bite it up."

They eat in silence except for a few appreciation noises.

Teacher : " Now an apple from the top branch. Yes, right high." (All on tiptoe and very absorbed.) " Oh, it's sour." (They react violently.) When they had coped with those fearful bitter apples, the teacher cried : " Now for two minutes just do what the music tells you." (They understand by that not what it orders but what it *suggests*.) Imaginative climax chord comes several times, so that the Children are relaxed and tense alternately. They lie down on the chord. That is the only true " direction ". Other than this they choose to do what they like. The music stops.

Teacher : " One line here, another there."

The Children run into line.

Teacher : " I want to hear the clock tick. Listen ! "

All are quiet at once. A far better and happier way than bawling at them to be silent. When the teacher has made them feel calm by judging the pause correctly, he makes a sign and they walk quietly, but glowing with pleasure, back to their classroom.

(7b) *Average age seven years.* (*A class of forty-two Children, in the school hall.*)

Teacher : " Turn yourselves into big, fat frogs."

They leap about silently.

Teacher : " Now little baby frogs."

As soon as there were signs of tiredness : " Now all asleep."

All lie down and relax.

Teacher : " Now show me how your father walks." The Children do so, proudly. " Now your mother." The mothers walked much faster.

Teacher : " Now a little baby." They waddle round ; some crawl. " Now show me how you come to school." Laughter. Then they walk slowly round.

Teacher : " Now, how do you go home ? " A roar of laughter and everyone runs round.

Teacher : " Now, what would you like to be ? "

A Child : " 'orses."

Teacher : " All right. Away with you ! " Many ponies dash round, tossing their heads or neighing.

Absorption was apparent within five minutes of the beginning of the class, and all were very live and gay but perfectly under control.

Teacher : " Wheelbarrows ! "

Partners seize each other and are pushed by the legs ; some imaginary barrows are pushed.

Teacher : " Circus." Two boys become clowns. Then two more—they are even better than the first two. Then eight more clowns come from those standing in the ring. Then it begins to get dull.

Teacher (ready at once) : " Who would like to be horses ? "

Eleven Children put up their hands.

Teacher : " Chariots ? " Others put up their hands.

Three chariots are formed, one of five Children with one horse, another of four Children with two horses, another of five Children with three horses. Drivers jump on to the backs of the " chariots ". Fast music starts. One horse falls over, and the " chariot " collapses.

PLATE 17

JUNIORS.   Typical circle, caught in pause to a long musical note during improvised dance.   (*See* p. 143.)

JUNIORS.   The King and Queen dance.   (*See* p. 143.)

By courtesy of the " Birmingham Post and Birmingham Mail"

PLATE 18

JUNIOR MIXED. These rostrum tables are easy to lift and nice to build with. (*See* p. 147.)

YOUNG SENIORS. Adventure story. The natives attack.

Photos by Victor Thompson

Teacher (quick to feel the drama subsiding) : " Now crocodiles—everybody." Crocodiles crawl all over the floor.

Teacher (when he sees them tiring) : " Dead crocodiles now ! "

All go limp and relax. Complete silence.

Teacher (after half a minute) : " Make nice trees for me."

All stand, stretching their bodies and arms.

Teacher : " Good. Nice sharp angles ! "

Teacher : " When the music starts, all the girls come and sit here (he runs to one end of the room and points) and all the boys form a ring here." Music starts, and they scamper to their places. The boys start a Nigerian game which they have played before. They all clap slowly. Then one boy comes into the middle of the ring and bows to another sitting in the ring. This is his chosen partner. They wrestle in semi-stylised manner. As the fight becomes more exciting the rhythmic clapping gets faster. The Children begin in this way to become sensitive to sound, appreciative of dramatic climax and develop a consideration for the needs of others. Claps become violent at any climax and break out into ordinary applause at the throw. The first Child conquered, then sat in the circle, and the vanquished chose a sparring partner. This continued for a time, then—

Teacher : " Everybody do what the music tells you ! "

Pianist plays a march. All march.

Pianist plays the gust of wind. Crash chord. All fall down.

The spacing was good for the first time. They fell and made good grouping over the floor space. This is one way we judge their progress in group sensitivity and general understanding of shape and beauty. This grouping always begins to occur where Children are given enough of this dramatic play, and improvement of the composition of their drawings and paintings comes with it.

Teacher : " Boys ugly trees, girls pretty trees."

Afterwards, an improvisation of " the Three Bears ". Four boys turned themselves into a table and three boys into chairs.

A Bear : " I looked agin on me bed and she's still there ! "

Teacher (when this had finished) : " Now, all be father bear." All then had a chance of playing this character. Then all became baby bear, tables and chairs in turn.

Teacher : " All the girls ! What would you like to do ? "

They chose to wheel babies in prams. " Now, the boys ? "

A Boy : " Be fathers."

Teacher : " Right, and how do you carry your lunch to work ? Better eat it soon." (After a time) : " Now what would you like to do ? "

A clamour of joyous suggestions.

Teacher : " All right—the boys are funny men, and the girls horses. Away with you ! " Off they scamper, the horses avoiding the funny men with great dexterity.

Music started at a sign from the teacher. The climax chord came and all fell down.

Teacher : " You are all fast asleep, I hope. I can't hear the clock tick yet. That's better."

A slow march was played. They got up quietly and marched off to another room.

Teacher : " Well ? "

Self : " There are some very good things there. Absorption is good for such big classes, and group sensitivity is developing rapidly, isn't it ? "

Teacher : " Yes. What about the movement, though ? "

Self : " Well, I was fascinated by the bond you have built so quickly, but their movements are all a bit the same. The music needs to vary more, particularly with the older group. They are doing the same things because they hear the same sounds. If the sounds were more varied we should see richer interpretation. But I'm very interested in this quick reaction work. They have wonderful chances of being so many things in a short time. And you have got them *happy*."

Teacher : " Yes, I was determined to do that. As you have always said, when they're happy they behave."

Self : " How often have you taken these groups ? "

Teacher : " This is only the third time. The first time I could not control them very well."

Self : " Well, it's a big class. Not at all easy until they are used to it."

Teacher : " I hit on the 'trees' idea and now they relax or become tense as needed, and that necessity for keeping their mind on the subject has brought control."

Self : " Yes, you've got it now. It generally takes three or four periods before they sense the responsibility they are offered. The dramatic qualities then develop properly."

Teacher : " And not before ! Am I giving too many suggestions ? "

Self : " Certainly not, at this stage. They are only just starting, so they

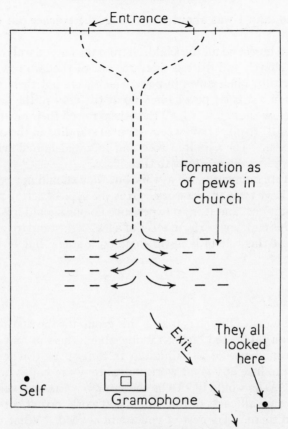

Entrance

Formation as
of pews in
church

They all
looked
here

Exit

Self

Gramophone

Fig. 8.—Example of calm spiritual Play not uncommon
after six years of age, though this had unusual quality.

need a lot of help. In a few weeks they will be giving *you* ideas. Then is the
time to withdraw one's own personality. But you are using this as a P.E.
period too, aren't you, when taking it at this speed ? It is all right so long as
you only suggest *what* to do and not *how* to do it. You are not blocking their
creative powers. Think of that wonderful example of 'running play '."

Teacher : " Yes, that's the first I've had quite like that."

(8) *Junior School.* (See Fig. 8.)
I watched their improvisation movement to music for some time ; it was

extremely dull, and I was about to go when the teacher put on a record of organ music.

There was a hush and all the Children from the far end walked slowly down the aisle of a church and drifted sideways out of the two rows in fours and fives on either side, knelt down in pews which were not there and started to pray. A boy in the front pew looked up at the door of the hall, and slowly and intuitively, without a word, all the others raised their heads also and saw the same vision. It must have been an angel standing in the doorway showing them heaven. The Children rose and followed him slowly out. Once outside they walked thoughtfully to their class.

There are rare moments such as this, but they should not be too rare with Children who have regular free work. It is the type of acting not seen under any other conditions, and it is an experience no one should miss. Once having drunk of this cup, few performances of a less high standard are acceptable.

The work at this school is never done on a stage, but on the floor of a smallish hall.

(9) *Nine years old*

A teacher student of mine is taking this group for the first time. He is in the centre of an interested circle, talking about the sun and obtaining the interest and confidence of the Children in himself as teacher. He knows they will not produce any good work unless they are happy with him.

Teacher : " Who would like to be the sun ? " (Six or seven arms go up.) " All right, you are all parts of the sun. You work in that corner. The sun will shine from there. The rest of you are in a wood. What do you do ? "

A Child : " Chop trees."

Teacher : " All right. What do you do at night ? "

A Child : " Go to sleep."

Teacher : " Yes. So when it's dark you go to sleep and when the sun starts to shine you—— ? "

Several Children : " Start to get up."

Teacher : " Good. Now, what would happen if it rained ? "

A Child : " Oo. We'd run 'ome."

Another : " We'd run under the trees."

Teacher : " Yes. Very well, we'll start now. Listen to what I say is happening and you can do what you feel is right. Ready ? Now it's dark. Everyone is asleep, even the sun——."

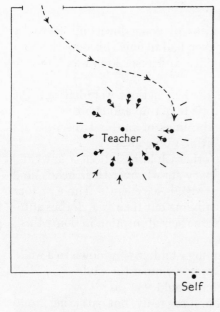

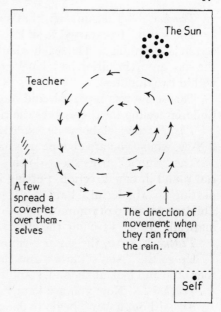

FIG. 9.—Shape of movement as Children entered and formed circle round the teacher. This is the time to stimulate interest and this is the typical shape of the class becoming interested.

FIG. 10.—General distribution of players when they had been stimulated.

The sun crowds together like a rugby scrum in one corner. All the other Children lie down on the floor to sleep.

Teacher : " The sun is slowly coming up."

The rugby scrum disintegrates a bit and a little forest of arms rises slowly into the air. The sun's rays are clearly being given off. Slowly, one by one, the wood-choppers rise to their feet. There is quite a good climax as the last one rises, yawning, and suddenly all mime their wood-chopping. The teacher supplies the noise by stamping his foot, and the chopping falls into time. Group work is developing. When the teacher is satisfied, he quickens the pace with his foot. The chopping gets quicker and quicker. They are being informed of, and are experiencing dramatic climax without it being talked about. The teacher stops stamping and the chopping ceases. Only one Child is out of tune with the group feeling, and chops two strokes after the stamping ceases. No one takes any notice, so he is not made to feel silly, but he knows what to listen for next time. That is clear by his expression.

Teacher : " The sun—oh, that's right."

The " sun " has started to sink. The arms are going down and the rugby scrum is reforming. The teacher had not even had to finish his remark about the sun, group intuition had developed rapidly, and absorption was complete within two minutes.

This scene was repeated, and most of the instructions were left out, the Children feeling for themselves the right time to get up and chop.

The Teacher (elaborating slightly on the lines of the first discussion) : " Now, whilst you are chopping, a nasty biting rain comes."

The " sun's " arms shoot down. The other Children let out a howl and run round in one direction, putting imaginary shawls over their heads, and putting on wonderful " hats ". The face work is excellent. Three or four Children get tired of running and sit out, wringing out their wet clothes automatically whilst watching the others. (Note their absorption in doing this.)

Teacher : " Ah, the sun is coming out again."

Up go the " sun's " arms, and the running Children slow down to a walk, then stop and look at the sun, standing completely quiet the while.

Teacher : " Now you are happy. What would you do ? "

All, without a word, begin to dance, at first raggedly, but gathering group form as they continue.

Teacher (as soon as he sees they are getting tired) : " The sun is sinking." He does not have to say any more. The " sun " sinks slowly in its own time, and at exactly the right moment the wood-choppers begin to sink to the floor in ones and twos, some of them leaning their axes against tree stumps or laying them carefully on the ground.

I felt the light dying. If not of a real sun, it was the light of " real theatre " when a great scene comes to its close. I glanced round. The few who had been sitting out in the corner were spreading a " coverlet " over themselves. A little boy jumps out of bed and runs to warm his hands one last time at a fire under a central-heating pipe (unwarmed), then runs back and gets under the coverlet, too. All is quiet, all is relaxed, and that perfect calm and happy control which this work brings can be felt over the room.

(10) *Junior School*

I asked whether they did improvisation at this school, and was told that of course they did.

The first play was the *Pied Piper of Hamelin*.

A collection of rats talked rather badly, obviously not sure what to say.

I whispered to the teacher : " Is this their work ? " The answer was " Yes ".

Certainly the words were not being improvised. They had been learned or partly learned once, and were now in the process of being forgotten. This is not improvisation. It is the relics of a polished production based on an improvisation, something quite different.

The Children were stilted, until a messenger burst in—the first live action of the play.

All the time the Children were conscious of my presence and of the other Children in the audience. The speech was clear, but the Children were not in the part. This happens often, and one has to come to a decision about clarity of voice or sincerity of characterisation. They seldom go together in the early stages.

As the play proceeded, the Children began to give up worrying about the old words and started to make up their own.

The mayor and council took courage and walked straight over and off the stage space several times, enjoying themselves, and this encouraged the audience to begin to prompt in loud whispers and to make suggestions. Participation was beginning.

Their own grouping began to appear. One line caused great amusement : " I wouldn't be in your socks—er—shoes for anything." That was the only vital part of the play.

I then asked for a real improvisation.

The teacher took a few of the Children outside to give an outline, saying : " You know the story of William Tell ; well, do that." The Children came in a few minutes later and arranged a chair, a hat, a stick and a basket in place, and then took them all back and put them in a different position. Not until a great deal of experiment had gone on in complete silence, during which the teacher was the only one showing any surprise, did the play begin. Backs were turned all the time. There was a mother and son. A chair was put in the middle. The Children passed it time and time again, bowing to a hat on the chair.

A boy called out : " Seize him, guard, for not bowing."

There was a gigantic struggle of about fifteen people clutching each other, a huge snowball which swayed from side to side of the room threatening some almost atomic explosion, which, however, never quite happened, for another cry came to our ears, and the crowd disintegrated : " If yer a good arra,

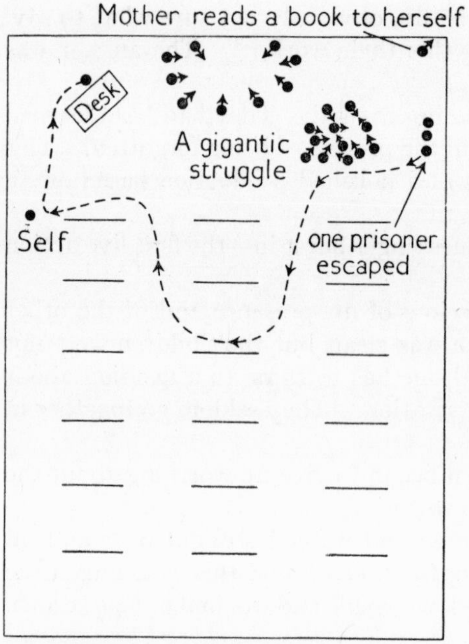

FIG. II.—At the top is shown general distribution of players, mostly with backs to the audience. The "snowball" of strugglers is on the right. The escape is charted also.

shoot yer arra and don't 'it 'is 'ead." There was a lot of " seize " again, and a number of people were put in a dungeon.

There was some good rhythmic roaring from those who did not want to stay in the dungeon. Then one man escaped and rushed about the room hiding under desks and once under my legs.

The excitement was intense. Everyone was fascinated to know whether the man would be caught.

He finally succeeded in making a break behind some rocks—the desk—and when the guards could not find him he said to a companion (who was also hiding behind those rocks) : " Oh, boy, I'm going home now." He went home.

His mother was reading a book in a corner.

Son : " Hey."

Mother (puts down book, quickly getting into part) : " What have you been up to ? You're in a mess."

Son : " Didn't bow to the hat, so they put me in prison, but I escaped."

Mother : " Just you get on and help me, and you'd better not go out again ever."

The play then ended, not only because the words were finished, but because everyone knew somehow, as Children do, that it was over.

(11) *Junior School*

The Head is very interested and has entirely the right ideas ; extremely keen on improvisation.

In a large hall, a teacher (male) is starting a nativity play in mime, to musical background. He had had only two other rehearsals. The Children were not used to this form, but he was doing well.

The calm control was beginning to arrive and he did not have to speak loudly. At the back of the room about twenty Children were reading until their time came for taking a part, and were rather interested in me, although I sat down as quietly as possible.

It was twelve and a half minutes before good absorption came into the acting. A nice procession came from the back of the room.

Teacher : " Yes, that was fair. Would music help you ? "

Most answered : " Yes." It did. Mime and absorption improved at once. The procession passed calmly before me and the first waves of sincerity came over.

Next came a lovely snowball scene, mimed to a background of music which broke off suddenly into carols. Some other Children arrived as " strangers from afar."

Very nice groups of conversing in mime.

There was, however, some bewilderment amongst the Children, clearly unused to this work. A Child near me : " Now what ? "—Another Child : " Just goo on, silly." They then continued to act. I can think of no better advice to any actor who is not bothering to think enough about his part, than to " just goo on, silly ".

One boy, aged eight, had to climb steps on to the stage, to a musical background. As his movement fell in with the music he clearly began to experience a quite new sensation. When he first climbed the stairs his steps were in time to the music, and he became so delighted and absorbed in this extraordinary experience that he climbed down again and repeated this piece three times.

The master in charge, who was experienced in this work, left him entirely alone, and so did the Children. Then they became absorbed in what he was doing, and shared a great part of his experience.

Quite suddenly they " came to ". The boy remained on the stage and the play went on. As they were kneeling to the Holy Child, I walked quietly out. It was time to go and no one noticed my going. They were all in that Other Land.

(12) *Junior Mixed*

I saw a badly acted carol and nativity play, having been invited out to help.

Suggestions were made on the use of a gallery and apron stage. Finally it was suggested putting the choir in the gallery. The positions were bad, but improved. I suggested that another time the audience might be in the gallery, or on stage, and the whole hall be used. Alternatively, the best way to produce this particular play would be to have the audience sitting in rows diagonally across the hall, half facing the gallery along one side, and half facing the stage. (See Fig. 12 on opposite page.)

The teachers were extremely interested in this idea and said that they would think about it for a further production.

Teacher : " Now, tell us honestly, what are our chief faults ? "

Self : " You say the Children have not done much Drama. That is perfectly apparent. They need much more improvisation and free movement. They are stiff, cannot be heard, do not say their lines with meaning, are waiting for instructions all the time and are very slow on cues. The show lacks speed and meaning, and does not have a calm slowness either. It is a typical product of the wrong type of work for this age group."

There followed a lively discussion on how to start improvisation. I promised to go again.

(13) *Junior Mixed*

The teacher here has an unusual knowledge of Children and has developed his own way of using Drama throughout the school. Much use is made of dramatic movement to musical background. A number of teachers from various places had asked to see the work, and five of us arrived quietly in the hall. The Children were slightly disturbed at our coming and it was made worse by our needing seats.

We saw various activities.

(a) *Listening*

This is not specifically a part of the training at this school, but it is always noticeable. Quiet is obtained before a gramophone record is put on, and the Children listen quite absorbed from beginning to end. This absorption is essential to the later reaction, because the Children then have opportunity to think about the sound and decide what they wish to express to it. When the record was finished they got up and moved about the room, expressing what they felt. The different moods of the music showed well in their work, the pattern on the floor space was excellent and there was a continual changing relationship by the various groups. Full absorption came in the first fifteen minutes, and they took twelve minutes to settle down after our entrance.

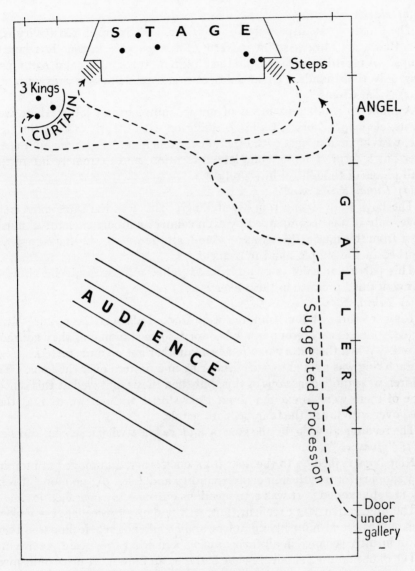

FIG. 12.—Suggested form of production for Nativity play, offering more space to those taking part. (See pages 201–2.)

(b) Hands

The Children sat dispersed over the floor.   Their group sensitivity is so good that they always sit in patterns, forming quite unusually beautiful groups.   A record was played and the Children expressed to calm, soft music, using only their hands.   Great subtleness and tenderness expressed.

(c) " The Circus "

A mime to a different mood of music, jumping and jolly; there were clowns, elephants, horses, Children riding on each other, walking the tight rope, weaving in amongst each other, never touching.   Relationship to each other has a form of tense, complete absorption, and extremely interesting small pieces of thoughtful interpretation.

(d) Hands (Girls only)

The boys were sitting round watching.   This was the same exercise as above, only it was accompanied by even calmer and more thoughtful music. Apart from this music, there was no sound, all the watchers being completely absorbed in the simple hand movement.

This particular calm is of undoubted value, and can only be obtained after continued practice in these exercises.

(e) Telling Stories

Rings of three or four Children were formed all over the room.   Music started.   One of each group mimed a story, some standing as they got more excited.   When their story had finished, another got up and started.

Each ring was related to each other ring in a pattern over the floor.   The Children were quite conscious of this, but then they paint well at this school. Some of them were so excited about their stories without words that they rolled over with joy at the funniness of the tale.

The record ended, so did the stories, and we knew when each one finished.

(f) " Jockeys "

Nine boys rushed on to the floor from one corner, and moved in jumping and galloping form with tremendous vitality and zest.   At no moment were they merely excited.   It was a tremendous outburst of controlled joy.

The integration was excellent, but, as the dance proceeded, the jockeys appeared to become more like tumblers, and I could not help feeling that there was an intuitive change in all their minds about what they were portraying.

The dance finished suddenly ; we had seen an important piece of inspired work, with many lessons in imagination and control of " body speech ".

(g) " Magicians "

Groups of four boys and girls, one being the magician and others dolls marched on to the floor. The magician in each group cast spells upon the other three dolls. Many different ideas were to be seen. One magician twiddled a screw at the end of a long string attached to the noses of each of his dolls. Another appeared to be conducting them forward on a sort of knife edge, on which they balanced with difficulty, making curious jerky movements as their doll-like balance was upset.

(h) " Searchers "

This included all Children reacting to the idea of searching, to a low-music background.

They walked calmly round the room, searching. There was hardly a sound. A tense feeling began to glow, and suddenly a Child pointed to one corner. They all then saw what they were looking for. It looked as if they had seen Christ.

(i) " Pandora " (A playlet, with dramatic movement to music, and some speech)

All the Children poured on to the floor, jumping and dancing to joy-music. A Child from the end ran in snakewise amongst the others and stopped at a point quite close to my foot. All the others stood still and shouted : " Who's this ? "

The Child began to mime the opening of a box, and one by one the Children shouted to her with such lines as, " Don't do it, Pandora ". Pandora, however, continued and the box lid flew open.

Actually what flew out I do not know, and I would give much to have known what was in their minds, for the scream which followed from all will take me a long time to forget. They fell flat on their faces for nearly half a minute, while the music on the old gramophone ground slowly on.

Slowly one boy pulled himself up on his arms, and pointing, cried : " Look, what is it ? " One by one the others watched whatever had come out of that box fly round the room.

When they were seeing it so clearly that I felt I would see something too, the play suddenly stopped, and the Children, some feeling their feet, some giving an affectionate slap to another Child, smiling, or scratching their heads, often in little groups with arms round each other's necks, drifted out of the room towards their class.

This is a happy school. I have never heard a cross word from teacher or Child. The school accepts the principles of Child Drama and develops all work from this starting-point. Their Child Art is as outstanding as their Child Drama. The two are closely allied.

Their scholastic attainment is high.   The Children write their own books and run their library.   School attendance is very regular.   Here the Children pretend to be well in order to go to school, and often ask for more work.   Obedience is wonderful.

I state these facts as a matter of interest, but would add that such tendencies undoubtedly develop where school attitude is based on joy rather than compunction.   Joy is the basis of Child Drama.

(14) *Junior Mixed (Nines and tens—C's)*

They are about to repeat an improvisation on a story theme.

Master (to Boy) : " You are a king.   Pick yourself a queen."

Boy does so.   He leads the queen all round the hall, sitting on various thrones, and then up on to the stage, where he places two chairs.   The stage is not used as an ordinary stage, but is now merely a symbolic higher level— the throne room in the king's house ; the rest of the hall is " the world ".

All the other Children set up shop behind light tables, close against the walls round the hall.   A tailor's shop is in one part ; a " bird " is standing opposite.   The bird goes to the tailor and orders a coat ; then he goes to the shoemaker.

Bird : " Ah want some shoes, see ? "

Shoemaker : " Wot size ? "

Bird : " Twos, but turned up at the end."

Shoemaker : " Orl right.   Done next week.   Wot colour ? "

Bird : " Yeller."

Shoemaker : " Oh, yeller ! "

Bird : " Yeller."

Shoemaker : " Oh ! "

Bird : " Yuss."

Shoemaker : " Yeller, orl right."

The bird goes to a girl behind a desk and buys a hat, then returns to the tailor and puts on a school blazer, then to the cobbler and puts on shoes (coloured socks).   He flies off suddenly in a burst of " running play " round and round the hall.   Then he flies off to the palace (on the stage).   He is plucked and eaten.   He (or would it now be his soul, for he has been *very* eaten) then flies into the middle of the hall complaining of cold.   An owl advises him to get glue and feathers.   He collects imaginary feathers all round the room.   Others help him.   (I remembered at this point that these

Children were supposed to be C. But they were behaving very intelligently, if not yet out-flowing. They were fully absorbed and behaving perfectly.)

Having collected the feathers, the bird flies back to the palace.

Bird : " The king in all his glory is not as fine as me ! "

King (in a rage) : " Eat 'im. Eat 'im. Oh, well—I'll let you off this time."

Bird dances off and the play ends.

Headmistress (to cobbler) : " Did the bird pay you ? "

Cobbler : " Yuss, miss—er—no, miss, sorry miss. 'E said ter put it on the bill." (A ' C ' Child ?)

Headmistress : " Oh, I didn't quite hear that bit."

Child (smiling meaningly) : " No, miss ! "

Master (to me) : " They are improving. But they hang around the walls and won't come away much. Their behaviour has improved a lot, though, since we sometimes let them act out bits of their home life as you suggested, and balance it up with other stories like this."

Headmistress : " What about the main actors ? "

Master : " Oh, they were picked as the best by the others."

Self : " If they are still shy, it is worth going back and doing even simpler things, as if they were younger. Try encouraging them all to be birds or kings together sometimes, until they get away from the walls. They are seeking protection still, and are not confident in out-flow. That will help them to get over their shyness."

Master : " I'll try that. Do you mean in the middle of the play ? "

Self : " No, that would spoil their absorption. Afterwards. You might ask them which bit they liked most, whom they liked best, and then say : 'All right, now every one be so and so'. That gives them equal opportunity, and gradually encourages them to take a bigger part by associating themselves with the leading characters, which they think they cannot take. When they have once been that character, even if not alone, it is not so alarming."

Master : " Yes, I'll certainly try that. I think they're shy because they've always been told to shut up and keep out of sight in their homes, and now they don't want to be seen."

Self : " How did you find that out ? "

Master : " By trying your idea of occasionally letting them improvise whatever they liked. They acted scenes from home. I think this don't-want-to-be-seen attitude has been largely responsible for their backwardness in everything."

Self: " Very possibly. Anyway, *we* are pleased to see them. They must be happy here. When they are happy their out-flow will be released. It will be interesting to see how soon after that their ordinary school work improves."

(15) *Eight to nine years*

I saw some work in classrooms.

Teachers had attended some talks of mine and were trying out the ideas.

(a) *First Group*

The desks and forms had been moved and the shape of the acting space was oblong, with a wall on one long side and audience on the other three sides.

Scene 1.—Improvisation started. A Child put on a bowler hat (real) which it had brought to school, and started to burgle a thick safe (imaginary) under a desk. Two boys and a girl came in and found him. A policeman entered almost immediately, wearing a conductor's cap (real) and took the burglar to prison.

There were two complete and separate ring formations in the grouping within three minutes, and during most of the playing time the players were in part circle against the one wall, and acting inwards with backs to audience.

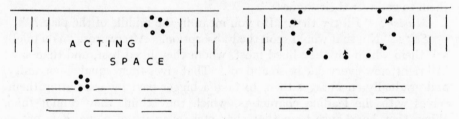

FIG. 13.—Position of desks and ring formations as they occurred.

FIG. 14.—" . . . during most of the rest of the playing time the players were in a part circle against the one wall and acting inwards with their backs to the audience."

This is very common when Children are left alone. The magic circle of our early ancestors' first attempts at Drama in the hunting dances occurs again and again. Its presence is one way of telling that the teacher is not interfering too much.

Scene 2.—About a tea-party. They ate lobsters and pins.

Scene 3.—Two naughty gnomes are stealing apples, an announcer tells us. The policeman enters.

Policeman : " I accuse you of pinchin' Mrs. Gum's apples."

A Man : " Take 'em to the Fairy Queen." Queen enters.

Queen : " I banish you from fairyland for being bad."

(Could anyone think of a better reason ? Good, sound Child logic this.)

Teacher (suddenly to a Child) : " I don't think you want that stick." A stunned look passed over the Child's face. Why had everyone else been free and she not ? What had she failed in ? The Child blushed, put down the stick and retired to a corner, stricken with embarrassment. My heart sank. How should one treat the inexplicable adult interferer ?

The play had come to a sudden end and a tense silence followed. Luckily, when I could bear it no longer, some jolly pirates entered wearing handkerchiefs, paper hats, and one had on the bowler hat, which had now taken unto itself a character of its own.

Fighting followed. Good use of desks was made. The players began to forget about the audience after nine minutes.

Then it suddenly finished and the Children went back to their desks. Most of these scenes had been introduced by an announcer, the Children improvising on what was announced.

Announcer (after hurried whispering with two players) : " The next scene is at Mrs. Brown's 'ouse ; they are 'avin' their dinner." Some dinner it was, too. The audience were fairly absorbed and grew more so. Their eyes bulged at the feast. Audience participation was clearly taking place, but of the quiet kind. Then, suddenly, two members of the audience beckoned to some pirates and asked for some food. The pirates mimed out huge helpings of indescribable delicacies into large dishes, and numbers of the audience jumped up, and, putting their hands into the dishes, ate in silence. Now you old-fashioned traditionalists, which was the audience and which the actors ?

Self (to teacher, afterwards) : " They are still a little too conscious of an artificial audience. Too many glances at those watching. If they did not constantly address the audience about the scene, they would have a chance of getting into their parts and staying there. Staying there is what they need."

(b) *Another Group :*

In an improvised play called " The Witch who went to the Moon ", a wizard needed four fleas, two flies, a pinch of strong snuff and a spider.

He took the fleas from a dog (under the collar of a boy), and jumped up to the blackboard to get flies from the window. The board was in a frame and looked just like a Child's picture of a window, black and empty.

It has often worried me to see these empty black windows in their paintings. Sometimes they fit in with the picture, but sometimes they are just black and empty. I was jarred again by the Child taking as its obvious window a black and empty space, taking it even into the dream world, where it stores its only riches.

(c) *" In a Waiting-room "* (A play often done at this school.)

Doctor : " Yer've got a bad finger, eh ? "

Patient : " Yus."

Doctor : " Look at that aeroplane." (Patient looks up.)

The so-called audience (grinning delightedly and chanting together) : " Chop ".

The meat axe came down and the finger came off, to be lost in an inkwell. All the audience looked in the inkwell to find it (Audience Participation).

(16) *Ten to eleven years*

(a) *Teacher :* " All right, just start doing things."

They started miming, quite happily. After a few minutes I wandered amongst them.

Self : " What are you shooting at ? "

Boy : " It's a fair."

Self : " Coloured balls or targets ? "

Boy : " Targets."

Self : " Get any bulls ? "

Boy : " Yes, the last shot."

Self (to another) : " What were you throwing ? "

Boy : " Balls at coconuts."

Self : " Did you get any ? "

Boy (absolutely decided) : " Yes, four."

Another boy : " That's right, 'cos I picked up four, and I'm in charge of the stall."

Teacher : " Do you want to say anything to them ? "

Self : " Only that I much enjoyed seeing you doing things. I was glad the people I asked knew exactly what they were doing. That is the best way to do it." I could have watched them for hours. There was great sincerity and everyone was utterly absorbed. It was completely satisfying, creative theatre of the quality you can't buy.

(*b*) In another class at the same school, five Children were improvising rather badly. The rest were sitting in desks, rather bored.

Teacher : " How you do link Art with Drama ? "

Self : " Well, look at that lovely green blackboard just behind the players. Their playing space is closely allied to that board. They could use coloured chalks for scenes to their plays, as the acting is just in front of them. It might be an added stimulus, but not necessarily—at least it would be a better background than the long-division sum. They might try drawing a window too, and everybody could tell in turn what they see out of it. That would break things up and give everyone a chance, rather than letting only these five act all the time."

(17) *Boys, nine years old*

When I went in, a great fight was raging, mostly with rulers, around an upturned desk which was a galleon. An outstanding thing here was the use

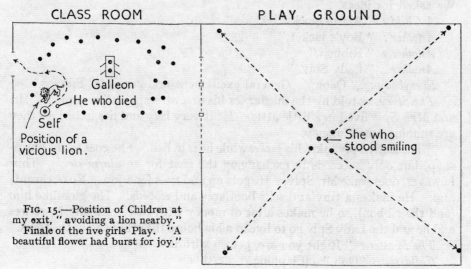

CLASS ROOM   PLAY · GROUND

Fig. 15.—Position of Children at my exit, " avoiding a lion nearby."
Finale of the five girls' Play. "A beautiful flower had burst for joy."

of make-up. The Children licked a bit of pastel and applied it to their faces, or to each other's.

We then had Child Art and Child Acting.

The playing was in a full circle, and we all sat round.

Absorption was good.

During this play, five girls, dressed-up and made-up in the same spit-pastel-and-polish way, were acting their own game in a playground outside.

A boy died, groaning at my feet. I smoothed his brow and laid him out for burial and slowly moved to the door, avoiding a lion nearby. The girls outside were dancing in a circle. Suddenly they threw up their hands and each fled from the centre outwards, to the edge of the playground, leaving one alone in the middle, smiling. A beautiful flower had burst for joy (Running Play).

(18) *Junior Mixed*

I heard some very poor choral speech, then asked about improvisation.

Master : " Oh yes, we do that. Is it any good ? "

We saw some, but he made so many suggestions that the Children stopped making up ideas and stood about waiting for direction. I took him aside and suggested less interruption, and told him about my " ideas game ". We asked for ideas.

A Child : " Alarm clock."

Another : " Boy's jacket."

Another : " Ribbon."

Another : " Lady Spiv."

Everybody : " Oooh." General excitement and cries of " Spivess."

The Story, as told by the master for his first attempt at this game : " Mr. and *Mrs. Spiv* lived in a little attic. He is very lazy and lies in bed, so they are running out of money.

" The Lady Spiv takes his *jacket* while he is in bed. She goes to the pawnshop, but only succeeds in exchanging the coat for an *alarm clock*. This, however, does wake Mr. Spiv. He gets up and tries for a job. No one wants him. He makes a tray and sells bootlaces and *ribbons*. The girls like him (and the ribbon), so he makes a lot of money with ease. Finally he retires and he and the Lady Spiv go to live in a big house the other end of the town."

The Master : " Right you are, get on with it."

Children : " Ooh." (Clapping.)

The master then chose Children for the parts.

A large coat, taken from a large boy, was hung over a chair. Quick but elaborate preparations were made for Mr. Spiv's bed and the attic window. Mrs. Spiv assumed a very hungry look. The pawnshop man just answered " nah " to everything, and had to be prompted by the watchers to say " alarm clock." It might still be in the shop to this day but for that, as neither the master nor I were going to say anything, and the haggling had been a heavy strain for us all.

The alarm clock was a great success. The spiv leapt out of bed with a cry which froze my blood, the watchers in the front desks were taut with excitement and leaned back away from the violence of the scene.

The scene suddenly came to an end, in a state bordering on collapse. There was a longish pause and complete silence, everyone thinking hard. Six boys then came out, and there followed a fascinating series of quick flash scenes, very much like the art of film, where six excellently defined characters as heads of business firms all turned down the spiv in quick succession, for such reasons as, " Yer 'air is too long, me man ", and " 'owja get inter my faktry with them wide shoulders ? The door's too narrah."

Spiv : " Ah, I coom in sidewiz."

The spiv then sadly walked about with bent back, his back having bent farther after each unsuccessful interview. All this gave us a lovely passage of symphonic production with an intuitive feeling for timing, and clear, unconscious group-agreement in rhythm.

The face of the spiv lit up and he leaped at the master's desk. Out of this came a cardboard-box lid, and a tray was tied round his neck with string which was not there. (This was done in the quaint convention, of which they could hardly have known, of two helpers coming on from the wings and retiring when the job was done.)

A procession of beautiful ladies was formed by some of those watching. Gold piled high on the spiv's tray as many ribbons were bought.

Finally the spiv was lifted up by his admirers who bore him round the available acting space three times, and then took him towards the door. There was a scuffling noise and the lady spiv shot (like a rabbit in the head-lamps) before our gaze, bewildered at first but then deciding, flung herself with open arms on the gentleman spiv.

The whole procession was halted by this onrush and fell back. The spiv was dropped, and the lady spiv cried, with tears in her voice : " My love, my love, we are successful at last."

It is difficult to relate in cold blood the dramatic effect of this onrush. The only other time I have seen or felt any piece of theatre like this was on the arrival of the airman after his running full tilt down the aisle of Lichfield Cathedral in Dorothy Sayer's *The Just Vengeance*. It had that same ethereal quality, and for violence and thrill it must be likened to the dash of devils from the auditorium in the Birmingham Repertory's production of *The Marvellous History of St. Bernard*.

To return to our spivs. They went arm in arm towards the door, and as they passed out on their way to happiness, fortune and their big comfortable house, the spivess turned and solemnly said : " The house is outside, sir, yer see." I did, indeed, for who could fail ? Who could fail to have been moved by this adventure of modern times, containing much that one could hope to see anywhere in experiment, absorption, calm, rhythm, pageant, sorrow and a happy ending ?

" Is improvisation any good ? "

You who have not felt it, do not yet know theatre as a whole.

Questions :

Self : " Did you like that ? "

All : " Yeaas ! "

Self : " Do you like choral speech ? "

Most of class : " Yes."

Self : " Which was best, the choral speech or this ? "

All : " This. Wot we've just done.

(*Note.*—" What we've just done " coming from ones who had watched. There is *no* audience as such in good Children's Theatre. They all participate. It is a land which they *go to*, when it is done right.)

Self : " Why ? "

Answers : " It's more fun. More real. It's nicer, you feel it more."

Self : " Do you like watching or acting best ? "

All : " Ooh, acting." *One :* " It's difficult not to join in when you watch." *Others :* " Yes, sir, with the words, I mean," etc.

Self : " When there's not much room it's different, isn't it, but perhaps you would like to have made the noise of the alarm clock all together ? "

All : " Yes."

A Child : " We could make the traffic sounds in the road."

Self : " Yes. What else ? "

Various : " Policeman's whistle. Snoring. Factory noise. Cars coming out of the factory for export."

Self : " Yes, of course. All these things could come in. What a lot of good ideas. Perhaps if you do that play again you might use those ideas, or in some of your other plays you might think of other things to do, if some of you have to stay in your desks. You'll all feel more in it then, perhaps."

All : " Oo yes, sir."

Will they ? I wondered afterwards. They may satisfy their need for expressing choral and rhythmic sound effects, but it is difficult to believe that they *could* be much more " in it " than they were that afternoon. But they will be participating more, which is slightly different, and very important indeed.

SENIORS

(19*a*) *Girls, eleven years old*

When I entered, nine groups of six girls were chatting and arranging mimes, the themes of which they had talked over with their teacher a day or two before. One group was asked to show its work, and we attended at a picnic scene (speech and mime), well spoken and well mimed. The audience sat in a horse-shoe shape on the floor of the hall. The acting shape was a circle.

(19*b*) *Fourteen years old*

I saw girls, dressed up, going behind a curtain on the stage. Three other groups were chatting in the hall, using chairs and tables and preparing themes for improvisation.

Teacher (noticing the girls going behind curtain) : " They fight to borrow the stage, but keep the curtains shut. I think they like to be enclosed so they can *really be alone* without being seen."

(Note.—*Even at this age the Child actor does not always want an audience.*)

Teacher (to girls in hall) : " Shall we see ' Just William ' ? "

All : " Yes."

They brought forms and sat as an audience. The curtains on the stage opened in jerks, and an all-girl cast proceeded to do an excellent rough portrayal of boys. Much use was made of the apron stage and drawn curtains. As the play developed, some girl characters entered. The spontaneous language flow was vital and interesting.

William : " Oh, Vylett, yer alwiz tryin' ter sit on men's laps. Get off, you."

(Later, looking very dirty) : " I don't think me mother'd like you, yer not alwiz as clean as I am."

The dialogue came bursting out in showers of quick wit, so fast and eager and pat that it sounded like an excellently learnt written play—but better.

At one point a door in the hall burst open and a stream of guests came up the steps on to the stage. This was the only happening by which William was put out. " He " was not ready for such eagerness for joining the play, but " he " managed to find seats for all who came to his peculiar party. Great gusto and absorption were now displayed ; hitherto there had been some showing off from the stage, quite unlike the quality of the first mime done by the other group in the middle of the hall. This, one would expect.

There was a piece of fur on the table.

Hubert's Mother : " Don't play with that dirty bit of skunk off the table, yer not at 'ome now."

Teacher (to me) : " For this, I just outlined in a few words a ' Just William ' story ".

Out of those few words the Children were creating a first-class script, which had already lasted half an hour and was still going strong.

I looked back at the stage. A " boy " had been tied up, and the front curtains came to. " His " legs still stuck out on to the apron. The other " boys " moved forward to play on the apron. Sometimes they paused for a second and the legs wriggled.

The curtains opened again. Enter mother, wearing fur.

William : " Why d'jer wear a dog round yer neck, Ma ? "

Girl (in high heels) : " Do you like me new shoes ? "

Boy : " Wer ! Yer've got stalks on 'em, I shud think."

Mother finally starts to sing, standing on a chair ; William pulls the chair and " Ma " falls over.

A lot of actors crowded on the stage when " Ma " started to sing. When she fell, all suddenly grabbed partners and started to dance. " Ma " pulled the " boy " with the legs (described earlier) out of the way. He had remained there all this time. The curtains came to again (someone was enjoying herself).

William and a few friends strolled like veteran Shakespeare players on to the apron, talking about the play—(a surprising convention this, rather like a modern propaganda or documentary play).

Teacher (whispering) : " This may go on a long time, I'm afraid ! "

Self : " Good. Don't stop it."

The curtains suddenly opened. The dance was still in progress. The dancers were fully absorbed and had completely forgotten about the audience.

William : " Silence, ladies and gentlemen. We will now do a play. ' King John, after 'is great wash '."

First Actor : " Damn and blast."

All : " Ooo, yer mustn't say that."

Ten shillings were given to William, and the play came to an abrupt end. It had taken 52 minutes.

The speed and zest were tremendous. I felt I had been present at the Commedia dell'Arte.

Teacher : " I would like you to meet William."

I braced myself to the task of facing the raw, dirty, brass-voiced, bullying little tike that had fascinated me with the busting horror of " his " loathsome personality. A shy, soft-voiced girl with large eyes edged up slowly and said : " Good afternoon, sir. Thank you for watching."

Consideration

Although this was largely a proscenium production, the apron stage was fully used. There was a sort of hinterland activity, too, behind closed curtains, when a number of dancers were absorbed and had forgotten the audience. Finally, guests entered from the floor of the hall and flowed up on to the stage. This is typical of the older Child who does not remain confined to the stage by choice, but, left alone, prefers a more elastic form of presentation.

(20) *Fourteen to fifteen years*

A semi-polished improvisation.

Two steps led up to a stage at one end of a hall.

A girl came on to the stage, straight down the steps and on to the floor. She announced : " Peter Pan in Kensington Gardens." I was handed a programme.

Peter Pan
In Kensington Gardens
Characters
In Order Of
Appearance

Peter Pan
Park Keepers
Nurses Policemen
Soldiers
Children
Maimie and Tony
Fairies
Trees
Brownie
Queen and Court i.e
  Doctor & Duke
  Serpentine Fairies
  Woodland Fairies
  Gnomes

Music started and one girl entered, dancing the length of the hall, and walked up on to the stage. She started to speak, with her back to where the audience would normally have been. Two girls in blue peaked caps (park keepers) opened imaginary gates. (See Plate 5, opposite page 80.)

The first girl announcer was rather conscious of my presence. The next girl dancer was quite absorbed and did not notice me, nor did the park keepers.

Then pairs of girls entered from the opposite end of the hall to the stage, wearing soldiers' and nurses' hats and coloured gym tunics. They

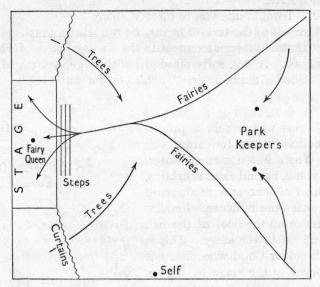

FIG. 16.—*Peter Pan.* Plan of entrances, showing pattern on floor space.

marched round in a circle. More girls in soldiers' hats came in and marched in a circle also.

" Children " then danced in freely through " the park ".

Maimie and Tony came in.

The park keepers closed those huge unseen gates, which I know were solid iron and heavily encrusted with gold. Then Maimie and Tony began to speak.

Trees entered in two streams from curtains on the outer side of the stage proscenium, and edged, with waggly feet, on to the floor of the hall. They wore leaf headdresses.

Absorption was fair within nine minutes.

The learnt speech seemed a trifle unreal against the sincerity of the movement. Grouping was good.

Fairies entered from the far end in two streams. Words came occasionally in the middle of music. Some of the fairy dances were a bit formal and self-conscious, though finished. Some gymnastic work and country dance were then incorporated in the fairy dances. There followed some much better acting-dance, with heavy rhythmic footwork.

The fairy queen sat on the stage with some attendants whilst the other fairies danced on the floor of the hall.

There was a good dramatic moment as the woodland fairies were surprised by Maimie and disappeared behind the stage curtains. Maimie danced frantically round trying to get out of the park gates, and finally fell despairing on the stage. The fairies peeped through the curtains and covered her with mimed leaves.

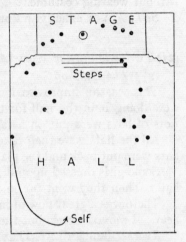

FIG. 17.—Plan of *Grouping* round Fairy Queen.

Peter Pan appeared. Maimie came off the stage and conversed with him. Dawn came. Peter became a statue again. As the sun burst forth, the park keepers opened their great gates. Maimie then slowly departed.

Back came the soldiers and nurses, marching round, and the play finished in a sad-gay mood with that tender atmosphere which a repetition of the beginning so often brings.

Teacher : " Some of them were looking at you. The girls who have been here longer are absorbed, the others aren't."

Self : " Absorption is a habit that grows."

Self (to girls) : " Do you like this ? "

All : " Yes."

Self : " Do you prefer this or the script play ? "

All : " This."

Self : " How did you build this up ? "

A girl : " Oh, over a long period, we sort of pieced it together."

Self : " Would you like more costume ? "

Some girls : " Yes."

Self : " Would you move so well ? "

Most girls : " Oo, no. Not so well. They'd stop us."

A girl : " I didn't think of that."

Another girl : " It's more clever if you make the audience understand without wearing costume."

Self : " Yes, exactly.   You rely then on the strength of your acting."

(21) *Twelve to thirteen years (A's and B's)*

(a) *"The Hatshop"*

This was an improvisation being done for the second time. The girls were doing it in the hall for the first time and were enjoying the change. Lots of hats were put on a table, below and in front of the stage.

All the hats were then taken off and the table placed on the stage ; the hats were put back and the play began.

Some girls dressed up and started to play on the floor with backs to the hall.   Then they went up on the stage—backs were turned all the time.

There was a great flow of improvised dialogue, most of which I could not hear.   I moved closer, but the play suddenly ended.

Teacher (amused) : " Thank you.   Just take away the hats."

The girls, who had been utterly absorbed in the play, turned to her with beaming faces, still full of the joy of their unheard creation.   They took away the hats and nothing remained to us save the memory of that strange scene, with many little women in dresses too big for them, and hats like fungus by moonlight.

(b) " *A Nice Cup of Tea* "

A girl announced the title from the stage.   Another girl started an interminable telephone conversation, answered by a voice off-stage.

Lady : " Come to tea at five."

Voice (off-stage) : " Four-thirty ?   How kind."

Lady : " Five, not four-thirty."

Voice : " Yes, I'll be there at four-thirty."

Then the lady and her maid rushed about a lot.

Lady (looking at cloth) : " I told you not to boil this cloth. It's got holes in."

Maid : " Well, that's where the jam spots was. "

Three ladies entered, wearing odd clothes. They chattered well. Absorption fair, but at times all were a bit conscious of the teacher and my-self instead of thinking of their acting. This was a direct example of where the necessity for coming out in front of the class (because of space, under usual conditions) had spoiled the acting. They were used to being funny *for the class* in the classroom, instead of getting right into their parts.

Teacher : " This has been done once before, but it's quite different now."

Self : " Good. That's creation."

A great deal of coughing started, and it appeared that the maid had left Oxydol in the teapot. All the ladies made a hurried and undignified exit.

(c) " Podgy's Lesson "

Scene 1.—The table which had been used in the last play creation was pulled off the stage and placed on the floor in front of it. Two girls came on to the stage and went to sleep on a gym rug. They were later called and came down to have a meal at the table. One of them was dressed as a podgy boy.

Scene 2.—An announcer : " Mother and Auntie go to the pictures."

There was a lot of chat at the table, and I think I am right in saying that soap and chocolate were put together in a sort of pudding and left on the table by the "grown-ups ". They then left for the pictures whilst the children were asleep again on the rug on the stage. The children got up. They had been pretending to be asleep. They came down off the stage and became absorbed in the pudding. They quite forgot the audience of four people, and turned their backs on us for eight minutes. Mother and auntie returned. Podgy and his sister scrambled under the table. They then made awful faces over the soap they had eaten, and I suppose they were dis-covered by the grown-ups. But this was not clear and the play fizzled out.

I do not condemn the play because I could not follow it. It is a privilege for an adult to understand Child Drama, but there were moments when things became disjointed and the playing was not so vivacious as in " A Nice Cup of Tea ", although there were passages of language flow from Podgy.

(22a) Twelve to thirteen years (C's)

"The Gypsies"

Singing started. Costume was used. Some of the girls used tambour-ines. Both stage and floor were used.

Teacher : " They asked to piece together bits of their school experience."

One girl danced part of a dance which fifty girls had done together on a former occasion.

There were two rows of audience, not very interested or absorbed.

Two big groups of girls on the stage did not move for a long time. It was nice singing, but very formal, and theatrically dull—a bad copy of some second-rate adult show they had seen.

It was difficult to believe I was in the same hall as that in which the statue of Peter Pan had lived his hour amongst the scents of that wonderful garden, guarded by the encrusted Child-created gates, those emblems of dignity.

I was then invited to see work in classrooms. During my journey to one of these there were noises coming from the stage. The curtains were closed.

Self : " What's going on ? " (Hinterland activity, I guessed.)

Teacher : " Oh, they use the stage like that for privacy quite often. They need privacy in their work, we find."

Self : " Yes, I have often found that. It is linked with this curious fact about the non-necessity for audience."

In the classrooms :

(22b) *Eleven years old (C's)*

There was some play based on an improvisation done for the second time. There was a dentist's chair in which a number of girls sat in rapid succession ; odd implements were used. Absorption very good.

Dentist : " 'Fraid we 'aven't any gas. You'll 'ave to 'ave kokane."

A " child " was being difficult. Its mother savagely helped it into the chair.

Backs were turned to us all the time, and the playing shape was the usual two-thirds of a circle which one sees in classrooms when there isn't enough room for them to act in-the-round.

The patients returned to their desks. After the last one had had a tooth screwed in with a spanner, a girl said : " That's all." The play had ended.

Children seem to be haunted by dentists, and invent play which is mixed with nightmare imaginative suffering ; they are helped to face the horrors of adult-controlled life by that boisterous humour which to me is one of the endearing qualities of Childhood, symbolic of a sort of jovial courage. Without this, how would they get through ?

(22c) *Eleven years (C's and D's)*

(i) An announcer : " The Hat Shop."

Self : " Did they copy this from the older group ? "

Teacher : " No. They did not know the others were doing it." Many hats were tried on. Backs were turned to us, and the near circle was formed.

A waste-paper basket was tried on as one hat. Some children thought this funny, but others thought it a sensible use of a nearby property.

The shopkeeper : " No, it's too big."

The logic of this was accepted.

The basket was then tried on each customer, but it would not sell. Customers returned to their desks after purchase. A fur was put on one customer.

Shopkeeper : " That's a nice one."

Assistant : " The Northpole wear them." (Geography coming out.)

Customer : " Nope. Don't like it. It's too 'ot."

Assistant : " Ding ding." (Effects noise for change put in the till.)

The customer had bought another mimed creation. Materialist hats were clearly not in vogue.

Shopkeeper : " That's the end."

(ii) *" Grandpa's Pills "*

The characters stood in front of the desks with their backs to the class. An announcer turned them round one by one and introduced them by their name in the play. It was about naughty children, I gathered, but could not hear or follow the details.

The language flow was there, together with great absorption. Voices subdued. There was music off. A service took place. A hymn was sung. Some of the audience joined in. Activity and language flow became rapid.

Teacher : " The shy ones are in this."

Self : " Excellent. They are happy now. Look at that wonderful absorbed playing."

Teacher : " Yes. You would hardly believe they are the same girls."

Self : " They will get even better if they do this regularly."

Later, *Self* (to girls) : " Do you like this ? "

Girls (all) : " Yes."

Self : " You like acting, then ? "

Girls : " Yes. This is nice. It's better than plays. You can get into this. It makes you cheerful."

Self: " But these *are* plays. They are your plays that you make up."

A girl : " Yes, it's all our own."

" All our own." That is the best description of any original and true work of art. It is the right description of Child Drama. It belongs *entirely* to them.

(23) *Senior Boys*

First Story : " Robin Hood "

When we entered there was an improvisation going on about Robin Hood. The system was for relays of boys to play one after the other. This was one relay. The rest sat all round on forms. The players were disturbed somewhat by our presence. After twelve minutes, absorption improved, language flowed more evenly, and the scene ended in a good fight with very fair dramatic climax ; several men were hanged by a hangman who stood on a gym horse and used a gibbet which was not there. Playing time twenty minutes.

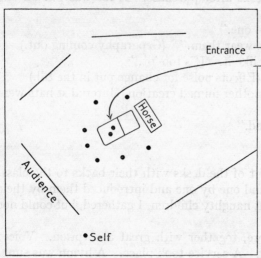

FIG. 18.—*Robin Hood.* The Play revolved round a mattress and a gym horse. (See Plate 19 opposite.)

Second Story : " The Greedy Boy "

A polished improvisation thought out beforehand and enacted before. A wonderful greedy boy with a huge tummy went through many adventures trying to obtain food. Action mostly took place between two points in the middle of the playing circle.

There appeared to be a parent, much smaller than the greedy boy, who kept hitting him when not reading a newspaper.

Language flow was excellent, pace and attack good. A good character

PLATE 19

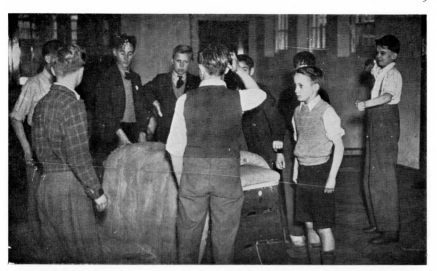

SENIOR BOYS. The circle appears, as Robin Hood gives directions. Note man with bow on right. (*See* p. 224.)

SENIOR BOYS. A man is hanged for being wicked. Example of *playing out.* They have not yet found proscenium. Acting-in-the-round, but a desire for higher levels is beginning. (*See* p. 224.)

Photos by courtesy of the " Birmingham Gazette"

PLATE 20

SENIOR BOYS. Enjoying the scene. Typical circular shape of the small gang formed in Child Play.

SENIOR BOYS. Beginning to feel their way up towards one end of a room, as proscenium theatre is approached. They have just arranged boxes and are beginning to climb on them. Benches are arranged for audience. Strong resemblance to Elizabethan Theatre. (*See* p. 70.)

Photos by Victor Thompson

of a doctor in a bowler hat with a stick and a limp came in from time to time, when the fat boy over-ate. He prodded the fat boy in the tummy with his stick, till I thought he would burst.

In a shop where the fat boy was buying food were some forgers who gave him a dud half-crown.

The parent entrusted the fat boy with a piece of meat made of a towel with some red on it. This he ate behind a gym horse, spitting out huge bones made of screwed-up paper, after which he had a terrible tummy-ache.

Somehow the dud half-crown was discovered, and the doctor traced the forgers. There was a well-controlled fight. Police came in and carted off the forgers, and the doctor, after prodding the fat boy, left him to lie alone with his tummy-ache.

The players came back again to our world. " That's all, sir," they said.

Self (to Master) : " It's good to see them using the

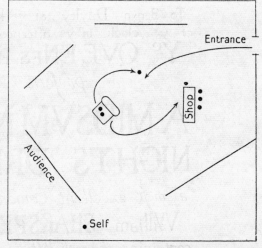

FIG. 19.—*The Greedy Boy*. Polished improvisation. Movement to and fro between mattress and gym horse.

right amount of space. They seem very comfortable, acting in-the-round."

Master : " Oh, yes, they like it."

Self : " How long have these been at it ? "

Master : " Half of them six months, the rest only three weeks."

Self : " How much of it was their own ? "

Master : " Every bit. I don't have to suggest ideas now. ' Robin Hood ' was done for the first time today, but ' The Greedy Boy ' has been done before."

The master had attended a six weeks' course on teaching method, and is beginning a second on how to take improvisation. He had " discovered " the work, though, before taking either course.

(24) *Senior Girls*

My companion and I were offered a playbill which informed us of a rehearsal at " Ye Globe Theatre ".

AT Yᵉ GLOBE THEATER

To Begyn Dayley at yᵉ hovver of **THREE**
of yᵉ clock in yᵉ afternoone,

Yᵉ QVEENᴇs PLAYERs

preſent

A MIDSVMMER NIGHTS DREAME

a moſt excellent Comodie VVritten by

VVilliam SHAKSPERE

containing, the moſt Pittiefvll tragedie and
crvel Death of Pyramvs and Thisby

There ſhal be Held this preſent Monday yᵉ
fivetene date of Nouember in the yeare of ovr
Lord 1597 at yᵉ Sayde Theater Alſo

A ReHeARSALL

at halfe paſt tvvo of yᵉ clocke, vvyche ſaide rehea
rſall yᵉ **PVBLICK** may iuſtlie attend.

Printed by *E. A.* and *W. I.* for *Richard Burbage*
at yᵉ Blue Bible, in Greene Arbovr, in little Old Bayly, London
MDXCVII

The school has been doing a drama project. They have finished the Early English Theatre and are now Shakespearian. Everything is Shakespeare, and today the whole school is dressed up. Everybody is moving and thinking and living in the period.

I slipped into the hall and crouched down by the apron stage to watch the crowds come in, hating my ordinary clothes for being so drab. The amplified voice of a hidden narrator was suggesting, to the room at large, points worth noticing. When the rehearsal had started I escaped by a side door and joined my companion and the head mistress at the back of the hall. All about us were families, mothers and fathers with their children, some rich, some poor ; they strode or shuffled through the straw on the floor. A few crowded round the hot-potato vendor, and an occasional cloud of steam from the raised benches down the side of the hall proclaimed where the lucky ones were contentedly nibbling their treasures. A few ate apples.

Some Children looked at us and came out of their setting, but they melted back fairly well, though none near us was absorbed. Our strange presence and idiotic clothes were enough to upset any Elizabethan family. Those nearer the stage were much more absorbed. But everyone in the room was participating—all in a part, audience and " actors " alike. This is eminently satisfactory for those who have not been chosen to be in the actual play (on the stage).

There were two " producers " on the stage, who were improving dialogue and giving instruction to the players. The rest of the dialogue (Pyramus and Thisby scene) was Shakespeare's. Two gallants passed by and bowed to a lady. Their tights were distemper on bare legs. A cloak flapped against my nose as they passed, and a rich smell of orange from a " daughter " near me impinged upon the animal odour of straw.

Suddenly the doors near us burst open and a further flood of colour poured in, talking in low tones, all improvising, disporting themselves in the manner of the day. It was an intoxicating experience. I was immersed in the wealth of colour, the mental concentration on the period growing all about me, and, over everything, the warm odour of the straw.

A girl with a jewelled cross worn on her forehead approached the head mistress. " May I introduce my family ? " she said. " This is my husband."

Headmistress : " How do you do ? "

There followed a conversation about the family and a query about the husband's fortune and activities.

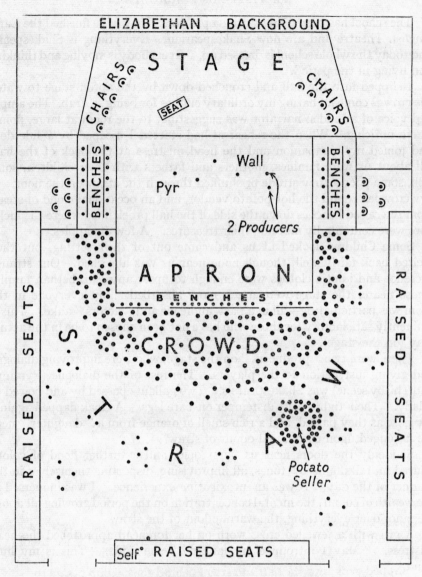

ELIZABETHAN BACKGROUND

STAGE

CHAIRS

CHAIRS

SEAT

BENCHES

BENCHES

Wall

Pyr

2 Producers

APRON

BENCHES

RAISED SEATS

RAISED SEATS

CROWD

STRAW

Potato
Seller

Self° RAISED SEATS

FIG. 20.—Senior Girls' Drama Project.
(See also Plates 21 and 22, opposite page 232.)

Husband (politely) : " I don't work."

Headmistress : " Oh, no. You are lucky. You have enough without."

Husband : " Yes."

I engaged another family in conversation. There were three children, Katherine, Ophelia and Othello.

Self : (To yet another family) : " Do you enjoy coming to the Players ?"

Lady : " Oh, yes."

Self : " Did you manage to get a hot potato ? "

Husband : " Unfortunately they had all gone."

Lady : " Yes, and that's a great pity, for our little boy has a pain ; the heat would do 'im good."

I was introduced to the school staff, all dressed up, and smelling strongly of scent because of the " rabble ".

Self (to another family) : " Do you like coming to the Players ? "

Husband : " Yes, very much. We always come when we can. It's nice to chat to your friends at the same time."

The play on the stage then came to an end.

Headmistress (to all) : " Don't leave the theatre yet if you don't want to. Stay and discuss the play with your friends."

Another mistress : " What did you feel about it ? "

Self : " Wonderful, but we should have been dressed up."

Mistress : " Oh, we thought about it. We even had two ruffs ready, but didn't quite know what you'd think about it."

Self : " What a pity. A ruff and an old curtain and I should have felt quite at home. The Children near us would have been more absorbed too."

We looked out of the window. All over the playground were families continuing their play-experience. They were still chatting and strutting and bowing, as if they had never been anything else, and had no interest in whether they were being watched or not.

Headmistress : " Well, you've seen half the school now."

Self : " How many are having this experience ? "

Head : " About six hundred. They've all made up their own costumes. The second half of the school will be in the hall by now. I see the flag is flying. "

I slipped back into the hall and stood behind the curtain beside the stage. This was a noisier " house ". Things were warming up.

Wall (to crowd) : " Shut up, you."

Crowd : " Yah."

At the words " I die " the groundlings yelled : " Wer, aren't you dead yet ? " The show ended in a roar of cheers. The atmosphere was electric.

Later we were talking to the head in the hall, while Children were clearing away the forms and collecting the straw.

Head : " We're very happy here. Everyone helps. I trust the Children. They will have this finished in a few minutes. That girl is a ' C ' Child, but she knows exactly where to put those chairs. They will be back in the classroom when they are needed."

(25) *Senior Girls*

The headmistress has long felt the necessity for the Child to act-in-the-round and to express its own form of theatre. She uses the school play traditionally about once a year as a social function. She has not liked festivals, and wanted to have a local Children's Theatre, by which she meant a place where Children could go and play, but she could not make people understand this. (What tragedy.)

I saw sets of improvisation.

(*a*) A teacher, having just started, showed improvisation of a Bible story. Instead of leaving the Children in the circle where they were, she pulled the audience to one side. In the resulting perspective theatre, only one Child out of seven was absorbed in the part ; the others fidgeted and arranged themselves until they thought they could be seen by the audience. The teacher was surprised and interested at my idea of the Children watching in a circle all round the actors, which would have eliminated the shuffling of the six minor characters.

(*b*) *Older girls, twelve to fourteen years.* The teacher wished to impress on me that this was the girls' work and that they would say different things today from what they had said before. It was quite clear, however, that many of the words had been learned by heart. It was polished improvisation, a Bible story in modern language, quite nicely done, good grouping, but the Children were giggling occasionally, and glancing at the audience.

This had been worked at for about a fortnight, and quite obviously not improvised lately, but prepared for my visit.

The second play by this group was an improvisation of *Hansel and Gretel.* No words had been learned in such a formal way, and none of the Children took any notice of the audience. The witch was absorbed within two minutes. Gretel had outstanding facial expression of fear (a very moving performance). The witch told Gretel to go to sleep, and the convention of the sleep lasting only three or four seconds appeared to amuse the class.

The players, who had till now been quite absorbed, were disturbed at the laughter, and remained so for four minutes afterwards. The interruption had been nearly as bad as if the teacher had stopped the show to make a suggestion.

Those watching participated by making noises with the desks. There was a moment when a tray should have been dropped. This had been done once before, and all the audience took out their rulers (on seeing the tray), ready to drop them, but the play changed its form and the tray was never dropped—to the disappointment of the would-be participators, who found their rulers quite an embarrassment and kept looking at me to see if I thought them foolish. I pretended not to see and looked only at the play. They then did the same, and became absorbed for the last few moments of it.

Head (to Gretel) : " Wouldn't it have been better to have waited longer during your sleep ? "

Gretel (rather nervous) : " Don't know, miss. "

Head : " What could she have done ? "

A Child : " Snored."

Head : " You'd better remember to snore next time, hadn't you ? "

Gretel : " I don't know, miss. I'm not sure. I can't remember."

Self (very calmly) : " What do you think about this snoring, Gretel ? Are you sure it would be right ? There have been two suggestions, one that you wait longer, the other that you snore. Think about it a little and make your own decision which is right for the way you play it."

Gretel (relieved) : " Yes, sir." (Laughter.)

Self : " Why do you laugh ? "

Child : " Please, sir, it's funny to think about a snore." (All of us laughed.)

Self : " Yes, it is funny to us, but it was serious for Gretel, perhaps. Snoring can be an important business. All that we do in acting (when we do it well) is important to us. Thank you very much for your plays ; do you like doing this ? "

Everybody : " Yes."

Self : " Do you prefer the book play, or this sort of acting ? "

All : " This sort of acting."

Self : " Do you like acting best, or watching ? "

All : " Acting."

Self : " Is there anybody here who does not like acting ? " (Nobody.)

(c) Ten to twelve years.

Room full of Children, taken by music teacher. A formal pattern of Children sitting and standing. Outline of story of *The Selfish Giant,* by Oscar Wilde. A few sentences were read by a narrator to musical background, which was too loud to allow one word to be heard.

The Children began to move to the music, and did rather obvious dances, but kept certain formations which clearly gave them pleasure. Once or twice a Child would break out of the form and dance its own movements, snakewise through the formal group. Included in these dances were raindrops, trees and flowers ; a number of players, having done their task, had been told to turn their faces away from those watching. This seemed a curious mixture of perspective tradition and the beginning of intelligent use of acting in a circular form.

Teacher : " We have also started a storm scene, but I don't suppose you want to see that, as we've only done it once."

Self : " I should be most interested to see it. That's just what I like." The teacher played storm music. A few Children danced on the spot where they stood, hearing the time beat, wagging arms and heads, and clapping. Others were encouraged to wave their arms and heads, where they stood listening to the music. Then they were asked whether they would like to join in and make wind noises, which they did, first of all as separate individuals, then, as the group sensitivity grew and certain intuitive climaxes were reached, in bodies of about ten in a bunch together. The result was not yet a whole climax by the complete group, but various groups were beginning to be formed as an entity. I felt that, given time, there would have been agreed intuitive climaxes by the whole group.

The Children then got on to the floor while the teacher repeated the storm music. This time they entirely forgot to make any noise whatever, and merely made an improvised dance. The movement, however, displayed group climax at the places where sound climax had been forming before. It was apparent that they were finding it easier to express by movement rather than singing.

Many delightful movements were made. There was a vitality about the whole group, some absorption, and good facial expression. Unconscious pattern was formed, space being well balanced between each Child.

PLATE 21

SENIOR GIRLS. Elizabethan Project. Flowing out from proscenium.
(*See* pp. 226–230.)

SENIOR GIRLS. Elizabethan Project. Rehearsal takes place.
Note stage projection. (*See* pp. 226–230.)

Photos by Reg. Cave

PLATE 22

SENIOR GIRLS. Elizabethan Project. Note acting going on quite apart from the stage. (*See* pp. 226–230.)

SENIOR GIRLS. Elizabethan Project. A family in the "audience" meets an actor. (*See* pp. 226–230.)

Photos by Reg. Cave

PLATE 23

SENIOR GIRLS. Beginning of a partly polished dance improvisation without words. Later, words could be included. (*See* pp. 81-83.)

SENIOR GIRLS. Absorption. Intended and sustained theatre, as the adult understands it, has arrived. (*See* p. 12.)

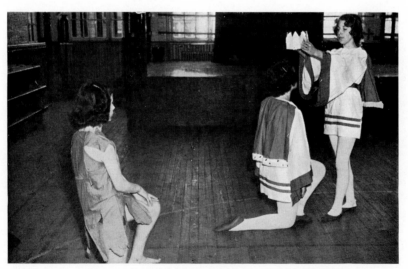

SENIOR GIRLS. Dance Drama. (*See* pp. 79–81.)

Photos by Victor Thompson

PLATE 24

SENIOR GIRLS. Dance Drama. A more formal circle. (*See* p. 79.)

SENIOR GIRLS. A tense moment. Note shape of flowers on floor. We have arrived at the polished improvisation, *dressed*. (*See* pp. 81–82.)

Action photos by Victor Thompson

(d) Group, fourteen years old.

A dance at one end of the room, which had been originally improvised but was now polished, appeared in this instance stilted and quite meaningless, arranged by an adult. The next dance by the same group was arranged by a girl, said to be gifted. She placed the Children lying in a circle with their hands inward. The Child arranging it was the chief dancer, absorbed, but copying facial habits of older actresses, which gave the most extraordinary mixture of truth and insincerity to her work.

Having danced away into the circle, she touched a number of Children (who were flowers) on the head ; they woke up and grasped after her. The grasping turned to menacing and the flowers closed in on the dancer ; as they got closer to her, three from the circle rose up and caught hold of her, making the most fascinating groupings, the whole thirty or so swaying rhythmically together with upstretched hands. The sudden climax came, and the main dancer was flung out of the circle.

Simple musical background. No words. Group sensitivity marked in this. The whole class took part. Absorption excellent. Great sincerity. Good theatre.

Last Dance

This, I was told, would be the masterpiece.

The choreography was arranged by the same girl. There followed a very ordinary copy of an adult improvisation, with a few of the best girls chosen. The grouping was good, and space well filled. But the performance lacked drive and purpose, and was in marked contrast to the previous dance where everyone had taken their place and the core of the dance was the absorption. In the last dance, only pattern had been consciously aimed at, and the result was precocious rubbish.

(26) Senior Boys

Play No. 1.—" The Artist's Model."

The boys had been given a choice of what they would like to act, a few days before, and had clearly talked about its theme and were now performing it for the second time. It was becoming longer and more elaborate, and the teacher was interested and surprised at the new features.

The model stood on a table (stage right). This main figure acted as the flagpole for the pennant of the other figures, who moved about in a rhythm

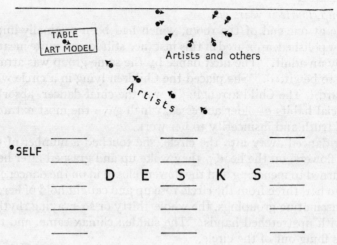

TABLE
ART MODEL

Artists and others

Artists

•SELF

D E S K S

FIG. 21.—Two main formations during the play. A near-circle against the wall. Even with Senior Boys no notice was taken of the audience during the play.

of their own, absorbed in painting the model.   The model, however, started to move, and the artists became annoyed and hurled insults at him.

An Artist : " Don't move."

Model : " I must, I am a ghost " (weaving his hands about).

Another Artist : " Yer will be a ghost when we've done wiv yer."   (Other insults of various strength and wit were hurled, and one infuriated artist rushed up to the model and started to paint him all over.)

Most of the class, who had been practically participating and only just remained seated in their desks, then shouted :

" Don't paint *'im,* paint the canvas."

There were a few more greater shouts from the artist, quite unintelligible to the teacher and myself.   All the actors then turned to the front and said : " That's all, sir."

Everyone else in the room appeared to be fully aware that the play had finished except us (teacher and self).

The degree of absorption and sincerity was most marked.   The play lasted half an hour, and it took fifteen minutes for them to become oblivious of the audience, everyone turning their backs.   There were no suggestions from the teacher.

Complete calm all the time, except for the emotional outbursts.

Play No. 2.

A different set of boys got up—about eight of them. They explained that it was a dentist's waiting-room, and then started " straight in ". Absorption was apparent within three minutes, those watching completely interested.

We witnessed the most harrowing and imaginative details of some fearful dream-dentist's apartment, where such things as pneumatic drills were used. Babies were hit on the head and held upside down.

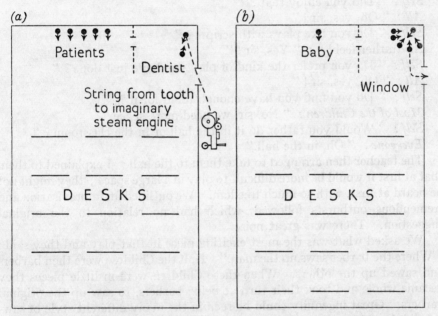

FIG. 22.—(*a*) Waiting-room and patients. Dotted lines represent imaginary partition and doorway. Teeth linked to steam engine. (*b*) The End. The dentist is cornered. One patient drops dentist's teeth out of window to rhythmic tapping by Baby.

When all the boys had been through interminable sadistic ordeals, in which all violence was mimed, the last character went back to ask the dentist for his walking-stick, which he had left in the room. When given back his stick, he smote the dentist over the head with it, whereupon all the afflicted patients rushed back from the waiting-room, fell upon the dentist and took out all of his teeth, dropping them out of the window to a rhythmic tapping sound.

By this time each Child had his back to the audience ; the atmosphere was electric with horror. They turned round with cherubic smiles and said, " That's the end, sir."

With many Children it appears to be necessary for them to state when they come back to our world, and if they do not actually say so it is quite apparent when they do.

Questions :

 Self : " Did you enjoy that ? "
 All : " Oh, yes, sir ! "
 Self : " Do you like plays with scripts ? "
 All (rather feebly) : " Yes, sir ! "
 Self : " Do you prefer the kind of play you have just done ? "
 All : " Oh, yes, sir ! "
 Self : " Do you find you have enough room for it ? "
 Most of the Children : " No, sir, we need more space."
 Self : " Would you rather do it in the hall or in the classroom ? "
 Everyone : " Oh, in the hall."

The teacher then arranged to take them to the hall. I explained to them that at first it would be more difficult to play in a large space ; they might not be heard at first, with so much freedom. We outlined an improvisation and tremendous outbursts followed, which had no relation to the original suggestion. There was great noise.

We asked what was the most exciting piece in that play and they said : " Where the barber saws up the man." Half the Children were then barbers and sawed up the others. When these Children were in little pieces they became whole and took their turn at being barbers, to saw up the original barbers. Great ingenuity could be seen in the many different style of sawing. Other ideas which they tried, with less success, were the use of various forms of weapon. It would be better for them to use a little less of the hall until they learn more control in the full group, but they clearly need more space than is available in the classroom.

Suggestion to teacher. " Allow them occasional outbursts of this kind, to free their emotions and enable them to ' Play out ' what they have seen on the films, at least once a month."

(27) *Secondary Modern School (Mixed)*

A master was taking a rehearsal of part of *Noah* (Obey) on the floor of the hall. I stood near. Three out of five players were reading the script with great difficulty and not speaking loud enough. Another group was rehearsing as animals on the stage, together with Mr. Noah. Presently I moved over to them. A mistress was trying to encourage Noah to get into his part more ; he was reading with great difficulty.

The Teacher (quietly) : " *How* do you get them to get inside the part ? "

Self : " They never will whilst they are having such difficulty with the script. If you want more meaning, which is the first sign of getting inside the part, I should try Noah without the book for a bit. Get him to make up his own words—words that he thinks he would say *himself* if he were really that person in that situation. That will give him a chance to create. He is enchained by his inability to read a script, at the moment. Look at those animals. They are quite different. They are *acting*, because they have no scripts. They are free." The teacher tried this. At first Noah was self-conscious.

Self (quietly to teacher) : " Go on. Persevere."

At the third attempt a smile came on Noah's face, and suddenly the language came. It poured out for about five minutes, sending the animals into stitches of laughter. The teacher then asked the boy to try the script again. The result was remarkable. He was now nearly Noah. I turned away to the other group again.

Master : " They don't read very well yet." I suggested the same device.

Master : " Would you do this often ? "

Self : " Yes, if it brings improvement. Even with professionals I often break off rehearsals if things are going dead, and improvise the scene ' in-the-round ' to get life. When life comes you return to the stage and carry on with the formal play."

Master : " How can you shorten the waits between scenes ? "

Self : " I should say rehearse your scene-shifters like a P.T. class until their speed is doubled, and reconsider your form of production in order to cut out curtain waits. Use the apron stage to keep scenes going.

" When I was producing this play with young people a little time ago we had, for instance, the cabin on the apron stage, lit inside. When the players went up on deck they passed through the flaps to the rear of the cabin, and up through the stage curtains, behind which the deck scene had been prepared. As the last player left the cabin, it rose (to a swirl of music) right up into the roof, out of sight ; the proscenium curtains opened on " sunlight " and the deck scene was before us without any waiting. The crane apparatus for the cabin was made by the boys' woodwork section and thoroughly tested by a professional mechanic."

The master was interested in the idea of coming out from behind the proscenium, and asked further questions.

Self : " This is the natural flow from floor to stage, which one expects with this age group.   If they are left alone they do it for themselves.   We learn much more by watching than directing.   That is the value of improvisation.   If used properly, it gives creative freedom to the Child and instruction to the teacher."

(28) *Grammar School*

Sixth-form boys were rehearsing a play, but in even a small hall it was difficult to hear what they said, and the acting was not very vital.

Teacher : " Would you care to speak to them ? "

Self : "Yes, if you wish."

The rehearsal was stopped ; I broke the whole group into pairs.

Self : " All the people on this side of the room think of something rude to say to the person opposite you.   Now let's hear you, one by one."   They started along the row, but it was unconvincing.

Self : " If you were angry, would you speak like that ? "

Boy : " No.   I'd be louder."

Self : " Right.   Be angry and *be* louder."

Gradually all the voices got louder.   They were beginning to attack their parts.

Self : " Now you are speaking loud enough.   Don't drop below that when you are on the stage or you will not be heard.   Remember, each one of you, the physical and mental experience of that loud talking.   It must become a habit whilst acting."

We then tried talking loud and *not* being rude, so as to keep the sound strong whilst portraying a calm mood.

There followed a discussion on the use of good manners.

Partners then tried both moods on the original speakers.   Those who remained weak were put at opposite ends of the hall so that they could not hear each other until they spoke up.   When all were fairly certain of speaking up, they were asked to improvise the scene they had been acting on the stage.   This was done with tremendous life, all over the floor of the hall. Pace and climax improved tremendously.

Self : " Thank you. That's quite different, isn't it ? "

A boy : " Yes, that felt real, somehow."

Self : " Good. It sounded real, too. Now let's try it on the stage and use your scripts again."

The acting was greatly improved, but was not as vital as the improvisation. The scene ended.

Self : " It has gone down a bit, hasn't it ? "

Nearly all : " Yes."

Self : " What will you have to do then ? "

A boy : " Improvise more often."

Self : " Yes, and what else ? "

Boy : " Learn the words better."

Self : " Yes. The words are not known. Some of you are using books, some trying to do without them. You won't be expected to act so well whilst you have the books, but I understand you have been rehearsing for some weeks now. Compare these words with your improvisation. You can never attain the same life until you *know* what you are going to say. That means learn the words absolutely pat as soon as possible. It is better to know a great deal about the words before you start moving on the stage at all."

A boy : " It's awfully hard learning the words."

Self : " I know. Do you get a lot of prep ? "

(Laughter) *Most boys :* " Yes."

Self : " It makes a lot to learn, I know. But you do see now that it is a waste of time if you *don't* learn the words, don't you ? "

All : " Yes."

A boy : " Couldn't we make up our own plays and do improvisation ? "

Self : " Yes, of course you can, but don't neglect the wealth of English literature. At your stage you should do both. Create *and* learn." I then stimulated discussion on improvisation by telling them a little about the Italian theatre.

After that we went on to trying moves from the rehearsed play, on the floor of the hall. Everyone had practice in using the right amount of space and in asking an imaginary lady for a dance, also coming into a room politely and then rudely.

At the end of an hour we stopped.

A boy : " That is the most interesting hour I've ever had on Drama. I never realised before what a wide subject it could be."

Self : " If you relate it to life it stays alive. If not, it becomes dead literature, beautiful but dead."

Teacher : " Thank you very much. What would you suggest we start with in doing more improvisation ? I never saw the value of it before."

Self : " I don't want to suggest too much. The ideas should come from them. But you might try with these lads the vast field of documentary plays. Everyone can be included then, and you won't get those bored ones sitting about pretending to watch a dull play, as when I first came in. That's the way to hate drama. They're a grand lot, though ; they responded very quickly and should do some excellent work."

PLATE 25

SENIOR GIRLS. Flowing up on to the stage. (*See* pp. 70–73.)

SENIOR GIRLS. Beginning to flow off stage. Fast action
caught by the camera. (*See* pp. 70–73.)

Photos by Victor Thompson

PLATE 26

SENIOR BOYS. Semi-stylised action to the clash of a cymbal. They are knights in armour fighting with battle-axes. The " din of battle " took his work seriously. It took four minutes to get them going. This could be linked to historical study, and further scenes enacted. (Acting before the stage.) (*See* p. 80.)

SENIOR BOYS. Their first attempt at imaginative rapier work. The man with his arm up has just been run through. Discussion on history of the period could follow. (Flow on and off stage is beginning.) (*See* pp. 70–73.)

Photos by Victor Thompson

PART III

OUT OF SCHOOL

CHILDREN'S THEATRE

MASKS AND MAKE-UP

PUPPETS AND MARIONETTES

FILMS

QUESTIONS AND REMARKS

Dedicated to

NELLIE HERRIDGE

In whose Cooking Palace I Fought
the Last Years of the 1914–1918 War,
and with whom I thereupon set sail for Canada
upon the Kitchen Table, and shot the Rapids
of that Noble Land

CHAPTER XV

OUT OF SCHOOL

If you are to be a Beautiful Person, you'll have to
surround yourself with flowers, not ugly stones.
Nine-year-old Child

... it must be permitted Children not only to divert
themselves, but to do it after their own Fashion. ...
John Locke [1]

In Parts I and II enough has been said, perhaps, to make it clear that out-of-
school work is as important as in-school work.   If it is not carried on, the
Child may run wild, and not only may the actual Art of Child Drama suffer,
but, particularly in the long summer holidays, the Drama of the streets may
cause trouble.   The gangs can be a considerable nuisance both to parents and
police.

On one occasion, a Child I knew well got into a particularly wild gang,
which slowly encroached upon my home and finally made its headquarters
in my garage.   The Child changed in a few weeks into a screaming monster.
Activities were anything from throwing stones or beating smaller Children
to rank theft.   In the end, the only way to save the Child we knew, and
incidentally avoid for the gang leader the necessity of going to an approved
school, was to close the garage and open our house.   *There was no Play
Centre for these Children to be in, and apparently no adult interested enough to
stop them getting into trouble.*   It was therefore necessary for us to turn our
house into the gang headquarters.   This was a bold and uncomfortable
experiment—looking back now, I wonder how we dared it.   There is not
room here to describe how we dealt with the matter ; that would take a book
on its own.   But, briefly, we started a small private Child Drama Centre, and
ran it as a place for Children to play in—a real Children's Theatre.   It was
not our first experience of running such a thing, but the first in our own
home, and at this time it was highly inconvenient.

[1] *Mentioned also in the Ministry of Education pamphlet*
"Out of School," published since this book was written.

By degrees we got the Children off the street and interested them in sounds and movement and speech. We had Red Indian attacks in the garden to " hot swing " background music. Behaviour began to get better at once ; within three weeks, honesty was noticeably improving (though we lost a lot of things one way and another). We had to give up because the place became too popular and we could not deal with the constant stream of wistful little callers, but the Child we knew was caught in the nick of time. She changed to another district after these Drama experiences, and this move crowned a precarious success.

This experience, of course, is not unique. The National Under Fourteen's Council[1] used to suggest Play Centres for the same reason.

I have made some mention in the section on Children's Theatre of Pete's Kitchen.[2] This is the type of centre needed, I believe. There are also suggestions for the lay-out and simple provisioning of such a " No-audience Play Centre ".[3] There should be fully trained people in charge, capable of nurturing Child Drama. We need lots of these centres in our cities, and there might be some open-air ones, too. They are an *urgent necessity*. Not only are they important for the prevention of delinquency, but would help develop further the joys and beauties of the Child's own Creative Drama.

Included here are a few short descriptions of out-of-school work. They may be of value in suggesting a manner of guiding out-of-school Play, and have some bearing on in-school Play, particularly for juniors and infants.

Mixed Age Group

Getting a group of various ages to do something together for the first time.
Girl : 11 years ; Girl : 7 years ; Boy : 8 years ; Girl : 5 years.
Adult : " What shall we play ? "
Chorus : " Let's play house."
5-year-old : " No, let's play hospitals."
Chorus : " Oh, yes." (Great glee.)
Adult : " Who will be the patients ? "
5-year-old : " I will." (Lying down at once on floor.)
Adult : " Who wants to be the doctor ? " (No answer.)
Adult : " Will you, Georgie ? "
George : " Yes."

---

[1] This is now merged with the *Save the Children Fund.*
[2] See Chapter XVI, page 293.   [3] See pages 301–304.

7-year-old : " I want to be the nurse."

The eleven-year-old girl felt rather out of it.

Adult (to her) : " Margaret, will you be surgeon ? "

The adult noticed that everyone except the patient was a bit wooden. It was clearly the time to stimulate. She therefore went for the doctor and started : " Oh, Dr. Snooks . . . "

Nurse (stimulated at once and issuing orders) : " Ring the bell."

Adult did so in mime.

After pause, doctor, thinking very hard, opened an imaginary door.

Adult : " I think you'd better get into my car."

The little boy got behind the adult, who made noises, and they both " drove round " the room. All the children laughed except the patient, who was very ill and quite absorbed.

Adult : " Let's get into the lift."

Doctor was still tongue-tied, but could open and shut doors. Noises were made. The lift arrived at the top floor, doctor and adult-suggester got out and approached the patient.

Adult : " Here is the sick woman. What is wrong ? "

Doctor (after pause) : " She's got the measles."

Adult : "I'll call the nurse." (Buzzes and mimes bell.)

Nurse (appears at once and starts to scold the doctor, ending) : " What yer going to do ? "

Doctor : " She's got the measles."

Nurse : " Yes, but what are you going to *do* ? "

The Play now showed signs of flagging because nobody knew what to do, least of all the doctor.

Adult : " I think the patient should be taken to hospital."

Nurse (stimulated) : " Oh yes, ambulance." (She rushs to the wall.)

Adult : " Two chairs ? "

Nurse (very crossly) : " No."

Adult realised too late that her suggestion was redundant. This is the mistake which is so easy to make.

The nurse luckily became absorbed now, and mimed opening the garage and brought out a stretcher. She indicated to the doctor that he should help her carry this. Doctor did this very well (he was beginning to get into it. They approached the patient, then went off and put two chairs near her, but did not use them, yet.

Play began to flag again.

Adult : " Call the surgeon."

Nurse rang a bell (imaginary).

The eleven-year-old girl then came to life and entered the game a bit, as surgeon.

Surgeon (rather self-consciously) : " It's 'er appendix." (Silence.)

Adult : " Will you take it out ? "

Nurse : " We must put 'er ter sleep."

The doctor suddenly began to pour gallons of stuff, which he produced from the air, over the patient's face. The patient relaxed and her eyes closed. Absorbed play now started in earnest. Doctor and nurse, making fearful rending noises, slit the body from chin to toe, and scooped out many hundred-weights of entrails. They were *very* busy. They then did up the patient as if with a zip-fastener, and shook her to wake her. They lifted the patient on to the two chairs that were waiting hopefully. But Play flagged again.

Adult : " Have you taken her temperature ? "

Doctor and nurse at once put a thermometer under each arm of the patient.

Nurse : " She's got a temperature of 150."

It was clear that all the Children except nurse had come to the end of their simple creative ability.

The Adult, therefore : " Now what shall we play ? "

Nurse : " Oh, she can't go home yet."

Adult : " Very well, we'll leave her in the hospital then."

This apparently satisfied nurse. The patient got up and the Children started to play with a toy engine.

The Child of seven years was the only one with much previous experience of creative Child Drama. She rather led the Play after the adult, and we notice that she alone at the end could have sustained the action. The five-year-old was extremely quick, too, and may have done Play at school. She was absorbed throughout. The others have had no proper opportunity to do this work at school, and, although enjoying what they did, were slow to enter into the action, and of course had no language flow. The boy began to speak with his body. The eleven-year-old girl has missed the best years of her life because no one has ever shown her how to find her own powers. It will be much harder for her now, and, though she is going to a school where she will have opportunities for creation, there is little hope that she will entirely escape the self-consciousness which comes soon after her age to

Children who do not receive the correct opportunities for expression in earlier years. The whole episode took only seven minutes.

When dealing with the beginnings of Child-Drama, the task of the adult is heavier, but we should be ready to drop out as soon as possible. It is unwise to keep things going too long with beginners or new groups. This adult was, of course, aware of these things.

Play to Music Background (1)

A record of the *Three-Cornered Hat* (Falla) was on the gramophone. A Child of seven and a half years, who had not done this sort of work for some time, came into the room.

Child : " Ooh, music ! Come on, let's play."

Self : " I'm making a pudding."

Child : " That's because you're a wild animal. You eat little children. Spit out the bones ! "

The Child then watched me eating Children, and started to copy rather badly. Through lack of help and practice it had lost some ability to create easily. I stopped, therefore, and the Child stopped too.

Child : " Go on."

Self : " There are no more bones." (I hoped the Child would invent the next thing.)

The Child lay on its back. I moved away. Suddenly the Child ran across the room and leapt at me. Things were warming up.

Child : " Aha ! I'm a savijanimal, a very savijanimal. I'm killing you now because you've been naughty."

I was dragged to the sofa and eaten in time to the music. I was glad that spitting out the bones was not copied. My bones were pulled out like large fishbones and laid in a row. The record ended.

Child : " Oh dear, do let's have it again."

The music began once more.

Child : " This is where we dance." We danced in a circle, the Child giving directions. Then invention gave out and the Child sat down.

Child : " Go on, you do something."

Self (knowing that invention in this Child would return with perseverance) : " I'm a stone." I lay on the floor, quite still. The Child got up.

Child : " I'm a little gnome friend. No, I'm a *little* wild animal and you're the mummy. Oh dear, I don't know what to do."

Self : " Listen to the music."

Child listens, then : " Aha, we are going for a walk."

I got up, and lumbered along next to the little wild animal.

Little Animal : " You are being very kind to me, today."

Mother Animal : " Yes, I'm all right till I'm hungry."

Little Animal : " There's a good mummy.   Have an acorn ? "

Absorption and movement to music were improving.

Child (suddenly, on recognising piece of music) : " Ooh, this is where I kill you."

The killing began.   It was better this time, and my coat suffered a lot. I was pretty dead by the end of the record.   It was not clear whether I was the original man of the first record-playing or mother animal.

We played the other side of the record and a good dance of the gnomes was invented.   My role was a wizard, but all the gnomes danced in circles and cast spells about, till the drawing-room looked quite different.   The Child played nine different parts.

Creation was now good.   I put on the first record again.   This time everything was strong, vital and absorbed, and it ended with the little animal growing up, and my death this time was definitely that of mother animal.   The Child wandered off to find its real mother.

Child : " Oh, I *am* happy.   Mummy, I'll finish your ironing for you."

Three washing-up cloths were ironed for the grateful mother.   Whilst the ironing was going on, the Child, happy and liberated by the play, had a calm flow of language spoken very carefully and beautifully.[1]

Play to Music Background (2).   " *Captain Hook Crucified.*"

Little Girl : " Shall we play ? "

Self : " Yes."

The little girl immediately becomes a boy.   I put on a record.   We fight rhythmically to a background of *Why does my Heart go Boom?*.   Some fine sword-play here.   Then the movement becomes stylised and a heavy blow occurs on each " boom ".

Child (serious suddenly.   Dialogue is clearly going to start, although the music is still playing) : " You are Hook."

I accept my part without comment.

[1] Chapter VI, page 103.

Hook is suddenly vanquished and gets carried off. We meet a policeman. I am ordered to be this too.

Policeman (Self) : " What have you been doing ? "

Child : " I haven't. *He* has." (Pointing to where I was before) : " It's
Hook. Will you put him in prison ? "

Policeman : " Yuss."

I am Hook again, and playing two roles at once (to no one's surprise). I
help to chain myself up and am " rewarded " (adult thought) by being
pushed into a corner by the Child, who is now boy and policeman. This is
quite clear to both the Child and myself (since our intuitive bond has now
been built up—with more players I have called this " group intuition ", and
under school conditions between adult and Child " student-teacher relationship "). No word has been said about the Child becoming policeman. It
has just happened. We both know it and accept it.

Child : " You may have your hands free though, just to play with and to
eat." (The quality of mercy is not strained, it would seem.) Hook (Self)
eats, but scratches his nose on each " boom ", as it comes in the music.

Boy (the little girl) then struts away, smiling slightly at the nose scratch,
but still in character.

I put on another record.

Hook is then taken along by the policeman (little girl), hooked in the
shoulder by the head of a hobby horse—(note the association of ideas being
experienced physically by action. The name Hook leads the Child to hook
Hook. This trait, which appears so often in Child Play, always reminds me
of Shakespeare's continual play on repeated words).

We march round to a background of *Basin Street Blues*.

Hook (Self) is pushed into a corner of the room.

Child (as policeman, and speaking to the room) : " I think we'll crucify
you now."

Child (as little boy) : " Turn round, so we can see you better."

Hook is faced to the room, and carefully crucified in mime.

Child (in own voice as stage director) : " Put your head like God does."

The Child then waited, watching with large eyes to see that I played this
with satisfactory sincerity. The moment passed.

Child (as little boy) : " They're lovely bright nails, aren't they ? "

Self (as Hook, bravely and trying to be nice about it all) : " Yuss."

Child (own voice) : " I'll fetch the pony now and see what *he* has to
say."

Child (in squeaky voice) : " I am your little pony coming to help you although you're bad."

The record came to an end.   There was some interruption by someone coming into the room, and the Child wandered off quite calmly, quietened by its natural outburst, to sit clicking a piece of tin to its doll.   I sat down and made some notes on my remarkable experience.

Later

The Child came back.   I sensed that it now wanted to continue its adventure.   I resumed my position with arms wide.

Child : " See—that's a man on a cross."

Child (own voice) : " Oh, where's the horse, I've lost it ? "   (She had taken it away before the interruption.)

Child : " Never mind—the doll can be the horse."

Self (in Hook's voice) : " Are you going to help me down ? "

The doll is lifted up by the Child and tries to take the nails out of my feet, as a baby might, the Child grunting for it.   The doll succeeds.

Hook : " Are you going to climb up and take the nails out of my hands ? "

Doll then climbs me and walks along my arm.   There is some rhythmic pulling to remove the nails.   The doll then slides to the ground.

Child (in voice of doll baby) : " There you are, Soldier.   Mummy said I was to take you home."

I take the doll by its hand to a toy wheelchair.   (I gather I am now Soldier.   One must be ever ready for a swift change of part in Child Drama, sometimes even being a number of people or things at once.   Consider, for instance, the position when the Child did the voice of the doll baby, who itself was acting the part of the pony, if only for a short time.)

Child : " Now we are going shopping."

Self (in ordinary voice, I am not Hook now) : " Shall I push the baby in the chair ? "

Child (in own voice, which is perfectly logical as the following is a stage direction) : " No, don't.   You just do it until the mother comes."

Self (to baby doll) : " Are you warm enough ? "

No answer.   I should have known better.   Attempts of this kind are irrelevant.   I should have done by-play in mime, and noticed that the Child was beginning to enter a new character, so couldn't answer for the doll.   She was walking round and round the table, then suddenly stopped near me.

Child (as mother) : " Well, did he find you ? "

Self : " Yes, he was a good baby."

Mother : " Where were you ? "

Self : " I was on a cross."

The word " cross " coincided intentionally with the beat of a drum at the end of the record.

Child (suddenly herself again, because the cessation of the music background has temporarily destroyed the dramatic atmosphere and mood) : " Oh, *Petie,* I would like it again."

Basin Street Blues starts again. At the opening of the record the Child walks along shyly, with me as her husband wheeling the chair with the doll in it.

Child (as mother, to doll) : " Good little thing. Sweet little thing." Doll laughs. (Child makes noise.)

Mother : " Let's go home now. They'll be coming with horsewhips to whip you back on to the cross again."

Self : " It wouldn't be nice if they put me back, except that it's good to be like Jesus."

We walk round faster and faster—escaping.

The Child is suddenly put off by an adult sitting in a chair watching. (So many examples of this I could quote. There should be no audience.) The play is going to crash. Luckily the adult knew Children. She quickly went on writing something and appeared to be uninterested. Actually she was writing notes of the dialogue of this play, otherwise it would have been lost to history.

Self (urgently brushing adult and chair aside) : " Let's push through these trees."

The Child at once accepted what was nearly audience as stage property. The adult is now a tree.

Child (as mother, reassured and beaming): "We're getting into the house." The wheelchair is pushed to a corner, and the doll baby put on a table.

Mother : " Where's that enemy ? "

Self : " I can hear him."

At this point the Child's movement was not very good. Some sharp drums came in the record music, so to relate the music as atmosphere to the play again I quickly repeated—" I can hear him " (as if the drums were him).

Child (fully alive again) : " Quick, you go into your office without any windows, so they can't see you."

She hides me quickly behind doll's wheelchair (which hides one-sixth of me).

Mother : " When they've gone I'll let you out."

Mother looks out for enemy, returns.

Mother : " They're coming—go up to the attic and hide."

I climb stairs, which aren't there, for dear life and hide behind my own hands, with one eye peeping through.

The Child broke out of character for a moment, with a conspiratorial sort of wink and shrug at seeing my eye.

There is a sudden change and the Child becomes the enemy, who tries frantically to open the attic window.

Child (as enemy, and suddenly speaking dialect) : " Oo, ah can't do thut winder. It's too stiff, yer see."

Child (derisively as mother) : " Ha-ha-ha."

Enemy tried again several times, finishing up with, " Oh, can't ", which came exactly on the drum beat and climax at the end of the record *Basin Street Blues.*

The wise teacher or co-player, in school or out, would here note that the Child is beginning to sense the dramatic feeling of " climax " and " ending ". The words " Oh, can't " were more consciously connected with the time beat and ending of the music. It was quite clear that that was the end of an episode " to be continued in our next".

Note.—It seemed that about the time that the doll baby ceased to impersonate the pony, Hook on the Cross became Soldier. For the reader's information, Soldier is the traditional husband of this particular doll's mother.

Consideration of the Above

What do we learn from consideration of these episodes ? Many things. This short summary might be of value, and I have added statements, in brackets, based on much wider observation.[1]

1. Music can help the Child to develop mood, atmosphere and climax. It may also give gentle suggestion as to *how* the Child might move.   (In fact this suggestion is generally better than anything we could give intellectually.)

2. The Child is happy to play many characters.   Often it slips from one into another.   (Pulling the Child up stops this easy imaginative flow.)

3. Audience may be a distraction.   (I do not base my conclusion on this

---

[1] For fuller consideration of the value of such work see Chapter VI.

example, though a clear one, but on twenty years of careful observation.)

4. A Drama expert is not necessary to help develop Child Drama, but a human being, responsive and sympathetic. (Add Drama experience, too, and the result may be even better. Drama experience without Child knowledge is valueless, and may even be harmful.)

5. The Child is happy about such experiences.

6. A Child may be quietened by such nurtured activity.

7. A Child may develop remarkable ability to invent good, interesting or exciting situations.

8. A Child can obtain a full physical and emotional experience. (It is doubtful whether it can obtain it so well in any other way.)

9. There may be sympathy, co-operation and a self-discipline in this Play, which is based on liberty but *not licence*.

The accompanying picture is the Child's illustration of the Episode of Hook. (See Plate 27.)

Child : " You see there are nails all over his body to make sure that he does not get away."

Note this is an added creative piece of imagination not in the original improvisation. It may be of interest that this particular Child shows affection by pushing people in the tummy and chest where the pattern of nails has been drawn in the body. This particular crucified figure of Hook has been pierced many times. Why? Out of love?

Child (continuing) : " There is only one nail in his left hand, as most people are not so strong with that hand. But on the *other* side he has a hook, and that's metal, y'see, so he had to have a nail through his arm."

Note the extreme logic and careful thought which has arisen from the experiences. And " he had to have a nail ", not " I put a nail ". The thing is a *sincere reality*—not a personal whim. That is what brings quality to acting developed in this manner.

Child : " Underneath is a little rabbit in his house, with lots of beds for his family. He is all warm in there, but above the ground old Hook is hanging—hanging on the Cross. And it's raining."

These last words contain the familiar ring of poetry to be found in good out-flow when Children thrive in confident freedom. There is a Biblical flavour about their simple strength. This is the way to obtain good English, not by directive speech training. And as for the rain, there was a storm when Christ died, too.

PLATE 27

Captain Hook crucified. (*See* p. 252.)
Photo by Victor Thompson

PLATE 28

PLAYING OUT OF DOORS. God's voice speaks to Noah.

The dove is freed from the ark. Example of Running Play. See Description in Chapter III. (*See* p. 64.)

Noah and family begin to build the ark. Note circular shape which so often appears in Child Drama. (*See* pp. 25–27.)

Photos by kind permission of the Educational Drama Association

Imaginative Play being Stimulated by an Idea from Immediate Surroundings

This is so easy that it often happens by itself ; at other times suggestion can help.

The family of four and myself were present.

Child : " If that cat tries to sit on my doll, clap at it with your hands like this."

The Child then clapped several times in an upward thrusting movement, very beautiful to behold, smiling at each clap.

Child : "Oo, that was like a cracker. Here's a cracker for you."

Twenty-one imaginary crackers were then pulled, and we all found caps, brooches, whistles and masks, in silent play. The masks were the most successful because when you had adjusted the " elastic " behind your head it offered great opportunities for making an interesting face, which was held until the imaginary mask was " taken off ". In this way we relieved our feelings tremendously in unspoken language, and entered into portrayal of a number of interesting characters in a short time.

If this had been stimulated by something or someone at school, it might have so happened that paintings or drawings of the characters, or scenes containing them, would have followed. The class might have been sent away to write a story about some of the people. The Drama enthusiast might have achieved real masks, painted and cut out by the Children. This achievement, however, would not necessarily be a triumph. It is merely the materialising of an idea, a normal development from Play, *and should not be considered more important than the original pulled face, which was the true experience.*

What follows the experience should be fulfilment, and it must be natural, voluntary, co-operative and not forced.

On this occasion, however, it was at tea, and that piece of enriched life having been lived, contentment brought the ever-accompanying calm, and the meal was set upon and devoured systematically in silence. That was certainly fulfilment.

Play to Music Background (3)

Cast—Girl aged six, boy aged five.

Girl : " The king will go riding with his speshull agent—Dick Button."
They rode for twenty minutes, galloping round and round without a word, to

Riding on a Blue Note (Ellington version).   Rest and pause for breath came only when I put on the record again.   At the end of that ride I, who had merely helped to supply the sound, felt as if I could go no further.   The Children were apparently much refreshed and wandered out of the house, chattering, to cook mud pies behind a hedge.

Play to Music Background (4).   *Sixes and Sevens*

I put on a record of the Intermezzo from *Escape to Happiness*.   The Children were not very interested at first.   They eyed me and the record.   Then I bent down and waved my arms and fingers in time to the music.
Self: " I am flowers in the wind."
This remark might be somewhat open to doubt by the adult mind, but Children see farther than the mere outside.
A little girl moved towards me.
Little girl: " Yes.   And the sun is too hot for you, isn't it ? "
Play had begun.
Self: " Yes, but the clouds help."
Another Child: " How ? "
Self (waving frantically and sagging alternately) : " When they cover the sun.   It's cooler then."
1st Child (miming watering can) : " There, have a drink.   There's a nice big drink."   Other Children then began to water me with buckets, cans and hoses, all mimed.   I began to sag.
A Child: " Hey, grow up.   What's the matter ? "
1st Child (now stage manager, producer and " directions ") : " You say —' you've got too much water ' ."
Self: " I've had too much to drink.   We poor flowers don't like too much water when the sun is on us."   (Simple gardening instructions.)
A Child: " Leave them alone a bit."   (Note the easy acceptance that I am plural, and the ever-present sense of fair play ready to be developed.)
Another Child (Fair play and leadership stimulated) : " Yuss, I am the gardener.   Stand back, everyone."
A ring was formed and, in complete silence, I began to grow slowly to the music.   Absorption was intense.   Suddenly a Child produced a bit of stick.
Child: " Here, lend us your torch."
A metal reflector was handed over by another Child and fitted on to the end of the stick.

(Then to me) : " This is the right amount of water."

A water squirt was then mimed, with noises. Several Children took up the noise, keeping together and working up quite a gusto of squirt in chorus.

I began to smile. The record was nearing the finish. I stood full up and flung my arms wide.

One or two Children : " Aw ".

The music stopped.

The Children stood around for a moment, then most of them ran off, miming squirts at each other. A little girl came up to me.

" Jesus has his arms like that," she said, and pressed a crumpled piece of paper into my hand.

I unrolled it later. It was a lovely present. Before me was a thin flower with long black hair, many fingers on its branchy arms, and it was smiling at the sun.

No one ever knows what will happen, if anything, and it is often dangerous for an adult to try to join in. We make better properties than anything. Perhaps on this occasion the flowers were in the nature of a theatrical property to start with, and so they kindly accepted me. This is always a great privilege.

Play to Music Background (5)

The story : A good father dog and a bad mother dog put their little puppy over a wall where the wolf was. The wolf is after the puppy all the time, but father dog protects it. Father dog and the puppy finally shoot the wolf, who dies at the end of the record.

Cast—*Child :* Puppy. *Self :* Father Dog and Wolf.

The play was repeated three times in exactly the same way. There are no words, only growls and squeaks.

First performance this day was to a background of *Wiggle Woogie* ; second to *One-o'clock Jump* ; third to *Swinging the Blues.*

There was a fearful death fight this last time, to the noisy drums at the end of the record, which made for very good shooting.

It will be understood, of course, that by " performance " is meant really " experience ". There was no audience. But this piece of Play had been done before, and its repetition in such remembered detail changes its classification from Play to *a* play. It is important to note the distinction, without necessarily believing that the piece is now more important. This is the sort of error that our own adult taste may lead us into. The first improvisation is probably the most important of all.

The occasion when this piece was first improvised was when Mr. Brian Way, Director of the West Country Children's Theatre, came to stay with me in order to go into the needs of Children (all ages) in detail, and to discuss their application to Children's Theatre in general. We talked for hours, using models occasionally for types of flexible stage and for use of floor space. I then invited him to join in an improvisation, for experiencing it oneself is very important. Being an extremely intelligent Child-lover, he bravely accepted. The story was developed by degrees by the Child's suggestions.

The Cast was as follows : Father Dog—Brian Way.
Little Puppy—a Child (age 6).
The Wolf—Myself.
Mother Dog—Nobody. " She is too bad."

The sofa was the wall. Mr. Way shot wolf clean through the chest as he was skulking along the window seat. He and the Child made a sort of fortress of the sofa and were firing over the back. Wolf died in a pool of blood in the middle of the floor, to the last strains of *Lazy Boogey* (Billy Penrose version).

NOTE ON BACKGROUND MUSIC

It may be wondered why the background music mentioned is often jazz. Why not better music ? it may be asked. Different music can and often should be used, but jazz is a happy sound and should not be despised. It contains a message of hope, even when it laments. The obvious time beat catches the Child's attention. The percussion sounds are recognised, and I am not at all sure that the undercurrent of prayer and slavery are not perceived half-consciously, too. The music is primitive and often very descriptive. Added to this, it arose from an improvised form.

Let me make it quite clear that this is a consideration of " hot " jazz and swing music, not dance tunes.

The young Child in particular is not often taken in by sentimentalised " sweet " music. Much of this appears to it to be as boring as an intellectual slow movement from a symphony. The music must be good of its kind, and even here one can help to form taste and judgement by carefully selected records of the best players.

Hot music is one small part of the experience of life. It is simple and quite different from the sophisticated wail to which we are more accustomed.

Appreciation of " good " music as background comes slowly and should not be hurried. In the early stages, music with a pronounced beat should often be used until the calmer moods can be appreciated and expressed at some length ; this should be expected any time from about six years on-wards, and comes with the dawn of seriousness which develops into such beauty in the seven-to-eleven age group.[1]

No particular plea is being made for the use of " hot " music. Other music is more generally used to encourage Child Play, but, just as it was once necessary to explain the beauties of primitive Drama (at least to point out that improvisation is important), so I merely add that primitive Music, which is truly based on an improvised form (and for that reason a sincere expres-sion), is not " altogether unimportant " either. It has its own uses, its own beauties and its own aristocracy. Those who do not like this idea will no doubt search amongst the " hit " writers of earlier ages, for the best musicians have nearly all been writers of dance tunes, and some of them very popular too. But the task will be harder, because the great masters were intellectual and in that sense sophisticated. What a music specialist finds a jolly tune is often doleful in the extreme to the man in the street. Unless exceeding care is taken over choice, the Child in the play-room will find it even more dreary because, for the most part, great music does not *begin* to express the things with which the young Child is concerned. Why should it ? It was written by great men, not little people. When the Child enters its " dawn of serious-ness " it may be ready to start searching amongst the great truths of great men.

Another form of musical background altogether is improvised playing on the piano. This has the quality of non-restraint when accompanying the Child, and offers greater freedom. It is valuable before the age of six years. But few people can do it well, and often the Child needs the discipline and inspiration of sound which it moves *to*.

When it no longer needs the discipline it is free to be free, and sometimes moves off the beat or is slow in changing tempo. But recognition of change of tempo and mood are not a bad thing. They are necessary as a Child grows older.

We are entering here again on the very delicate balance between liberty and licence. With a bad improviser on the piano you get licence, and liberty is lost. With a sensitive one you get liberty.

But at any age when a Child is searching for the security of a pronounced

[1] See " Observation," Chapter II.

time beat (not at all unassociated with the birth of interest in mathematics), carefully selected gramophone records are very important. Their subtle dogma has an undoubted effect upon behaviour and helps to create obedience.

This may be of comfort to those who are still unsure of activity methods in general, when considering work in schools.

Out-of-school adult attitude is often more generous.

YOUTH CLUB REPORT

To show the development of this work at a later age, I include here one report of a youth club. We find a continual interest in domination of space, but a marked progression **towards** " theatre " as the adult understands it.

Evening in a Youth Club

This was a first experiment by a teacher, of using with youth age what is more normally accepted as a form for young Children. He had tried to produce a whole evening of work in the arena form.

The first half of the programme was dramatic movement to a musical background. The room was arranged with chairs all round a space left in the middle. There were three rows of seats at either side of the hall, and about ten at either end in a semi-circle ; one of these ends was on the proscenium stage.

After the National Anthem, the lights faded and narration over a microphone started on black-out. The actors took their places in the gangways and the lights faded up on Scene 1 : Four husbands were walking about, absorbed in the sound of rhythmic baby cries. A nurse entered with a baby, followed by other nurses from the gangways. One husband was left alone in the arena, utterly distracted. This was a good portrayal of mood, and relation to music was highly satisfactory. Four other nurses made an entrance from different angles, each with a child. Four children were placed in the father's arms and the father collapsed under the burden and was held up by the four nurses, who formed a sort of flower pattern round him. There followed a number of scenes in mime—fathers bringing up children, a throwing game, a morning walk.

There was complete silence in the hall ; the audience was absorbed after the first twenty minutes ; each round was applauded. The scene was lit up by lights on top of the centre of the hall.

At 7.30 p.m.—(a) Scene : " Out in the Fields." A group of boys and girls, aged about fifteen to twenty-five, wavered from side to side as the light faded up and fell on them. There were a number of moods expressed, depicting personal relations. Odd ideas worked into a sound background, and the floor was well covered and group sensitivity was fair.

(b) " Cricket Match." The boys were very lively, expressing extreme gaiety. The music accompaniment was quiet jazz. The movement slowly developed into a game of cricket. Various strokes were played, and finally a ball was hit very high. Being so close to the actors it was easy to watch with them the ball which was not there. They moved towards the centre trying to catch it, and as it came down they knocked their heads together. The ball fell uncaught and the players flopped down on the ground. Blackout.

(c) " In the Park." Various groups expressed such things as old men, gentle ladies, shy maidens, and lastly a special dance in silence. This last was an excellent characterisation and moved the audience to a spontaneous burst of applause.

(d) " Shipwreck." An older man as ship's mate walked amongst men hauling fish. I saw some rhythmic netting. Only the man amongst the boys was lacking in group sensitivity—I noticed him bumping against the others three times, but it was interesting to see that he showed more force in interpretation than the younger people. The space was excellently covered all the time, and, as I was considering this, the sailors were flung to the ground by a heavy wave. Absorption in characters at this point was fair. The change of mood was not outstanding, and the dramatic effect would have been greater if lights had flashed on and off as lightning during the storm scene. The lights faded out for night.

When they had slowly faded up again, as the sun rose, we found only one survivor, who tried to revive a number of his mates. He found one alive, but this one eventually died also. The survivor then walked slowly off. (I have seen this more effectively done by boys aged seven to eleven, who all survived the storm and saw " land " next day through a dirty school window. It was a Promised Land.)

Morning came and the survivor was discovered alone in the centre, after narration had told us what had happened. Music changed, and other men entered as natives. They stalked him, but he showed them a flash-lamp, at which they were over-awed and fetched him food. I noticed at this time that the audience was too big for the actors to hold fully. They had not enough experience of playing in this theatre form, and absorption was only great enough to hold a comparatively small audience. This was slightly disturbing as those watching began to cough.

The witch-doctor began to move in the centre, the natives grouped around him doing a tribal dance, rising from a kneeling position with hands over their heads. Pattern work was good, foot work was poor. To start with, the audience found this dance funny, but as it continued they became quieter. Some of the girls dancing were in slacks, some in shorts and some in dresses. Those in dresses seemed to find them a help and danced much better.

The castaway appeared in one corner and was brought in by a number of natives. He over-awed everyone by his torch, and they took away the totem pole (a human) and put him in its place. Then the torch gave out. The natives seized him and put back the totem pole, but the inevitable girl cut his bonds and helped him to escape from the opposite corner of the arena to which he had entered. When the natives came back they tied this girl to the totem pole and the dance was resumed. All the actors now danced anti-clockwise, and the light of day faded slowly on the despair of the girl. This faded into narration. It was explained how the castaway sailed off in a native boat, which happened to be lying idle on the beach.

(e) " Mayfair Saloon." Girl shop assistants were discovered cleaning and opening shop. Their actions were unsatisfactory. They were not giving enough thought to what they were doing, and the audience immediately sensed this and began to get bored. They continued moving and coughing until a lady came into the shop and tried on a dress ; immediately they became interested and silent. One of the shop girls laughed at the lady when wearing a funny hat which we could not see. The lady was furious and, although the other shop girls tried to prevent her, she walked out and the light faded.

The narration before this scene was still talking about " I ". It seemed to me that " I " was connected with the sailor, but I did not think the sailor appeared in this scene and the narration became redundant.

(f) " Moonrakers." There was a half-light and a nice entrance, from one corner, of a long line of men describing a snake pattern on the floor. The moon rose suddenly and all the smugglers fell prostrate. They started to hide their ill-gotten goods, and pretended to be doing other things as three excise men came on the scene. There was excellent change of mood at the exit of the excise men. (About now I found myself longing for some speech.)   Just then the smugglers made a beautiful group exit carrying their stolen goods.

(g) " *Life on the Ocean Wave.*"   Various duets and relationships between the sailors were noticeable.   Clearly one or two people was the right number of actors for the space allotted for playing in, and it was a relief to see only two people after so much crowd work.   Arena theatre presentation needs change of every kind in movement, speech, music, lighting and grouping ; it is through such contrast that a long programme can hold our attention.

For this evening's entertainment there were too many people acting for a prolonged period in a small arena, and this gave one a feeling of mental indigestion—it would have been far better in a bigger place.

During the latter part of this scene a slim dark girl, about sixteen, with slim-fitting white shorts and blue blouse, with a handkerchief over her face, vamped a thick-set sailor in light blue shirt and trousers.   The mood was excellent and imaginative, with quick small contrasts.   Backs were shown a little too long to one portion of the audience.   This was the first time in one and a quarter hours that I noticed any discomfort at backs being turned towards me.   The scene ended in a lively movement when the girl discarded her veil.   The sailor then made advances, received a quick slap in the face and made a hurried exit.   The sailor gave the impression of being much more experienced in life and was able, therefore, to add greatly to the interpretation.

The narration at this point had become somewhat dispirited.   By nine o'clock a great number of people had risen out of their seats to climb up on to any higher place they could find, such as the old proscenium stage, radiators, piled forms, making for themselves the type of gallery which is really necessary for this work, i.e. a raised place so that one can look down on the movements.   Lighting can then easily be done by spots below audience eye-level.   But it is important to note always the difference between method of training which is *preparation*, and the final detail necessary for *production*.   Many faults of this evening should normally be part of the experience of groups and individuals in the hall and classroom, and will be perhaps passed over during early rehearsals ; but these, of course, must be polished away before production takes place.   Freedom for acting without audience and for early rehearsal ; polish for production.

(h) " *Church Yard.*"   A nice oval grouping of figures with outstretched arms, representing trees and tombstones.   A dog came in sniffing round, and a ghostly figure suddenly played a fiddle at him. The dog exited, scared. Two lovers came in and embraced. They were frightened at the place and went out. Then came a drunken man, but when he realised where he was he became extremely frightened and tripped over a grave. The ghostly figure played a fiddle at him and he ran away rapidly.

Trees and tombstones then appeared to come to life, and the result was a ghostly dance, but not dissimilar enough from what we had seen before. This could only have been effected if excellent lighting, sounds and music had been used.

The sun began to rise. By the dawning light the figures took their places once again. The dog and the " drunk " came back, the " drunk " to sleep, the dog to sniff happily around and move as happily off again. Black-out.

At the end one felt that the dancers, although they had made an extremely interesting attempt at it, were not quite up to the standard of giving such a large number of different interpretations as were required to fill so long an evening.

(i) " *The Wraith of Wrath.*" A play produced in the arena form. It was a relief to hear speech at last, in contrast to so much dancing. The lighting was overhead centre, and a red glow for a fire at one of the longer sides of the oval. The light fell on players' faces in a nice way. Unfortunately it fell on the faces of a number of the audience too, because they were not raised in a gallery. The play was much more intimate than the dance had been, and I felt it would have been more pleasant to be much closer, whereas for the dancing I had wanted to be farther off. Excellent use was made of all parts of the floor. It soon became clear that this could have been better produced in the oblong than in an oval. Light from the fire need not then have fallen on the faces cf the audience, and we could have felt the fire coming straight from a wall.

During the play, two men dissolved to one end of the oval and mimed billiard playing, during an important scene between an older man and a girl. Although this was a nice idea and worked in naturally, my particular line of sight showed the movement immediately behind those speaking, and it seemed an unnecessary distraction. The producer had here not known how to deal with these two actors, or had been tempted into this mime usage.

A long, slow entrance was made by a young girl seeing a ghost. This was quite wonderful and could not possibly have been so effective in any other theatre form. The actors were all absorbed. A ghost entered in full light.

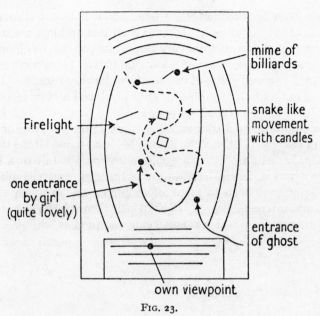

Firelight

mime of
billiards

snake like
movement
with candles

one entrance
by girl
(quite lovely)

entrance
of ghost

own viewpoint

FIG. 23.

I found this light too strong for this moment of the play. The audience was silent, but, although they were held, I felt it would have added considerably to the play if either half-light or clear spotlights had been used for this entrance. The scene ended and a short interval was announced. This appeared to be disastrous to the continuity of the play, for what had just been built up was entirely thrown away. The time was now 9.45 p.m., and as I sat there I wondered how the scene could ever be built up again.

Scene 2. (A year later, the announcer has told us.) It is a very pleasant sensation being one with the actors as they move closely to you. The arena offers much that the close-up on the film offers, but with added effectiveness of reality as well as imaginative show which includes real actors. At only one period so far during the play had I noticed a person's back being turned towards me. That was when the young girl said some very important words, and could have moved round so that all parts of the audience had a chance of seeing her facial expression. All doors were mimed, and the pace of the show was a little slow in places. This is a normal fault in amateur production, but it seemed far less a distraction than it would have been on the proscenium stage. The extra detail offered us by the closeness helped here.

The scene built up its atmosphere again about half-way through, and the audience was utterly absorbed. I found their feet and legs a nuisance when the lights were up. The answer every time is (in the ring or oblong form) for the audience to be raised, but even a low ring barrier (as at a circus) would be helpful. Much use was made of candles in a darkened scene. The drifting movement of actors holding these candles produced a type of beauty quite unobtainable on the proscenium stage.

The scene built up to a tremendous climax at the end, finishing with the chief actor of that part of the scene having his back to me all the time. As he fell forward, the light from the fire glimmered on the hilt of a knife in his back. There was a fearful scream from the girl, and the play finished. There could not have been so great an ending on any ordinary stage. It is the curious and interesting angles of sight which enrich the play for us in the enchanting theatre form which is now being accepted as " arena ".

CHAPTER XVI

CHILDREN'S THEATRE

THERE is much talk and propaganda going on just now under the heading of "Children's Theatre", but people do not always mean the same thing by it. These are some of the things they do mean :

1. Children acting to Children, in the proscenium form.
2. Children acting to adults, in the proscenium form.
3. Adults performing plays for Children :
   (a) Big plays, big productions, in large theatres to large numbers— acting at them.
   (b) Small plays, small productions, in small rooms—amongst and *with* Children, not at them.
4. Children acting in " productions " in the arena form, watched by large or small audiences.
5. A large building of which grown-ups can be proud.
6. A small building where Children can be happy.

Types 1 and 2. There is something to be said for older Children acting for other older Children in the proscenium form, but only because the sort of training suggested in this book is not yet used everywhere, and there should be no sudden break away from tradition when Children have not been allowed to develop their own Art Form. But where this activity is contemplated an apron stage jutting well into the audience would be a beginning of better things.

For juniors, however, such activity is really sad. Some of my most uncomfortable moments have been when watching the unnatural efforts of young Children to disport themselves in front of an audience in a proscenium production (often in our plays), when one knows what lovely work they can do under the right circumstances. It is just the same as looking at the dry dead leaves that Children had to draw before Child Art was understood. Even Children up to fifteen are likely to show off if adults are present in the audience ; they find it difficult to get really into a part and their acting deteriorates.[1] When young Children act before grown-ups, they are often disturbed by the adult laughter, and spend a good deal of time smiling out at their loved ones or grinning cheerfully at their stage companions. This is a sort of social affair, a dress parade. It has nothing to do with theatre. It is neither acting nor art. A number of courageous teachers and parents are beginning to notice this and to consider what improvements can be made.

Type 3(*a*).   The idea of Children's Theatre that still holds powerful sway is that of the adult team acting to Children.

At the basis of this activity, if we are honest, is the idea that Children do not really know what acting is or what beauty is, so ought to be taught them by seeing wonderful productions, thus adding to their culture. This is the sincere opinion of a number of professionals, and, where such productions are confined to Children of about twelve and over, not much harm is done, particularly if it is difficult for many Children to see these productions more than once or twice a year. But there are two rather negative effects, both of which are worse with Children under twelve :

(i) The Children copy these productions for long periods after, and the copies get worse and worse ; they lose confidence in their own ability to dress, make scenes and write plays.[2]

(ii) They copy the actual production *form* of the adult actor, and, when acting after seeing the play, they act at being the actors acting that play. They tend to stop their own real acting. The position is aggravated further whilst these large productions continue to play entirely in the proscenium form, and it is high time that professional actors, drama advisers and educationists got together to discuss what theatre form the productions should take for various age groups ; for the truth is that the Child, even of twelve and over, often does its work off as well as on the stage, and loses confidence in its own Art Form if it sees " perfect " productions by professionals in another acting shape.

What are we to do about this problem ? The big companies are here, and one would not want to destroy their efforts. Well, of course, they will probably stay, and in the meantime there are real signs that all those interested *are* beginning to discuss these matters in a friendly manner.

[1] I am not here talking of the professional Child actor who has to undergo rigorous training of a specialised type and who may hardly know anything of the joys of Child Drama.
[2] See Parts I and II.

Much more urgent is the case of professional and/or amateur actors performing plays in the proscenium style to *Junior* Children, as this means there is no proper understanding of the Child's needs or capabilities. It is sheer nonsense for any adult to think that he can show Children between the ages of six and eleven how to act by acting *at* them.

Type 3(*b*). If, however, he studies the Child's real approach to acting, watching it test out by turn the whole history of Drama and its forms of presentation, and then with very great humility attempts sometimes to act *amongst* Children and *with* them, performing almost as pockets of " resistance " (or more accurately " insistence ") amongst the little inhabitants of the Land, and sharing an experience with them at very close quarters—that is something quite different, and if not done too often may be of some value. But let us face the disturbing truth—the young Child will get on quite well without these efforts, though they do sometimes make it happy and, most important of all, they do not destroy, to such an extent, its confidence in its own Art Form. Why ? Because we are being fair to the Children and are doing it their way, not ours. (See Plates 33 and 34, opposite page 296.)

The actors in this type of playing must be specially trained in group sensitivity, and fully understand the methods of elastic forms of presentation and audience participation, again being well trained in avoiding obstacles without loss of character, and in avoiding treading on small heads, tummies or toes. Somewhat revolutionary ? Of course it is. The Child's world is quite different from ours, and we are, as yet, extremely backward in our efforts to explore that world. But we have one big excuse—we are grown-up.

Type 4. Here we have an extension of the Child's own Art Form, and a sincere attempt to expand the work of classroom Drama and Children's Festivals. There is continuity of the old tradition that there must be a " production ", and that this must often be dressed, and audiences are usually present. The *advantages* of this type are that people are trying to find out more about Child Drama, and are offering Children more space, without too sudden a break from former teaching. The *disadvantages* are the presence of an audience not trained in how to behave in the presence of Children acting, and not knowing what to look for, thus inducing the wrong atmosphere—this will, of course, improve in time—and the tendency to curtail the Child's freedom by polishing the wrong things and, in some cases, by too much dressing up.

Type 5. A large building of which grown-ups can be proud cannot accurately be said to be a Children's Theatre.

Type 6. A small building, where Children can be happy, may vary from a room to a medium-sized hall of special design.[1]

A compromise version of Children's Theatre *type 6*, and even to some extent of what a few people have in mind regarding *type 5*, may be found in the following reprint [2] of parts of an article I was invited to write in January 1948 :

" Children's Theatre is a *Land* not a building. It is the Land of Imagination and Emotion set in the Empire of Dreams. If we do not realise this, or worse, if we do not want to realise [it] because of our own blind adult conceptions, we shall get the wrong sort of theatre and it will not be a children's one at all. There is a danger of its becoming merely the sentimental symbol of those who are no longer young, the showcage for little dead puppets directed by us, and not by their own delight. . . .

" Real Children's Theatre has hardly been conceived yet. It should be something quite different from what we know. It may be that the theatre of the future will not have a stage because future generations of actors will no longer tolerate such absurdities. If we are thinking of a building for children, one thing is certain : the built-up stage, one end of it, should not be the most important item. It should be as elastic as possible, with many rostrum pieces and good floor space, with possibly a gallery running round the greater part of, say, an oval hall. A limited audience could look down, less noticed, upon the group patterns and verbal outbursts beneath. Chairs might be kept in side rooms ready for the occasional more formal show. A good canteen, comfortable changing-rooms, bright colours, a size-convertible auditorium, good air-conditioning and plenty of rooms off, away from the main hall, to chatter in and continue improvisations, are important characteristics.

" I was invited lately by the directors of the Young Vic and West Country Children's Theatre Companies to give my ideas for the best

[1] *Since this was written, a new and exciting development has taken place at the Drama Centre in Birmingham, where the Educational Drama Association has started a Children's Theatre evening. Here, first junior, and then senior Children perform their own dramas for an hour or more; there is no audience, as all the Children come to act.*—EDITOR.

[2] From the Educational Drama Association's magazine *Children's Theatre*. Reprinted by kind permission of the Editor.

immediate development in this country. I answered that there should be :

" 1. Professional " A " Companies (since they already exist) show-ing occasional big productions to older children (children to the theatre).

" 2. Local professional or amateur ' B ' companies, on the lines of the West CountryTheatre and the late Pear Tree Players, which take Drama into the classroom (theatre to the children).

" 3. A nation-wide education of teachers in Drama method, the core of which would be the full realisation of the importance of mime and free dramatic play as stimulation to scholastic attainment, balanced happiness and pre-conditioning for obedience."[1]

There are a great number of professional teams which claim to have built up suitable programmes for Children, but, apart from the fact that we should not overestimate the value of theatre played to Children anyway, the number of these teams in England that, at the time of writing, have any pre-tensions whatever to a knowledge of Child need, could be counted almost on one hand, certainly on two. When I was asked to speak on Child work at the first British Theatre Conference (1948), only one other person supported me. He was not an actor. Yet a number of actors came up afterwards and said how interested they were to hear these ideas, which to them were new.

Since then, however, the director of one of the biggest professional com-panies has almost entirely swung round to my own view,[2] at least for the younger Child, and other companies have been kind enough to form a link or to make inquiries. We must still be very careful, though, of " fully educa-tional " play-bills. I do not want to suggest that Children do not obtain pleasure from seeing theatre, but I do suggest that they can obtain more

[1] These three points were, of course, suggested during a conversation chiefly centred round Children's Theatre as acted by adults to Children. The order of the three points is not necessarily the order of importance. Considering all Children's work as a whole, apart from this specific context, it might be correct to say that order of importance should be three, two, one ; and this whole book, particularly Parts I and II, is in a manner suggesting further reasons for recognising the importance of point three.—AUTHOR.

Since this section was written, research into all three of these suggestions has been carried out continually in Birmingham at least, under the guidance of Mr. Slade and for the Educational Drama Association.

A variation of the first suggestion has also arisen in experiments in Manchester where small groups of adults have used stage and auditorium to produce a play with the whole audience taking part.—EDITOR.

[2] *Since this was written he has come round fully—but has stopped presenting plays.*—EDITOR.

pleasure in other ways, if aided ; that theatre is not yet thought out carefully enough for them—so is not the inspiration it could be ; and that if they see the wrong theatre at the wrong time their own work suffers. One cannot escape the conclusion, after long observation, that such theatre is not *necessarily* a helpful experience. This is exactly the parallel of what happens to Child Painting if the wrong visual experiences are given to Children too early.

There is one other form of pressure that teachers and educationists should constantly guard against. In the name of the " theatre " many mistakes are made, not the least of which is that it has come to be thought that we may not or cannot make our own pleasures, but must be dragooned into being an *audience* whilst someone else does the work. That, it would seem, is to be our main form of culture. " Audiences of the future ", we hear on every hand.

S. R. Littlewood, the critic, speaks of " tendencies of mass entertainment, against which intelligent criticism has always had to struggle and is still struggling".

A symptom of this is that Drama, we are often told, must not be used in any other way than going to see theatre, lest it harm the sacred word " theatre ". (The extraordinary and inexplicable energy of the amateur actor and producer should only be allowed rein as long as the professional theatre is copied, the argument runs.)

Even supposing one accepts as good what has to be watched or copied, one cannot escape the fact that, somewhere, one finds underlying this propaganda the word " box-office ". Perhaps this cannot be helped, for theatre is run as a business. But how far have we come away from real culture !

The whole attitude is wrong, and the Child in its natural environment rebels against it. Educationists may feel they have to stand quite firm here. Drama is the great science of doing and struggling. It has been, since the beginning of time, Man's activity, whereby he finds himself. Let us not make the mistake of going quietly, going in chains, going without thought, lest custom or regulation force us as doomed slaves to sit in serried ranks in the theatrical prison, after paying a savage fine at the door. Let us rather be free men and choose to go when and if the fare is good enough, and if we want to. Let us also be free and energetic enough to make our *own* fare if we want to. Above all, we must preserve this freedom for the Child, even if we have been gulled ourselves. Drama is " what you do ". Theatre has come to mean " what you sit and watch others do ". The first notion is essentially virile, the second is in danger of being decadent. Of course theatre has its place. It can be wonderful and beautiful, but it is only a small part of Drama, and we shall not get the balance right unless we see this quite clearly ; and, unless we do see, it is difficult to understand the supreme and innate culture of Child Drama. We have the chance of a sound culture in future generations if we go the right way about it, using our own minds and hearts, and helping Children to use theirs. But if we all just sit down and watch, future generations will only sit, probably even forgetting how to watch. Life is bound up with doing. "Drama" means "doing". "Theatre" does not.

Some professional actors do not understand this point of view, and it is not easy for educationists to know what is best to do under the circumstances. Perhaps we should remember that all healthy growing is a somewhat slow and organic business. Too much sun is not the best thing for a young plant. Because Drama is becoming recognised as a most valuable subject, there should be no sudden rush to the quickest and most obvious source of wealth. When dealing with Children, to be a brilliant actor is not enough, to be a wonderful producer is not enough, to own or direct a famous company is quite beside the point. Lengthy and detailed observation in the educational sphere is much more important. The real wealth of Drama is in the heart of the Child, and that is where we should look for it. The manner of handling is what matters, and, because of this, some of the best work with Children is done by experienced teachers *who really understand what they are doing*, and yet, strangely enough, have very little knowledge of Drama.

Nearly all " Children's Theatres ", started by professionals, have first started and then made some attempt to find out " Child need " afterwards. This is the wrong way round, I submit. There are very few companies that have not started in this way, and they had very great difficulties, because their theatre was so different from other theatres.

Is all this a condemnation of professionals ?

Of course not. They have their very particular place, but there should be no haste about what we do with Children. Professionals are busy people, and they are not always at home in discussions on education ; but educationists should always be consulted on Children's Theatre. I, too, started taking professional theatre to schools in the early thirties, and made the usual mistakes. But unusual opportunities for unbiased observation have come my way since then. Many, many Children and young people have my undying gratitude for showing me a completely New World.

I have been rather plain spoken about Children's Theatre because I know that most of those interested are very genuine about what they believe to be of value, and, by speaking freely of our thoughts on the matter, it has been possible to come to agreement on many points.

It might appear, then, that there is some good cause for thinking that: (a) Adult companies might play big productions occasionally to older Children, though production with some projection out into the audience would be a more suitable shape.[1] (The Intimate Theatre Group attached to the Highbury Little Theatre has begun to play in this style, and it is a very important experiment.)   (b) For younger Children, playing " amongst and with " (again not too often) is undoubtedly better.

As this latter type of theatre is less well known, I include some reports on a company that was finding its way towards the right method, and which subsequently invited me to make reports on its work and offer some training. The reports are in the order that shows how progression may be developed from the formal to the intimate and more elastic form of presentation. Playing is not fully elastic yet with this group, but there must be slow organic development.   The ideal of more active audience participation[2] is now gaining more ground, when actors are sensitive enough to break off and allow Children actually to join in.   Also I would prescribe trained actors who, in any place, could act an improvised play immediately, to or with Children, on a theme suggested by the Children themselves. This means taking improvisation seriously, not as a parlour game. It means regular practice.

For the work in school hours, further consideration of " teacher-actors " might be of value.   By this I mean persons who are primarily teachers (not necessarily school teachers) and know how to take work with Children. They come to the school with the freshness of outsiders and may be dressed up.   They come for acting.   They are trained actors.   Actor-teachers, a new profession.

Imagine the wonder of the spiral entry of happy Children finding one day, say, three dressed-up (or partly dressed-up) characters in the corner of the room.   The characters would then begin to act (or even be acting) and come out farther into the centre, as they sensed confidence grow out of wonder.   Then, as the Children clustered round, they would begin to speak to

---

[1] See considerable further discussion of this point in Parts I and II.

[2] *Since this was written, " audience participation " has been incorporated with some success in the Arena Theatre Company's production of* Pinocchio, *written and produced by Brian Way and Warren Jenkins.*—EDITOR.

them and perhaps ask them to join in Play. A half-mask, a hat, a sword might be handed out. This is the prelude to adventure and personally experienced Drama which has no boundaries. Approach can be quite direct by this method, e.g. *An actor* (to Child) : " Hey, Mr. Policeman, he's taken my hat. Will you arrest him ? Here's your truncheon."

If the Child is unreleased it may not start Play at once, but another may offer to be policeman. Others may join in. If not, the actor, unabashed, goes straight on : " Oh well, if you're busy I'll have to catch him myself." Then the fun would start. Music might be put on by the third actor and a stylised chase could begin.

Actor (to two or three Children) : " Ah, there's my motor." He gathers the Children round him and drives off with them hanging on to him. They are the motor.

This sort of approach seldom fails to stimulate Play and lovely experiences—it was one of the methods of the original Pear Tree Players with junior groups, and, not only does it stimulate great joy on the actual day, but often offers many further opportunities and suggestions to the teacher for carrying on after the actors have gone. The word " theatre" should not be used. The occasion should be thought of as : " Do you remember the day those PEOPLE came and we . . . " What did " we " do ? There is no end to this kind of Doing. This is Drama.

Much misunderstanding about showing plays to Children arises from the non-recognition of the two main types of Play [1] (personal and projected). Watching plays does not satisfy either, but, because of the intense need and desire for personal Play, we find pathetic attempts at major or minor forms of restrained or unrestrained audience participation—from jumping up and down to making faces and calling out—and the answer to inquiry is, " I would rather be acting than watching." But a continued habit of watching strangles the will to do, and a reaction towards something like the calm projected Play sets in. The Child thus tries to find satisfaction in the two ways that belong to its nature.

This calm is ultimately typified by the quiet staring and open mouth. But when watching a play the Child is not observing its *own* creation, so it is not even genuine projected Play, and, as it is therefore essentially non-constructive, apathy sets in. This is what brings laziness.

After this, creative Play will be considerably less vital, and at various intermediate stages we find copying. The actors are copied, and the shape

[1] See Chapters I–IV.

of playing. This can continue sometimes for years, to the utter destruction of new characters and situations.

As to seeing proscenium theatre too soon, we have already considered that the emotions and the material form may be linked, and that there is personal Play and projected Play, and that projected Play contains shapes which are the result of an inner state ; watching a play does not guarantee a balance of these, nor does it guarantee the right balance of in-flow and out-flow in learning, because general theatre conditions (certainly for younger Children) are far too cramping to behaviour. It may even be that the circle, which appears so often, is a form of unconscious Monument lying half-way between personal and projected Play ; this is linked with out-flow. Shape has a tremendous effect upon the Child, and, where conditions impose an unavoidable disciplined *in-flow* (as in ordinary theatre, because audience participation—out-flow—cannot properly take place), the Child's entire emotional state may be altered by the violent emotional education received through an outward shape, such as proscenium theatre, coming too early. At least it is most noticeable that Children grow up much more quickly when they experience proscenium theatre too early, and they are also noticeably more shallow.

So the proscenium should not be the form of exhibition until after puberty, and, as this still does not conform quite to the Child's natural creation, one cannot avoid casting doubt even upon that. At a time when perspective is being slowly approached, and the body itself is developing, it would seem that some projection out from the proscenium is nearer the need. It conforms with both conscious and unconscious shapes, and is nearer the Child's own Play at this time.

Some suggestions for a possible approach to both the younger and older Child may be found acceptable in the above, and, for the younger, the attitude of approach inherent in the following reports may prove of interest.

FOR CHILDREN UNDER TWELVE YEARS

Report on Children's Theatre Players (I)

We saw three plays—the story of *Cinderella*, a mime *The Dark Tower* and a play *The Blue Rock Inn*. The plays were presented by adults to Children in the proscenium form, and a number of adults were present in the audience.

The first play was quite charming, with a story-teller, music, dancing and colour built up quite simply. The coach was mimed, Cinderella stepping in between the two coachmen, and the imaginary door being shut. There was an experiment here in bringing the actors out into the audience, but the production would have been better if the whole show had been presented in the arena form.

The second play was a mime. The Children enjoyed the funny parts, but became slightly restless during the slower parts.

In the last play, which was a thriller, the young audience had had enough. The two Children in the play could not be heard for more than one word in twenty. The acting was dull during most of it, and brightened up only towards the very end. The best part (contrary to the opinion of those who feel unhappy about presentation in the arena form) was when the young actors turned their backs on the audience for quite a long time and threw stones, which did not exist, into an imaginary sea. Even though this was on the proscenium stage, it held us perfectly. It seemed that the Children. aged about seven to eleven, became tired after about an hour.

During the interval I walked round and asked a number of Children what they thought of the show.

Self : " Did you like that ? "

Answer from thirty-five Children : " Yes."

Self : " Did it worry you when the actors came down the centre ? "

Children : " No."

From ten asked : " What do you think about it ? "

A Child : " It's nice."

Another : " I like it."

Another : " They're closer."

Another : " Please, sir, it is more like what we do."

Another : " You would hear easier if they did that."

Another : " You could see the clothes easier and see what they're made of."

Another : " Couldn't they play near us all the time ? "

Twenty-one other Children were asked : " Did you like the actors coming near you ? " and all answered : " Yes."

Self : " Did you like the first or the second play best ? "

Fourteen out of twenty replied " the first ".

A Child : " I like some talking."

Another : " It is long when they don't speak. Makes it more lively to have some talk."

This was the beginning of the players' preparation for the right Child

Form, but even here the Children were so nearly participating, at the few moments when they were excited, that it would have been better for them to have been taking part. Their own answers, of which these are typical, also lead one to think that they would prefer to be closer to the actors and more a part of the play. Acting " at " Children by adults is not what is needed.

Children's Theatre Players (2): *After some Lectures.*

Adults were acting a play in the Chinese style to Children in a school hall. There was no proscenium, only background screens of painted scenery.

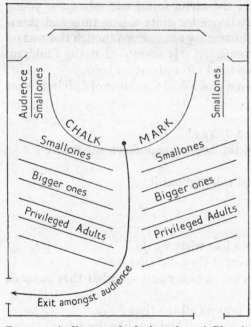

FIG. 24.—Audience and playing plan of *Play in Chinese style.*

The audience was seated in front and at the sides of a round-shaped playing space. A wide gangway was arranged.

The players needed more attack (attention flagged at times because characters did not get voices over), and should learn to be more elastic in movement, and more sensitive to judge the need of the occasion as it arises. For instance, an old man, whom the Children took very quickly to their hearts, had walked out down the gangway. The Children rose to view him all the way, and a teacher started saying : " Sit down, sit down." This was a great pity, as they would have sat down soon. Children often stare into space where loved ones have been, till they have had their fill ; then they come back from " the Land ". But during all this a character began to sing at the playing end, which was by now *behind* the Children, as they had all turned round, and some adults were perturbed that the Children took no notice of the singer. The gentle way for the singer to attract their attention would have been to have walked down the gangway singing, and to have returned, still singing, to the main playing area. Attention would then have been back by the end of the song without any fuss.

Some sellers of trinkets and coloured clothes came running in from the back offering them for sale to the Children. This pleased them greatly. Then their dear friend, the old man, came in. They were delighted to see him again, particularly when he said : " Be off, you young rascals ! " to a bunch of small boys. If there had been more room, these boys might have run to another part of the hall with him chasing them.

One or two small Children stole on to the playing space to peep down the gangway to see the old man coming. They were escorted off. Why ?

Other characters began to speak too soon sometimes, when the Children were enjoying a particular person. We must be very careful about timing in this way ; quite a long wait is sometimes necessary when Children are enjoying something very much. This is quite different from adult theatre, where good timing is very important in a different way.

Another point which should have been clear : the seating was practically like that in a proscenium theatre, though the players were acting in a horse-shoe-shaped space. The audience therefore *had* to stand at times, to see at all. Adults then shouted, " Sit down ", and the usual dumb animal look passed over the Children's faces as they obeyed mechanically. We should do everything to avoid spoiling things like this. If the players had acted along the length of one side of the hall, or in the middle, there could have been a wider near-circle, or a complete one, with *less rows* of chairs. This means easier sight—one of the great advantages of arena theatre.

Crashes on the gong or cymbal were used to help quieten the Children. This is better than shouting at them. Noises accompanied characters at entrances and exits, according to the convention of the play. There were some nice examples of audience participation when Children mimed making the noises they liked, particularly the cymbals. They joined in also with stylised hand and head moves at times.

Bottle-tops and cake-tins were used on the dresses, adding considerable richness.

Why did the Children love the old man so ? Because he was a charming character. He was simple and *was utterly sincere and absorbed the whole time*. Not for one moment did he try to show off. So he went straight to their hearts.

The character of an " author " had a good attack and often held the Children, even in speeches they might not have quite understood.

There were two funny magistrates with pompous walks. These were much enjoyed. They carefully avoided overplaying. The effects noises did not always back up the actors well.

The property man who behaved like a naughty boy was enjoyed too.

The best audience participation was when, near the end, the " author " said his oft-repeated words, " I bow ". Half the audience timidly joined in, but finally, the whole audience, rapt, said sturdily with the author, " I bow ". (I " bowed ", too.) The characters made an exit down amongst the Children. There began a faint clamour, but, as their loved ones passed slowly by them and out of their lives, the clamour swelled to a roar of cheering, which continued long after the characters had disappeared.

One false note was brought in. When the characters were introduced for the last time in a sort of curtain call without curtain, there was no clapping at first. We had our rare chance at this moment to get their true assessment of the worth of the players. They would, I know, have cheered or done something when certain characters appeared. This would have been absolutely right. But some kindly adult started a strong, resolute clapping to give a lead. All the Children then joined in and so, of course, we got no true assessment. Adults should be allowed in only if *quite silent*. We have to learn quite a new code of behaviour. It is something of a shock to find that most of us do not know how to behave at a Children's theatre.

The cheering thing about this evening was that the players showed real signs of beginning to act in a quite different, sincere way *with the Children*, not *at* them. We must train further in this and persevere. Next, we must learn to be elastic. After that we must learn judgement of when bad behaviour or audience participation is taking place.

The Children, except for the few rare moments mentioned, were not quite absorbed enough to avoid looking round when people came in at the entrance door. (Everyone in the audience came and went at will.) But there were discernible moments of genuine joy this night, quite unlike the crowd hysteria which the big theatres stimulate with their bogus follow-up of adult-inspired letters from Children, which players delight to receive. Alas, they mean nothing.

But tonight showed the beginnings of something real, something potentially great. It can only become great, though, if the players fully understand the instruction offered by the Child behaviour, and work hard to become masters of what they know to be the next steps in this great adult education. For it is we who must learn. The Children teach us.

Children's Theatre Players (3) : (*After some Training.*)
  Performance of Cinderella *at Children's Hospital.*   (See Plates 29 and 30.)

Some of the cots in the ward had been pushed together, and, in places, little groups of rather sad, quiet Children, obviously not too well, sat together, occasionally banging a heel against a chair, rubbing a nose or just looking.

Small tables had been put in the middle of the room as rostrum pieces. Enter the narrator, wearing a high hat and wonderful gown.   In the training and general consideration which the group has been doing with me, we have gone into the matter of sensing the atmosphere of a group of Children.   The narrator sensed at once the quiet, slightly listless feeling of the Children. She walked about, speaking quietly but clearly, improvising until she had the Children's attention.   (No brazen sudden " attack " on the Child's reserve.)

Then, *Narrator* : " I'm going to read to you.   Can you see what I'm going to read ? "   She held up an enormous book.

Children (near her and now interested) : " Cinderella."

Narrator began reading, and each character ran in from one side of the ward, was introduced, and ran out.

The play then started and broke from narration into dialogue.   Action took place down the whole length of the ward, working outwards from the high centre.   There was some nice rhythmic brushing by Cinderella, which went on just long enough for one or two Children to join in saying quietly, in time to the brushing noise : " Shush, shush " (audience participation). Then came the ugly sisters, both of whom are experienced in more formal productions.   They did not always make full use of all the space, but their work was absorbed and well in character.   One of them improvised lines occasionally with great success.

After their exit, the fairy godmother told us that she was going to get a fairy coach for Cinderella, only it was so very magic we wouldn't see it like ordinary coaches.   The pumpkin and mice were shown to the Children by Cinderella running all round the room with each.   Fairy godmother then did a dance all over the ward to soft music, " working magic ".   She made occasional remarks to Children near her.   This was very charmingly done, with full use of floor space.   Finally, the " pretend " coach arrived.   Coachmen mimed the opening and shutting of the door.

The ugly sisters had made an exit in the wrong place and had to re-enter there, but, on coming to the ball, made one of the most successful moments of

theatre by improvising the line : " Sister, you've brought us in at the back
door ! "

Two of the players, not yet fully used to the arena theatre form, were not
very sensitive about being seen from certain angles. Interestingly enough,
they forgot at certain times to act " in-the-round " and played as if still in a
proscenium theatre to the place where the narrator was sitting (the only
place where no audience was), largely, I suspect, because that is where I had
sometimes stood during my final rehearsal with them, and possibly also
because they entered from the other side and unconsciously " played out "
away from their entrance.   Apart from a few such mistakes, it was clear that
the actors were taking well to the arena form, and a quiet appreciation began
to glow in the faces in the cots.   It was an interesting individual feeling
coming from each little person, as the Children were not all bulging together
giving off a mass audience feeling.   It was quieter and more genuine than
anything I have ever experienced.

The performance went down a little near the end, but brightened up just
at the end.   The Children joined in three cheers for Cinderella.   Afterwards,
the fairy godmother and Cinderella went round to each Child and gave them
a little silver shoe, bought with a sum subscribed by the cast.   Nearly every
Child tried this little shoe against their own foot, both boys and girls.   Members of the cast went round talking to the Children.   Nearly every Child
wanted Cinderella (played by a young girl) to talk to them.

Three girls and one boy were distressed by Cinderella being so poor.

A little girl : " Her dress was in such rags ! "

Another : " I would have sewn up the hem for her.   I suppose she had
to look after those ugly sisters.   They *did* make her work hard."

(In the play there had not been much indication really that she worked
hard, except for the telltale hem.   But that rhythmic brushing, which com-
pelled some of the Children to join in, had brought home the message
tremendously.   This is the sort of truth we learn about Children's Theatre
from what is done in the classroom.   I have called it " the power of the time
beat and its imaginative association with words and action ", which I
suggest for classroom work.   It is an introduction to the love of sound,[1]
whilst the Child is in the stage of speaking chiefly with its body, which aids it
in speaking ultimately with joy from its mouth.)

From conversations with the Children we discovered that practically all
liked Cinderella best.   One liked the herald, another the ugly sisters best—

[1] For type of training see " The Teacher ", Chapter X, page 137.

PLATE 29

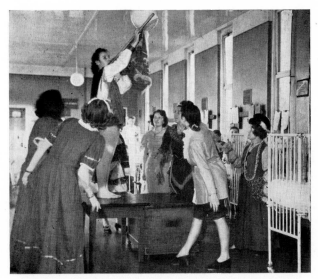

BIRMINGHAM CHILDREN'S THEATRE PLAYERS.
Proclamation of the Herald. Boxes and tables are used
to help the line of sight from beds during important
climaxes. (*See* pp. 279-282.)

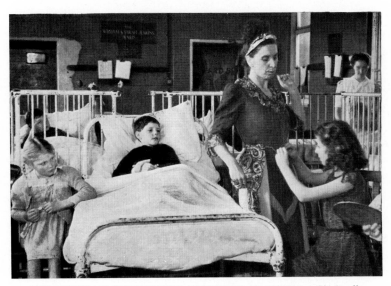

BIRMINGHAM CHILDREN'S THEATRE PLAYERS. Cinderella
helps an ugly sister. (*See* pp. 279–282.)

Photos by Reg. Cave

PLATE 30

BIRMINGHAM CHILDREN'S THEATRE PLAYERS.　The final procession.
(*See* pp. 279–282.)

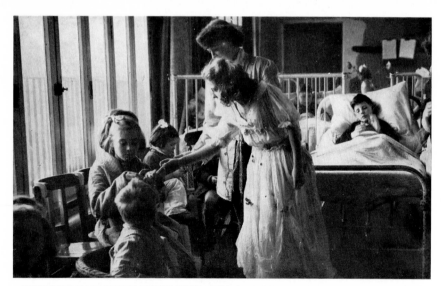

BIRMINGHAM CHILDREN'S THEATRE PLAYERS.　Cinderella presents little
silver slippers to each Child after the show.　(*See* pp. 279–282.)

Photos by Reg. Cave

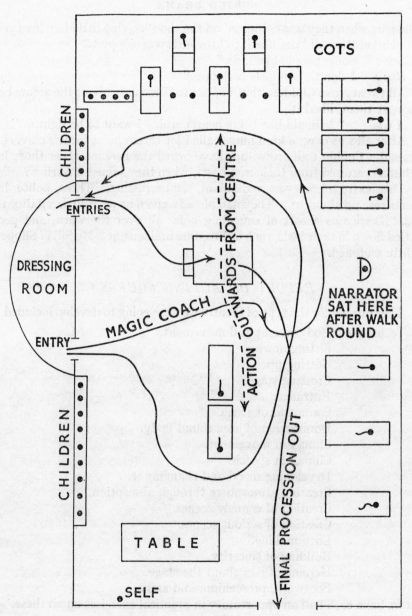

COTS

CHILDREN

ENTRIES

DRESSING
ROOM

ENTRY

MAGIC COACH

ACTION OUTWARDS FROM CENTRE

NARRATOR
SAT HERE
AFTER WALK
ROUND

CHILDREN

FINAL PROCESSION OUT

TABLE

SELF

Fig. 25.—Indication of shape of production of *Cinderella* in Children's Hospital.

"the part when they was crammin' on the shoe". One little boy (five years) out of all of them did not like it : " the girls was sloppy ! "

Self : " Some people like girls."

Boy : " I don't. All girls is sloppy."

All twenty-two Children that I spoke to personally about the actors being amongst them, liked it.

A Child : " I should like being nearer still. I want to be right *in*."

After all was over, a kind nurse called for three cheers for the players. I was sad. Couldn't all grown-ups have heard the genuine cheer those little ill birds mustered from their iron nests, when they joined in earlier ?

This extra cheer was redundant, embarrassing. Three polite little efforts rose up about us. They had already given us what little vitality they had. There was a sort of snuggling noise all over the ward, and people settled down in their beds, each one to stare in silence at " My Silver Slipper ", tightly clutched.

REPORT ON ACTING COURSE.[1]

The training for the type of theatre we were going to develop included :

Technique : Body weight and movement.
Sitting down.
Getting up.
Crossing stage.
Entrance.
Command of scene.
Domination of area round body.
Climax in movement.
Climax in speech.
Developing mood and changing it.
Creating atmosphere through absorption.
Creation of comedy scenes.
Creation of serious scenes.
Love making.
Building of sincerity.
Helping others about the stage.
Footwork, proscenium and arena.

Actors have each had an opportunity in practical exercises on all these.

[1] This report was made to the Committee of the Educational Drama Association.

We went very carefully into tempo and the use of sound—mood in sound and relation of right sound to scene. Much work was done on learning to play in an elastic form. We played numbers of the scenes whilst putting many obstacles in the way, so that actors could get used to avoiding them without spoiling their acting. Special time was given to actresses who might take men's parts as princes. The flow of language in improvisation improved enormously, and group sensitivity became quite good. It was even possible for someone to ride a bicycle in and out of dancers without their being upset or changing tempo. Numerous people had a chance of producing small scenes.

We dipped into created documentary plays, exercised on dramatised poems of different mood, expanded a scene from *The Dog Beneath the Skin*, spent the whole of one evening polishing technically a play in movement to narration and music, made up by members of the course. In fact, we developed the whole group slowly up to the point when script plays might be tackled, with continued reference to the general principles practised in improvised and other scenes.

It has been interesting to watch improvement and the absorbing of theatre knowledge, particularly of the arena and semi-arena form. Actors began to co-operate quite quickly in either dominated or free production. One or two, though, stood out as actors of a set type, and after all our work still quite clearly conceive of theatre as a somewhat rigid and directed affair, and I rather doubt whether they realise the extent of the training which was there for them to absorb. This is no criticism necessarily (though it is a very great pity) ; it depends largely upon previous experience and subsequent attitude to the work. It is interesting to note that Miss Lutley's [1] first arena production for the Children's Theatre Players was extremely well conceived, though here again one or two of the actors whilst playing seemed to have quite forgotten what we had practised at the course. Yet one thing stood out : the moments of improvisation during the performance at the hospital were often the best dramatic moments of the play.

Quite early in the course it became clear that it would not be possible to pick out ten members as a team at this stage, as had been suggested at one committee meeting. I therefore concentrated on the things which were needed most, and first of all tried to develop a good group spirit. It is not certain that a group so varied in experience can be welded into one, but I took note of the advice I sought from the committee early on in the course,

[1] At that time Programme Director, Birmingham Children's Theatre Players.

and have begun to divide out in my mind those who could and could not play together so well in certain forms, and I now feel that separate and further training in actually produced plays should be the next step. We are about ready for this now. Only just. We most certainly were not ready for it before now.

An Experimental Evening promoted by a Festival Committee normally concerned with Proscenium Theatre

A member on the committee of this festival had seen that there was something lost in Child Drama within the usual dominated production, and had arranged an evening when a few spectators (adult) sat on the stage, and the Children performed on an open floor space.

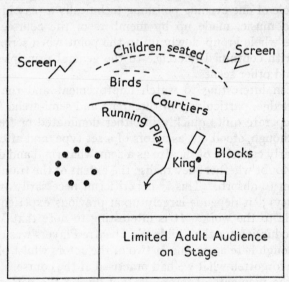

FIG. 26.—Play I in Festival Experiment.

1. *Age six to seven years. An Infants' School.*

The infants came into the room, and a Child rather self-consciously announced to the audience on the stage what was going to take place. The teacher sat on the floor with some of the Children and told a few other Children where to go. There was some choral speech, or rather a group of Children on the floor talking together, led by the teacher, saying what was happening. The rest moved and ran about the room, mainly in circles.

Absorption began in three and a half minutes. There was some " running play ", but this was not very virile. Some of the Children ran round and round until they became tired, and this part of the play then began to flag.

There was a little too much narration. This has the result of making Children conscious of the audience, and of course the idea of such narration means that the originators of the play had separate audience in mind, and had not fully understood the play without this narration, which nearly always makes the whole business a little unnatural.

This play had been thought of by the teacher and the Children together. The Children were dressed up, and, although this was nice to see, it evidently hampered their movement.

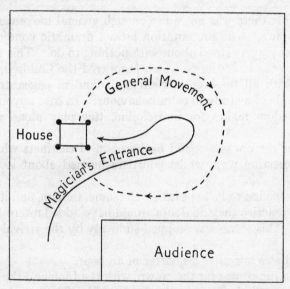

FIG. 27.—Play II in Festival Experiment.

2. *Age seven to eight years.*

There was much more absorption in the next play ; the Children were wearing masks, headdresses and notices on their tummies. Many of them were trees, and wore leaves on their heads and greenery round their wrists. On the whole, they were wearing too much, which made it almost impossible for them to move properly. There were, however, some very good moments in this. The house of the magicians was four human pillars holding a piece of material attached to their heads. They stood, one at each corner of the square. There was a magnificent magician's entrance. The movement was done to a background of music.

3. *The Lion and the Unicorn.*

This was really an historic pageant, and had been intended to be done in a field, but bad weather had driven it inside.

Somebody brought in two ladders over which was thrown black-out material. These were mountains. The whole play was dressed very well with lovely paper headdresses and masks, but such a number of Children were taking part in a confined space that at times there was a little confusion.

On the whole there was not quite enough general movement, but some very fair grouping. The presentation lacked dramatic content, in that a large number of players stood about with nothing to do. This was no doubt due, in part, to the headdresses which hampered the Children, beautiful as they were. With all these groups circling round in pageantry, we had a supreme example of a study in calm behaviour. In case anyone still thinks that some freedom makes for indiscipline, this play alone would be an answer.

At one time there was a sound background of castinets which was used in a most interesting way, whilst courtiers hurried about looking for the king.

The tempo tended to be kept rather the same, though, and if the Children had had more practice they no doubt would have added interesting rhythms of their own. This scene was stopped suddenly by the arrival of the town-crier.

Absorption was fair after a quarter of an hour.

There was a tug-o'-war for the crown, with the Lion and the Unicorn first in line, then many little figures following behind. The tug-o'-war was done to a clashing of cymbals. The struggle was brought to an end because it seemed to be decided to do something else, and a sort of rejoicing took place to music on gramophone records. Banners were suddenly shown, saying such things as " Long live Lion ", " Vote for Unicorn ".

There was a big display of circular movement, all the Children marching round. A joust was then arranged between the Lion and the Unicorn.

A watchful teacher moved a screen which was in the way of the group just after the Lion had won the joust. (This is just the sort of way that a good teacher should make judgements in this work, ever watchful to do and ever humble in retirement.)

There was some more marching round and then the play appeared to have finished. When it had finished, two rows of Children were seen to be sitting in the middle of the floor space. They were fully absorbed—so absorbed that it was at least half a minute before they awoke to find that the play had finished. This is another example of how Children go to " the Land ".

4. *Senior Girls. The Story of Jephthah's Daughter*

The audience on the stage was informed that this had been an improvisation on a play done once before. It was clear that some of it had been rehearsed, but most of the dialogue had still the freshness of real improvisation. There were very nice camels, which transported the judges. Two girls, the front one standing, the back one with back bent and holding the waist of the girl in front, made a camel. The rider sat on the bent back.

This was the first play of the evening which was not dressed, and the acting was far better. Great battles took place with such cries as : " God is be'ind us."

The action and movement were exciting, and there was a reasonably good flow of sincere language. So far, one might say that this was the most real approach to Child Drama in the evening.

5. *Junior School.*

The Children sat round in a circle. This play the Children had done before as a proscenium production during the preceding days of the festival, but had said of their own accord, " Need we have it on the stage ? " This was an improvisation, but it had been polished a little. The words had been grouped together by use, and extracts from a literary text were used occasionally.

6. *Alice in Wonderland.*

A wrangle took place between Alice and some gardeners over the colour of some roses.

A few properties were used here, but the Children were absorbed and unaware of the few adult watchers on the stage, and turned their backs to them, placing the properties so that the right side could not be seen.

A squad of club cards entered, singing. Many other things happened in a jumble, but finally the Queen of Clubs called in a loud voice, " Off with their heads ". There was a loud scream and all the Children disappeared. A most satisfactory ending to a most extraordinary show.

7. *Senior Mixed. Mime of Theatre.*

This was explained as a mime of a " theatre ". It was, in fact, a sort of dumb-show play.

It was the Children's own idea and they made up their own clothes by bringing assortments which their parents provided.

To begin with, a lot of chairs were brought in and placed, not (as one might think) in straight rows, but in a slight horse-shoe. (No doubt how they think a theatre of the adult type might be improved.) The " audience " entered first, in dispersed groups, good silent activity going on. Suddenly someone brought in ices, and nearly the whole audience jumped up and ran to form a queue. The ices were sold quickly and the " audience " returned

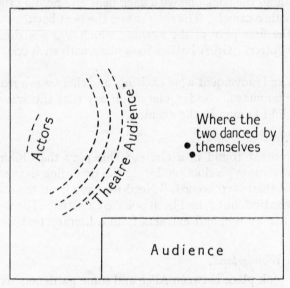

Fig. 28.—Children completely indifferent as to whether real audience could see or not.

to their seats. The " audience " had not considered the watchers on the stage at all, and most of them had their own backs or left shoulders to the adult watchers (us, the real audience). (See Plate 31 opposite.)

PLATE 31

CHILDREN'S FESTIVAL.
The circle. Note imaginative
cave in background.

CHILDREN'S FESTIVAL. Example of floor space being well
covered during a moment of some relaxation.

HILDREN'S FESTIVAL.
airs arranged for an impro-
sed play about the theatre.
pying adult theatre. (See
pp. 284–290.)

PLATE 32

Photo by Victor Thompson

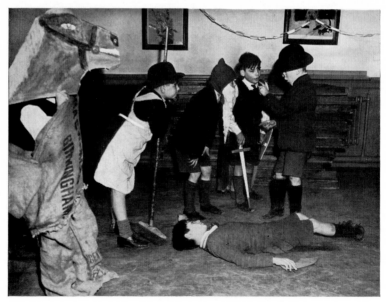

Children acting a story in their own genuine manner.

Photo by Victor Thompson

Sometime about now, though I could not see very well, the " play " commenced. A jester, clown, king, queen and dancers played before the " audience ". There was some quite good clowning.

Finally, all the actors came on and stood in a row. At once all the " audience " stood up too, and a Child from somewhere else ran to a piano in the corner of the room and played " Good Save the King ". The second this was finished the " audience " rushed out of the room. During the play, one small boy and one small girl, interested in the dancing of the actors, became absorbed and danced also behind the " audience ".

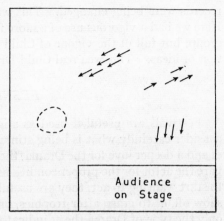

FIG. 29.—Dance I. An outstanding formation of moving groups.

8. Senior Girls. Dancing.

(a) We saw some quite pleasant dancing to a simple tune.

(b) The girls had heard the record of *The Sorcerer's Apprentice* and had asked to make up a dance to it ; we were seeing what they had made up after a pause of one year. The whole thing was very alive and full of joy, the presentation being somewhat stylised. Moves vigorous, fingers were well used, and all of the body beautifully expressive. There was absorption from the first.

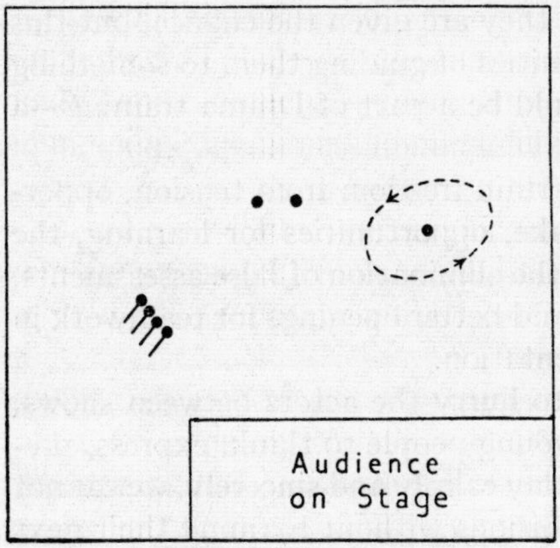

One nice bit was when four Children lay in a row on one side of the room, the magician and the apprentice were on the far side of the room, whilst another group of Children danced in a ring, so balancing floor space in an interesting manner.

The Children were still in their parts and continued to act even whilst

FIG. 30.—Dance II. Circle formation and parallel bodies on floor.

C.D.—19

records were being changed. This was particularly true of the apprentice. Here we had a vigorous use of a more formal type of dance by a slightly older group, but full of the vigour of Child creation with their wonderful association of ideas. This was real Child Drama.

FESTIVALS [1]

Festivals are useful if used as stimulation, but it is important that we consider carefully what is being stimulated. If it is a better understanding of and a deeper love for the Drama, then festivals are useful. If festivals prepare the actor for the proper conditions of work, and if they help young actors to start wanting to act, they are useful. But if they teach young people to show off, or to grasp after trophies, or to expect personal praise, or to play only the type of Drama the adjudicator will like, then they do definite harm.

A form of festival must be found which fosters the right motives. A step in the right direction is undoubtedly the non-competitive festival, where the teams come to do Drama purely for the love of it and to learn more about their art from a constructive commentator. There is no thought of placing, and less thought of drilling in production. Drama cannot really be assessed by numbers, and if it is, there is a tendency to lay too much stress on matters such as choice of play. Acting out the characters of their imagination is the important thing for young people, and it is far more valuable than pleasing an adjudicator's personal whim. Choice will come with time and guidance. Children will often choose competition if they are given the chance, but this may be because we have missed opportunities of guiding them to something better than the old tradition. This should be a part of Drama training—a guide to better things.

The non-competitive festival offers certain freedom from tension, opportunities for doing a thing for its own sake, opportunities for learning, the elimination of jealousy to a large extent, the elimination of false assessments, better chances for programme selection, and better openings for teamwork in production as against a " striving " presentation.

But even this type of festival tends to hurry the actors between shows, out of necessity, and if we are to teach young people to think, express, prepare in the dressing-room, and finally to play calmly and sincerely, we cannot persistently drive them into festival conditions without harming their next

[1] This article is the reprint of a Report to the National Advisory Committee on Drama in Education of *Theatre News Letter.*

step forward. For these and many other reasons, it is suggested that

(*a*) Festivals be used only for instruction and stimulation.

(*b*) Non-competitive festivals do this better than competitive.

(*c*) As soon as possible groups pass on to form the beginnings of little theatre groups, or teams to supply a theatre centre, or to prepare presentations for a specific audience.

(*d*) All opportunities should be taken at once to give the Child and young person what is *really* needed for them, rather than what is useful for the credit of organisers, advisers, or adult producers and teachers. Large festivals are useful for credit. Competitive festivals are more useful for credit. Let us leave credit out and see what we have left when there are no axes to grind.

Let us also examine carefully what the outlook of the young person is before contact with the advanced adult conception, and try to weigh up the value of spontaneous imagination against sterile intellect. Which would you mark the higher in an old-fashioned competition, and why ?

LET THE PEOPLE ACT

The following report [1] arises from an invitation to mention another band of players, the Pear Tree Players, with whom I was earlier closely associated. I consider to this day that as a team they produced moments of theatre of a standard which I never expect to see again. They played with and to Children, adolescents and adults. Their training, therefore, had to be very wide and varied. I know of no words to express my admiration for what they achieved. They were the first full-time professional company entirely devoted to educational work.

The magnitude of the influence of local drama committees and drama advisers is only rarely appreciated. The setting up of drama committees is the first serious attempt at wide and proper representation of interested persons and bodies, and the appointment of drama advisers constitutes the most important step in providing adequate training.

The ordinary professional actor cannot really do this advisory work because it needs a wide experience with a very special training and outlook. As the work gains growing recognition as part of education, it will call for even greater specialised training of those who intend to teach and advise. The two main effects that the work of advisers has had on the professional

[1] Reprinted by kind permission of the Editor of *Theatre News Letter*.

theatre are the stimulation of audiences and the growing dissatisfaction with the general standard of performance.

This is the background to the experiment of which I am writing. The background is as important as the experiment, which grew organically out of these conditions. It happened in Staffordshire in 1945. As part of my work, I had been running training courses for leaders. A few members of one group announced that they wished to become professional at the end of our run of *Strange Orchestra*, and asked me to direct their team. Nothing would stop them. Finally I agreed to train them further, although most of them had already worked under me for eighteen months.

The team came into being, and I insisted that it should be entirely autonomous under its own directors, but work closely with me. This was agreed ; the result was a most fascinating set of aims and principles. We planned to found a school which they wished me to direct, but in the meantime they wanted to use my approach and methods as their own, and to appear as an exhibition team. It was from this basis of the school that the idea of the Pear Garden arose, and we chose the name Pear Tree Players. Serious training started, every Sunday, every available free moment of the day and most evenings. As one of their aims was to break away from the proscenium arch and develop group work, they were drilled in group dance improvisation and every imaginable type of production, including the arena form.

After working at fever pitch for a considerable time, I considered the group ready to act anywhere to any audience. But they were not only actors. They had to be teachers too. They produced in youth clubs, made lighting sets and improvised. There were three to begin with, and finally six. From this experiment I was able to start the county paid panel, for which only trained people were accepted. We played all over the county, on flat floors, in barns ; we improvised, played excerpts and one-act plays.

In the course of a year, hundreds of people had seen numerous types of productions and heard many talks with illustrations. The interest stimulated was tremendous, but it was not a box-office success. I do not think an educational team can be. It must be aided by grants. It may be necessary sometimes to play to ten people only, or to a few children.[1]

Our team was never aided. It was an equal-sharing company and I paid the deficits and would be paying gladly still had I the money. When all that

---

[1] The words of the original manuscript were " with a few children " not " to a few children ". It is interesting that someone responsible for the final copy may have thought this was a slip, or was it thought that the average reader would not have understood it at the time ?

I could afford had gone, the members, who were knit into the best small professional team I have ever known, split up. Some are in commercial theatre, some are doing advisory and club work. We still keep to the same principles and frequently correspond. They are professionals of a new profession, and their work will never stop. Instead of concentrating on one place, the Pear Tree Players are now cultivating little gardens all over England.

REAL CHILDREN'S THEATRE

Perhaps this is the time to mention Pete's Kitchen. Pete's Kitchen is just a room, but a very special room. It is where I and my friends cook dreams and brew spells. It is special because it is a big room, it is special because it is at the top of a house and right away from everyone, it is special because it is full of special things and because hardly any grown-ups go there except me. It is a Children's room, a room full of romantic things, things to make you want to be all sorts of wonderful people, and dare most mighty deeds. Some of these " things " would not be very exciting to grown-ups, but they are wonderful to the cooks of Pete's Kitchen, wonderful.

These are some of the things, though do not take them at their face value, for the everyday stupid practical value of a mere thing is not at all the cooking value which that same thing has in Pete's Kitchen. The values are different in this Land, and do not forget it, or you will not even begin to understand the wonders that are experienced in this place.

But the things :

There are a grandfather clock, some old boxes, two small divans, a chair, a long thin green cupboard, an old English square piano, which once graced the West End set of a famous play (some of the notes work), a gramophone, a baby's playpen, a red tent, some old green curtains, a wide brown drainpipe (new), a green oil-drum (old), a fireguard, a red candlestick, and a large black pot with a tap in it. There is a big cardboard box and a big wooden box painted red and black. In the cardboard box are smaller things. Some of them : three pairs of brown shorts with animals' tails ; some coloured waistcoats ; a few pieces of bright materials ; belts ; paper hats ; six wooden revolvers made from scraps ; some bits of tin (for banging) ; some bits of tin (not for banging, for wearing ; they are bright) ; some bits of wood for wands, swords and other things I have not learnt about yet ; a little box full of cardboard noses ; a piece of a dragon ; a pair of castinets ; part of a mermaid's seaweed ; some gold wrapping ; a one-stringed fiddle ; the horn from the one-stringed fiddle (they have to be separate generally) ; some silver wrapping ; the horn from inside a loudspeaker (on loan ; it's for crashing noises, or a dragon's voice) ; a cymbal (for crashing noises without a dragon's voice). The rest of the small things vary from time to time, but bricks, stones, old iron and bits of wood are common at any time.

On the walls are pictures (rather unusual). Oh, I forgot to mention there is a divan, but this is for me. I sit on it when I get tired, because I cannot go on acting or dancing as long as the other cooks. Their energy is greater than mine, and of course more often than not I merely sit. I am only the chief cook and bottle-washer. They do the creating. I sleep on the divan, too, if I have been working very late devising new utensils for cooking.

There is one last thing, which I love very dearly. We all do. It is a broken blind spring, encased in a tin roller. You can rattle it or bounce it lengthwise, and it goes clanging and jumping in your hand long after you have stopped annoying it. " It is a naughty snake really, who won't come out of the wizard's wand." I was told it. So it must be true. You see how different things are in Pete's Kitchen.

Now what are the other things used for ?

To date :

Grandfather clock : Big Ben, Nelson's Column, the sun standing on a long leg, a lamp post, an oak tree, where the witch lives, the flying tadpole's house, pillar-box, dungeon, grandfather clock.

Old boxes : For standing on, eating off, making castles, throwing down to make a good noise, " tapping gently for being sad and when your friends leave you or you leave your mother or when a puppy is hurt ".

Two small divans : For standing higher than other people, for jumping on. " You can jump to the moon very high on these." They make good mountains if piled on each other, and a slide at the fair. They are high walls to keep in naughty Children, and you shoot well from behind them against the enemy. They are ships.

A chair (its back twiddles) : A factory, baby's cot, canteen, prison, throne, bit of a church, ogre's hat, chair.

Long green cupboard : A tree ; lying down (with door open) a canoe, coffin lying upside down (door shut), a crocodile, a raft, a horse, a bridge, a rampart. Standing up, it is Lot's wife, and " the thin house, squashed by two trakershun engines for being wickitt ".

An old English square piano : Table, shop counter, operating-table, rabbit's house, Pandora's box, giant's cigar box, organ, harp, piano.

Gramophone : Witch's spell machine, washing-machine, mincer, sausage machine, for playing gramophone records and learning to listen to sounds. When the sounds have been listened to, you dance " on purpose " for, with, to or because of the sounds, or you act, with the music helping you to know what to do and what words to say. This is how you learn to talk properly and mean it.

Baby's playpen : Tent, ladder, low wall, sheep pen, garden, part of a ship, large lens to look at the moon, pond, " me own own own room all to meself 'cos I've never 'ad it, see ? " (This room has windows all round, " so yer can see the sun whenever it smiles, see ? ")

Red tent : For wiping feet on, blood, disappearing cloak, parachute, and on very important occasions it is used as a red tent.

Old green curtains : Grass, blankets, tents, hammocks, table cloths, tying up enemies, cloaks wrapping the dead, long hair, being married in, and when hung on special wooden beams they are part of a tree.

Brown drainpipe : For looking through, speaking into, calling down with a funny voice, " for being bigger than you are " (by shouting into), wastepaper basket, clown's roller, " trakershun engine ", cannon, trunk of the tree of which the green curtains (when hung) are the leaves.

Green oil-drum : Tea urn, high stool, table, ship's funnel, to roll about, to kick in time to music, cannon, lectern.

Fireguard : Breastplate, gunfire, thunder, gate.

Red candlestick : Drinking horn, headdress, candlestick.

Large black pot with tap in it : Tea urn, petrol pump, " place where the sea comes from ", witch's cauldron; pirates' treasure cask, milk-bar machine, lemonade holder, bath filler, air pressure pump, " for blowing up tyres or babies ".

Big red-and-black wooden box : For standing on, sitting on, hiding in, drowning your enemy in, banging for guns, and eating off the red if you are happy and off the black if you are sad. It tells the weather, too. When the red side is showing it is going to be fine and when the black is showing you must " quickly very fast hurry home 'cos of the big storm coming. And it rained. But Noah was safe wasn't he, because of the Ark ? "

The *cardboard noses* and *half-masks* I made and adapted from basic designs of the Commedia dell'Arte. It seemed right for a number of reasons. Chiefly because the Child can speak better with the mouth free or nearly so, and these masks are less hot for vigorous adventures. Full masks are used, too, to help them experience head angles and for improving their speech by very reason of the difficulty. But the half-masks are used more for the plays of which they are to get into the skin. The Children seem to get the best out of these. It gives them a character, but enough of themselves is still visible for them to have to act hard too. The half-mask becomes more a part of themselves.

It will be understood, of course, that there are no script plays in Pete's Kitchen. It is all genuine Child Drama. Everything is improvised. The art of the Commedia was improvised too. It has been called the dead art, yet it is, above all, the *live* art. But it has been sleeping for many years. The Children are now showing us what this must have been like. They are recreating something in modern yet age-old terms. It is not unnatural that the best masks for spontaneous Child Drama seem to be on the lines of those used when the art of improvisation was practised and understood as an art, and not thought of as something just easy and unimportant.

Although there are a lot of properties in Pete's Kitchen, they are not always used. The best work, as in school, is done when the least dressing-up takes place. But they have occasional opportunities to use everything. The great point is that they do not pretend to be actors and play at acting, which often happens when they go on a stage. There is no stage, so they just act. And what acting it is. " But Noah was safe wasn't he, because of the Ark ? "

Pete's Kitchen is an ark, too. Everyone is happy here. It is not possible to describe all that is done, but this outline of the imaginative use of properties may give some idea. There is no audience, no axe to grind, no stage, no grown-up titter to disturb the acting, no showing off, no worries, no clapping, nothing is done for propaganda. It is all done for the right reason. Here we are absorbed in creating real Child Drama because we love it, and because we believe that we are creating something wonderful and beautiful. We work *very hard*, because we want to.

This, for those who are interested, is a real Children's Theatre, and I believe that probably nothing else *is* a Children's Theatre. The other things are neither theatre nor " Children's " in the full sense. They are too often places for copied adult work to be done to please us, or for adults to let off steam in front of Children. There is nothing Childlike about them. Big buildings are good propaganda, big productions are, too. But all that is really wanted is a place where Children go to the Land, with the help of an understanding adult. There should be many such places. Their need is great, and they alone might be termed Children's Theatres, though, if they

PLATE 33

EDUCATIONAL DRAMA ASSOCIATION. Audience Participation.
(*See* p. 267.)

Photo by Victor Thompson

WEST COUNTRY CHILDREN'S THEATRE COMPANY. Audience
participation. A scene of rejoicing. (*See* p. 267.)

By courtesy of the " People "

PLATE 34

Photo by Victor Thompson

Adult actors acting amongst Children in arena and/or horse-shoe-shaped
presentations.   (These can of course be done without a theatre if necessary.)
(*See* p. 267.)

Photo by Victor Thompson

PLATE 35

SENIOR BOYS, FOURTEEN YEARS.   The pirate chief is run through.   No proper arrangement has been made for flowing on and off the stage, so the work of the attacker has been absolutely spoiled.   The picture is of an improvisation period I took in school, but has an important
lesson on the needed shape of any Child Theatre building.   A compromise theatre must cater
for all shapes observed in Child Drama.   (For diagrams of shapes see pp. 160–161, and 302-304.)

Photo by Victor Thompson

PLATE 36

INTIMATE THEATRE GROUP. Arena Theatre. Photo showing the auditorium, rig and canopy, all partly erected. (*See* p. 92.)

INTIMATE THEATRE GROUP. Arena Theatre. *The Servant of Two Masters* by Carlo Goldoni. Production as shown to Birmingham School Children of thirteen years and over in a special season in the Parks, Summer 1949. Note bulge into audience, the Child's general playing shape at this age. (See Parts I and II.)

Photos by kind permission of " Birmingham Post and Birmingham Mail"

are, it will be the first mistake. In this Children's Theatre which I have described, the " theatre " is never mentioned. It is Pete's Kitchen. But some of the best theatre I ever hope to see is created in that place. It is fresh, vivid, virile, full of contrast, full of surprise, full of zest, full of imagination. You cannot guess at every moment what is coming next, like you can in our theatre. It is eternally new, terribly moving. It has moments of *great* theatre, within the framework of the as yet unrecognised art of Child Drama.

THE CHILD AS TEACHER

In approaching Child Drama, the best results are obtained by believing that the Child is not only an original artist, but an important Person. With this in mind I hold discussions with Children from time to time, particularly out-of-school, when frank answers are obtained. One learns much from this.

The following are questions that I have put to Children, and all the answers have been given recently.[1] All are from under eleven's.

Question : " If you were a teacher, would you punish Children in a Drama class if they were being naughty ? "

Answer : " No, 'cos if the class was proper the Children wouldn't be disobeying." (Note—this was Cizek's point in Child Art. Student and teacher are co-workers.)

Question : " When did you start to act ? "

Answer : " When I was a baby."

Question : " What's the best age to start the sort of acting we do together ? "

Answer : " Young 'as is ever everest possible."

Question : " Do your teachers teach you to act ? "

Answer : " Yes, some of them talk at you all the time. You don't. It's better then, 'cos you really know what to do before you start."

Another Child : " Talking stops you doing things."

Question : " Do you like your own plays or ones that have been written by other people ? "

Answer : " Ours is best."

Question : " Do you like lots of hats and swords and belts and things to play with ? "

Answer : " Hats sometimes, but I've got a hat I made—oo, long *long* ago. Don't need belts, yer can fit swords into a bit of string."

[1] These discussions took place in Pete's Kitchen, but are relevant also to In-school work.

Question : " If you got stuck when you were playing, would you like to be left alone, or is it nice if a grown-up helps you ? "

Answer : " It's nice to finish, but it must be a *nice* grown-up or it's not nice. Some grown-ups aren't nice about helping. They tell you what to do too much."

Question : " Do you like lots of ideas for stories to act, or a few ? "

Answer : " Just a few."

Question : " And long ideas or short ? "

Answer : " Just little ideas. You can make them big after."

Question : " Would you rather dress up a lot or not ? "

Answer : " Act in your own clothes unless someone is watching. Then you've got to go and dress up."

Question : " If you felt a bit crochety, would you like to act an angry person ? "

Answers : " 1. Yes, you can't be naughty then.
2. Yes.
3. Specially if you're hot.
4. It would be comfy."

Question : " Do you like to have acting just sometimes at school, or often ? "

Answer : " It would be nice if acting was in all subjects."

Question : " When you're acting, do you sometimes think you're acting *you* ? "

Answer : " Yes, sometimes, not alwiz."

Question : " Is it easier to get ideas for playing when you are by your-selves or when you see other people acting ? "

Answers : " 1. Your own plays.
2. By yourself."

Question : " What would you prefer the teacher to do when you are act-ing your own plays ? "

Answer : " Just watch—except if you like the teacher *very* much they could join in just sometimes."

Question : " Is it nicer to copy or make up your own things ? "

Answer : " It's easier to copy, but it's nicer to make things up."

Question : " If you were acting a play and a teacher kept trying to help, when you were talking, what would you feel ? "

Answer : " I'd think she was horrid—I mean crool."

Question : " If you were acting a play about history and someone stopped you to tell you how the people you were acting behaved a long time ago, would you like it ? "

Answer : " No, I'd think they were interruptin'—and I wouldn't listen, either."

Question : " Oh ! Would you pretend to listen ? "

Answer : " Yes."

Question : " Why ? "

Answer : " Because I wouldn't want them to know."

Question : " Why ? "

Answer : " Afraid I'd get into trouble."

(Formal producers take heed.)

Question : " Some teachers want to help you very much. Do you like it when they do ? "

Answer : " Depends what they do. I don't like how they do it at my school."

Question : " How do they do it ? "

Answer : " Tell you how you ought to act it like."

Question : " Isn't that nice ? "

Answers : " 1. No. I think they're stopping me.
          2. It doesn't help."

Question : " Do you like to be told about acting or invent it ? "

Answer : " Invent it myself."

Question : " When you do acting as *you* like it, would you call it work or play ? "

Answers : " 1. Work or play. It's the same both together, all lumped.
          2. Don't be silly, '*course* it's work, you know it is. You learn in it, don't you ? "

Question : " If you can't think what to act today, what would you like me to do ? "

Answer : " Help us to think of a story."

Question : " If I said that's the wrong-coloured dress when you were acting, what would you feel ? "

Answer : " Oh, horrid. I'd think I was all quite wrong, all my acting. It would be awful. But you don't say that."

Question : " Is it easier to act in the town or in the country ? "

Most of the children answered : " In the country."

(They had all known town and country. I cannot give the exact number of answers, my attention was taken away.)

Question : " If you were in a play, would it help if I told you all where to stand all the time ? "

Answer : " No, I'd like to make it up while I was doin' it."

Question : " What would you say was a *young* Child ? "

Answer (from a nearly eight-year-old) : " Under seven. I began to be old at seven. I just knew I was different." (Child had had dawn of seriousness.)[1]

Question : " Do you like music on when you are acting ? "

Answer : " Yes, it tells you when to be puppies or fairies or when the enemy is coming."

Question : " Do you prefer to act the same play lots of times or do a new one ? "

Answer : " I like to finish a play three times, then I like to do something new or be helped with a story."

Question : " If you couldn't think of something, would you like someone to suggest a story, or would it be annoying ? "

Answers : " 1. Yes, I'd like it.

2. It's nice to be helped when you *can't* use a gun or a sword, but while you're trying it's as annoying as a—a kick."

Question : " Can you act about things you've never seen ? "

Answer : " Of course. I act about Brontasasurasis."

Question : " Do you often feel you want to act ? "

Answer : " Yes, only *some* days not. Nearly always I want to all the time."

Question : " Does acting help you to know things ? "

Answer (seven-year-old) : " Yes, I'm sure I know a lot about life, 'cos I act so much. I'm alwiz *being* someone."

Question : " What would you think if I suddenly said : ' That's all wrong ' ? "

Answers : " 1. I'd be very surprised and sad.

2. It's like our teacher.

3. I wouldn't know what to do. I'd think I wouldn't try any more 'cos of not knowing if I was right."

Question : " Do you get acting at school like we do it here ? "

Answer : " No, it's a pity, most of our teachers don't let us act. They keep suggesting all the time."

Question : " Can you think of any way of using marks for acting ? Would you like to ? "

---

[1] See Chapter II, page 51.

Answer : " It would be absolutely silly, Petie. That's for correcting work and things like that."

Question : " Do you find it nice to act this way ? "

Answer : " Yes."

Question : " Is it easy ? "

Answers : " 1. Yes. You sort of mean it more.

2. It's easy to act when you're here. *You* don't stop and ask why we did it like that or tell us things all the time.

3. I can't *never* do it like this wiv our teacher. She says it's silly."

In the past year alone, I have had some personal contact with over thirty-two thousand Children under fourteen. Out of these, three Children have said they preferred the script play to their own Child Drama.

PLAN FOR CHILDREN'S THEATRE

It will be seen that the following diagrams and suggestions cover a very wide section of human activities, and a considerable age range, if we include adult actors as amongst those interested and/or partaking.

I would repeat that probably the only real Children's Theatre is something like Pete's Kitchen, which is a No-audience Play Centre. But we would not call it a Theatre. It is more accurately an intended Child Drama Centre. The other things are buildings where Children can copy our adult theatre or be shown theatre.

If, however, we seriously and fairly consider the Child's genuine Drama, any building known as a Children's Theatre should cater for *their* way of doing things. For this we might expect :

(*a*) *Age five to seven years :* Regular stimulation of Child Drama by one adult present (not dressed up). A fair stretch of level floor is used.

(*b*) *Age seven to eleven years :* As above, but with more space. Also occasional visits by adult players (dressed up) playing with or amongst the Children. Children participating or not.

(*c*) *Adolescents :* Creating Dance or imaginative Drama with one adult (not dressed up), acting in script plays or producing them in their own theatre shapes, with or without stage ; seeing theatre presentations in arena or horse-shoe shape, presented by adults dressed up.

(*d*) Occasional proscenium production by adults shown to over fifteen-

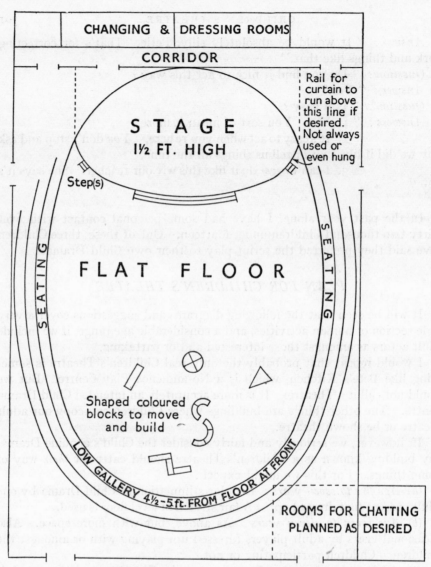

FIG. 31.—POSSIBLE OUTLINE FOR CHILDREN'S THEATRE.
(Building where Children act. No proscenium.)

SHAPE : *Square* for *Sound*, but *Oval* for *Influence*. General shape to appear oval. This would serve for production, pageants, semi-proscenium, arena theatre, play centre, hall for improvisation.

Lights : from front of gallery, ceiling. Floods to move on stands where needed. Curtains to hang from front of gallery to floor, if desired. Rooms off for chatting and creation.

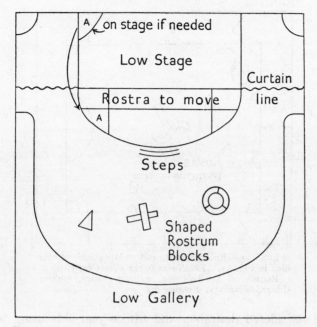

FIG. 32.—Another possible *Children's Theatre* outline. More traditional.

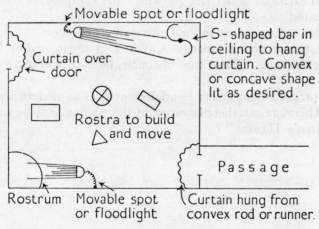

FIG. 33.—*Pure Play Centre*. No audience. Room adapted for every town, in large numbers.

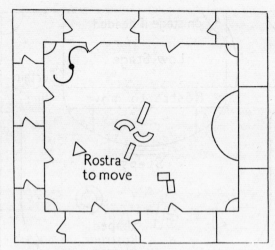

FIG. 34.—Enlargement and adaptation of the
idea in Fig. 33. *The No-audience Play Centre.*
Rooms off for painting, writing stories, making
things, occasional dressing up.

year-olds, if considered desirable, and fifteen-year-olds using proscenium
form if they want to.

Plate 32, opposite page 289, and Plates 33 to 36, opposite page 296, show
the two main divisions of activity for which any compromise theatre building should cater.

1. Children acting a story in their own genuine manner.

2. Adult actors acting amongst Children in arena and/or horseshoe-
shaped presentations. (These can, of course, be done without a theatre, if
necessary.)

Theatre proper belongs more to adolescence. The modern adolescent is
no Child. Therefore can there be or ought there actually to be such a thing
as a " Children's Theatre " ?

PLATE 37

THIS IS A FIRST THEATRICAL MASK. *Child* : " It is a man with bulges at the side of his face—a funny man—you have to cut out his eyes so you can see through, and he has a childerblain on his chin. A funny man like that has to have a ball, so I put that in too. That's the ball, next to him, to match his hair." (*See* p. 307.)

JUNIOR SCHOOL. Examples of " near masks " where unconscious knowledge of the drama of other periods and lands is beginning to show. (*See* p. 307.)

Photos by Victor Thompson

PLATE 38

JUNIOR SCHOOL. Interest in beards. Background shows pattern found in Child Make-up. (*See* p. 307.)

JUNIOR SCHOOL. Picture of a face. Note the pattern. This appears in Child Make-up. The nose pattern is similar to African Art. (*See* p. 307.)

JUNIOR BOYS. Their first experience of using such masks. They are searching for a bag of gold. But I have it, and the man at the back is just coming for me. The scene was created and acted within four minutes. The masks helped us to decide on the story. Note typical circular group of the small gang. (*See* p. 312.)

Photos by Victor Thompson

CHAPTER XVII

MASKS AND MAKE-UP

MOST of us recognise in ourselves, from time to time, moments when we wish we were someone else—or at least slightly different from what we are. This desire manifests itself in many ways and can be a powerful motive for good or evil. Related to it are envy and ambition, but also the desire to be better in character. It can be a desire consciously connected with inner or outer achievement.

The desire is recognisably fulfilled in the realms of theatre, as we know it and understand it, and make-up and masks both play their part in the realms of outer achievement. They form rather the materialist outer skin of the character portrayed. They can make things easier, in some ways, both for actor and audience, in the process of believing in a changed character, but such is the intricate balance between outer and inner self that they do not always make things easier. For instance, an actor may come to rely too much on clothes, make-up and scenery, and become lazy about the work of inner creation. The audience may then, to some extent, be gulled into accepting an outer vision of something, but they receive less emotional message. It is therefore more difficult to believe in and understand the character in the play, not unnaturally, because less of it exists. Sometimes the actor does hardly any work on inner creation, particularly when concerned with showing off. At these moments very little, if anything, is created. There exists, in fact, no character. We cannot share what does not exist, and the audience leaves the theatre emotionally unmoved, except perhaps for the pleasure of the spectacle. The intelligent theatre critic feels cheated.

In the best theatre work of the usual type, we would hope to find the make-up or mask used as a blended part of creation. The inner creation is the core of it all, then comes technical achievement, the make-up or mask being added to it and becoming thereby a crowning of the achievement.

It is important to understand this process, for it is undoubtedly the basis

The noses above I discovered in a primary school magazine, soon after making half-masks like them. The pupils had not seen my masks.

of genuine Child Drama. The young Child is often concerned with becoming another person, and does this chiefly in its own inner self. It can even be several people at once, or different people (and/or things) in quick succession. It may, on the other hand, be one person (and/or thing) for long periods on end, or intermittently over weeks, months or years.

This inner acting, with its swift mental associations, naturally affects the outer acting and makes the use of properties, clothing, masks and make-up of debatable value. A Child will often tear off or discard what is " in the way " creatively, and, because of its natural ascetic taste and tremendous inner creative energy, will entirely do without outer aids on many occasions, relying on magnetic imagination. Such *belief* exists in their creation, and such energy of work, that the creation is indeed *created* and needs no extra crowning. We believe it absolutely. At these moments, the Child and the sympathetic adult may come together in intense moments of emotional sharing, which one so often seeks in the adult theatre and so seldom finds. Because of all this, Children do not automatically turn at first to masks and make-up as an aid to their Drama. These things dawn in time (if they have not been imposed), according to the Child's inner need for further outer aid.

It is interesting to note that many make-up books, written by well-known experts, stress the fact that, owing to the strength of light on the stage familiar to most of us, the face of an actor appears somewhat as a flat plane. The art of the make-up expert in the purely technical sphere is to make this flat plane appear to mean something and cease to be flat. He is, in fact, painting a picture. This is exactly the Child's approach to both masks and make-up, and often the first Child-created masks arise out of painting a person's face on a flat plane of paper. Then a bigger face may be painted, with the idea of cutting out the nose, eyes or mouth—not necessarily all three. But very often these early half-intended masks are never cut out and never used, and often would not fit a face if they were. So they remain as painted pictures, a monument of some imagined character. It will be remembered that the young Child does not yet use perspective in drawing or painting, so that this " flat " approach, which the experts suggest, is in one sense both easy and natural for the Child.

Because of this, in its own turn, the reality of the painted face—i.e. its photographic likeness to the human face—depends largely on its intended connexion with a playable character. When this intention, or at least part intention, exists in the young Child's mind the colouring appears to be simple as a rule. There is a tendency to use only a few plain-coloured washes or

smears. We note also a certain hurry in the creation. It is often un-
finished, like the early attempts at writing a play. There has been too much
rush to get through with the emotional idea and too little time given to
craftsmanship and creation of the actual picture itself. Nevertheless, unlike the early written plays, the early mask attempt does often contain
" character ", born no doubt somehow on the tide of the original urge, and
we can enjoy this whilst forgoing the detail. We have to do this with many
adult modern painters, so we can also do it for the Child. There are joys in
simplicity.

But by far the most interesting examples of both masks and large-face
pictures, which have a link with masks, are those where the Child has either
taken the logic of the " flat " plane approach to its furthest limit, or has
forgotten the original emotional urge in the middle of creation and has
become absorbed in the actual pattern of the picture. Then, indeed, do we
find a garden of colour and intermingled lines. Stripes, chevrons, circles,
crosses and dots are our heritage. These may appear not only on the outer
edges of the picture but on the face also. The unwise teacher will then
reprimand for unreality, when the artist at that moment was not in the least
concerned with " reality " in the sense of " photographic likeness " ; this
does not enter much into Child Art of any kind in the early stages. (See
Plate 37, opposite page 304.)

For those who are familiar with the Drama of other countries, and with
the general history of Drama, these paintings will not come as such a shock.
The masks of the East, for instance, particularly the Chinese, are concerned
with lines and dots, though here the ornamentation has become consciously
linked with symbolic meaning and " type " (in the sense of stage character).
With the Child, pattern is not necessarily linked with " type " or character,
owing to lack of life experience, but there is *some* link on occasions, and symbolism is generally unconscious. The African mask and the totem pole look
rather like the early Child pattern mask, both in colour and in shape of
pattern. By " pattern mask " I mean the face picture where pattern rather
than character type only is perhaps the more noticeable. (See Plate 38.)

So the general line of development goes through painting, and particularly through portraiture. Suddenly the faces get bigger and we notice
pattern developing on them. This is the unconscious approach to the primitive mask (and earlier-known masks based upon tradition), though the creation must still be described as a picture of a person with a face like a known
mask. Then may come the sudden flash that a life-size picture (or attempt

at it) *might* fit over the face.   In general it would appear that only Children receiving a good deal of nurturing in Child Drama get this flash early. Sometimes it never comes until an adult suggests it.   It is the urge of the flash that may make the first fully *intended* mask, and its early successors, of inferior craftsmanship.   Most Child painting, though, shows some general approach to masks as we know them, arising out of the Child's ordinary observation of the human face.

Unless it has been brought to the Child's notice early by the adult, the discovery of make-up appears to follow the mask.   It is very difficult to obtain a clear organic development here, as the influence of general street make-up of older girls and mothers may make itself felt early, though the rather more " natural " trend of the street make-up does not occur to the Child as being Art.   It is rather a suggestion to try out colour on the face. So, just as being forced to do adult Drama is hardly connected with Child Drama at first in the Child's mind, so, too, adult make-up has little to do with masks at first, or with Child make-up.   It is rather a temptation to daub, if noticed at the stage of application.   But this leads on to discoveries.

However, the organic development, which appears to be via the mask, is logical, because masks have limitations and Children have their strange ascetic sense.   So there inevitably comes the time when this property, the mask, will be cast aside, and the next more comfortable and logical step is to paint your face instead.

Whatever way the Child comes to make-up, we find two distinct manifestations—the simple rushed make-up which looks like a colour wash, and the pattern make-up.   We should not be in the least surprised at this, for they denote the two differences in the types of Play.[1]   The quick, rather clumsy, wash type is hurried through so that the Child can start upon personal Play (Action) ; the pattern form is slowly, carefully built up, often in absorbed silence, and may be worn just to show a few friends, perhaps, or to make a few faces ; it will not necessarily be used for acting at all.   This is connected with projected Play ; quietness is present, and the stillness of sitting doing things, not necessarily followed immediately by acting.   There is equidistance, too, in the patterns very often.

When discussing this at a meeting of teachers, a member of a Training College staff said : " Yes, we notice that so *often* when we go round to school practice.   Children who dress up or use masks a lot, and properties, do not do very good acting.   They march up and down.   Their best acting is done

[1] The two types of Play are considered in Part I, Chapters I–IV.

when they go to a corner. Sometimes playing, say, near the Wendy House, not necessarily with it, they act hard and use no properties at all."

So, then, the mask and make-up are arrived at rather by considering the face as a flat plane, and when a make-up is rushed through in order to start rapidly on personal Play, often the front of the face only is coloured and half the sides are left bare. Only a flat frontal view, easy to see in the glass or through a companion's eyes, has been considered. This is far from confined to Children, though ; one has seen many adult actors who have forgotten that we must not see the mechanics of their art, leaving a hard edge of make-up at the side of their face or neck.

Children help each other with make-up, and paint their companions' faces just like a canvas. They may use all sorts of things—burnt cork is an old trick, but generally adult imposed—boot polish, pencils, wall paint—anything may be seized upon. In the section on schools [1] is a description of attempts at spit-and-pastel. These are examples of making the best of a bad job ; they may go on often without our knowing it, and be the cause of perplexing skin troubles. Perhaps we should provide more materials.

An adult making-up a Child does it in a quite different way, often for somewhat different reasons. The mental attitude is not the same, particularly the mental " Art attitude ". The make-up is generally devised for productions on a stage, whereas Child make-up, whether pertaining to personal or projected Play, is intended to be seen at close range in a Land where Drama is all about you. Too early an impact of adult stage make-up (as opposed to street make-up) will shatter the Child's own attempts, and we may never see the occasional wonders of pattern which rock our grown-up self-satisfaction by their overwhelming dignity of association with things fundamental ; most of our make-up is merely trivial and representational. The type of make-up used in ballet would seem to resemble most nearly the best older Child work. But then this is nearer the Children's Land, in many respects, and is the most fresh of our adult arts.

Typical of the pictorial approach to make-up is the following : I was sitting at a table opposite a little girl of seven and a half who had been drawing. I said : " You've got a lovely mark just under your nose."

Child : " Oh, have I ? Let's see."

She rushed to a mirror, made a face and rubbed off the mark. Then she stared at herself, and with her blue pencil drew a line just where she had rubbed out the original line. She turned to me to see what I would say.

---

[1] Chapter XIV (No. 17), page 211.

Self : " That's smart.   Do you like that line ? "
Child : " Yes."
She pulled a face to fit in with the line, then started on a small piece of acting.   The line just happened to fit in with a natural shadow, so perhaps suggested realism and personal Play.   But the fascination of this new thing was too much—the Child returned to the mirror.   She stared for some time, then slowly drew, with ordinary pencil, a flag with a cross on it on her forehead and another on one cheek.   On the other cheek she drew a blue line.   She drew a red stripe on her nose, then a cross, then a blue line under her lower lip, and finally a circle on her chin.   She then laughed delightedly.   I shared the delight.   Then she rubbed off the marks on her nose and the two flags (note : all the clear " pattern " marks).   What was left were the simple swift lines in natural places.   She stared again, then rubbed off the circle on her chin.   This left only the blue shadows.   Personal Play started at once. The Child walked fiercely round the room.   Then suddenly : " Oh, dear, I suppose I'd better wash."
Self : " Yes, I think you'd better.   Did you enjoy that ? "
Child : " Yes.   It was the wonderfullest thing of *all* day today."
So does it start, as a process or by accident.   But that day I was present at this great birth, this discovery—" drawing on my face in colour ".   More often we are not there when the idea dawns, or perhaps we do not recognise the birth of make-up if we are.   Sometimes we can guess the progress of a Child's approach, and judge the time of birth very nearly.   Sometimes an accident will bring discovery very early.   The Child mentioned above had long ago been through the painted (on paper) mask stage, but had discarded her attempts, and had not found make-up till now.   In the meantime, though, she has been going through the larger-faced portrait stage with more details filled in.   She was due for the final discovery.
If make-up is discovered late it is nearly always bad at first, as we would expect, as years of missed practice, discovery and judgement have to be caught up with.   By then the Child is well on with personal Play and has made many dramatic discoveries.   It therefore tends to indulge in very rapid smears or washes of make-up, in intense haste to get on with personal Play and acting things out.   This may go far into adolesence, though we often hear the older Child ask pathetically, " Is that all right ? " of a wash which is very bad indeed.   But such a Child has missed the Summer of Child Art, perhaps, and may not have been aware of make-up by seven years or so, which might have been an added happy experience.

Some mention has been made, in the section dealing with older Children, of the use of make-up as an aid to confidence. At any age we may find shyness reduced by either masks or make-up at particular times and with certain Children. But these are often the ones inclined to be self-conscious, and it is not kind to give continual chances of protection. Judicious moments without protection (i.e. without make-up or mask) are necessary for *extending* confidence once gained. It is necessary to understand the difference between mere escape and sheer creative joy, though it is not impossible for these to be intermingled.[2]

The Teacher

The following points are merely indications of a way, but each teacher is an artist and will find his own way.

Child make-up is an Art Form.

This form is an extension of Child Art, but lies somewhere between it and Child Drama. The general handling should therefore be the same as for Child Art.

Early approaches come organically through painting and drawing. The flat mask may arrive. You may recognise it if you are aware of its existence or probable existence.

Do not mistake any sudden wish for using scissors to cut out nose, mouth or eyes for wanton destruction (as differentiated from mere snipping about). There may be a reason. Look carefully at the picture and judge. Allow accordingly.

This desire for cutting *may* come early in the Child's life, if anything like Child Drama as outlined in this book is done in your school.

Never force the use of masks. Some Children are bewildered by them. Be very careful how you introduce them—see that they are simple and not too heavy.

Introduce them sensibly so that they hamper movement as little as possible. *E.g.* do not expect dance to be so good if full masks are worn and dancers cannot see.

Allow Children to make their own.

It is possible to use masks for improving speech, by playing a game of wearing difficult masks and asking Children to stand at opposite ends of the room

[1] See Chapter IV, page 77, and Chapter XII, page 154.
[2] Charles S. Parsons, in his book *A Guide to Theatrical Make-up* (published by Pitman), which Sir Cedric Hardwicke describes as the best book he has read on the subject, mentions this point, and even builds upon it in the first chapter.

and still be heard.   This can be great fun if kindly taken.   "Attack" on words, volume of tone and diction all improve by this.   Use these special masks only in this intentional way, not in free Child Play unless the Children ask for them.

During Play I find that, at least for the younger Child, the part-mask is better.   You may find this so, too.   It may cover only the eyes or nose, but more freedom is left and more of Self exists.   Result is more movement and more life.   Dance is sometimes enriched by the half-mask, by the full mask seldom.   I made experiments with these masks, after very considerable observation, in an attempt to find something lighter, less hampering, and still of some " new " joy.[1]   I made them with odd noses, which I believed to be in sympathy with Child thought.   Two days later I was rewarded with not only a delighted reception, but with finding similar noses in a primary school magazine, drawn by Children who had never seen my masks.   Later I discovered further paintings of the same nose shapes, and further outstanding examples of patterns on faces.   I used the simple, bright, plain wash colours on the masks, as this seems to pertain to make-up and masks which are used for personal Play or obvious Drama.   If you make masks yourself, remember to make them small enough.   (See Plate 38, opposite page 305, and Plate 41, between pages 360 and 361.)

Before making *any* masks, spend a long time considering Child Art and Child Drama.   You are likely to make better masks—i.e. more right for the purpose.

Look out for the difference between pattern and wash in the painting. Use similar shapes yourself.   Colours bright.

On no account whatever make anything approaching a natural life-like mask for any Child under twelve at least.   If you do you may ruin its Art, and probably its approach to make-up also.

If noses are cut out it is joyful to have colour ready to dab on the wearer's real nose.   This may aid the approach to make-up.   *Use bright colours only*, not natural shades.   Primary colours are best to begin with.

Allow Children to paint each other's noses.   Use good theatrical make-up for this.   Take care of the silver-paper edge.   Keep tearing it down on the paint stick, or little noses get scratched.

Have very few sticks of make-up.   You keep control better.   Have them handed back to you after use.   Later, trust and manner of using are understood.

Be ready for first make-up attempts, and for discarding of masks once this has started.

[1] See also Chapter XII.

I am inclined to feel that there should be yellow, blue, white, black, red and green grease-paint in every primary school.

Do not tell Children how to make-up. *You do not know how they should make-up for the Character in their mind.* They do. Still less can you tell them what pattern to draw on their faces. Only guide over avoiding mess and taking-off application, if asked.

Expect and allow patterns. Share the joy.

Compare with their paper paintings. If some pattern is not appearing on faces the Child Art on paper may not be right. Consider. Judge.

Instruct only if you are asked. Prepare yourself in knowledge. Questions are more likely from over ten upwards.

Be ready to explain the use of Number 5 as base.

Be bitterly disappointed if you have not seen many intricate patterns on faces during the primary school years. You have missed much. So have your Children.

As the Child nears twelve or thirteen, more reality may creep in, more lifelikeness. Allow this.

Keep something for wiping off. Be in charge of some cream or remover. Do not put grease or greasy cloths on or near important papers, or allow Children to do so.

As experience comes, have occasional make-up period with glass and paint for each Child sitting in desk. Treat entirely as an Art class. Do not necessarily expect action or class drama. Judge whether to allow it, should it be stimulated. It may be a complete period of projected Play creation, with no desire for personal Play in action.

Expect patterns. Expect foreign faces with older Children.

Older Children can be helped, and may ask for aid. They are coming nearer our theatre and our make-up. Watch their painting. Girls tend towards finding out about street make-up, and boys make trials over beards and moustaches. These are more realistic than junior attempts. Be ready with tactful, not overbearing, advice. Do not be silly and say all beards are awful or anything like that.

Be prepared for unusual developments in older Children with blemishes. Do not draw attention to them. Consider. Judge. Act accordingly, or generally decide not to.

Allow Child make-up to approach and turn into ours—slowly and naturally. It may always be different, perhaps better.

Do not force make-up. Children may only want to use it for special purposes and times. Discover. Judge. Act. In general, and with all age groups, do not start out with the idea that Child make-up will necessarily be anything like ours. It may not be. For younger Children, know your Child Art, for older Children, study the ballet, and particularly Robert Helpmann. Consider, too, the masks and traditional paintings of other times and climes. Get a good book on make-up and use it like a cookery book if you do not know your subject well. Look at pictures of Indians, Chinese and Japanese actors ; African Art, Aztec and Inca Art ; and study the marks on the faces of Red Indians, also Greek patterns.

Lastly, free yourself from any immediate association with the make-up of the ordinary adult theatre. It is mostly done for a special purpose, for special conditions, and does not always succeed. The worst Children's work is a hurried copy of this, the best is an Art Form of its own, drawing unconsciously upon the great historic treasures of the world. It lies halfway between Art and Drama, but the better part of it pertains to what is more obviously Art. Child make-up has great comedy and an immense wisdom about it. It does not necessarily belong to movement or theatre. It is an Art Form hardly developed at all as yet. Its existence is even less suspected, I believe, than Child Drama itself.

CHAPTER XVIII

PUPPETS AND MARIONETTES

So many people ask about these that a short section on the subject is included. Puppets can be of immense interest, and become an absorbing part of Child creation. There are, however, certain difficulties about them. But let us take the things in favour first.

In Favour :

Puppets encourage concentration. Long periods of constructive play can take place with them.

Their very toy-likeness makes them beloved. There are many trials of behaviour to be obtained by play with them.

They provide a valuable incentive for playing out violent themes, difficult themes, themes that pertain to personal fears.

Older Children can find out a great deal about stage performance by them, also stage production.

They teach about colour, design and organisation. There is an obvious connexion with crafts of many kinds.

Puppets can take the place of companions, brother or sister.

They teach patience. They can aid speech.

They stimulate imagination and become thereby a source of inventiveness.

They can be useful for aiding shy Children, who will only begin to " live " through puppets or speak through puppets, or speak and live when hidden behind puppets or puppet stages.

They can aid us with " difficult " Children, as well as aid these Children themselves. Periods of release and temporary co-operation either with other Children, with adults, or both, may become apparent during Play.

Puppets can become life-like in one sense, but are seldom actually "photographic " to look at, and so are nearer Child Art.

They are often genuine products of Child Art.

They are the living essence of projected Play and can be, therefore, very valuable treasures for the best adventures into life experiences, in the sense that all these terms have been used and described in this book.

They can be used as a half-living visual aid to many educational subjects.

Against Puppets :

They are often too ready-made ; in a way, often too glamorous. This implication will be understood if the earlier suggestions about the clear relationship between happiness and creation, arising out of the Child's ascetic sense, have been understood.

Apart from this, most of the drawbacks are connected with the lack of understanding on the part of the adult.

Puppets often become a sort of fetish. If this happens, it is quite possible for Children to become arrested in the doll stage.

The adventures of personal Play are renounced ; in shy Children quietly avoided. The Children spend far too much time in projected Play and can become quiet, wide-eyed and odd, instead of healthily using their whole bodies, speaking out as themselves, or courageously and personally being different people (personal Play). And, although shy Children can obtain cover enough for release and build up confidence with puppets, too much use of them brings the habit of seeking cover, which is the very opposite of this.

In addition, we often find continual concentration on one body position, which causes round shoulders and drooping head. The other position, as from underneath, is better, but the whole body is cramped.

The workers of puppets can never be quite sure whether audience reaction is the result of success or failure in achievement. Both can be entertaining in a puppet show. This can lead to a slapdash attitude, even ultimately affecting moral awareness, particularly from six upwards.

There is (by reason of adult handling, suggestion and imposition) too much stress on audience and show. This is foreign to the best in Child Drama, and, by overdoses of the wrong kind of puppetry, the delights of Child Drama, even the attitude necessary for it, are pushed farther away. We have seen earlier how one of the beauties of Child Drama is the immense concentration on immediate creation and the desire to participate, which often makes audience redundant. Despite concentration on the puppet and his part, there comes an overconsciousness of audience too often and too early, where too much puppetry is done.

As well as this feeling of " show ", the adult often unthinkingly introduces the proscenium form and conceptions of theatre, as differentiated from Dramatic Play, far too soon. This, in turn, can lead to overmuch showing off and trying to be funny through the puppets, and we lose much serious thought and character building.

So the puppet can be less useful than the true doll, and, because of its frequent association with being mentally and materially confined to one area, cuts right across the whole attitude about " journey ". The " journey " is a most important adventure and life trial. It is obtained by Child Drama with its full use of space and creation of a world about one. It cannot be attained in the more usual manner of using puppets.

Enough has already been said about early introduction to perspective theatre upsetting the Child's slow approach to depth-consciousness for us to see the difficulties of the puppet theatre, even though an audience of Children appears to see past the proscenium arch in puppet plays (rather like disregarding the edge of the film screen) more than in live theatre. Perhaps this is the attraction of the " dolls " themselves, and partly because here proscenium openings are less obvious and dominating, smaller and less obtrusive. But there is some effect of proscenium consciousness, and more so upon those who work the puppets, as projecting personality out towards audience, depth, sight lines and grouping, however primitive, are all involved.

One of the joys of Child Drama is that many little people can frequently take part at once. With puppet performances we are back at the old difficulty of formal theatre and plays—only a few can normally take part at a time.

So, then, there are complications about puppetry, and these are only a few of them. But most of the complications, or the worst of them, arise out of the attitude of the adult. The more the adult confines all Drama activity and energies to puppets, the less likely are Children to discover the vast other realms that belong to the whole of Drama. A judicious use of puppets can be helpful. Injudicious use betrays itself by obvious results, which can be observed with ease, the most obvious of which is that even the Child sometimes rebels, begins to cease puppetry and starts to play with the puppet purely as a doll. It will make off with the doll and start a journey. In this way it sometimes finds or refinds, space, courage and life.

The Teacher

A few suggestions only. These may be of no value with some groups. With others, where there is already an understanding for the place and use of puppets, the suggestions may be redundant. But these suggestions form a link with Child Drama and the whole general attitude to the subject.

Do not think that puppets must be confined to one place or one small acting area.

Do not think they must necessarily live in a theatre of any kind.

Do not think that there must be shows all the time, and an audience.

Given this mental attitude, understand that puppetry (to the Child) can arise organically out of such early things as " little pig went to market ", where fingers impersonate pig and undertake the action of tickling, progressing say to " sh " noises with finger on lip, and thence to beckoning. All of these are copied in time by the baby. When the first dramatic entry is mastered (running to the threshold of a door and dashing away [1]) and when " peep-bo " has progressed to the door and the Child's head pops round the corner of it, we may see this followed by a hand, or an object, or a doll popped round the door.

Then may come the hand animals and shadows on the wall, a " bird " with finger and thumb. This sort of chain of experiences is the direct mental lead up to glove puppets.

So use glove puppets before other puppets. (Suggest for *circa* five years of age or over.)

Once having started on puppets, *do not use them too often*. Realise the necessity for other kinds of Play, particularly personal Play, which becomes more necessary and natural as movement is mastered.

If the Child wants to use puppets too often, because imagination or physical effort is being cramped, give tender suggestions which lead away to chances of personal Play, or arrange (if in school) for puppets not to be seen during certain periods.

Do not imagine that puppets are better than dolls for the young Child ; they are often less valuable in every way for general Drama progress.

When first using or allowing use of glove puppets, do not confine them to a stage ; let them pop up over chairs, desks or tables, anywhere. This introduces space, and puppets lead their little masters and mistresses to move about, so that space and journey are experienced just as and when needed. Drama is all about us. Actors and audience are one. This fits the Child's mental state.

After glove puppets, a doll on one string (either attached to the head or the back of the neck) may be found interesting. Any introduction then of sounds or music, as earlier suggested, tempts the doll to dance. Simple time beat will be experienced in a new and exciting way. New rhythms may

[1] See Chapter I.

be discovered.   Group sensitivity can enter by an " ear " for the time beat of a companion's doll.   Sometimes a whole room full of dolls ends up with dancing on the same beat.   The sound is percussive, can lead to interest in percussion bands, but is anyhow most exciting in itself.   Consider resemblance to African dance and all stamping dance movements.   See the circle appearing.   Understand why.

Watch for any disinclination, though.   Strings may not be used for dangling, they may be wound round.   There may be a desire to pick up and fondle the doll.   Allow this.   It is important affection, and may anyway be a smoothing over from concentration on the doll as actor, to use of doll as mere treasure [1] in wider Drama.   The doll's master may now be going to become the actual actor (personal Play).   This is healthy and more important.

Any frustration of personal Play as just described starts the arresting of the Child in the doll stage, and localising of Dramatic Play.   Either in glove puppets or dangled dolls, any set habit of this kind is very difficult to eradicate.

If you come upon a group of Children bound in a habit of puppets and experiencing no other Drama, forms of liberation may be discovered by finding space *somewhere*.   Spread Children out, suggest picking up of dolls, stimulate Drama by story, singing, sounds, music or mere running.   Dolls will become treasures [1] or will even be discarded.   For bad cases of permanent glove puppetry, try a puppet on one or both hands.   Find space if you can and start simple dance or Play with Children spread out.   I have known Children dance happily about with a puppet on each hand, but slowly discard one, then the other, and finally, with bursts of energy, enter with happy liberation into the free personal Play of full Child Drama.

With older Children, when judged ready for manipulation, more strings can be used with dolls.   They can walk about the floor just like other people, and chat.   Do not send the puppets to prison in a rotten little theatre box. Immense and wonderful crowd scenes all about the room can take place, either with forests of glove puppets held high, or with manipulated " people " (marionettes).   Look out for interesting examples of the circle and equidistance in this crowd work.   We have a mixture here of personal Play and the patterns of carefully placed objects found always in projected Play.

Do not object to this way of doing things because the sight of strings upsets *you*.   The Child may put up with them for a long time, and look through

1 " Treasures " are described in Chapters I and II.   Also Footnote 1 on Page 23.

and past them and only at the doll. Children have stronger imaginations than we have. Take account of this. If you understand the importance and strength of projecting ideas outwards from Self, this will present no difficulty.

As you note understanding of depth coming into painting, and into other forms of Drama, so you will discover the right and natural time for the puppets to go slowly to their prison in the smaller perspective theatre. But they will go happily *at the right time*, and by volition, as we all do. But one of the difficulties about puppets is that they hurry their masters towards the perspective theatre, because of their limitations. The intelligent Child in the junior school will discover the value of puppets being enclosed long before wanting to be enclosed itself. This can set up a tension. Watch for it and dispose of it, first by more Child Drama of a wide nature, lastly by death of the puppet if necessary.

Where space is restricted without hope of relief, or where proscenium puppetry is found to exist too early, slow liberation can be achieved by audience participation[1] as earlier described. Puppets are accompanied by sounds made by audience, or may react to such sounds. I have known puppets jump right out of their theatre box with excitement at this experience, leading their masters with them.

A link can be made with wider Drama by occasional personal acting (the Children acting) of stories previously acted by puppets, and, vice versa, stories for puppets to act may arise out of personal Play. This is a way of breaking a set habit. Watch, though, that it does not lead to laziness through not wanting to create new stories.

Creation of stories has, of course, so far consisted entirely of improvised speech. Language Flow is *greatly* assisted by some use of puppets. Stories from books, etc., should form only the outline. Much interesting talk will be created around them, but can also take place entirely without them.

Take care not to overburden with heavy stories because *you* do not like the ones the children make up.

Be careful not to overdo puppetry between eleven years and thirteen. This is an expanding time for personal acting, and many more important Drama and life discoveries are being made.

If interest persists after thirteen years or so, or if Children suddenly find puppets or marionettes then, there will be interest in craftsmanship, which should be more polished. This is the time for insistence on good details.

---

[1] See Chapter III, page 59.

The proscenium puppet theatre will be more correct for this age, even the script play.

From the earliest employment of puppets, full consideration should be given to the Child's ability to make things.   Puppets are often more loved if made by Children, and the organic development of Art and of Crafts is not so upset as when ready-made puppets are given out.   These last can be a menace.

With older Children we should expect the dolls to be really well made, and shoddy workmanship should be challenged.   This does not infer that earlier attempts *will* be badly made ; that need not be so, but judge earlier attempts by a different value—Child value, not adult standard.   Work of thirteen years upwards is more like adult standard.   But do not be harsh, and do not hurry anything. Encourage. Differentiate between the swiftly made toy and an important piece of craftsmanship at this age.

Teach history—particularly costume, setting and manners—by puppets and marionettes, with older Children.

So, in conclusion—do not let your own mind be cramped by puppets and marionettes or your own vision of Drama as a whole be limited, either by them or by one sort of theatre connected with them.

Puppets can be of value, but their value is limited.   They can be done without, though they can be a pleasant enrichment of experience if used with discretion.   They are not nearly as important as the Child itself acting.   It will often use dolls during Play, and in fact thereby use " puppets " according to the natural laws of its own Drama.   Dolls are discarded in time and are not used all the time.   That is as it should be.   Avoid becoming sentimental about puppets, saying, without due thought of Children, " but they love them so ".   Children love anything that gives them joy.   So they love puppets, but they love Child Drama more ; and, not altogether unimportant —it is better for them, both physically and mentally.   It offers more opportunities.

CHAPTER XIX

FILMS

SOME people are not altogether happy about the influence of films.

The chief concern seems to be with moral content, and with the fact that violent, even sadistic, scenes have a bad effect upon the behaviour of Children, as also the modern trend to accept Man as he is rather than to glorify him, and to show heroes who are not golden all through. Another view is confined somewhat to professional actors, some of whom decry the long queues outside cinemas when theatres are not always full.[1] Lastly come those who have been considering the Child much more in recent times, yet find difficulty in accepting any suggestion that the Child should not go to adult theatre too young, or see proscenium productions too young: " But Children see films," is their usual cry, and they feel a genuine sense of rebuff, even of insult, to the theatre they love.

It is very difficult to know just what effect films do have on Children, for much goes on inside the Child, but we have some chance of observing behaviour, by which we can tell something. Even so, the influence of the film is much more subtle than that of the stage, for a number of reasons, and it is this which makes for difficulties in judgement.

All Child attitude is fluid, so it is not possible to deal with these points in a neat and tidy way because they all run into each other ; but we might consider first the professional attitude, for it stands alone rather more than the other two points.

Many professionals are proud to say that theatre is a business, and that actors are hard working, practical people like everyone else. This is true, though it would be a poor look-out for our theatre if this were all that actors thought of themselves. There should be no over-riding self-satisfaction at being practical. People who brag about this so often merely mean that their vision, aesthetic wisdom and ability are strictly limited. Let us therefore add to this somewhat uninspiring idea of the modern " worker-actor " that, besides being sensible, he is an artist, at least in intention.

[1] Since this was first written the development of television has altered the situation considerably. Cinemas, in turn, feel somewhat threatened, but the main argument in this chapter about film itself remains unchanged.

But supposing theatre is a business, it might be treated as such. There is some resemblance between the way shops are run and the way theatres and cinemas are run. There are big and little shops, and their art is to cater for the customer ; the more his tastes are considered, the more popular the shop.

Cinemas, in a way, are not unlike good chain stores. The cinema considers the mental standpoint of the age. It is mechanical, it is still new, it is always improving. Regarding the comfort of the customers, in winter the houses are warmer than outside, in summer more and more houses are cooler. Swift and smooth and regular publicity drives home the message of comfort and attraction. Food is often served on the premises. The seats are comfortable, and you can both see *and hear*, and, except for London, the prices are cheap for what you get. Both the product and its salesmanship allow for many customers at one time.

The personal question enters too, and this is where we begin to interweave with the Child and its needs.

In an age where life goes fast—too fast, perhaps—where labour is, for many, more a burden than a creative joy, people are seeking a place of mental refreshment and physical comfort. The cinema offers both of these things. There is no effort to see and hear. The dark itself brings tremendous mental rest, shutting us off from the outside world. Both adult and Child take joy in this. We forget our troubles.

Now for the fare. We are well warned by advance publicity that it will be funny, sad, sentimental, gripping, fantastic, bestial or spectacular. If we are too lazy to find out about the piece, or, not being regular visitors, drop into our seats for a rest or with a " chance-it " attitude, we may go to sleep if we do not like it, and no one will be insulted. But generally we become interested. One very important point—the people we are to meet are brought right out towards us. We can see every particle of expression in their faces without effort, so we get to know them well ; we love them more, hate them more ; we become one with them, almost at once.

In nearly all main films the acting is good. People do not always agree about this, but it must always be partly a matter of opinion. If we concede on the one side that it is not so often good, then we must at least admit from the other that we see things from interesting angles, and that people move and talk like people in real life have been known to move and talk, and that the reality of the scene is not continually destroyed by obvious stage tricks. The tricks are more concealed—not scenic ones, but human ones. Much can be done by the actors merely standing and looking, because we see so well. In better films it is often the silent moments that are most telling. The scenic tricks are, for the most part, well carried out, and at their best transport the spectator into breathless dream visions of another world. Is it not all very wonderful ? And two and threepence, even less in many places, gives you a very good seat indeed. There are many of these wonderful places in each city, and at least one in most small towns.

Now for the theatre. The business side is often run by business men, but not always. Sometimes the artists take a hand, or have to run it themselves, which is not always an advantage. But when business men do enter, there are often two sets or more of them between the theatre and public. Sometimes we find an efficient chain, but nothing like the solid-thought-out promotion of the cinemas. I am not necessarily suggesting that there should be, but, with the state of theatre as it is at the moment, we have to admit that prices are very high. The actor and manager argue that they have to be, as theatre rents are high. That may be so, but is not of interest to the public.

Most theatres in this country are draughty in winter and too hot in summer. The seats are not always comfortable, except the most expensive ones. The bars are small and crowded. In most parts of the house you only see very badly, or, in a great number of seats—to be quite frank—not at all. Owing to the practice of actors attempting to be more " natural ", one never hears more than three-quarters of the show, except in the best seats ; yet in the stalls one is overwhelmed with seeing through the tricks of scenery, make-up and acting, and rewarded with a crick in the neck, whilst paying an enormous sum for a seat. To be alone is to be very alone in the audience— intended to be a social gathering. And for a period one suffered agonies of depression at " canned " music in the interval ; perhaps this may cease, though, with new rulings. Half-heard canned music with the lights on can be very depressing.

The average plays provided have not much in them of joy, experience or message. We occasionally see again great plays that we know already, very rarely good new plays that we do not know. Nearly every play is split into three parts. Lastly, the acting is not always very good ; we cannot see the best actors *at the same time* in many parts of the country. We only rarely see them, and we generally see merely a competent but often second-rate performance.

To go back to our shops. The theatre, if big and more likely to pay, makes the fare more difficult to appreciate. If small, it is often uncomfortable and is unlikely to pay. Lovers of the theatre will put up with everything, but there is no earthly reason why they should. One cannot escape the implication that this shop is not run with an eye to the customer's needs. If it is a business, is it a good business ? How far is it considering what is necessary, and how far admitting the good sense of competitors ? Between the theatre and the cinema then—if you were an average person who had never known Child Drama or perhaps much of any other Drama, even at school—which would you go to ? Some Children do occasionally go to the theatre, of course, and more and more are seeing something of the realm of Drama at school, but many more go to the cinema regularly. From their own answers they like to go because it is easy, interesting, exciting and cheap.

Without launching into lengthy explanations, most of which we may know already, of why theatre is not cheap, it may be judged that there is some cause for theatre people to consider their business. If they cannot improve their shops, wares and prices, they may have to see their customers go elsewhere, and, in full justice to the general public, one might add that it would be gracious to suffer this without recrimination.

As to the moral content of films, it is true that many have exciting and violent themes, but it is also true that excitement is part of entertainment— and part of adventure. Adventure is a healthy emotion, but it is not always recognised for such because of the Child's varied ways of using it. The Child has as equal a right to adventure as the older person, and to entertainment also. Many intelligent adults read detective novels, don't we admit it ? The Child does not read very well, so it likes to experience detective and violent stories in the cinema. The whole of Childhood is concerned with doing right and wrong, and if Children are so often on the side of the evil man perhaps it is because, more often than not, they too are held to be sinners, under adult correction and according to adult standards. It is not unnatural that there should be sympathy. But it is in the realm of emulation that critics have their strongest case. If Children copy, then they may copy behaviour of film characters. There is much self-indentification in films because of, among other things, the close-up, the subjective camera, and modern editing processes. This self-identification may affect behaviour.

Behaviour appears to be affected in two main ways, either of a general kind or during Play.

Behaviour becomes generally affected in so far as play situations are taken for reality. We have considered that play to the Child is very much like reality,[1] being often more real (because more understandable) than adult-

---

[1] See Chapter I.

run life itself.   This is where Child Drama is of great importance.   Unsupervised Play of the street and playground often tends to become violent and can develop into habits of reality, from which arise some of the complications of irresponsible personal or gang behaviour.   Connexion with films, where this exists, can be seen in outward wearing of clothes, facial expression and movement.   With boys, hats are worn in sinister ways, walking becomes a permanent slow entry into dangerous doorways, faces become hard, gum is chewed.   Language becomes strange.   With girls, similar things happen, but with expected differences.   Hair styles, flashy clothes and make-up are our sign-posts, as also sulky expressions.   This is true of the older girls and boys.   Younger girls are often men.   Gum-chewing is shared by both sexes according to the amount of American influence of the moment.

Child Drama affords an outlet for all this, as also continuations of simple improvisations at older ages.   Play stories are much influenced by films. Some teachers even go so far as to give up allowing any improvisation because they (note *they*, the adults) cannot put up with the strong note of adventure. But it is extremely important that violent Play should take place in a legal framework and atmosphere.

Frequent opportunity may be given for " playing out " of situations, as this becomes a constructive form of " spitting out ".   *If sympathy, encouragement and careful tending are given to these outbursts, it is perfectly possible to lead Children away to other near-themes, and eventually to quite other themes.* That is the art of nurturing—the point of the adult's connexion with Child Drama—to guide gently, and, almost unnoticed, to add our part to the general creation and experience.   The leading away becomes easy in exactly that period when the Child, of its state and its nature, ceases to need to " play out " so strongly—when the emotion is, in fact, to an extent fulfilled. Thus it is that the potential evil of a story is arranged for and the habit of " doing badly " gently broken.   In the wild Drama of the street there is no checking, no guiding, and the wrong habits may be formed.   If formed— often by sheer bad luck or lack of adult guidance—the Child enters upon a period of trouble as uncomfortable and perplexing to itself as it is to parents and police.   Frequent opportunity for " playing out " is needed, and, if our films are full of the wrong moral content[1]—which they are not always—and if general standards of behaviour are not as good as they might be, then we must expect even more " playing out ", and allow for it.   Where this happens there is a marked result on general behaviour, and what appears by

---

[1] The same could be said of television.

arranged intention in the classroom and the club appears less or not at all outside of them.

The slowly dawning connexion between the beloved, arranged-for Play periods in school and club and the " spitting out ", help the Child to recognise what is real and unreal—ultimately what is Play and what is not. And the presence of the adult helps to turn behaviour the right way, where wilful disobedience unchecked, or thought unaided, would lead to difficulties. Typical of this is that the unguided adventure Drama of the street may include, say, beating a prisoner. In the street this may become too real, and end up in bullying. This cannot happen under proper supervision, and it has already been shown that the emotional desire to fight or strike may be guided away and almost entirely worked off by, say, mime with imaginary weapons.[1] Adventure stories are the simpler form of similar urges and can be used to advantage.

This then is the realm of " important moments " mentioned earlier. At its worst " playing out " is a bore and a puzzle to some adults, at its best it is a great source of discovery, relief and decision for the Child, and may in many cases be the basis of a most important form of preventive education, having results, far-reaching both on health and happiness, which so far have not been widely nor fully explored. There can be no full " in-flow " until the needs of " out-flow " are also considered and in part satisfied.

Reading was mentioned just now. I once heard an English lecturer, speaking on the value of " comics ", suggest that ultimately the Child obtained the actual practice which made it able to read fluently at all, *by reading comics*. Though many people look down on this form of literature, its appeal could be constructive none the less. For our purpose we might note that the comic strip of any kind is not unlike a short film. There are pictures. Story is told largely by movement. There is humour and adventure. Plot moves. Comics are also coloured, and, though people sometimes call them crude, they are often of strong, happy primary colours. Better literature is more generally sombre, and the cheaper editions are often in small print, or with each page crammed. (Shakespeare and the Bible are the extreme examples of this, if indeed we expect older Children to read them by choice.) As films are now taking to colour as well, it is probable that they will be even more popular with Children.

So we come to our third consideration, that of " but Children see films anyway, why shouldn't they see theatre (meaning proscenium theatre) ? "

[1] See Chapter IV, page 80.

This overlaps with what has been said about behaviour arising out of the experience of films. But what of the actual form of presentation itself ? The most direct answer is that there is considerable difference between the forms of presentation of proscenium theatre and of films. Apart from comfort, easiness of access and cheapness, the film is closer to the Child in many ways.

To start with, there are those moments of " close-up " contact with the characters. Children take great note of small details on faces and other objects. They will stare at faces and, often in a dreamy or an urgent voice ask for explanations of what they see. (This is the embarrassing realm of what we call personal remarks.) Babies will often pick up a tiny crumb ; they will also, if not prevented, pull or fondle part of a face they have scrutinised. (This also can be an embarrassment.) The screen close-up looms suddenly at you—the character is right up at you, on top of you. It is almost the same as you. Hence the easy self-identification. It is very literally right " in your life " or " out of your life ". To this extent it shows great similarity to the " peep-bo " of early Childhood, and must look very much the same as what we should remember of first years if we could. It is not unlikely, though, that a half-remembered chord is touched, for the " close-up " affects most of us strongly, just as the large gentle face of mother near and close is, for the lucky Children in life, an important thing indeed, and a close, angry face a thing of terror. At any event, this extreme intimacy in the cinema can be an experience of immense shared sympathy or repulsion.

This is by no means the only form of seeing and experiencing which is similar to the Child's world, for the actual angle at which things are " taken " is of extreme interest, and secures for us a firm mental suggestion of what we are to look at.[1] We might also consider that the fining down to an intense and temporarily limited viewpoint, on to some part of a person or object, is something that the Child shares with the film, and also to some extent with great painters and sculptors. The great artist is often minutely concerned with an experience in a given locality, with a small group of objects or a part of one ; so also is the Child, for this is the basis of projected Play, and is the process which leads directly to Absorption, the great Child virtue.

The absorption too, and the ability to concentrate strongly on one point, thing or character at one time, to the exclusion of all else, including audience,

---

[1] This point was raised at the 1949 Highbury Conference on Children's Theatre, though at that time it was suggested as an argument *against* films.

is the basis of " acting-in-the-round ".[1] It has been suggested that this is the Child's way of acting, as clearly seen from its behaviour, so that this concentration, either of vision or awareness, on particular objects to be found in films is often in accord with the Child's mental process.   In a sense we too, as adults, experience something akin to coma-acting during these moments, and, to this extent, seeing films comes close (at these moments) to the actual mental state of projected Play, characterised always by some quietness, stillness of body, staring, assorting of objects, and concentration on and awareness of a particular limited area.   But at other times films also spur on, by their ready invitation to self-identification, a state very near personal Play, and it is at these moments that audience participation takes place and cheering and jumping up and down breaks out.   This is, of course, more noticeable when it is a Child audience, but may take place partially when adults are present also.   So, then, films provide something very close to both types of Child Play—personal and projected—and we must expect that the film will be loved.

Associated with this concentration on certain things or people is again the angle at which a shot is taken.   We may see a shot through grass, through low foliage, through legs, or even upwards from a low level, so that slight distortion takes place.   These are all the angles of sight which are common, everyday experiences to the Child and may enable it to get " into " a film situation much more than a theatre situation.

This brings us to the actual shape of presentation.   It is not necessary to repeat the suggestions about proscenium theatre presentations being of doubtful advantage at certain ages, except to note that in proscenium acting there is, as a rule, a very conscious attitude towards the audience. There is generally a projecting of the actor's personality outwards (to say nothing of the school of thought which bases this acting on showing off), and because of this there is a regular, often traditional form of grouping and move-ment, which *can* become unreal (in the sense of " un-fitting " rather than of " fantasy ").   It is a tyranny which the shape of the theatre imposes, and against which " moderns " self-consciously rebel.

This consciousness towards audience, and the actual shape of the pros-cenium itself, are a far cry from true and genuine Child Drama.   In the cinema, the darkness makes the edge of the picture less of a conscious pro-scenium than in the theatre, which takes delight in the arch, often leaving straggly curtain edges about.   But there is something more important than

[1] See definitions in Chapter II, page 48.

this, even more important than the fact that many actors in a proscenium theatre can neither be seen nor heard well.   It is that the film transports you well past the edge of the screen and shows you moving pictures of life seen at many angles, and, very important indeed to the Child, life in which people are acting (or seem to be) *because they are sincerely absorbed in the situation of the moment and not half-conscious of audience.*   We see them as we would in life.   Backs are often turned naturally towards us.   Figures pass suddenly in front of our noses.   There is no obvious, irritating grouping going on all the time.   It is the Doing of Life, which we see before us.   That is Drama. We are, in fact, looking on at something very similar to acting-in-the-round, for the better actors in a film become absorbed in the situation during certain scenes,[1] exactly as the Child does, and, when they are absorbed enough, the camera takes them.

The Child, then, can find in the film similar experiences and sight angles to those of its own Play and its everyday life.   Much more space is used in films, and there are many natural circular groupings.   The camera can offer us searchingly precise experiences as well as large community and group experiences, and also include " journey ".   The stage simply cannot give us " journey " except in a stylised, unreal or amusing way, and its hard, help- less trees of woodland scenes do not compare well with the wind-tossed forests, which can even move to music if desired.   Even the film " cuts " are similar to the Child's swift mental change of scene or character during Play.

That all this is true is not only suggested by the experience which all adults can achieve by being familiar with Child Drama, films and the theatre, but is shown largely by the Child's own behaviour.   If it goes to proscenium theatre it copies the actors acting, afterwards.   It copies their manners, their movements ; it cramps its own movements and often demands curtains. It shows off, and demands audience.   Characterisation is confined to an overplayed type, which gets progressively less interesting the longer the disease lasts.   But from films the Child obtains vivid experiences, and its Play is enriched by exciting and believable characterisation and situations, and the stories are strong.   Creation is always added to these.   All that we can say against them is that we often do not like the stories, or that they are *too* strong.   But an intelligent adult can help lead on to other and further creations, whereas nothing can be done with the stub-ends of proscenium theatre experience—one often has to hope that the Child will forget them.

---

[1] Further consideration of creative drama, as a whole, and such things as demonstrations of the Method type of acting should help to make this point more clear.

So, then, films are quite different from the ordinary theatre, and accordingly have a quite different effect on Child behaviour.

Is this a tirade against the theatre? Of course not. We are trying to find out the truth about *Children*.

Now, regarding the theatre. If we want the best experience to come to the Child, we must study its ways and reactions. Some suggestions have been made on theatre in the chapter on Children's Theatre, but I would add here that something of what is experienced by the Child at films can also be experienced at *specially devised* theatre performances, which approach as nearly as they can the Child's own viewpoint and shape of acting—i.e. theatre which takes Child Drama into account. Thus one considers the affirmations of some theatre groups with great interest. For example, the old Pear Tree Players : " to bridge the gap between actor and audience " and " to be able to play in any place or shape ". The Adelphi Players also mention the first as an aim. The West Country Children's Theatre plays " in and amongst Children ". The Birmingham Children's Theatre Players of the Educational Drama Association play " with and amongst rather than at Children ". The Highbury Theatre gave birth to a horseshoe arena theatre in " an attempt to bring to the theatre something of the intimacy of the film ". Other theatre groups are also becoming aware of some desire for change, and, whilst we are not concerned with necessarily urging change, we are concerned with the needs of Children, and that may imply change. Except for a few Children's Theatre groups, the theatre is not nearly so close to the Child's way as the cinema.

This chapter has not been written necessarily to defend films, but rather to question the increasing tendency to make films a scapegoat. This is unjust. It is nearly always the adult who fails, and an excuse is found. The films provide many wonderful experiences, and are very close to Child attitude and Play form. Let us be honest about that. If it is true that they tempt violent outburst, let us see it as adventure. (It is not healthy to stifle adventure. Do we want a wet nation ?) We have seen that these strong impulses can be dealt with by the adult who cares.

It may seem that the strongest argument against films is that of moral content and its effect on behaviour. But this does not take into account anything of good moral content, and it would not be accurate to dismiss films without considering this. The older adventure books of Henty, Kipling, even the *Boys Own Paper*, make a strong point of justice and moral behaviour. So have, and do, many films. I know of people who declare they have learnt much of their moral judgement from films ; very fine people they are too. Much could be learnt, I think, by impressions of the behaviour of the late Sir Aubrey Smith, for instance ; his dignity and character must be indelible in the minds of all who saw him. The daring of Fairbanks, the pity evoked by Chaplin, the determination of Cagney—all these must also have an effect. Does one lightly forget *Disraeli*, or the moment when the younger Pitt on leaving Downing Street says to the coachman " A lovely day " ; or the determined search by John Mills as the resolute little cockney husband in *Waterloo Road* ? And, for the ladies, does one forget Mrs. Miniver, the sophisticated grace of Myrna Loy, the gay bravery of Kay Francis, the incredible emotional range and ability of Ginger Rogers, the immovable rock-like strength of Nancy Price, or the tremendous sympathy of Glynis Johns in *No Highway* ? Does not every film offer just as many lessons in courageous, decent behaviour, particularly in suffering of every kind, as in bad behaviour ? And does the bad man often get away with it ? I have mentioned a few names that leap to my mind ; there are new ones every week. Courage and justice do not die out of Drama. All tales of adventure are based upon these things.

After six or seven, Children begin to recognise morality quite clearly. At puberty there is another dawn of seriousness. It is difficult to believe that only the minus is absorbed. There must be some plus. And their remarks support this view ; so does their Play.

As there is a way of dealing with bad moral content, the effect or potential effect need not be so great. But even this has now been questioned, for the research department at Birmingham University that has been considering the cinema does not admit that inquiry reveals an adverse effect on moral standards. Does this wipe away our last objection to films ? Certainly it calls it in question. (We may have to fall back on crowds, infectious diseases and eye strain.)

But observation is as important as inquiry, and the fact that Children act film characters and situations cannot be denied. All depends on what happens to this acting. It is not wholly evil.

It is interesting to note, though the two things may be entirely unrelated, that the film inquiry took place in an area where more and more " playing out " is being encouraged.

CHAPTER XX

QUESTIONS AND REMARKS

REMARKS

Typical remarks by Children about Child Drama :

Girl, age six : " Oh, that was wonderful. Dancing like that is being a wind high, high, oh high in the sky."

Girl, age six : " I'd like to do this alwiz and alwiz."

Boy, age seven : " Couldn't we alwiz talk through the music like you let us ? It sort of *makes* yer talk."

Girl, age seven : " Put it on again, Petie. We're never going to stop this. It's better than Fairy Land."

Girl, age seven : " Most girls don't fight to music, you know. Think of it, not even to music. But I can shoot Brontasasurasis. They won't get up ... I think. (Note room being just left for resurrection.)

Girl, age eight : " *When* can we do this again ? "

Girl, age eight : " May I run with you ? It would be like that playing we once did all over again."

Boy, age eight : " I'm gonna add bits (kick) an' bits (kick) an' bits (kick) of me own to that wot we just done. Ha, you'll see." (He was kicking a hot pipe in joy.)

Boy, age eight (backward) : " Tis the only thing, man."

Boy, age nine : " This is bestest of all we done at school."

Boy, age ten : " Let's dance football."

Boy, age thirteen : " We're 'aving much more fun now. None o' that readin' stuff, on an' on. We're doin' Columbus now."

Girl, age fourteen : " Drama's the best period now, we use all the room as well as the stage."

Adult Remarks :

A Headmistress : " I thought it was jsut talk at first about Child Drama. But I feel very humble now ; everything you have said has happened in my school."

A Teacher (Senior Boys) : " Their speech has improved tremendously through improvisation . . . it is clearer since you last came, and there is better choice of words and expressions."

A Teacher (Infants) : " I have tried your idea of using noises, particularly the

333

tambourine. I never have any worry about control now. They seem so interested."

A Teacher (*Junior*) : " The C's do so well in this work."

Head Teacher (*Junior Mixed*) : " We do Child Drama throughout the school now. It has made a tremendous difference. Children and staff seem to be happier."

Head Teacher (*Infants*) : " Two of my teachers and I have started to try out ideas mentioned in your course. After only three weeks we are getting results."

Head Teacher (*Senior Boys*) : " I can see what you mean, but we haven't time for much of that sort of thing here."

Headmaster (*Grammar School*) : " You think that even in this type of school short periods of Drama would be of value ? I would like you to come and talk to my staff."

Head Teacher : " I would like everyone to see how much better Drama is with rostrum blocks than with a stage."

Head Teacher : " What they do is so beautiful."

Head Teacher : " I tried this twenty years ago. It didn't work then and it won't work now. There isn't time for Drama—not in my school anyway."

Head Teacher : " I can't see how Child Drama can aid education."

Drama Teacher : " There can't be a Child Drama."

Professional Producer : " It is obvious you are right. There does exist a Child Drama. Now I've seen it I am convinced."

Head Teacher : " I'm not going to agree with you yet. You're upsetting my old-fashioned ideas. But it seems to work—at least as far as I've tried it."

A Garage proprietor : " Your broadcast [1] was most interesting. It seemed to get right at what Children really want. I remember doing it when I was a kid."

Office Clerk : " I must say your talk was most interesting. It's seldom one hears anything like that, but I know you're right, as I've seen it happen."

Education Official (N. Midlands) : " If we all did as you suggest we might have a new and wonderful theatre. You have shown us how to make theatre out of nothing—moreover, to do it with people many of whom have never acted before. I see now that the principles suggested may be applied to any age group. Before, I could only see their application to Children, and I wasn't even sure about that."

A Teacher : " Although I am a Modern Dance specialist I have also found that you cannot tell young children how to move when they are playing, or they just go dead and try to copy. They surprise us with lovely movement that we would not think of, as long as we leave them alone."

Self : " The last words are the secret—so difficult for most specialists to accept."

---

[1] " Teaching Children to Act."   B.B.C. Midland Home Service.   15th July, 1948.

A Teacher : " It is clearly important that children should act out their worries, and I have always found it an admirable way of helping new children to settle into their new environment.   Three little girls who came here the other day could not fit in properly, but managed to find some friendliness from each other.   I left them alone, and for almost a week they played the three bears by themselves in a passage. At the end of that time they appeared to be quite happy.   The play was finished and from then on they fitted quite easily into the ordinary school work."

(This is a full acceptance of the value of Child Play.)

A Head Teacher (after visit to Midlands school) : " You have backed all that I have felt for years, and you have given confidence to the intuitive efforts of my younger teachers who were frightened by those who have had success with polished proscenium theatre."

Member of a Training College Staff, and a Speech Trainer (S. England) : " Your lecture makes everything more plain and helps tremendously with detail on how to guide the Child.   We have felt that something of this kind was the proper approach."

Member of Training College Staff (N. Midlands) : " You are the first person to point out the real link between Child Art and Child Drama, and make us fully aware that the latter exists as an Art Form.   We had suspected it, but could not see how it could be recognised."

Member of Training College Staff (Home Counties) : " This links educational and psychological theory with a practical everyday method, and at last makes sense of Drama as Education."

Head of a University Staff dept. (S. England) : " You ought to be grant-aided for research and investigation."

Professor of an English University : " I would not have missed your lecture for anything.   It opens up new worlds.   Of course you are right.   We are only at the beginning."

Professor of an American University : " Where I am in America, we are swinging more and more to your views.   I am particularly interested in your suggestion of experiments in acting without audience.   We'll try that."

Education Official : " What I have seen and heard is very revolutionary.   I see it as something of great importance, which opens up vast avenues.   I would like to keep in touch with you."

Head Teacher (Midlands) : " It is very inspiring to have such encouragement. Nobody has understood so well what we are trying to achieve here."

Head of a Training College (Midlands) : " What you have said has shaken a good many of us.   It explains what my English staff are always trying to tell me and it links up with Child Art."

Head of a Training College (S.W. England) : " What you say about the Child will be welcome to half my staff.   The rest will be plunged into gloom—even so, the force of your argument and the immense practical detail you have laid before us may convert quite a few, when we've had more time to consider the matter."

Head of Training College (Midlands) : " I cannot quite accept what you say, though on logical grounds I find it hard to pick a hole in the argument. It links up with the free activity methods so well."

Canadian Education Official (after lecture) : " You say you are actually doing this work. It must be marvellous. I would like all Canadian teachers to see it."

Indian Teacher : " This is all new to me, but is very interesting. I can see great possibilities in my country, but do not know enough to convince people. May I keep in touch with you ? "

American Professor : " Why don't you come to America ? Only one Drama trainer I know has got so far. Even he has missed some of the forms of movement and has never applied them to older age groups in the way you describe."

A County Drama Adviser : " But you surely don't mean that adults must learn about the theatre from Children. Doesn't the professional stand for anything ? "

A County Drama Adviser : " I just don't talk about Children at conferences now. People don't understand. I know you are right."

A County Drama Adviser : " May I come and see the work ? It would help me to sort things out."

Chairman of a County Drama Committee : " What you say fits in with many things I have found for myself. We would like to try some further."

Director of a professional Children's Theatre (S. England) : " You are the first person to raise a thoroughly reasonable argument against what we do. Actually we are experimenting with some projection into the auditorium, but not with Children's Theatre."

Director of another professional Children's Theatre (S. England) : " I am very interested in what you say, though I always argue against you."

Director of a Children's Theatre : " What you have said and what we have done as a result, has made the whole relationship with Children quite different. Wherever we go head teachers have noticed the improvement."

Member of a Children's Theatre : " What I have seen and heard today may alter our whole outlook. I am going back to talk to our group before the new season starts."

Director of a professional Children's Theatre : " I am sure you are right. We *must* break away from the proscenium."

A well-known Actor : " I can't agree with you at all."

A very famous Actress : " What you say of Children is *most* interesting. It raises completely new problems and opens up tremendous possibilities in production."

QUESTIONS

Many interesting and important points arise from questions and discussion. For this reason a few of the questions put either after lectures or by visitors, have been included. Where it was possible for careful notes to be taken, the outline of discussion, as well as question and answer, has been preserved.

I am indebted to many kind people who have taken these notes for me. In the case of questions by letter, or of the same question coming from different places, I have given a shortened version on the lines of the answer given at the time. The questions and answers here included have been selected by practising teachers as being of most interest and use.

Infant Teachers (Midlands) :

(1) *In defining the two forms of Play, you made us feel there is more projected Play in the earlier years. Is that correct ?*

Yes. From one to four years there is a great deal of projected Play. I think one would expect this, as the Child is not yet a very good mover. From about four onwards there is a change. But it is after seven years that personal Play really comes into its own, though, of course, it occurs earlier, too. The early forms of personal Play are rather experience trials of doing a certain action or of being in a certain mood. Early projected Play is still closely associated with sense trials, though Art patterns occur.

(2) *I've never heard it explained before, but I've noticed this difference, too : In personal Play, Children seem to wake up suddenly, assume a character or a mood and get cracking. Is that it ?*

Exactly.

(3) *Would you say many Children suffer from the wrong family or school atmosphere ?*

Yes, undoubtedly, and clinical evidence supports this view.

(4) *Do you feel then that Child Drama is a special thing of its own, and by its use Children become happier and healthier?*

Yes.

(5) *Briefly, why is this ?*

Because Child Drama is part of real life and has its deep origins in the activity and nature of Man. It is quite different from any conception of theatre, which is a small—though attractive—bubble on the froth of civilisation.

(6) *It is difficult to stop thinking in terms of theatre. It's the only part of Drama that people bothered to teach before. But it clearly does not cover the fields we have been discussing. What would you suggest ?*

C.D.—22

It is helpful to remember that Drama means " doing " and " struggling ", in fact—Life. The various parts of Drama then fall more easily into place and are seen for what they are. Theatre is only a mirror of Life. Drama is Life itself.

(7) *You are not actually against the theatre, are you ?*

Not in the least. I love it very much. But I am against its interference in the wrong places and at the wrong times. Theatre lovers too often try to impose not only their love, but the thing itself, where it is neither needed nor wanted. In a way, to speak for Child Drama is a sign of justice for the Child.

(8) *It's rather a shock to find that Children have their own Drama. But I saw what you mean even before leaving Training College. After hearing your first lecture I tried out things myself, and the Children reacted at once. Does this always happen ?*

Nearly all normal Children start Play eventually, in the right atmosphere. In school this is created by the teacher. But Children do not always react at *once*. It depends on the state of the Child and what has gone before.

(9) *Isn't the shock one gets really to one's pride ? We grown-ups think our theatre is the cat's whiskers, and, when we find something else, we don't always like it. Isn't that so ?*

Yes. But it is also, for many people, a blow to their own adult love (i.e. the theatre), until they learn to love Child Drama too. This makes it hard for some people to be open-hearted in welcoming Child Drama, and they don't recognise its beauty.

(10) *Don't you think it depends on the general attitude towards teaching ?*

Undoubtedly. Those in favour of very formal teaching tend to prefer the discipline of the script play, even for quite young Children.

(11) *You said that the young Child should not have too many properties. But if it is inclined more towards projected Play, oughtn't it to have a lot to play with ?*

My point was that we should not overload it when it was attempting *personal* Play. When finding its way towards acting and other things through personal Play—which is the right development—we can hold back the Child in something near projected Play, if too many treasures are used.

(12) *I know that's true. I've seen it happen, but its true even of the junior school, isn't it !*

Yes. Genuine Child Drama relies on inner creation, not on outer materialism. If we help them not to become greedy, Children develop great taste in using only that which is necessary. If we do not overload them, they tend to take eventually what they need and no more. Not only does this enrich their Art, but it is also a good preparation for Life.

Birmingham Teachers' Training College. (Infant and Junior Students) :

(13) *How far and in what way should guidance be given ?*

For the young Child, suggestions by stories may stimulate Play. Sounds are even better, such as jumping noises, " spreading out " chords on the piano, and pony noises. Many Children want to be the same thing at once. Allow this. Arrange for frequent moments of relaxation in contrast to movement and tension. Detailed directions should not be given to the younger Child, but general encouragement about where to go may be a help. The tiny Person finds crossing a room quite a big adventure. If stories are used they should be short and simple.

(14) *Is it possible to tell the Children a story and expect them to dramatise it ?*

Yes. But we must be kind, and get things warmed up. It is not fair to expect the young Child to pick up a scene " cold ". It may not want to, and there must be no forcing. But joining in action as a story is being told, sometimes prepares the way for genuine story acting afterwards.

(15) *Do we encourage the Children to talk while miming ?*

You mean should they talk when acting ? Yes, allow them to do so whenever they wish. Much speech comes through the body with the younger Child, though. Gesture is language, so is pulling faces. Special times of suggested " do it without talking this time " are of value if you want to concentrate on movement. That is according to the teacher's wisdom. But speech cannot start too early.

(16) *At what age should Children begin to dramatise their own stories ?*

I have known five-year-olds do it perfectly well, though it is not general until seven. Between seven and thirteen one expects a rich flow, if the Children have been handled well.

(17) *How can all the class participate in the limited space of a classroom ?*

The main players can be made to feel free to approach those who have to sit in desks. One often sees buying and selling, for instance, going on in this way, or a fugitive will ask for cover under a desk. Finally, everyone can join in with effects noises ; soft tapping of pencils for rain or leaves on the window, desk lids for explosions, chubby fists for feet of unknown animals, whistling and sighing for wind. Drama is then all about us. There is joy and creative experience.

(18) *Is it better to repeat plays, or always have fresh ones ?*

An improvisation may be repeated out of love. This is good and natural. Sometimes little improvements take place. Play repeated is the embryo of the stage play as we know it. This is how Play gradually grows towards *a* play. Repeated Play needs watching, though, as it can grow worse and lead to laziness. There should be constant fresh creative attempts to balance this.

(19) *Should teacher or Child choose the cast ?*

It depends on the circumstances. Both should have a say, sometimes one more than the other ; tiny Children are less able to choose than older ones. In more polished improvisations the teacher may have to organise a little. Children are at times capable of choosing, and grow to be good critics of each others' work. The teacher learns to *feel* what is needed ; this is part of the necessary sympathy and sensitivity which teachers can develop further from working with Children.

(20) *Should the teacher give a running commentary on what is going on, to keep the class interested ?*

It would be a clever teacher who could do so when genuine Play was going on. Often the Children feel, understand and hear more than we do. They sometimes feel it necessary to inform adults when they have finished. I think that in most cases the commentary would be redundant and a disturbance. Forgive me if I say, too, that it might possibly be inaccurate. We are not that close to the Child's mind.

(21) *As Children grow up and leave the junior school they often grow self-conscious What are we to do about that ?*

That is the problem of the senior school. The self-consciousness is connected with puberty, and one of its chief immediate causes is undoubtedly the break in atmosphere and teaching approach which the Child encounters in its new school. We need continuity of similar methods for at least the first year in the secondary schools. Continued creative opportunity is necessary, and the attitude of the teacher must be more constructive. We tend to give in too easily sometimes. We must give *more* aid, *more* opportunity. It is largely our fault if self-consciousness ultimately prevails.

(22) *Are people less self-conscious in roles that they want to be ?*

Yes. They get into the skin of the part better, because of real affection for and affinity to the person they now are. That does not leave so much room for self-consciousness.

(23) *How do you cope with the able and dominating Child ?*

Without cramping its leadership, ensure that others get a chance. It may be necessary to step in sometimes and suggest that other Children do something. The immediate reaction will tell you whether you were right to interfere, or whether healthy, normal leadership was taking place. Having felt the line of direction, pursue it until you feel the next emotional pull.

(24) *Is it good to let Children have masks and costumes ?*

Yes, occasionally. Let them try to create their own. However, the best work is done without these things. Use the half- or part-mask for the younger Child. It gives more freedom and is less hot, and therefore interferes less with creation.

(25) *How can a teacher control a class working in simultaneous groups ?*

If the Children are really interested enough to *be* working in simultaneous groups, it is unlikely there will be lack of control. If such work has been started too early, walk round amongst them or break it up, if need be, and revert to one group at a time, while the others sit round in a circle. Alternate with group work for sensitivity development, such as getting obedience and reaction to a mere hand movement from you instead of the verbal command. Children often become interested and quiet if you use body speech only (gesture), because this touches a note in themselves.

(26) *Why are Children shy in school but not in their Play outside ?*

It is sometimes a result of previous experience of adults—this is not the teacher's fault. It is sometimes entirely due to the atmosphere of the school ; they do not trust the atmosphere and there is not enough happiness. A good teacher will seek to change this, but in some schools fear is still the main force. Where fear or restraint are uppermost, you get rowdy play outside and anything from shyness to despair inside. This is entirely the teacher's fault.

(27) *Time is often a difficulty. Is the twenty-minute lesson possible ?*

Certainly. It can be most fruitful. Only twenty minutes a week even would be a help. Play in short bursts can be valuable and is often obtainable. Only the other morning I met five Children in a school corridor, while I was waiting to see their Headmistress. In seven minutes we had made friends, created a complete playlet between us, acted it out, waved good-bye and tiptoed away. This is possible where Children have trust and are unafraid. Learning to be quick is part of the training this work brings.

Birmingham Training College :

(28) *Would you enlarge upon your remarks about the use of sound ?*

Language contains vowels and consonants. Sounds are roughly divided into elongated sounds and short, sharp ones. Strings, bells and gongs offer us long sounds, unless specially arranged otherwise. Sharp sounds come from percussion instruments, tapping and banging things, though of course there are intermediate sounds, too. These sounds are enjoyed by the Child. It will often act or dance because it has heard a sound. By carefully nurtured love, first of sound itself and then of special sounds—short and sharp—then of sounds containing mood, it is possible to associate sound of many kinds (starting with the vowels and consonants) with language in general. The Child then transfers its love to speech. Parallel with this should come spontaneous Play where speech enters. Practice in speaking creatively and learning the love of sound is the best approach to language. Out of this grows a genuine love of literature. Good sound (literature) is recognised when heard. This develops genuine taste rather than imposed taste. Love of sound can be begun in the infant school. Movement to a tambour or tambourine brings great delight, and, because of interest in listening, behaviour improves and the teacher gains wonderful control. Many different sounds can be incorporated in Play, and add greatly to its joy and beauty.

(29) *Is " imposed taste " any good at all ?*

No. It is not genuine and it does not last. And while it does last it is often responsible for a sort of pose.

(30) *Should Children enact scenes from a socially or morally undesirable background ?*

It is not really quite a question of " should ". Children *do*. It is their first form of liberation. They spit out much that is undesirable in their lives this way, and we thus learn much of their background. They offer us a confidence. They can be led away to other ideas, in time. If this does happen, sympathetic handling is essential.

(31) *Should Children be precluded from using words in their early attempts at Drama ?*

I do not think so, though it is true that the young Child speaks much with its body. Only a few words may be used throughout one whole scene. They are generally the right ones. Where Children *are* stopped from using words, they sometimes fail to obtain enough early practice in creative speech, and, though movement may become beautiful at a later age, speech often remains poor.

(32) *Should Children be prevented from really fighting in Drama ?*

If Children start this Drama late in life, you can't prevent it at first. Boys always want to. It is possible, though, to smooth this away a bit. I generally suggest stylised fighting to a background of sound, or more concentration on acted stories. This breaks up the primitive urge to grip the nearest bloke come what may. But many *good* Drama climaxes revolve round the fight, and conquering is an important part of adventure and confidence-building in the masculine spirit.

(33) *How does this Play differ from natural Play ?*

Play is natural to the Child, but Play left entirely alone often tends to become more violent as the Child grows older. Play associated continually with beauty, and with the treasures of knowledge through the agency of an understanding adult mind, leads to better creation, more joy, has a marked effect on behaviour and results in the discernible phenomenon of an Art Form. This is Child Drama.

(34) *Should desks be moved ?*

Yes, if you need more space, but a lot can be done even in and out of the desks. Children sometimes find the first joys of a higher level by using desks, too.

(35) *How do we overcome the Child's diffidence ?*

By continual opportunity, continual encouragement and by creating the right atmosphere, not by forcing.

(36) *How do we overcome the domination of the class by one group ?*

One way is to split the class into several groups and have separate creation by each group. Keep your audience participation going strong to hold interest, when the others aren't acting.

(37) *Is Shakespeare possible in the secondary modern school ?*

Yes, but some teachers and educationists question the acting of Shakespeare in schools. As far as Child Drama is concerned it would come into the category of the script play, which does not appear to enter by *genuine Child choice* and obvious preparedness until about thirteen or so. One must say, of course, that many much older actors are quite incapable of either understanding or acting Shakespeare, though I have seen fourteen- and fifteen-year-olds get at some of the essence of Shakespeare, whilst obviously only understanding half the words.

(38) *Can you give an instance of the curative value of Drama ?*

Yes. I have found that Children who suffer from nightmares can be helped to face their fears through Play, and that the dreams may disappear afterwards. Children and adults suffering from pain will, when acting out a story, often perform movements which they cannot do in cold blood. Thinking of something else helps them. Realisation of their achievement brings hope and confidence, and the actual inducing of the movement may be necessary to the cure.

Building of confidence by acting little scenes, like having to go into a shop and buy things, is useful too, after certain forms of treatment. The patient slowly finds the courage to face the world again in this way.

Children who are backward or upset obtain release through creative Drama, and often find a way to mix with their fellows again by realising afterwards that they got on perfectly well in dance or Play. Opportunity to act out in a legal atmosphere a character that haunts and tempts, particularly during adolescence, can save a young person from actually becoming the character in real life. They face and choose, this way, their course of conduct.

Dramatic Play is used as an aid to diagnosis in Child Guidance Clinics and also, in part, for curative purposes.

I think that in the future the wider use of Drama will prove of great value as a preventive, quite apart from therapy.

(39) *What would you expect to find in good Drama lessons ?*

If you are speaking in terms of Child Drama, not of script plays, I would say : they should be joyful.

There should be a good, encouraging atmosphere.

The teacher should be obviously keen, quiet, kindly and observant, and know how to stimulate if necessary.

There should be variety and new creation.

One would expect clear defined shapes in the Children's movements, and good use of space.

Questions should be answered adequately.

There should be complete control.

Children's suggestions should be encouraged and used.

There should be good contrast—noise and quiet.

Speech should be flowing, rapid and unhesitating—one expects it to be of poetic and philosophic language between *circa* six and ten years, and increasingly witty and gay between ten and fourteen.

There should be great zest in the acting, good group sensitivity, marked sincerity and absorption, bringing high moments of " theatre " as we understand it.

I would hope to see things, animals, people or movements I had not thought of, and it would be good to get an example of " running play ".

The unconscious grouping should be exciting.

Everybody would get an equal chance of creation.

I think that would be a pretty good lesson, though you understand the teacher would not teach. He would guide and nurture ; he too has to be a creative artist ; he does not just sit back, but is constantly attending and ready to offer aid if needed. There are no short cuts to this work, no hard or easy rules. Each Child is different, each group has its own peculiarities, and each teacher has to learn to handle things his or her own way. But before starting we must love the Child, love the work and know why we do it. And if we cannot at all times love, because of tiredness, then we must develop a deep and strong sense of justice. For at the bottom of all creative opportunity in school lies an elementary justice for the Child. Together with the Child a wisdom is built, and an emotional sharing is experienced. Out of all this grows the indefinable and extraordinary knowledge of life that constitutes for the Child " education " in the full sense of the word.

North of England (after lecture) :

(40) *Do we often spoil spontaneity by the presence of adults ?*
Yes.

(41) *Should a teacher show a Child how to move ?*
If the teacher does, it is not Child Drama. There may be some general suggestion on *what* to do, if imagination fails, but not *how* to do.

(42) *Does the audience hear Child work ?*
There is no audience as such in true Child Drama ; the Children are creating because they want to. When this work first starts, adult judgement would often say speech is poor : (*a*) because practice and confidence in speaking at all are badly needed ; (*b*) because words are invented that do not appear in our dictionary. Speech becomes clearer and louder in time. A hint dropped once in two or three weeks about being a little louder is often enough to have a marked effect, where a good student-teacher friendship has been built up.

(43) *Would you make such a suggestion while Play is going on ?*
Never, it would break absorption. Interruptions shake confidence. If an adult interferes too often, Child Drama dies. This is different from sensitive, well-timed suggestion.

(44) *Can teachers trained in the old way ever be any help in this work ?* (Laughter.)
Most certainly, if they see the point of Child Drama, and suffer a change of heart. (Laughter and clapping.) Sympathy, understanding and ability to observe and assess are the needs of the teacher—and of the Child.

(45) *Does this training militate against the usual education and Child training ?*
There is no need whatever for it to do so. Some periods of creative Play have

been known to be of value even in the most formal schools. After all, periods devoted to games and P.T. are considered a useful balance. Drama sensibly used has the same effect. But it *does* tend to make Children more open, friendly and direct. The straight-laced teacher sometimes mistakes this for impudence. It is the same with painting and other creative activities. Much depends on the teacher.

(46) *Is there a lack of co-ordination between primary school and secondary modern?*

Yes. It may be possible in future for senior schools to know more of junior schooling, and, for Drama at least, this is most necessary, and I would say it was true for Art and other things also.

(47) *You said something about similar work to the junior school taking place at the beginning of the secondary modern. How much of this do you think should go on ?*

At least the first year should be much the same as in the junior school. No noticeable break comes until about thirteen or over. In general terms, puberty brings a new outlook, and about that time the outward form of Child Drama changes—there is a tendency towards using a stage up one end of the room.

(48) *Do you actually mean there is a shape you can see, like the circle in junior work ?*

Yes. It is rather like a long tongue coming out from the stage, and movement flows on and off stage, when genuine Child Drama takes place. If there is a cramping of space at this time, we find only a bulge out from the stage. The bulge is more the true shape for the over fourteens.

(49) *When does the script play come in ?*

Usually between thirteen and fifteen. The best play-writing begins about that age also.

(50) *Do you find Children can write plays*

Yes, if they have had enough creative opportunity.

Birmingham (after lecture for teachers) :

(51) *Do you get noise when you first start this work ?*

Sometimes, yes. Older boys make noise, particularly if they have not had much freedom. But they soon learn that undue noise spoils creation. The personal responsibility for restraint is thus slowly smoothed over on to them. It is part of the value of the work.

(52) *If a teacher is not too confident about keeping control in the hall, what would you suggest ?*

There may be difficulties when first using space. It may be better to use a smaller space first. By grouping the class in a ring (sitting on the floor, if necessary) and letting relays of players work in the middle of it, you can keep somewhat similar conditions to the classroom. The ring can then be enlarged as desired, and more players can take part at one time, until the whole group is able to take part all over the room if necessary. Quiet and control can thus be built up slowly. But noise is often necessary to good Drama at certain places of climax. Most Children need to blow off steam, and the more they have been cooped up the more they tend to burst out at the first opportunity. But they get over this with our help, and become calmer. Then they start to create more thoughtfully.

(53) *You spoke of Music and Drama. Can Children make their own music ?*

Yes, indeed, and my personal opinion is that this might be developed much further. One finds it when Children have been unusually delighted by a Drama or dance experience. They then make sounds to accompany themselves. It is a spontaneous outburst.

(54) *How do we deal with an audience such as parents on parents' day ?*

An audience of parents really belongs to the more formal display. Child Drama itself is quite different, and deteriorates with audience as generally understood. A great deal could be done by interesting Parent Associations in Child Drama though, and, with their co-operation, visits of one or two parents at a time might be inconspicuously arranged, until that time when there are balconies to raise observers above the Child's eye-level. Only then could Child Drama be shared by greater numbers of those interested. Complete quiet is a necessity.

(55) *Could one use " audience participation " on parents' days ?*

It might work, if parents know of the reason and procedure. They might be grouped round and add noises to the play. But this would be likely to bring self-consciousness to the Children to some extent. It would not be the same as Children making the noises, with their *great* potential for being " in it ". Grown-ups might tend to make a joke of it all. It is joyful, but not our sort of " fun ". There is a difference.

(56) *Isn't an audience necessary for some plays ?*

Yes. For set plays it may be. For Child Drama it isn't. The two are quite different. We mustn't muddle them up.

(57) *When our present Children become the grown-up audience, will there be true audience participation ?*

That is quite likely. If the attitude is understood, and if it remains of interest through the years, sincere audience participation may take place by a common unspoken desire to create together. One already finds grown-ups doing it with each other, Children with grown-ups and Children with Children.

(58) *What about taught speech ?*

Formal training can be run parallel to Child Drama, if the teaching is really well carried out. The two can balance each other. Child Drama is largely out-flow, formal training is rather in-flow. Both are necessary in life and in education, but bad formal training brings stilted, unnatural speech with no meaning in it.

(59) *How would you teach speech ?*

By full liberation, and plenty of creative trial. That is *practice*. Practice during Play brings " language flow ". Speech improves, and it is the delight of speech taught this way that what is said is meant. This method only works in a true, sympathetic atmosphere. The teacher is responsible for that.

Teachers' Training College (Worcestershire) :

(60) *Is it harmful to take Children to the theatre ?*

It is not always helpful to take *young* Children to the theatre. After about twelve years of age is best. For younger Children, bringing theatre to them is better, doing plays *with* them rather than at them, and certainly not in the proscenium form. We have to guard against shaking the Child's confidence in its own work.

(61) *What about Children writing their own plays ?*

They should never be discouraged, but young Children often write better and use their heads more if encouraged merely to write stories about what they experience during improvisation. Their written plays are generally rather bad, and as great a disappointment to them as to us when acted. Their improvised plays are better. Over thirteen or so, their script plays evolve well, if developed slowly in this way.

(62) *How do you link improvisation with the play later ? How does it develop ?*

True improvisation comes first, then a polished improvisation (i.e. an improvisation done again, perhaps several times, with some moves or words kept the same because of joy in them). This last is getting nearer to what we would call a play. Then sometimes words or a few sentences are written down to help keep an outline of the play. Finally, the whole or nearly all a play is written down. Stories are written parallel with this, and finally we launch on the better attempts at a script play, and study of plays by adults.

(63) *Do you use costume ?*

Yes, but in small doses. Lengths of stuff and bits and pieces still offer the Child a chance of creating. The ready-made piece is already created. Movement often gets worse with costume. Care must be taken to balance stimulus with real need.

(64) *Surely if children at school did what you say, they would grow up less of a social bumpkin ?*

Yes, of course. Drama has much to teach in the way of manners and social grace. With fourteen years upwards the matter is constantly arising, and even technical stage movement can be associated with everyday life in many of its aspects.

Birmingham :

(65) *Do you think that improvisation is more important than theatre training ?*

It is the basis of Child Drama. It *is* theatre training as well as education. Doing plays is different, and is not always good theatre training or education.

(66) *Why do you want the old theatre to die ?*

I don't.   It will die if something better succeeds it.   But for Child Drama we are not concerned with it.   We are only interested in what is really best for Children.

(67) *What will happen to our good English plays ?   Are there no modern plays we could save ?*

Good plays live on, and there are good modern plays, of course.   Children don't save plays, though.   That is not what they are there for.   Adults do that. Children have their own Art Form, but *can* partake of ours too, though not so well until they are older (*circa* thirteen years and over).

(68) *Are Children's festivals of educational value ?*

It depends on how they are run.   I think competitive ones are very harmful. It would be better for older Children to take part in non-competitive festivals.   It is, however, possible for younger Children to play in their own way (not pro-scenium) on certain evenings, if that is considered valuable.   All depends on *why* you do the festival.   If you really think of the need of the *Child*, most questions answer themselves.   Let us say that there are other things of *more* value than festivals.[1]

(69) *What about Shakespeare, and our old English plays ?   Could older Children act them " in-the-round " ?*

Certainly.   The old English plays were not written for the proscenium theatre, and Terence Gray of the Festival Theatre, Cambridge, said Shakespeare died behind a proscenium.   The Shakespearian Theatre form used a large apron and different levels.   Shakespeare can be acted anywhere.   The intimacy of the Arena form often lends itself to soliloquy.

A Conference of Teachers of Speech and Drama (Stratford)

(70) *Do you get Children to do movement and speech together ?*

Yes, I help them to find the rhythm of each and to experience the fitting of one to the other.   They obtain joy from this experience.

(71) *Do you always use music ?*

No, not always.

(72) *Do you allow children to speak whilst the music is on ?*

Young children, yes.   The music stimulates mood, action and words.   They do not listen in the same way as we do, but emotionally and pictorially.   As we get older we tend to get more intellectual about it, and more ashamed of our emotions.

(73) *Can one stimulate what you have called " language flow " easily ?*

Yes, it is there to an extent in every child, and is the true basis of good litera-ture and joy in speech.

---

[1] A Report on festivals appears in Chapter XVI, pages 290 and 291.

(74) *Would you do away with formal speech training altogether ?*

Certainly not for older Children.   But all Children need a great deal of their own creative opportunity.   That is " out-flow ".   Formal training is part of " in-flow ", and cannot have full significance without the balance of imaginative creation.

Under formal training we must also include the benefits of speech-therapy. But, interestingly enough, creative work has been of value even in speech-therapy, and I know of cases which improved by drama-therapy, which did not improve through speech-therapy.   On the other hand, I know of numerous cases where an application of creative work (sometimes used as part of drama-therapy) and formal training have together been effective.

North England :

(75) *Would you advocate peripatetic teachers or members of staff to take improvisation ?*

It is better for a member of staff to take it.   The ideal is that most or all teachers in the school should have some ability to provide the right environment for Child Drama ; then the work becomes part of a community expression and of general education.   The teacher *in* the school has the chance of knowing the Children better.   An outside teacher has more difficulty in building up a friendship bond with the Child (though of course it can be done), and the specialisation of the peripatetic brings with it attendant dangers of domination.   Outside specialists *can* be very useful, but they need most careful training, particularly in adaptability to different traditions and in assessing accurately the exact needs of the Children in close relationship to the attitude of the school staff.   It is very difficult for the outsider to fit in, and with Drama as education everything *must* fit, because of the endless link with all subjects.   Without this link, we often lose Child Drama and are back again at teaching the Child to act.

(76) *Where does the specialist come in then ?*

He should advise teachers, and run courses for them, if desired.   Taking a class himself is only part of the business.   The *teacher* must eventually take the class, therefore it is the teacher who must be helped.

(77) *Doesn't taking the class help the teacher ?*

Very seldom, because the Children react quite differently to a newcomer and would not react like that to the teacher.   So, although the teacher might see new ways of handling, they would probably be different from those that the teacher would need with those Children.   You see, there are no short cuts, and there is no escaping the responsibility.   The teacher has to try it, and to learn by " doing " and by experiment.   The specialist helps best by making suggestions after seeing the actual handling by the teacher.

(78) *Is there any way of seeing a specialist at work then ?*

Yes, when taking teachers' courses, or if the specialist finds time to actually run a class of his own with Children, in or out of school. Even here, though, the problem of an audience is considerable, as the Children are disturbed by audience.

(79) *When using improvisation, aren't we merely bringing into school what is already going on in the playground ?*

No, it is more than that. We are leading the mere personal spitting-out process, by friendly guidance and occasional sensitive suggestion, to an advanced form of creative art. Child Play may be the foundation of Child Drama, but we can help Children enormously if we understand and respect their needs and efforts, and lead without dominating.

(80) *The free work often expresses quite an ugly background.   Are we to allow this ?*

Certainly. It is better out than in, and is often the first attempt at creative truth. It is life as the Child knows it. Shut it up too quickly and you completely break the Child's confidence in truth. It need not be always left in this stage. By building the bond of friendship, a teacher can become the guide who gently leads to the contemplation of lovelier things, and creative beauty follows. Children who act out their ugly home life in front of you are doing you the honour of extending a confidence. Don't distress them by snatching away freedom and friendship directly you have offered it.

(81) *Shouldn't teachers enjoy and have a good deal of experience in improvisation themselves ?*

Yes, I run courses for them all the time. We meet and move and speak together, and every teacher has a chance of taking the group.

North Midlands :

(82) *How can we go on with what you have told us ?*

Try out what you believe in. Take it slowly. Keep in touch with me if you care to. There is an Association [1] which helps people in this work.

(83) *However did you find out about all this ?   You are right, of course.   It is very disturbing.   I have been doing the wrong thing for twenty-five years.*

The only way to find out the needs of Children is to observe them impartially. I begin by believing they are each one of them important individuals and original artists.

(84) *We have a small hall with a gallery.   Can we use this ?*

It sounds ideal. Child Drama can take place on the floor, and anyone who wishes may observe it from above Child eye-level, and will be less noticed than the formal audience. Adult intimate arena theatre presentations and youth Drama could also take place in such a building.

(85) *What is the place of audience in all this ?*

In real Child Drama the audience has no place at all. The Children are fully absorbed and audience is either unnecessary or a disturbance. In Children's

---

[1] See answer to Question 141 on page 363.

Theatre, if there be such a thing (or *ought* to be), the audience should be as inconspicuous as possible, or the Children become self-conscious and their acting deteriorates.

(86) *Would you say something more about " Child Theatre " ?*

Yes. There are moments in Child Drama when activity, sincerity, absorption and emotional sharing of experience are so wonderful that one can only call it a form of " good theatre experience " or just " good theatre ". It is quite different from what is generally understood as Children's Theatre with plays, scripts, stages, actors, costumes and audiences. In this type of theatre we seldom experience Child Theatre. Child Theatre is a part of the *very extensive* Art Form of Child Drama, which has nothing whatever to do with what has hitherto been called Children's Theatre.[1]

(87) *Do you mean that by " group sensitivity " Children or grown-ups can know what the others in a group are going to do ?*

Not quite. That is " group intuition ". " Group sensitivity " is the first step only, in which we develop a sense of the needs of others. Later comes group intuition. This may be present first, but can be clearly developed by training in group sensitivity.

(88) *Have you actually done this training ?*

Yes, many times with Children and grown-ups, amateur and professional actors. A number of professional teams have been trained by me in this manner, notably the Pear Tree Players.[2]

(89) *This is fascinating. Will a new theatre arise ?*

There are signs of theatre development. There is an increasing interest in Arena Theatre, in which personal qualities are necessary. Some such training will be essential—we need a new school of acting for it. But group intuition and group sensitivity enrich the proscenium theatre, too. To my mind they are necessary for all good theatre, but one seldom sees any evidence that actors are conscious of the existence of such things.

(90) *Why is acting on a normal stage bad for young Children ?*

Because it destroys Child Drama, and the Children then merely try to copy what adults call theatre. They are not successful in this, and it is not their way of playing. They need space, and don't need to be embroiled in the complicated technique of an artificial theatre form. It makes them conscious of audience, spoils their sincerity and teaches them to show off. The logical end of all this is a bombastic little boaster who wants to go on the stage. Professional repertories are plagued by this type of product ; it makes their work more difficult. The constant flow of romantic and unbalanced individuals towards the professional stage was undoubtedly one of the reasons for the recent suggestions on " entrance

---

[1] For full discussion of this subject, see Chapter XVI.
[2] An article on these players appears on page 291.

limit ". Children need equal opportunity for co-operative play. Out of this arises the beauty of Child Drama.

(91) *Do you approve of competitive festivals ?*

No. They are based on a misguided premise and cause jealousy. The internal individual strife, as well as the group strife, eventually destroys the elements of good theatre which the festivals are there to stimulate. One never sees good group sensitivity in the acting at a competitive festival.

"Non-competitive" festivals offer the finer ideal of merely having an evening of prepared Little Theatre. There can be a commentary—useful for adults, youth groups and older Children only. We are there to experience, learn, and to act as well as we can, not to win a pot or try to prove we are better than some other team. (Marks do not prove this, by the way. They are merely the outward symbol of the adjudicator's personal impressions if he is good, and of his prejudice if he is bad.) Organised interchange of teams to build interesting programmes is better than elimination. We may thereby consider the primitive and its merits side by side with the " slick ", without being so tasteless as to try to compare them. By elimination we often arrive at a series of nondescript " bests " which tend to be similar not only in standard, but also in theatrical conception and mistakes. Could anything be more boring or stultifying to imaginative development ? No Child should be allowed *near* such a festival. It would be wiser if only older Children were in non-competitive festivals, and one can only hope that competitive festivals will one day cease to be.

(92) *At last you have explained in precise detail what I, and I know many others, have felt for years. You have got nearer than anyone I have ever heard on the Child's need. Have you written on this ?*

Not much yet. But we always have personal experience and observation. They are even better than words.

(93) *Is it possible for you to run courses ?*

Yes, but I am naturally confined to instruction of people in my own area. Members of the Educational Drama Association have opportunities of joining in some of these courses though, when the courses are organised by the Association.

(94) *What numbers do you take at courses, and what do you consider the best-sized group for training ?*

It depends on the immediate object of the course. My last one had three to four hundred students. That was on general principles. Twenty makes a good practical group for movement and improvisation. Half a dozen is best for advanced work. A dozen is about the most difficult number for Drama.

A Midland Group of Teachers :

(95) *Is the ordinary teacher qualified to take Child Drama ?*

The ordinary teachers who are human beings are the *best* people to do this

work. If they learn more about Drama they may be better at it, but not necessarily.

(96) *Would you start with sounds first ?*

Yes, in most instances. But ordinary Play with words should go side by side
with movement to sounds.

(97) *Would you repeat an improvisation ?*

Certainly, if the Children wish it. This may develop into laziness, though.
Care should be taken to see that fresh improvisations are being done very often, as
well as the beloved repetitions.

(98) *This work is clearly of psychological value. How does it go with " C "
Children ?*

Very well. The so-called " C " Child needs it very much, and often does it
better than the intelligent Child, who gets caught up in other preoccupations until
it re-finds Play and happiness. But there is no evident " stream " in Child Drama.
All have equal opportunities. In experimental mixed groups the " C " Child often
catches up, and it is difficult or even unnecessary to try to distinguish any Child as
belonging to any category. In the Land they go to there are no distinctions.
This helps the superior type to be more human, and the shy type to gain confidence.

Midland Training College :

(99) *Don't you find that Children want stage properties ?*

They do sometimes, but not all the time. When playing at their best they
invent properties out of their environment, or do without them. It is when Play
has not really got going or never been developed right that they need constant
stimulation. By properties I take it you mean definitely intended provision of
toy swords, headgear and so on. They have their uses. But, if the Child comes
to rely entirely on them, laziness follows and imaginative creation diminishes.

(100) *When Children have only had formal proscenium Drama, how would you
start ?*

Continue with plays as they know them. Begin to use other entrances off
stage in the hall. Let the Children flow on and off the stage. Use processions
round the hall. When a particular part of the play is unsatisfactory let them play
a short piece of that part in dumb show, or begin to say in their own words what
they would say if the event happened in their own lives. Build, in fact, slowly
back to what they should have been doing, and bring in as many children as possible. With older Children, who are ready for plays anyway, some improvisation
should be done regularly. It adds a sparkle to their work and keeps them mentally
alive.

(101) *When should Children do script plays ?*

When they can read *really well, with meaning*, and appear to understand the
major part of what they are saying. Before this, script plays are harmful, as they

C.D.—23

teach the Child the appalling habit of never getting into the part (how can they if they don't understand it ?) and of reciting lines whilst grinning out at the audience. There is no educational, theatre or dramatic value in this. Do not think they are learning to appreciate good English this way. They are not thinking of what they do or say.

(102) *Would you " make " a shy Child join in ?*

No, never. If it is present at regular Play sessions it will join in at the *only moment when it is absolutely right and proper for it to do so*—that is at the moment that it *wants* to. Preceding this moment a long and courageous battle has gone on. This does not mean that there should not often be strong suggestion and encouragement. All depends on the common sense of the teacher in deciding on the needs of a group, or a particular Child, just as you would judge what sums to set.

(103) *Isn't this all rather impractical ?*

Not in the least. It is pure common sense. Just because we are talking about the emotional sphere, which has a bearing on every practical thought and action in life, you must not be misled into thinking it is vague. Think of it in terms of numbers, money, action, any sort of materialism that assists you, but don't think it is impractical. What every Child in fact *does* when given the chance is the most complete form of practicality. That is what we are talking about. The wrong application of a wrong form of work to the wrong age group, as has happened in the past, is what is impractical. It is worse. It is thoughtless and has caused much harm. The work I describe is being done by hundreds of teachers now. They help to substantiate that what exists and what works is not impractical. Finally, all these conclusions are based on observation, trial and experiment, and not on theory.

(104) *What would you do if a difficult Child started to break up the group ?*

It is hard to generalise. Each Child is different. But I would suggest : first of all, try giving responsibility. Make the Child the arch-good or arch-evil character. If this becomes overdone, quell by giving a more important part to someone else. Bear in mind there is a reason for the behaviour. Very often it is a symptom of a longing for expression, and for that reason opportunity is what is needed. If in doubt, keep near the Child. Physical nearness often helps. If behaviour improves, move slowly farther away, so that responsibility for self-discipline is almost imperceptibly taken over by the Child. If behaviour still does not improve (which is very unlikely), take away the opportunity of expressing and of being leader, and invent a static character like a lamp or tree, first left alone, then, if necessary, get the play moving round the Child so that it feels itself to be the centre again. By alternating obvious, less obvious and no responsibility, you are likely to get a changed reaction.

Speak strongly only as the second resort, and deal strongly after that. The strong words will change the whole atmosphere in the room and make the work difficult. It should be avoided whenever possible. Anything you do should be to get the changed reaction. With that comes co-operation. Very often the other Children begin to get fed up and the Child subsides.

(105) *What would you do if it wouldn't take the part you told it to take ?*

I would avoid at all costs " telling it ". Don't say " You be a tree ", or " You take the robber chief ". You then put yourself in a position to be disobeyed. One way is to say " You *are* a tree " or " Johnny is chief robber ". You then state a fact (as if accomplished) which is accepted by the other Children. You have not told the Child to do anything. With a very difficult Child, " Johnny is " is better. The other Children are more likely to make Johnny play the part than you are.

If you judge otherwise, however, you might invent a job outside the play, apparently to help you and near you. But it is better to try all ways of getting the Child to join in. An experienced teacher nearly always can, because a Child being a deliberate nuisance is playing a part anyway, so our job is to find another part acceptable to the Child *and* ourself. The Child is really longing to join in, if it can do so without apparently losing face. It is often showing off to the others. We must try every device to remove its hold on that audience. If the Child and/or the others can be absorbed in something else, the trouble ceases.

Teachers and Producers (London) :

(106) *Do you think there is a quiet revolt going on by amateurs against the professional ?*

It is certainly true that many more people are becoming increasingly critical of the professional standards of work, and many amateur companies take the lead in local areas. The old idea that the professional actor was the only person who mattered in the Drama world is passing. This was only true when " theatre " meant everything and a few people acted whilst the rest of the world watched.

(107) *Has Children's Theatre had anything to do with this ?*

Yes, in part, particularly where professionals have been closely in touch with educationists. Those who work with Children every day have given advice which has had a definite effect on presentation form by some professionals. But the main thing is that many more grown-ups and Children act now, rather than watch, and it is found that there are many excellent actors and producers who do not actually earn a living by the stage, but act and produce for love. These people do not always see the sense in going to professional theatre and merely watching, when they could be " doing " elsewhere. This, I think, is essentially healthy.

(108) *But isn't it true that the professional is always better than the amateur ?*

Certainly not, particularly since the formation of County Drama Committees and the appointment of Drama Advisers. Technical training is now open to the amateur and the standard is often very high. Background knowledge is often more sound, too, which makes the amateur more valuable in educational matters. But we are dangerously near trying to compare separate things here.

(109) *What would you say are the separate spheres of the amateur and professional?*

The professional's life is an intricate technical affair based on hard work, with the ultimate object of earning money by pleasing or interesting the public. His exertions are always delicately balanced between these two last things. If pleasing fails he must force an interest.

The amateur does theatre work for love and to educate himself by experience. He visits the professional theatre when he likes or when he can. His balancing is in the decision as to whether he should act or watch. He has a foot planted firmly in real life as it is lived every day. This gives him many advantages over the professional. He has a much wider outlook.

(110) *Where does education come into this?*

Education is outside it all. It is first concerned with balancing and developing individuals, and preparing them for life. One thing to be quite clear about is that it does not exist in order to train everyone to be professional actors.

(111) *Who should do the advising on Drama and theatre, then, in the educational sphere?*

The professional should stick to the theatre and the educationist should deal with education and with Drama. Consultation is often valuable, but it must be based on the full assumption that both sides know their job. The educationist only goes to the professional when in need of technical help. The professional should not try to direct education. The final decision on what is best for the Child must be made by the educationist. The professional has a lot to learn here from educational work.

The gap is, however, bridged by the emergence of a new profession, that of the Drama Adviser, who should have adequate training and experience in professional theatre, amateur theatre and in education. Only by a proper balance between these three will we obtain a clear vision as to the importance of various sides of the work in relation to actual human needs.

Miscellaneous Questions :

(112) *Isn't all this a training for Utopia when Children won't meet it?*   (North England.)

No, it aims at providing a balance to and enrichment of the Child's life, together with a sense of confidence, all of which is urgent if the Child is to be able to face life as it is today, and also to have any influence on the world of tomorrow.

(113) *Would a fuller knowledge of the history of Drama help people to understand this work ?* (London.)

Yes, if they do not get muddled between Drama and theatre. They might at least recognise dramatic and theatre tendencies in Child Drama more easily. But the human factor is more important. Drama is the Doing of Man. It is more important than the art of the theatre, which is a small part of Drama and changes all the time. Even judgement on what is good or bad art changes. The Child is unconcerned with this fluctuating intellectual instability.

(114) *If Children act more in the way you suggest, will it affect the theatre of the future ?* (Stratford-on-Avon.)

Yes, it will enrich it and change it in many ways. It is already less rigid than it was. But the experiments of adults and professionals seem somewhat timid when compared with the *virile Art Form of a seven-year-old.*

(115) *Do you believe in Child Art ?* (London, Birmingham, Smethwick, Worcester.)

Of course. I was an early member of the Society for Education in Art. I am an ardent admirer of Prof. Cizek and Dr. Viola, and all those who have helped Children to the point of self-controlled freedom when they could create their wonderful works.

(116) *Is Child Drama connected with Child Art ?* (Bristol, Halifax, Manchester, Stratford-on-Avon, London.)

Yes, they are inseparable. Drama means *all* the " doing of life ". But the basic philosophy underlying our approach to Child Art is not just because of painting and drawing. It is concerned with an eternal truth about the Child, so, of course, it is as true for Drama as it is for Art.

(117) *Would you agree that Child Drama could help considerably in discovering the correct approach to every school subject ?* (London, Coventry, Worcester.)

Certainly Child Drama will open many doors when it is fully understood. I have not yet discovered any subject which cannot be approached by some form of dramatic method.

(118) *Have you done much research on the link between Drama and ordinary school subjects ?* (America, Canada, South Africa, Brazil, Paris.)

Yes, I have been working it out somewhat extensively since 1934.

(119) *Wherever I go in London I hear your name mentioned. Are you aware that you have added a number of terms to our vocabulary both for education and to the theatre in general ?* (Visitor to Birmingham.)

So I understand. I even sat as Chairman to a speaker from London the other day, who said : " I don't like this term much (but he used it), it's so hackneyed." Terms are useful only in so far as they help to express ideas more accurately. If certain terms are too much in use at one time, it at least means that people are thinking about the ideas they are intended to express.

(120) *Would you say your most important drama experiment was the founding of the Pear Tree Players?* [1] *They have certainly made history.* (Birmingham, London, Paris, Newcastle, America.)

I think what they stood for and the work they did was very important and their courage was great.   There is no other team like them.

(121) *Is it true that you have already developed a complete system for training in arena theatre, amongst your other contributions to Drama?* (A professional producer, London.)

Yes.   But the contribution is from countless members of Women's Institutes, Youth Clubs and Children.   A few brave professionals have invited me to train them in this, from time to time.   Apart from that, I have merely co-ordinated certain experiences of the past fifteen years, which have all helped to show an absolutely clear method of progression in this form of theatre.

(122) (the same person).   *Did you not use part of this method even with your earliest professional companies?*

Yes.   Much of the creative work, as well as the technical discipline, I hold to be common to all good theatre, whatever form of presentation one chooses.   But in arena theatre there are certain things which must be developed further, particularly from within, and in relation to the group.   Observation of the Child helps us here.

(123) *Why don't you start training and directing professional companies again?* (London, Manchester, Bristol, Hereford, Stratford-on-Avon.)

At the moment my time is fully occupied.   I think, too, that education is even more important than the theatre, and that anyway the theatre will only be enriched by a broadening of its horizons.   Working with the next generation is part of this process.

(124) *Are you training teams now?* (London, Manchester, Birmingham, Bristol, Hereford, Stafford, Stratford-on-Avon.)

Yes, I am training an amateur Children's Theatre group, amongst other things, composed almost entirely of teachers.   I believe it is the biggest group in the country.   A number of teams, both amateur and professional, are receiving indirect training also, through the Educational Drama Association.

(125) *Why shouldn't you " drill " Children in production?* (North Midlands.)

By drilling them you are only making them copy an adult performance.   They will do what you say, as far as they can, but it will not be genuine.   It will have a dead quality.   Behind all this you are breaking down the Child's belief in its own Art Form, or you may have even prevented it from realising the existence of such a thing.   Morally, you are teaching the Child to depend on you entirely and are removing from it emotional responsibility, the acceptance of which forms strong habits leading to personal stability.

---

[1] For further details about these Players, see Chapter XVI, pages 291–293.

(126) *I can see that Child Drama might be linked with English, History and Social background, but what about Geography and Maths ?* (Oxford.)

Geography can be introduced by study of foreign costume, manners, custom and philosophy, as well as exports, imports, type of animals and social views, climate and geographical position. This can come in by discussion, story or reading before or after spontaneous work. Knowledge can even be imparted sometimes in the middle, if Play fades out suddenly, or if a question is asked. There is much scope for ingenious characterisation and imaginative development. There can also be study through a kind of geographical documentary play with older Children.

As to mathematics, I know schools where they do this by movement. Each Child personally experiences plus or minus by moving forward or backward. Other methods are group formations for adding or subtracting. I have used a game sometimes, which I call " domino marching ", where the pattern formations are experienced personally. With older Children, of course, numbers of paces, consideration of angles and geometrical formations are constantly calling for attention when learning about angles of sight (proscenium or arena theatre) and distribution of players over the playing space.

(127) *Why haven't these ideas been developed years ago ?* (Oxford.)

Because people could not distinguish between theatre and Drama, and because the acting of drilled plays on a stage was thought to be the only thing which mattered. It is not surprising that educationists were slow to accept a wider vision of Drama, when most of the old teaching was at second hand from professionals who knew little about education and often thought merely in terms of audiences of the future. Amongst amateurs, the philosophy of the competitive festival raged like a disease in the 1930s, and this is no premise for a wide philosophy on Drama and Life. During the second World War the National Festival collapsed, and for the first time serious thought, experiment and consideration became possible on a wider scale. This was followed up rapidly by the Service of Youth, which showed up the lack of good creative work in schools. New experiments began during evacuation, and new teachers and new methods have been added. But, behind the scenes, a few people have been fighting for what they believed in down the years, and, when they were impeded, quietly observed, until the time was ripe for speaking out.

(128) *When did you first begin to link Drama with education ?* (Stratford-on-Avon.)

About 1925, before I left school. By 1928 I had developed my own system of Athletic-Drama-Movement, which I tried out abroad.

(129) *When did you first start doing Drama in schools, and what did you do ?* (London, Birmingham, Newcastle, Stafford, Oxford.)

Apart from my own school, in the early 1930s, I gave talks on the link between

Drama and other subjects and also took round my own players, who acted early English Plays.

(130) *When did you first think of Drama as therapy?* (Gloucester, Bucks, Stafford, London, Belgium, South Africa, America.)

About 1926. I developed this further whilst abroad, with the help of expert advice, and began experiments in 1936. The ideas were further developed, together with medical advice, from 1938 to 1941. During that time I felt what I had been personally convinced of for a number of years to have been proved, namely, that prevention was even better than cure and that the introduction of simple play methods into the normal school curriculum would bring about a natural happy development with a considerable balancing effect on character, the building of confidence and an improvement in scholastic attainment and taste generally.

(131) *Do you get much opposition to your ideas?* (Birmingham, London, Worcester, Dudley, Stafford, Reading, France, Canada, America, Argentine.)

Only from those who care for the artificialities of inanimate " theatre " more than Children and real Life.

(132) *Do you advocate masks for younger Children?* (Stratford-on-Avon.)

Yes, to be used occasionally.[1] But part-masks are better for some things, as they allow eye and mouth freedom and yet still provide a fascinating experience. Full masks help shy Children, but are rather hot. Masks with no noses are cooler, and there is a special joy for each Child in choosing what colour to dab on its own nose—good primary colours too ! No adult nonsense about natural shades.

(133) *Do you believe in make-up for the Child?* (Birmingham.)

At times. It is better to let them develop their own Art Form in this and not to instruct until they begin to ask questions—*circa* twelve or later. Child Art in make-up is sometimes connected with the action which precedes or follows in the form of Child Drama. One may stimulate the other. But there is another part of this Child make-up, which is like painting a picture. Acting does not come into it then at all.

(134) *How do you introduce your method when a Child is not used to it?* (Kent.)

It is not my method. It is the Child's method. That is an advantage. All is based on Play. So the first thing is to provide the right atmosphere and environment. Stimulate by suggestions, ask them for ideas, and the rest comes slowly as you and the Children gain confidence in the work and in each other. Before starting, though, you must believe in it and know why you do it.

(135) *Is the work you describe useful to the backward Child?* (London, Coventry, South Africa, Birmingham, Stratford-on-Avon, Stafford, Jamaica, Hereford, Slough, Belgium.)

Yes, very, in most cases. It is the best way for the Child to express, and often

---

[1] See Masks and Make-up, Chapter XVII.

PLATE 39

INFANTS. Repeating an improvisation with some suggestions by the teacher. The typical large circle shape found in Infant Play has been incorporated. Trees grow whilst the princess sleeps. (*See* pp. 131–135.)

INFANTS. The end of an improvisation. The courtiers rejoice. This is a happy school. Note equi-distance between couples beginning to appear on the floor space, which will later affect composition in painting pictures. (*See* pp. 131–135.)

Photos by Victor Thompson

PLATE 40

JUNIORS. Rhythmic fly-swatting. The bad fly is underneath the board.

JUNIORS. Cooks prepare a meal. Notice equidistance in the pattern.
(*See* p. 43.)

JUNIOR MIXED. The people beg Archbishop Hatto for bread.

Photos by Victor Thompson

PLATE 41

JUNIORS. Noah prays while his sons prepare logs for the ark.

JUNIOR BOYS. Wearing half-masks made by the author. Two men are haggling over the sale of a bird, which can't stop sneezing.
(*See* p. 312.)

JUNIOR MIXED. TOP CLASS. Polished improvisation including Child ideas. A man comes to the door begging for bread. The owner is sitting in the house (back turned) with the door open. Note the gables of the roof. Choir for choral speech in the background. (*See* p. 361.)

Photos by Victor Thompson

PLATE 42

JUNIOR MIXED. These are dolls. The two boys standing on the left are the wheel of a ship. Here we perceive how limbs begin to fill space and make for good grouping. (This is an action picture.) Children find and notice this in Child Drama. It affects their composition in painting and drawing.

JUNIOR MIXED. Trees, and their leaves dying on the floor.

Photos by Victor Thompson

PLATE 43

YOUNG SENIOR BOYS.   The counter-attack.

YOUNG SENIOR BOYS.   Whites versus natives.

Photos by Victor Thompson

PLATE 44

SENIOR BOYS. The plot is hatched over a meal. Improvisation
entirely of boys' making. (*See* pp. 73–75.)

Photo by Victor Thompson

SENIOR BOYS. Adventure story. The criminal shoots himself
before the inspector can stop him. (*See* pp. 73–75.)

Action Photo by Victor Thompson

PLATE 45

SENIOR BOYS. Acting up one end of a room, but still the circle manifests itself. The ammunition blows up.

SENIOR BOYS. The pirate ship is attacked. Imagined weapons are swords, boat-hooks and cutlasses. This is their first time at this work. They are not immersed in the character yet; we are at the first stage of live movement, and delight at a new experience. Note flow towards stage. (*See* pp. 70–74, and p. 80.)

Photos by Victor Thompson

PLATE 46

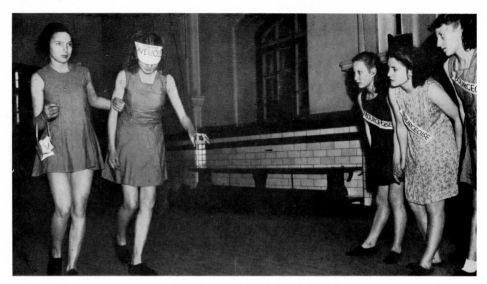

SENIOR GIRLS. Taken from in front of the stage as they flowed right past it through the proscenium " pass door " curtain, without using the stage. (*See* pp. 70–74.)

SENIOR GIRLS. The head of a procession that formed a long *tongue* flowing up towards the stage. (*See* pp. 70–74.)

Photos by Victor Thompson

PLATE 47

SENIOR GIRLS. An " aside " to the audience in foreground. This shape is what has been called the *bulge* out from the proscenium stage. Note *hinterland play* on stage, unconcerned with audience. This is an action photo, not posed, but taken during second time through. Hinterland Play went on all the time. (*See* p. 82.)

Action photo by Victor Thompson

SENIOR GIRLS. Child Drama is often interesting when seen from above. Note how the space is filled by the hands and feet of the two central figures.

Photo by Victor Thompson

PLATE 48

SENIOR GIRLS. Pageant and pattern as floor space is used. Seen from above. Conscious theatre has arrived.

SENIOR GIRLS. "In Church."

Photos by Victor Thompson

the only way in which it can equal a Child considered its intellectual superior. Also, by observation of what it does, we learn what it needs.

(136) *What about the shy Children of about fourteen years ?* (Sussex.)

They are probably shy because they have not had enough of the work before. With girls, try movement to music ; with lads, stylised fighting in dumb show with imaginary weapons to music background. One thing, because Children get self-conscious at this time, do not believe they cannot be helped or that the shyness cannot be avoided. Most of us let them down at this age and take their state for granted, instead of doing all we can to aid them.

(137) *What about choral speech ?* (London, Manchester.)

Choral speech has some value in helping Children to discover team spirit and group sensitivity, if they are not having full opportunities for discovering these things in other ways. In the hands of an expert good results are sometimes obtained, but it is a complicated and skilled form of art and there are few experts. If the trainer is not an expert, choral speech induces into the Children's voices a sort of dead whine, which often remains a constant factor in all their public speaking. It is the same unnatural sound that arises from attempting script plays too early.

Forms of group outcry and unconscious agreement of group sentences occur from time to time during Child Play, which can be developed as a basis for choral speech in later years. Choral speech as we understand it is an adult form of art and should not be imposed on Children as early as it usually is. When great choirs of young Children chant earnest poems at adults in public, on subjects only fit for ardent over-twenties, one is often at a loss to know what the point is—either as education or as training in taste. Perhaps choral speech is better used for class groups. The only way of making sure that the speech is kept sincere and full of life is by lots of improvisation going side by side with it. Voice is an individual thing and should not be confined only to herd utterance, which, in the wrong hands, can become a most undemocratic form of training. You will understand that I am not condemning choral speech as such—only challenging its unthought-ful use and its far too common use by inexpert trainers. Sometimes it is the only speech training Children get, and that is harmful.

(138) *Would you advocate moving to jingles ?* (London, Bristol, Manchester.)

Only if you can't find anything better. One point to be rather careful about is not to overstress rhyme. Children have a deep sense of poetry in their minds, but their own poetry does not rhyme. Rhyme is something which is too often (perhaps always) brought to their attention by adults—like baby-talk—and it is then copied. They may learn to love rhyme, and will, in early stages, tell you rhymes by the dozen ; these rhymes, by the way, usually don't rhyme. But once they have really got the rhyme craze they lose confidence in creating in their own way. Their own genuine poetic utterance is severely weakened. Their poetry, at its

best, is more akin to the Bible and the " Moderns ". Thus their utterance may be
Psalm-like in character, or like T. S. Eliot in shape, kaleidoscopic like Laurie Lea,
or soulfully moving like the translations by Spender of Garcia Lorca. By this, of
course, we see that they find plenty of opportunity for expressing many ideas,
which may be full of conscious joy or unconscious dream symbolism. Once the
disease of rhyme has been badly caught, all poetic expression shrivels into the
meagre canal of the rhyming ballad, and may remain thus thin for many years,
perhaps for ever. You see, there is a Child Poetry, and it is for teachers and parents
to recognise this, without emotional outcry, and to develop it as they learn how.[1]
I hope this won't upset too many people's happy memories of their own youth.

(139) *Do you believe in Comics for Children ?*

Oh yes, of course. But that isn't what matters. *Children* believe in them—
that's really the point, isn't it ? Comics have bright colours—we say vulgar.
They are full of adventure—we say dangerous and immoral. They are full of
primitive humour—we say sadistic. They are full of new worlds—we say the old
world is better. Is it ? They are very up-to-date—makes us feel old-fashioned.
Really, you know, most of us are very hard to please ; even when Children learn to
concentrate, perhaps for the first time in their lives, or even learn to read by them,
we still deride comics. Let's not be hypocritical—most adults either go to immoral
films or read detective stories, and live for an hour the lives they cannot lead in
civilised society. Children need this relaxation, too. Now—more seriously—
safeguards : we can select comics, and we can read *to* our Children from other
literature (we should do this often) ; we can put other books in reach. We can
wean them from comics. We can perfectly well arrange for comics to become
simply a useful stage in development. Comics need not remain a habit, continuing into adult life. It depends on us. It is dishonest to deride comics out of
hand, and, so long as strip cartoons remain a permanent feature of so many adult
newspapers, we have no just premise from which to argue. Oh, if only ours were
coloured, too ! [2]

(140) *How would television come into this ?*

It is as yet very early to say, but some things are already quite apparent. The
shape of television, as with the shape of films and film screens, does not appear
to upset the shape of Child Play too much, because the intimacy takes the viewer
right through the square, round, or hideous lozenge, into that other " land " where
another complete miniature life goes on. (This is not true of the proscenium arch
in theatres.) And Children use television themes sometimes, just as they do with
film and radio, and enrich their Play tremendously. But this is only where
adequate adult supervision takes place ; so far, television is apt to become a craze

[1] See Chapters VI and XIII on " Language Flow ".
[2] *There has been a great deal written in the Press about comics from other countries, and it is
because of these that adults should take the trouble to select. But the point made in this answer is
that comics are not bad in themselves.*—EDITOR.

in too many families, and then Children spend all the time they can crouched round the set. Disadvantages : they get eye strain, and don't do their school work properly ; they get thoroughly lazy and expect to be entertained instead of being up and doing and living and playing in their own way. It is not a good thing mentally to be too dependent on the habit of projecting, in the years when personal physical Play is very necessary. The false idol of the television personality might become dangerous in the same way as the film star. As to the Drama itself, as so far televised, this could have a harmful effect on Child Play, for much of it takes little opportunity that the new medium offers ; the plays are presented in a very unimaginative manner and in a style that is provincial and fifty years out-of-date. It would be a pity if this were copied as the modern ideal. Luckily such plays do not generally interest Children very much, for they can do better themselves. The danger for Children (and perhaps all of us) lies in indiscriminate and full-time viewing. Permanent viewing both ways (into the home and out of it) may be a horror of the future. Fortunately, some families, having had their existence somewhat upset by a television craze, suddenly grow tired of it and give it up altogether. Perhaps this is a disease like many others —a sort of " Chicken Pumps ", as a five-year-old said the other day—and after the craze, after the pause, we return to discriminate viewing. May the service be worthy of that hour. Meantime, we have the many excellent plays on the sound radio, where each of us makes his own production in his own mind.

(141) *Is there any Association one can join which helps and advises on developing this work ?* (Smethwick, London, Derby, Maidstone, Birmingham, Stafford, Hayward's Heath, Rugeley, Dudley, Worcester, Hereford, Leicester, Stratford-on-Avon, Coventry, Norfolk, Kent, Oxford, Reading, Burton, Cambridge, Australia, Belgium, France, Holland, Eire, South America, India, South Africa, Austria, New Zealand.)

Yes, the Educational Drama Association.[1]

Training in all aspects of this work is now carried out each summer, having been instituted in Festival of Britain Year.

[1] Hon. Sec., Miss P. H. Lutley, The Drama Centre, c/o Reaside School, Rea Street South. Deritend, Birmingham.

INDEX

A photograph is referred to by means of bold type, indicating the number of the Plate and the page opposite which the illustration will be found.

A

Abandoned things 34, 133
  definition of 23 n; of the mind 33
Ability, to address companions 125; to concentrate 328; to create 69, 246; to discern good and evil 12; to get into a part 126; to lead 125; to learn 29; to make things 321; to mix 125; to observe 106, 344; to recognise repetition 93; to write 66; to write plays 266
Absorption 13, 14, 24 n, 28, 29, 39–45 passim, 58, 59, 89, 90, 107, 111, 127–162 passim, 247, 254, 259, 277, 282, 285, 289, 328, 330, 343, 344, 351; **49 (Pl. 2)**; **Pl. 23**
  and audience 49; in dance 79; definition of 12; developed from projected play 36; examples of 182–235 passim
Accidents, road 47
Accomplishment 27, 30, 88, 105, 119, 151
Achievement 13, 172, 253, 316, 343
  crowning of 133; dramatic 153; inner or outer 305; standard of 109
Acting 14, 25, 26, 36, 40, 55 n, 59, 66–69 passim, 120, 123, 136, 148, 196, 201, 220, 231, 237, 252, 296, 308
  ability 105; Christmas story 50; course 282–284; dance 219; developments from personal play 35; exercises 18; and films 323; without proscenium stage 151; and running play 63; and speech improvement 156; stories for 138; and theatres 324; ungenuine 80
Acting-in-the-round 50, 59, 70, 71, 78, 126, 144, 152, 222–230 passim, 329, 330; **224 (Pl. 19)**
  definition of 13; description of 48
Acting out, characters of the imagination 290; evil 109; of situations 48, 53, 119, 121, 146, 310, 343; of worries 335
Action 20, 30, 45, 52, 66, 70, 82, 106, 116, 138, 151, 185, 222, 280, 287, 313, 337
  and words 39–42
Active imagination 118
Activity 20, 25, 31, 33, 45, 105, 112, 122, 124, 351

and drama projects 115; co-ordinating 122; free 336; hinterland 13; importance of circle in 25; methods 19, 258; nurtured 252; personal 56; purposeful 109; and rules 120
Actor 24, 25, 35, 70, 101, 126–139 passim, 149, 201, 227, 296, 305
  and audience as one 318; but no audience 57–59; future 164; professional 267
Adjudicator 290
Adlerian school 118
Adolescence 73, 114, 304, 310, 343
Adolescents 77, 82, 83, 116, 125, 127, 152, 291
Adult, actor 25, 301, 304; artistry 26; attitude 52, 317; conception 291; correction 325; direction 124; drama 27, 123, 136; education 278; laughter 99, 266; mind 60; plans 108; plays 79, 82, 291; standards 83, 321, 325; taste 256; theatre 57, 58, 89, 105, 151, 159, 258, 277, 301, 306, 314, 322; thought 248; view 41
Adventure 22, 23, 39, 47, 68, 70, 106, 110, 214, 225, 249, 273, 315, 325, 342 passim, 362
  of crossing space 49; in Egyptian Passion Play 84; in investigation 22; of tearing 21; walking 21, 134
Adventure characters 74
Adversity 31, 107
Aesthetic, development 94; excellence 111; experiences 105; joys 52; movement 114; values 153
Affection 12, 33, 132, 319
Africa 62, 88
African dances 85, 319
African masks 307; **305 (Pl. 38)**
Age of reason 51
Aims 105–122
Alice in Wonderland 287
Amateurs 159, 267, 355, 356, 359
America 92, 335, 336
American negro 88, 89
Analytical psychology 118
Anxiety 24
  speed 30, 31
Apathy 273

Apron stage 201, 217, 227, 237, 265
Archetype picture 118
Area, domination of 161, 282; mastery of 44
Arena Theatre Company 272 n
Arrested development 127
Art 19, 21, 23, 25, 28, 35, 42, 52, 65–68
    passim, 81, 105, 110, 115, 121, 125, 138,
    143, 148, 155, 211, 345 (See also Child
    and Child Art)
Art creations 65, 71
Art-drama 88
Art forms 22, 28, 40, 61, 68, 92, 112, 121, 266,
    267, 290, 311, 314, 335
Artificial, compartments of school life 28;
    effort 113
Artist 19, 322
Art processes 124, 126
Arts, the, 121, 158, 321
    as therapy 104; value of in modern psychol-
    ogy 117
Attention 39, 64
Audience 12, 25–32 passim, 48, 49, 55, 57–59,
    72, 81–92 passim, 121–139 passim, 144,
    147, 149, 154, 156, 162, 165, 167, 178,
    199, 200, 208, 214–237 passim, 234, 250–
    255 passim, 270, 272, 288, 296, 305, 316–
    318, 344, 351
Audience consciousness 148, 154, 329, 351
Audience participation 267–279 passim, 320,
    329, 342, 346; 296 (Pl. 33)
    definition of 12; examples of 59–60, 85, 140,
    149, 169, 209, 210, 227
Awareness of society (See Social awareness)
Aztec art 314

B

Baby 21–37 passim, 50, 93, 101, 125, 131, 132,
    164, 166, 297, 318, 328
    early experiments of 20; early speech trials
    165, 166; joy in sound 163
Baby-talk 94–98, 361
Background, of hot swing 124, 343; home
    57, 71, 341; musical 169, 200, 202, 232,
    233, 246–258, 286; of painted scenery
    276
Backward child 31, 35, 49, 116, 119, 343, 360
Backwardness 208
Ballet 80, 155, 309, 314
Ballroom dancing 123
Bashfulness 99
Behaviour 20, 22, 24, 26, 35, 37, 38, 44, 48, 56,
    57, 60 n, 72–77 passim, 99, 107, 109, 110,
    116, 120, 139, 142, 147, 149, 151, 163,
    207, 243, 258, 274, 278, 286, 315, 322–
    332
    and films 341, 342, 354

Behaviour problems 119
Birmingham Midland Institute 62
Birmingham Repertory Theatre 294
Birmingham University 332
Birth, in story themes 148
Blemishes 77, 313
Blowing-off steam 106, 109, 152,
Blues, the 124
Body speech 137, 166, 204, 245, 280, 331, 340
    definition of 12
Bond 83, 93, 106, 141, 146, 167, 175, 185, 189,
    248
"Bop" 123–125
Boredom 59, 73, 124, 179
Bossiness 75
Box-office 270
Boys 74, 77, 120, 121, 124, 153, 159, 193, 204,
    233, 235, 361
    and dance 79–80; and films 326; and make-
    up 155, 313
British Drama League 62
British Theatre Conference 269
Bulge shape 59, 72, 92, 126, 155, 345; Pl. 47
Bullying 327

C

Cambridge Festival Theatre 90, 348
Camera angles 330, 331
Canada 336
Capacity for learning 74
Casting 138, 146, 339
Catharctic treatment 118
Catharsis 118
Centres of interest 60
Chamber music 88
Chanting 101
Characterisation 29, 30, 34, 64, 77, 78, 80, 199,
    259, 359
Chases 85, 181, 273
Child, acting 35, 108, 212; actor 266 (see also
    Professional); art 21, 65, 88, 90, 108, 113,
    148, 205, 212, 265, 297, 307, 310, 311–
    315 passim, 335, 357; creation 123, 153,
    158, 185, 290, 315; dance 24 n; expert 44;
    guidance 119; guidance clinics 343;
    language creation 96; make-up 311–314;
    mental state 318; music 62, 346; nature
    71, 82; needs 34, 269, 350; own pace 31,
    108; own plays 152; painting 82, 270,
    308; poetry 362; as teacher 297–301;
    thought 312
Child Art 26 n, 50
Childish 31
Childlike 31, 296
Child-teacher relationship 112, 144, 248
    definition of 12

Child-theatre 351
 definition of 12; examples of 183, 184
Children's hospital 281
Children's theatre, 87, 149, 214, 230, 256, 265–304, 336, 351, 355, 358
 real 242, 293–297
Children's Theatre 268
Children's Theatre Players 274–284, 331; **280 (Pl. 29)**; **281 (Pl. 30)**
China 88
 masks of 307
Chinese theatre 88, 169, 314
Christianity 50
Christian standards 113
Christmas story 50
Cinderella 274, 281
Cinema 70, 322–332
Circle 246, 274, 287, 310, 319, 340, 345; **137 (Pl. 10)**; **224 (Pl. 19)**; **225 (Pl. 20)**; **253 (Pl. 28)**; **Pl. 45**
 examples of 23 n², 36, 46, 48, 49, 50, 55, 56, 59, 68, 72, 80, 85, 86, 87, 92, 124–143 *passim*, 149, 154, 167, 176, 184, 188, 193, 196, 197, 208, 212, 215, 218, 222, 223, 225, 234; filled-in 49, 56, 80, 168, 187; importance of 25–27
Circles of attention 48
Civilisation 28, 33, 70, 72, 106, 337
Civilised life 52
Civilised society 85, 362
Classes 54, 62, 65, 175
Classroom 19, 59, 72, 87, 92, 112, 137, 140, 142, 149, 154, 155, 167, 168, 185, 192, 208–211, 221, 222, 230, 261, 269, 280, 326, 339, 345
 dramatics 112, 267, 313
Cleanliness 81, 125
Climax 20, 22, 23 n², 24 n, 33, 47 n, 53, 54, 64, 80, 93, 94, 132, 137, 139, 166, 172, 189, 191, 193, 232, 233, 238, 251, 264, 282, 342, 346
Clock-time 28–29, 34, 72, 75
Close-up 263, 325, 328
Clothes 64–65, 40, 53, 87, 326
Clubs 69, 85, 123–127, 149, 326, 327
Clumsiness 77, 81, 83 ,159
Collective unconscious 48
Colours 53, 117, 118, 154, 268, 274, 312, 315, 360
Coma-acting 45, 56, 138, 148, 329
Comedy 70, 87, 282, 314
Comics 327, 362–363
Commedia dell' arte 89, 90, 217, 295
Common sense 12, 75, 106, 120, 122, 354
Communication 40, 93
Community 25, 62, 70, 121, 330
 efforts 53; expression 349; spirit 156, 158

Companionship 43, 57
Competition 62, 99, 290
Competitive festivals 348, 352, 359
Concentration 12, 28, 29, 31, 35, 39, 40, 63, 78, 81, 107, 115, 134, 143, 157, 170, 182, 227, 315, 316, 319, 329, 342
Confidence 12, 13, 21, 24, 29, 38, 45, 52, 54, 56, 58, 61, 63, 73, 79, 95, 106, 112, 113, 115, 116, 124, 125, 134, 141, 143, 177, 181, 196, 266, 267, 272, 311, 316, 343, 353, 360
Confidences 55, 125, 342
Consonants 93, 137, 165, 166, 167, 341
Construction 22
Constructive play 315
Contrasts 72, 137, 139, 148, 170, 261, 339, 343
Control 139, 142–144, 148, 155, 175, 179, 180, 190, 192, 198, 201, 236, 312, 334, 340, 341, 343, 345, 346
Co-operation 32, 112, 145, 148, 153, 284, 315, 355
Copying 20, 24, 35, 37, 44, 77, 93, 98, 233, 266, 273, 298, 318, 325, 330, 334, 351, 358
Costume 49, 64–65, 87, 115, 156, 166, 188, 220, 221, 229, 321, 340, 347, 351, 358
Country children 70, 299
Country dancing 27, 74, 79, 123, 155, 219
County colleges 157
Courage 31, 79, 107, 155, 179, 222, 317, 332, 343
Crafts 117, 158, 315, 321
Craftsmanship 76, 107, 117, 153, 307, 308, 320
Created names 96, 145 n
Created sound language 94
Creation 19, 27, 28, 32, 34, 38, 41, 44, 49, 51, 54, 56, 58, 60, 62, 63, 64, 68, 70, 73, 75, 80, 82, 87, 93, 96, 103, 134, 136, 142, 143, 150, 154, 163, 164, 168, 220, 245, 247, 273, 274, 305, 306, 307, 316, 320, 330, 344
Creative, ability 83, 123, 245; activity 122, 345; adventure 124; attempts 134; drama 13, 19, 343; efforts 132; energy 41, 306; expression 13, 98; joy 95; language 95; needlework 64; opportunity 340, 344; outbursts 100; play 54, 273, 344; power 108; release 170; rhythms 27, 46, 114; speaking 114, 342; study 76; theatre 211; use of bits and pieces 64; work 29; writing 114
Crime 81
Critic 19, 305, 325, 339
Critical faculty 153
Criticism 19, 20, 58, 154, 270
Crowds 32, 332
Crowd scenes 319
Culture 80, 266, 270, 271
Curative value 343
Cure 116, 360

Curiosity 73, 109
Curriculum 121, 360
Curtains 82, 215

D

Dance 22, 24 n, 26, 29, 35, 40, 47 n, 55, 56, 61–63, 79–81, 85, 88, 107, 115, 123, 126, 133, 140, 143, 152, 155, 181, 183, 187, 198, 204, 217, 219, 232, 233, 239, 246, 262, 292, 295, 301, 311, 312, 319, 341, 343, 346; **80 (Pl. 5)**; **Pl. 23; 233 (Pl. 24)**
Dancing 63, 87, 123, 125, 181, 188, 205, 212, 260, 262, 274, 289, 319
Dark Tower, The 294
Davidson Clinic, Sixth Annual Report of 21 n
Dawn of seriousness 50–51, 54, 58, 62, 73, 101, 170, 257, 300, 332
　definition of 12
Day nurseries 135
Death, in story themes 34
Decisions 57, 70, 73, 327
Delinquency 110, 150
Dentists 74, 222, 235
Dependability 127
Depth 44, 50, 58, 66, 69, 70, 72, 107, 139, 148, 151, 317, 320
Descriptive language, examples of 95
Design 60, 76, 268, 315
Desks 43, 59, 60, 140, 149, 169, 185, 208, 209, 215, 234, 318, 339, 342
Destruction 22, 33, 133, 311
Development 35, 37, 41, 50, 55, 60, 133, 273, 340, 352
　and comics 362; in community efforts 53; of ideas game 145; from Infants' school 146–149; of masks and make-up 307; of noise experiences 62; of the personality 108, 117, 156; from play 338; of play 252; towards play-writing 66; from self outwards 52; in speech 39–40; towards understanding of depth 66
Diagnosis 116, 343
Dialects 96–97, 100, 251
Diction 93, 112, 312
Difficult child, 98, 113, 315
Diffidence 342
Discipline 53, 61, 63, 75, 112, 141, 147, 169, 252, 257, 338
Discovery 106, 146, 163, 176, 308, 310, 319, 327
　of space 42–46
Discussion 82, 120, 157, 158, 238, 297–301
Documentary plays, 81, 126, 158, 216, 240, 283, 359
Dog Beneath the Skin, The 283
Dolls 23, 32, 37, 38, 48, 317, 318, 319, 321

Doll stage 318, 319
Drama, advisers 266, 291, 356; centre 268 n; as doing and struggling 22, 23, 25, 34, 37, 108, 132, 158, 163, 270, 271, 273, 330, 338, 357; in education 112, 335; experi 252; as a form of life 26; and life 92; to the street 70, 85, 242, 326, 327; therapy 349; training 158
Dramatic, activity 33; climax 24 n, 33, 182, 193, 197, 224; content 286; endeavour 113; entry 137, 318; fulfilment 51; history 113; movement 202, 205, 258; sense 43; values 107; work 79, 112, 120, 123
Dramatic play 36, 39, 42, 43, 45, 47, 48, 49, 66, 96, 316, 319
　on floor space 44; of gang 68; and grouping; and language flow 163; leaders 51; shapes in 50; and sounds 40; stimulating poetic language flow 172; as stimulation 269; and treasures 38; **49 (Pl. 2)**
Dramatisation 19, 145, 182
Drawing 49, 50, 57, 67, 91, 117, 122, 193, 252, 306, 311, 357
Dreams 104, 116, 343
Dream-world 101, 172, 174, 210
Dressing-up 40, 50, 64–65, 78, 80, 87, 106, 148, 187, 212, 215, 227, 267, 285, 296, 298, 308

E

Early English theatre 227
Education 42, 54, 67, 105, 113, 116, 119, 120, 122, 150, 157, 158, 161, 175, 269, 271, 291, 327, 334, 344, 347, 356
　of the emotions 119; through art 122
Educational Drama Association 64 n, 114, 158 n, 268 n, 269 n, 282 n, 331, 352, 358, 363
Educational psychologist 117
Educational system 121
Educationists 266, 270, 271, 342, 355, 356, 359
Ego, how formed 23, 26
Elizabethan theatre 72; **225 (Pl. 20)**
Emotional, activity 112; atmosphere 91; balance 25, 113; beating 98; character 107; climax 141; conquest 26; control 106; development 94; education 274; essence of language 97; experience 24, 30, 54, 93, 140, 146, 252; hurry 30; intensity 89; joys 52; language of sound 143; message 305; outbursts 234; participation 12; reaction 112; responsibility 358; shared experience 79, 93, 306, 344, 351; sound training 88, 137, 161, 167; spell of spontaneity 89; tension 117; training 73–75, 76, 106, 119; urge 307

Emotions 25, 28, 32, 33, 37, 43, 63, 73, 94, 106, 116, 119, 121, 126, 236, 268, 274, 325, 326, 348
Encouragement 21, 62, 78, 100, 142, 143, 169, 326, 339, 342, 364
Energy 34, 35, 41, 49, 53, 54, 73, 112, 113, 117, 143, 152, 158, 163
English 253, 354, 359
Equidistance 43, 49, 53, 60, 125, 133, 138, 143, 148, 159, 308, 319; **360 (Pl. 39)**
Equidistant pattern 43, 133; **49 (Pl. 2); Pl. 40**
Evil 73, 74, 109
Exams 55 n, 76
Experience of life 54, 256
Experimental psychology 26
Experimental stages 126
Eye strain 332, 363

F

Facial expression 39, 60, 64, 166, 231, 232, 263, 326
Faith 31, 36, 41, 106, 146
Family, atmosphere 21, 21 n, 25, 97, 132, 337 place names 96, 97; symbols 95, 96; terms 97
Fantasy 70, 79
Fear 20, 21, 53, 56, 81, 116, 121, 181, 231, 315, 341, 343
Festivals 230, 267, 287, 290–291, 348, 352; **288 (Pl. 31)** *(See also* Competitive festivals and Non-competitive festivals)
Fighting 35, 45, 55 n, 85, 111, 124, 153, 193, 209, 211, 224, 225, 327, 342, 361
Films 322–332, 66, 87, 92, 213, 236, 263, 362
Film screen 317
Film stars 77, 363
Finger sucking 23 n²
Floor space 43–45, 48, 49, 55, 56, 62, 70, 73, 78, 87, 115, 138, 143, 147, 148, 151, 159, 193, 202, 218, 221, 256, 262, 268, 284, 289; **361 (Pl. 48)**
Flow on and off stage 70, 71, 72, 87, 88, 91, 151, 152, 217, 238, 345, 353; **Pl. 45; Pl. 46; 240 (Pl. 25); 241 (Pl. 26)**
Folk drama 127
Folk-lore 121
Footwork 107, 159, 219, 260, 282
Form 117, 217, 230 of acting 48; of life 52; theatre 230
Formal, dance 152, 153, 290; plays 27, 237, 317; poetry 165; productions 69; speech training 100, 136, 137, 346; stage 87; teaching 125, 338; theatre 152, 317; training 79, 100, 152, 153
Forms of expression 57, 119, 151, 163

Forms of presentation 267 elastic 272
France 90
Free dance 187
Freedom 19, 22, 59, 61, 63, 66, 69, 80, 110, 114, 132, 141, 142, 143, 145, 169, 179, 181, 236, 238, 252, 257, 261, 270, 286, 312, 340, 345, 380
Free speech 134
Fresh creations 56
Friendship 44, 45, 52, 73, 98, 99, 106, 141, 145, 167, 181, 349, 380
Frustration 29, 132
Full finish 46
Full life 124
Fullness of personality 105

G

Gallery 183, 201, 261, 268, 350
Game, 102, 114, 120 beginnings of the 19, 23–25; development from 29; examples of Ideas 154, 189, 212–213; Ideas 35, 45, 60, 144–146
Gang 55, 56, 60, 61, 62, 68, 70, 76, 106, 143, 149, 150, 242, 326; **185 (Pl. 16); 192 (Pl. 17)** activities 32 n; description of 53; leader 53, 56, 76, 77, 84, 147, 242
Gang stage, the 21, 32, 57, 147 description of 53; reason for development 52; sign of 55
Geography 150, 223, 359
Gesture 20, 27, 39, 41, 124, 125, 132, 136, 167, 339, 340
Girls 74, 77, 115, 120, 123, 153, 157, 193, 204, 215, 361 and dance 79–80; and fantasy 70; and films 326; and make-up 155, 313
Glamour 90, 316
Glove puppets 318, 319
Grace 39, 62, 64, 79, 107, 125, 138, 143, 147, 153, 189
Grammar 66, 147
Gramophone 61, 124, 143, 166, 169, 202, 246
Gramophone records 286, 295 use of 61, 256; *Basin Street Blues* 248, 250, 251; *Intermezzo from Escape to Happiness* 254; *Lazy Boogey* 256; *One-O'clock Jump* 255; *Riding on a Blue Note* 254; *Sorcerer's Apprentice, The* 289; *Swinging the Blues* 255; *Three Cornered Hat (Falla)* 246; *Why does My Heart go Boom* 247; *Wiggle Woogie* 255
Grease paint 313
Greek, dance 79, 80; patterns 314; theatre 91
Green pastures 88

Group 12, 53, 56, 61, 62, 76, 81, 82, 92, 149, 181, 183, 213, 230, 232, 279, 330, 340, 344
  adventures 56; agreement 143; creations 53, 55–57, 82, 138; decision 52; dynamic 31, 53, 56; feeling 53, 57 n; integration 61; intuition 12, 61, 62, 63, 198, 248, 351; plays 126, 158; reasoning 159; rings 49; sensitivity 12, 53–54, 61, 62, 126, 147, 182, 193, 194, 204, 232, 233, 259, 267, 283, 319, 343, 351, 352, 361; spirit 283; work 107, 147, 292
Grouping 286, 317, 329, 330
  examples of 143, 148, 193, 199, 201, 204, 219, 230, 233, 261
Guarding 86–87, 109, 132, 270
Guide to Theatrical Make-up 311 n
Guiding 19, 25, 37, 140, 150, 183, 290, 326, 338, 344
Guilt 21
Guilty secret 100

H

Habit 13, 63, 162
  of attack on words 156; of clarity in speech 100; and comics 362; of listening 170; of reality 326; of speaking loud 238
Hall, happy entry to 49; no use of 140; oval 268; and running play 60; and rostrum blocks 60; school 58, 87, 92, 154, 268; use of 61, 73, 137, 142, 167, 168, 181, 201–203, 206, 220, 229, 236, 261, 345
Hansel and Gretel 230
Happiness 19, 22, 38, 55, 63, 73, 106, 114, 121, 163, 269, 316, 327, 341, 353
Happiness development 56, 64, 182
  definition of 12
Happy entry 137, 143, 167
Hate 37, 38, 106, 136, 323
Health 29, 105, 106, 122, 327
Highbury Little Theatre 272, 331
Higher level 46, 60, 64, 70, 71, 73, 87, 147, 149, 206, 342
Higher planes 64
Hinterland activity 82, 154, 217, 222; **Pl. 47**
  definition of 13
History 114, 150, 152, 156, 298, 321, 359
  of drama 60, 72, 84, 105, 126, 140, 267, 307, 357; of the theatre 92
Histrionic declamation 163
Holidays 69, 242
Holy Bible 327, 262
Home 25, 37, 45, 85, 147, 165, 171, 242
  atmosphere 97; drama in 134; dream perception of 32; glimpses of 136; and language flow 163; life 207, 350; music of 100; truths 169

Horn dance 85–87; **88 (Pl. 7)**
Humour 23, 24, 327, 362
Hurry 45, 50, 66, 116, 147, 290, 307, 321

I

Ideas 12, 39, 53, 61, 65, 66, 67, 74, 94, 170, 177, 205, 208, 236, 240, 360
  association of 104, 248, 290; imaginative 13, 143; language of 93; new 45; projecting 320; for stories 298
Ideas game 144–146, 154, 189, 212, 213
Imaginary words 95, 170
Imagination 31, 35, 41, 49, 76, 91, 95, 106, 113–118 *passim*, 140, 145, 177, 204, 268, 291, 297, 306, 315, 318, 320, 344
Imaginative, adventures 126; approach to production 105; climax 191; creations 55, 126, 136, 152, 162, 349, 353; creatures 70; drama 301; dream life 30; expression 114; forms of production 152; ideas 13, 143; interpretation 107; notions 173; play 29, 253; theatre 127; work 62
Imitation 80, 94 (*See also* Copying)
Impersonation 23, 37, 76, 153
Impertinence 145 n
Improvisation 13, 19, 55, 63–66 *passim*, 74, 85, 88, 89, 115, 116, 123, 126, 148, 162, 170, 252, 257, 268, 272, 283, 287, 292, 296, 326, 333, 339, 349, 350, 352, 353; **81 (Pl. 6)**; **360 (Pl. 39)**
  examples of 176, 177, 179, 180, 181, 185, 195, 198, 199, 200, 202, 206, 208, 212, 214, 215, 222, 224, 230, 233, 236, 238, 239, 240; first most important 256; flow of dialogue 55; ideas game and 145; mental freedom by 179; movement in 195; over-dominated 176; play-writing and 81, 347; repeating of 56; script plays and 155; sound and 169; to swing 124
Improvised, dance 61–63, 87 n, 90, 123, 147, 232, 292; **Pl. 23**; dialogue 220; music (piano) 61, 169, 189; play 272; speech 150, 170, 320; stories 138
Impudence 98, 345
Inca art 314
Infectious diseases 332
Inflow 58, 74, 76, 93, 98, 99, 106, 142, 152, 274, 327, 346, 349
  definition of 13; and outflow 54–55
Influence 20, 37, 71, 72
  of adult attitude 52; American 326; of child drama on the child 123–127; of films 322; of lighting 41; of the stage 41, 151
Inner, clarity 57; condition 55; creation 305, 338; instinct 72; loneliness 32 n; **self** 40, 67, **71**

Inspiration 45, 114, 257
Instinct 33, 110, 111
  destructive 22; of maternity and paternity
  32
Institute of Pastoral Psychology 117
Integration, and equidistance 148; personal
  and group 61; of self with others 44, 50,
  53; of sound and body 166
Intellect 94, 101, 126, 291
Intellectual, expression 163; interest 127; joys
  52, 79; showing off 96–97
Interference 32, 133 (See also Interruption)
Intermediate personality 53
Interpretation 39, 181, 194, 204, 261
Interruption 28, 29, 75, 94, 146, 148, 153, 170,
  177, 180, 185, 249, 299, 344
In-the-round 48, 70, 237, 280, 348
  definition of 13 (See also Acting-in-the-
  round)
Intimacy of film 328, 331, 348, 362
Intimate theatre group 92, 272; 89 (Pl. 8);
  297 (Pl. 36)
Introspection 32 n
Inventiveness 315
Investigation 22, 28, 133, 335
Italian theatre 79, 239
Italy 89

                    J

Jabber-talk 95, 101, 164, 166, 170
Japan 88
Japanese theatre 88, 314
Jazz 88, 89, 125, 256–258, 259
Jibberish 93, 133
Jitter-bugging 123
Jive 123
Journey 42–43, 50, 60, 84, 85, 88, 91, 92, 124,
  125, 140, 174, 317, 318, 330
Joy 13, 24, 27, 30, 48, 54, 93, 95, 97, 101, 107,
  131, 137, 138, 153, 181, 211, 278, 289,
  311, 312, 321, 324, 339, 346
  in acting-in-the-round 126; aesthetic 31;
  basis of child drama 206; in creation 103;
  in doing wrong 74; of dramatic play 49;
  and higher levels 60; in learning 76;
  nurturing 170; personal 33; and running
  play 63; sharing 77; in sound 93, 163,
  164, 166; in speech 170; in time beat,
  rhythm and climax 53; in work 12
Joyous outburst 98, 204
Judgement 37 n, 41, 256, 322, 357
  adult 344; early expression of 20; with
  dawn of seriousness 51
Jung C 118
  collective unconscious 26, 48; and shapes
  in dramatic play 50

Jungian psychologists 104
Juniors 265, 268 n, 273 (See also School,
  junior; School, primary)
Justice 21, 31, 117, 332, 338, 344
Just Vengeance, The 91, 214
Juvenile delinquency 85

                    K

Knowledge 42, 44, 52, 54, 58, 70, 76, 98, 112,
  127, 159, 178, 344, 356, 359
  capacity to absorb 152; of child needs 269;
  of drama 271; of dramatic art 157; in-
  flow of 142; of lights, etc. 155; of right
  and wrong 172; technical 127; theatre
  283; unconscious 28

                    L

"Land" The 55–56, 82, 101, 104, 267, 276,
  287, 296, 353
Language 94, 115, 326, 341
  beginnings of appreciation 22; child's first
  approach to 93; after dawn of seriousness 51; developing in Junior School 146;
  development through play 35; flow of
  from sound use 40; gagging of 41; of
  gesture 339; of movement 39, 167;
  musical approach to 170; and showing
  off 99; strong 121; and playwriting 66
Language flow 136, 139, 143, 146, 149, 150,
  215, 221, 224, 225, 237, 245, 247, 283,
  320, 347, 348, 362 n
  beginnings of 63; definition of 13; examples
  of 75–76, 85, 93–104, 100–104, 163–175,
  171–175
Language of music 96, 99, 132, 144, 165
Laziness 38, 56, 58, 104, 164, 273, 320, 339,
  353, 363
Leader 32 n, 125, 292, 354
  and bossiness 153; club 123; discussion 25;
  in dramatic play 51; natural 161; unbalanced type of 110
Leadership 32 n, 35, 147, 189, 340
Leading away 152, 170, 318, 326
Learning, basis for 12; behaviour of people
  and races 159; capacity for 74; find own
  method of 109; foundation of 177; frame
  of mind for 106; opportunity for 290;
  pleasure in 76, 141; to walk 21
Legal, atmosphere 343; framework 73, 74,
  326; opportunity 21; outbursts 100; outlet 106, 150; surroundings 56, 146
Leisure 31, 76
Levels 68, 87, 126, 329 (See also Higher
  levels)

Liberty 114, 141, 252, 257

Licence 132, 141, 252, 257

Lie-legends 54, 146

Life experience 30, 33, 66, 70
    adventures into 315; and shapes in dramatic play 50; sharing with company 52; pre-experience of 107, 159

Life occupation 35

Life situation 23, 32

Life trial 77, 141, 153, 317

Lights 41, 82, 126, 155, 261, 262, 292

Lines of sight 71, 78, 154, 159, 317

Listening 34, 63, 170, 202, 203, 341

Literature 22, 79, 81, 82, 94, 107, 114, 126, 146, 156, 158, 170, 239, 240, 341, 348

Little theatre groups 291

Local drama committees 291, 355

Local place-names 34, 97

Logic 12, 21, 22, 51, 74, 96, 132, 174, 209, 223, 252

Love 13, 23 n², 32, 33, 37, 38, 44, 56, 83, 106, 107, 136, 323, 344

Love of sound 40, 94, 139, 165, 280, 341

Loyalties 125
    in gang 56; training in 76

M

Make-up 64–65, 78, 85, 148, 154, 212, 305–314, 306, 308, 313, 324, 326

Maladjusted children 121

Malvern Festival 91

Manners 81, 107, 124, 153, 238, 321, 347, 359
    training in 54, 76, 157

Margaret Morris Movement 121

Marvellous History of St. Bernard, The 91, 214

Masks 65, 78, 85, 88, 90, 148, 253, 273, 285, 286, 295, 296, 305–314, 340, 360; 304 (Pl. 37); 305 (Pl. 38); Pl. 41

Mastery of the body 36, 41, 60, 65

Materialism 40–41, 75, 338, 354

Mathematics 42, 258, 359

Mechanics of writing 66

Mediaeval central stage 60, 72, 87, 127, 140

Medical psychologist 117

Medical support 116–122

Mental, absorption 148; activity 112; agitation 66; associations 306; attitude 309, 318; block 116, 164; changes 34; concentration 227; defect 119; development 91; energy 109; freedom 179; health 121; hesitation 41; ill-health 119; indigestion 39; laziness 104; liveliness 113; process 329; relaxation 152, 323; standard 49 n; suggestion 328; vision 153

Mentally retarded girls 115

Mime 86, 90, 116, 121, 123, 145, 178, 190, 197, 200–201, 204, 205, 209, 210, 215, 216, 235, 244, 249, 262, 269, 274, 288, 327, 399

Mind, broadening of the 80, 159

Modelling 57

Model theatres 35

Modern dance 79, 123, 155, 334; 81 (Pl. 6)

Modern floor shows 88

Monuments 33, 34, 60, 67, 97, 134, 274, 206
    definition of 32

Mood 20, 23 n², 39, 47 n, 61, 63, 72, 79, 132, 137, 181, 182, 202, 204, 238, 250, 251, 257, 282, 283, 337, 341

Moral, awareness 316; behaviour 331; content of films 322, 325, 326, 331; decisions 125; discernment 125; judgement 331; responsibility of 51, 80, 107; standard 113

Morality 332

Morris dance 86

Movement 12, 27, 34, 40, 42, 45, 53, 70, 71, 72, 80, 86–87, 106, 114, 123, 125, 137, 139, 156, 232, 243, 247, 261, 283, 286, 287, 314, 318, 326, 329, 334, 339, 341, 343, 359
    of Christmas story 50; in classroom 140; 184 (Pl. 13); Pl. 14; climax in 282; dramatised to music 182; and dressing; up 62, 64, 285; early creative 20-economy of 158; elastic in 276; graceful 143, 153; hand and arm 57; improvised 195; language of 39; like speech 166; and masks 311–312; in personal play 29; and properties 49; rhythm of 133; sincerity of 219; street play 46

Music 20, 23 n², 27, 28, 34, 35, 61, 62, 63, 97, 114, 115, 122, 124, 132, 138, 143, 166, 181, 201, 202, 243, 261, 262, 274, 295, 300, 318; Pl. 15
    beginnings of appreciation of 22; "canned" 324; language of 88, 93, 96, 133; play to background of 246–258; and running play 46, 47, 64; and sounds 94, 169; speech through 147, 165; as stimulation 348; and stylised fight scenes 80; thoughtful 204; words through 219

N

Narrator 149, 209, 218, 220–221, 277, 232, 258, 260, 263, 279, 280, 285

National Advisory Committee on Drama in Education 290

National Association for Mental Health 119

National Association of Girls' Clubs and Mixed Clubs 158 n

National Under-Fourteens Council 243
"Near-finish" 29, 42, 45, 55, 101, 111, 133, 134, 146, 153, 164, 168
Negro music 88
Nervous children 111, 121
Neurosis, and family atmosphere 21 n; prevention of 122; and speed anxiety 164
Neurotic illnesses 122
"Night", the 127–128
Nightmare 74, 116, 134, 343
Noah (Obey) 236
No audience play centre 243
Noise 35, 80, 94, 97, 98, 142, 164, 197, 236, 343, 345
Noises 59, 61, 62, 134, 137, 138, 140, 166, 167–168, 169, 214, 231, 244, 277, 278, 333, 339, 346
Non-competitive festivals 290, 291, 348, 352 (*See also* Festivals and Competitive festivals)
Nō plays 88
Nurturing 19, 40, 45, 66, 109, 122, 140, 162, 163, 170, 243, 308, 326, 344

O

Obedience 29, 55, 61, 98, 99, 106, 143, 148, 167, 170, 206, 258, 269, 340
Observation 19–20, 26, 35, 37, 53, 54, 58, 116, 122, 188, 251, 252, 270, 271, 312, 332, 354, 358, 361
Occupational therapy 117, 118
Only child 32 n, 43
Other Theatre, the 91
Outbursts 27, 124, 148, 249, 331
    emotional 234; of speech 40, 81, 94, 97, 100, 170, 268; spontaneous 346; street gang 81
Outflow 14, 58, 74, 76, 93, 98, 99, 106, 152, 182, 207, 208, 252, 274, 327, 346, 349
    definition of 13; and inflow 54
Outlet 110, 326
Out of school 77, 120, 149, 155, 242–264, 297, 350

P

Pageantry 86, 87, 152, 183, 214, 286
Painting 25, 55 n, 57, 58, 66–70 *passim*, 91, 107, 117, 122, 151, 180, 210, 253, 307, 311, 313, 320, 345, 357
    child 270; closely associated with drama 49; improvement of 193; of faces 148; picture in make-up 306; and spilt food 132; understanding of 108
Parents 19, 33, 37, 150, 242, 266, 288, 326, 346, 362

Parents' associations 346
Participation 145, 148, 199, 227, 276, 316
    audience 57, 59–60
Patience 19, 22, 35, 52, 54, 141, 315
Patient 116, 117, 118, 122, 343
Pattern 22, 23, 42, 112, 132, 133, 204, 232, 233, 260, 307, 312, 313, 319, 359
    in dancing 181; on floor space 202, 218; group 268; make-up 208; mask 65; work 107
Pear Tree Players 90, 268, 273, 291–293, 331, 351, 358
"Peep-Bo" 24, 46, 133–134, 318, 328
Percussion 27, 80, 87, 88, 188, 256, 319, 341
Percussion bands 153, 165, 319
Performing in the round 48
Peripatetic teachers 349
Personal, acting 320; action 33; activity 56; control 35, 106, 157; creation 44; credit 108; development 32, 41, 48, 49, 52, 68, 76, 78, 106, 115, 116, 120, 121, 162; experience 47, 106, 136, 273, 352; expression 61, 123; fears 315; fulfilment 65; growth 26; identification 78; integration 61; mastery 67; movement 49; music 100; opinion 77; organising 75; praise 290; problems 81; relationships 76, 134, 259; remarks 328; responsibility in behaviour 142, 345; rhythm 31, 41, 42, 48, 106, 119, 164; secret 38; stability 358; trial 164; viewpoints 47
Personal play 32, 41–43 *passim*, 59, 67, 76, 106, 136, 159, 273, 274, 337, 338, 363
    definition of 29; developments from 29–30, 35–36; and drama projects 153; and films 329; and masks and make-up 308–313; and movement language 167; and puppets 316–320; and running play 47
Perspective 50, 58, 66, 67, 71, 72, 91, 274, 306
Perspective theatre 67, 71, 152, 230, 317, 320
"Pete's kitchen" 293–297, 301
Philosophy, foreign 359; philosophic creation 63; philosophic quality 13; philosophic references in language 51; philosophic things said 170; philosophical content in dialogue 55
Piano 147, 166, 169, 181, 182, 189, 257, 339
Pictures, first signs of perspective in 49, 50; same shapes and signs as in play 50
Pinocchio 272 n
Plato 121
Play 12, 19, 24 n, 29–32, 33, 34, 35, 39, 106–108
    acting as work or 299; audience 59; basis of everything 360; best on floor space 44; child works hardest at 76; class control

179; criticism 58; definition of 42; deteriorates with audience 49; development to dramatic play 36; evidence of abandoned things 23; films 325, 332; fully conscious recognition as drama 37; gangs 55; general approach to 120; growing creation of speech 93; Hinterland activity 82; inborn part of young life 41; indistinguishable from work 109; inflow 98; joining in 273; knowledge of right and wrong showing in 172; language flow 163; link after dawn of seriousness 51; and masks 312; more obviously drama 130; music background to 246–258; normal children 338; not end of theatre 56; participation 60; playwriting 65, 66; playing out 70, 74; puppets 319; remarks and behaviour 38; rostrum blocks 60; same shapes and signs as in pictures 50; sharing space 43; showing off 99; simple elements of life in 47; and skill 67; special room for 134; and speech 40, 63; spontaneous 45; stimulated by adult 134; and suggestions 140; and television 362; themes in 152; as work 23; with water 133; without words 142 (See also Personal play and Projected play)

Play centres 37, 149, 242–3, 301
Playground 45, 98, 212, 229, 326, 350
Playing-out 38, 70, 73, 74, 77, 82, 116, 119–122, 170, 236, 280, 326, 327, 332; **224 (Pl. 19)**
Playing shape 155
Playing space 60, 211, 276, 277, 358
Play reading 155, 158
Plays 62, 116
  adults performing to children 265; created group 126; from play to a play 339; made up by teacher 139; not write for children 150; one-act 156; books 181; put on by children 143; second-rate funny 153
Play to music background 248–258
Play trial 23, 38, 46, 53, 77
Play-writing 107, 266, 307, 345
  beginnings of 65–66; polished improvisations and 81–83
Pleasure 27, 64, 69, 93, 124, 141, 167, 269
  aesthetic and informed 19; of attainment 94; of hating 38; in learning 76
Plot 76, 327
Poetic, attempts 94; creations 63; expression 362; flow 51, 126; imagination 34; language flow 172; quality 13
Poetry 75, 122, 361
  formal 165; in outflow 252
Point of view 21–22, 34, 39, 52, 61, 64, 98, 132, 164

Polished improvisation 56, 66, 81–83, 89, 96, 115, 139, 143, 148, 153, 169, 217, 224, 225, 230, 339, 347
Polished production 199
Power instinct 23, 118
Practice, and ability to create 246; in adaptation to new environment 157; in movement 106; in reading 327; in speech 63, 81, 97, 106, 112, 150, 341, 342, 344, 346; in using space 239; in writing 81
Pre-experience, of life experiences 107
Prep 239
Preparation for life after school 77–78, 156–157, 159–162, 338, 356
Prevention 21 n, 104, 150, 360
  drama 119; of neurosis 122, 132
Preventive 343
Preventive education 327
Primitive, art 26; communities 25, 27, 28, 38, 71; tribe 70, 71
Processions 84, 201, 213, 353
Production 31, 35, 70, 107, 123, 126, 156, 157, 162, 261, 281, 290, 337
Professionals 266, 267, 271, 322, 355, 356
Professional stage 107, 127, 150, 237
Project 57 n, 76, 115, 153, 226–230; **232 (Pl. 21); Pl. 22**
Projected play 33, 38, 41–43 passim, 47 n, 67, 76, 106, 159, 273, 274, 337
  definition of 29; developments from 29–30, 35–36; and drama projects 153; and films 328–329; and masks and make-up 308–313; and puppets 315–319
Projecting ideas 320
Projecting personality 161
Projection, into audience 272; into auditorium 336; balance with self 35; mental 30; from proscenium 274; in school theatre 91; square 126
Properties 23, 33, 34, 40, 42, 49, 53, 75, 86, 90, 106, 134, 136, 137, 148, 166, 187, 223, 250, 255, 287, 296, 306, 308, 309, 353
Proscenium, arch 67, 69, 71, 144, 238, 292, 317, 362; consciousness 71, 317; form 126, 265, 266, 274, 304, 316, 347; production 217, 287, 301; puppetry 320, 321; shape 148; stage 69, 71, 72, 127, 151, 258, 261, 263, 264
Psychic trauma 118
Psycho-drama 116
Psychological, balance 114; theory 335; value 353
Psychologists, educational 117
Psychology, use of drama in 26, 117–118
Psychotherapist 117
Psychotherapy, use of drama in 118–119

Puberty 28, 62, 67, 71, 72, 73, 78, 274, 332, 340, 345
Punctuation 66, 165
Puppets 35, 315–321
Puppet stages 315

Q

Questions 51, 54 (*See also* chapter on Questions)
Quietness 24 n, 35, 143, 148, 168, 308, 343, 346

R

Radio 66, 70, 362, 363
Rate of progress 48
Reading 35, 78, 125, 126, 153, 236, 237, 327
Real children's theatre 293 (*See also* "Pete's kitchen")
Realism 62, 70, 79, 80, 310
Realistic play 29
Reality 14, 29, 30, 39, 42, 65, 80, 84, 91, 101, 104, 136, 172, 174, 252, 263, 313, 323, 325
Recluse tendencies 32 n
Recognition of good and evil 48
Reductive analysis and techniques 118
Relationship between actor and audience 25
Relaxation 42, 115, 183, 189, 339, 362
Release 116, 117, 126, 315
Religion 118, 121, 170
Remarks 38, 59, 99, 328
Remedial drama 125
Repetition 27, 42, 48, 56, 85, 89, 93, 101, 132, 219, 255, 353
Repressions 112
Research 113, 335
Results 56, 76, 118, 126, 143
Rhyme 361, 362
Rhythm 20 n, 22, 30, 42, 46, 47, 53, 62, 63, 64, 93, 94, 102, 107, 121, 139, 146, 170, 172, 181, 188, 214, 233, 286, 318, 348
agreement in 213; baby's speech trials 132; distinction from time beat 27–29; in speech 164–165
Rhythmic development 106
Ridicule 31, 77, 81, 99
Ring shape 25, 36, 49, 68, 70, 87, 126, 183, 186, 187, 190, 204, 208, 254
Ritual 47 n, 121
Road safety 102
Roller skating 47 n
Roots 25, 71, 126
Rostrum blocks 60–61, 64, 71, 87, 134, 139, 140, 147, 149, 268, 334; **65 (Pl. 4)**; **193 (Pl. 18)**
Rostrums 60–61, 64, 91, 126, 279; **184 (Pl. 13)**
Rudeness 45, 52, 77

Running 35, 319
Running commentary 35, 340
Running play 138, 147, 183, 184, 189, 191, 195, 206, 212, 344; **64 (Pl. 3)**; **253 (Pl. 28)**
definition of 13; bud of 49; later stage 46–47, 63–64
Running play of the street 46, 47

S

Safety valve 73
Save the Children Fund 243 n
Scandinavia 27
Scene changing, speed in 154
Scene painting 82
Scenery 155, 162, 276, 305
Scene shifters 237
Scholastic attainment 55, 106, 206, 269, 360
School—General 37, 44, 45, 61, 63, 64, 67, 69, 76, 85, 94, 100, 106, 110, 112, 113, 118, 122, 123, 126, 134, 142, 171, 253, 258, 287, 318, 338, 341
School—Infants 53, 55, 62, 63, 87, 136–140, 141, 143, 176–185, 243, 284, 341
dawn of seriousness 51; developments from 146–149; dramatic play and bumping 43; effects of lighting, stages and scripts 41; language flow in 165–170; ring in 49; running play 57
School—Junior 185–215, 243, 287, 305, 312, 313, 320, 338, 345
and stages 55, 63, 64; language flow 66, 67, 69, 70, 87, 91, 115, 141–180, 151, 165, 167, 170–171
School—Nursery 135, 163, 165, 167–170
School—Primary 113, 141–150, 185–215, 243, 287, 305, 312, 313, 345
School—Secondary Grammar 55 n, 149, 238–240
School—Secondary Modern 67, 149, 151–162, 215–240, 342, 345
School—Senior 67, 87, 91, 92, 116, 149, 151–162, 340
School—Special 117
School-leaving age 123
School play 120, 230
School practice 308
School stages 64 n
Script plays 41, 69, 78–79, 115, 123, 126, 139, 141, 152, 153, 155, 156, 162, 216, 219, 231, 236, 237, 239, 283, 296, 301, 321, 338, 342, 343, 345, 351, 353, 361
Scripture 150
Secrecy 82, 106
Self-centred preoccupations 112
Self-confidence 115, 157, 158

Self-conscious creation 99
Self-consciousness 114, 131, 152, 166, 190,
    219, 237, 245, 311, 340, 346, 351, 361
Self-control 157
Self-defence 32, 174
Self-discipline 252, 354
Self-experience 47
Self-identification 325, 328, 329
Selfish Giant, The 232
Self-protection 20
Senior boys 111
Senior girls 287, 289
Senior mixed 288
Senses 12, 26, 47 n
Sense trials 53, 337
Sensitivity 51, 68, 98, 112, 185, 190, 193, 259,
    339
Service of youth 359
Shakespeare 327, 342–343
Shakespearean theatre 91, 221
Shapes 36, 55, 59, 67, 68, 76, 80, 91, 112, 138,
    140, 148, 151, 155, 197, 262, 273, 331,
    343, 345
    acting 47–49, 266; examples that appear in
    play and pictures 50; grouping 139;
    horse-shoe 301; joy in 126; presentation
    329; production 281; repetitive 45;
    rostrum blocks 60; running play 47, 64;
    tongue 70–72; understanding 193;
    variety of 126; wrong, and effects 44
Shared creation 97, 145, 156
Shared experiences 97, 140, 201, 267
Shared intent 53
Shared sympathy 328
Sharing 27, 28, 32, 32 n, 38, 44, 61, 82, 83, 87,
    92, 114, 132, 133–134
    discovery with an adult 45; experiences 24,
    25, 26; joys 131, 164, 166; life experiences
    52; pleasures of attainment 94; space 43–
    44; trials and mastery 77
Shouting 35, 277
Showing off 24, 25, 28, 39, 40, 49, 57, 58, 64,
    96, 99, 126, 133, 134, 136, 149, 159, 216,
    265, 277, 290, 296, 305, 316, 329, 330,
    351, 355
Shyness 53, 69, 73, 78, 80, 134, 207, 311, 315,
    341, 354, 360, 361
Sideways thresh 21, 23 n², 27, 34, 39, 132, 167
Simplicity 31, 40, 75, 307
Sincerity 40, 45, 58, 62, 79, 86, 89, 107, 126–
    127, 136, 139, 143, 147, 156, 162, 199,
    201, 211, 219, 233, 234, 248, 277, 282,
    343, 351
    definition of 14; developed from personal
    play 36
Singing 35, 221, 319
Skill 19, 51, 60, 67–68

Slang 96–97
Slap-stick 87
Sleep 29, 104
"Slow developer", definition of 31; after
    dawn of seriousness 51
Social, adjustment 21, 134; awareness 12,
    32–35, 53; background 359; behaviour
    152; conditions 33; consciousness 31;
    effect 109; ethics 120; function 110, 230;
    gathering 324; graces 32, 123, 347; gulf
    in ages 135; learning 34; living 33; moral
    questions 109; moral values 158; obliga-
    tions 32; practice 32 n; problems 81;
    situations 34; standards 32; studies 158;
    training 81; views 359
Society 61, 71, 76, 105, 106, 120, 122
Society for Education in Art 357
Sound 12, 20, 27, 33, 34, 66, 87, 88, 96, 106,
    133, 137, 139, 143, 146, 164, 202, 214,
    243, 262, 295, 318, 319, 320, 338, 341,
    353
    and audience participation 59; background
    of 286; beauty of 63; and communication
    94; dancing to 188; examples of use of
    167–171; of feet 62, 64; helps use of
    floor space 49; hot swing 124; importance
    of in play 35; and improvised dance 61;
    inspiration of 257; joy in 98; love of 40,
    94, 139, 165, 280, 341; **136 (Pl. 9)**; mood
    in 283; sensitive to 193; stimulation of
    40, 166; and toys 165; vocal attempts 93
Sound effects 88, 90, 215, 223
Sound experiences 50
Sound talk 64
Sound trials 97, 99
Sound value 23 n², 95
Space 50, 53, 59, 60, 62, 64, 66, 69, 72, 79, 80,
    137, 139, 143, 148, 155, 159, 169, 181,
    208, 227, 232, 236, 239, 258, 267, 279,
    301, 317, 318, 320, 342, 343, 351
    discovery and use of 26, 42–46
Space relationships 62, 66, 71, 126, 137
Spain 27, 62, 188
Speaking through music 63, 169
Specialist, music 178, 257; modern dance 334;
    place of 349
Speech 12, 35, 45, 57, 79, 106, 112, 126, 133,
    137, 139, 140, 156, 167, 181, 199, 205,
    215, 219, 243, 261, 262, 333, 339, 361
    appreciation of 146; beginnings of language
    flow 63; choral 165, 212, 284, 361–362;
    climax in 282; control 143, 180; de-
    velopment of 39–40; dialects 100; early
    creative 20; growth of with sound 169;
    imaginative expression through 114;
    improvement in 157; and inflow 98; and
    love of sound 94; and masks 296, 311;

message of the soul 99; and music 165; outbursts of 40, 81, 94, 97, 100, 170, 268; practice in 63, 81, 97, 106, 112, 150, 341, 342, 344, 346; and properties 136; and puppets 315; release of 163; spontaneous 152; therapy 349; training 253; trials 100, 133–134, 166

Speed, anxieties 30, 31, 164; in creation 154; in stage management 237

Spelling 66, 147

Spiral 71, 137, 143, 164; **48 (Pl. 1)**
shape of happy entry 49; in painting 49 n; in play and pictures 50

Spiral entry 49, 56, 272; **48 (Pl. 1); 136 (Pl. 9); 137 (Pl. 10)**

Spiritual, awareness 62; beauties 68; experiences 106; play 195; quality 50, 88; standard 131

Spontaneity 27, 88, 89, 110

Spontaneous, delight 110; imagination 291; outbursts of language 170; play 121, 173, 341; productions 121; speech 152

S-shape, in play and pictures 50; in running play 64

Stability 25, 71, 97, 125

Stage curtains 82, 151, 219, 237

Stage entry and exit 159

Stage, management 154; performance 315; presentations 162; production 315

Stages 216, 239, 296, 301, 318, 322, 334, 345, 351
approach towards 152; and audience participation 59; effect in Infant schools 41, 139; experimental 126; first use of 70–73; flexible 256; and floor 221; formal 87; and hinterland activity 82; influence in Junior schools 151; more use of at thirteen years 153–154; not confine to 155; not in Junior school 147; and running play 64; and script plays 78–79; and showing off 58; as symbolic higher level 206; tricks 14, 323

Stammering 31, 116, 164

Starting things up 141, 144–146, 181, 246

Stimulation 39, 61, 63, 114, 140, 180, 353
by adult 133, 244, 273, 301; of audience 292; and child art 148; of discussion 120 n; fashion of 41; and festivals 290–291; free dramatic play as 269; by gramophone 169; by ideas game 145; of the imagination 113; by make-up 313; by music 348; by noises 137; by objects 27; of poetic language flow 172; by properties 40; by puppets 315; by sound 166; by stories 338; successful example of 177; by suggestions 360; by teacher 343

Stories 49, 66, 74, 76, 82, 115, 142, 180, 319
acting 138; adventure 327; Bible 230; built by children 53; creation of 320; detective 110; film 330; gangster 152; ideas for 298; and play-writing 347; simple 182; stimulate play 338; by teacher and children 169; telling 204; told by children 146; told by teacher 145; with sound 167; writing of 147

Story form 45, 106

Story play 49

Story-teller 274

Story themes 48

Street play 45, 46, 56, 64, 81, 326

Streets 45, 98, 100

Study, drama as a means of 134, 152, 156–159; distaste for 164

Subjects (other) 69, 73, 99, 107, 108, 142, 157, 357

Substantives 95–96

Swing 124, 125, 243

Symbolic meaning, and masks 307

Symbols 26, 72
in child behaviour 48; common to art and drama 138; of home and preservation 97; and Jung 104; recurring 49–51; for safety 124; of the unconscious 117; unconscious dream 362

Sympathy 86–87, 102, 106, 117, 122, 123, 132, 140, 146, 151, 163, 326, 328, 339, 344

Symphonic production 27, 31, 43, 107, 164, 184, 213

T

Task 39, 54, 65, 117, 150, 162, 163, 170, 246

Taste 64, 106, 127, 154, 170, 256, 338, 341, 360, 361

Teacher 13, 19, 25, 44, 50, 54–59 *passim*, 62, 64, 69, 70, 82, 89, 90, 99, 105, 111, 115, 117, 137, 140, 142, 145, 150, 158, 159, 163, 167, 177, 182, 183, 189, 197, 215, 221, 238, 266, 269, 286, 287, 291, 307, 311–314, 317–322, 326, 338, 362
the child as 297–301

Teacher-Actors 272

Teacher-Pupil relationship 112, 181, 182, 184–185

Team 31, 107

Team dynamic 33

Team spirit 31, 76, 361

Team work 112, 290

Technical, achievement 305; discipline 358; excellence 80; knowledge 127; training 356

Technique 72, 80, 159, 282–284
Television 362–363
Tests 55 n, 76
Theatre 60 n, 64, 72, 91, 113, 128, 132, 136, 147, 161, 165, 211, 214, 230, 233, 258, 270, 305, 313, 322, 324, 331, 334, 337, 338, 347
  arena 13, 48, 72, 126, 127, 258–264, 265, 275, 277, 280, 283, 292, 301, 304, 348, 350, 351, 358, 359
  centre 291
  lovers 158, 324
Theatre News Letter 290 n, 291 n
Theatre News Service 112, 113
Theatre—proscenium 31, 58, 59, 84, 140, 159, 274, 284, 327, 329, 330, 335, 351, 359
  as main wrong shape experience 44; approach to 66–68; at fifteen years 162; dramatic play unlike 48; effect on dramatic play 45; and make-up 65; not end of play 56; not in Junior school 144; and running play 64
Theatrical experience 47, 79, 139
Therapy 104, 116, 117, 122, 343, 349, 360
Third dimension, first appreciation of 50
Three-dimensional drama 91
Thrift 75, 106
Tidiness 22 n, 33, 75, 125
Time 20, 27, 44, 63
Time beat 20, 20 n, 21, 23 n^2, 27–29, 34, 42, 46, 53, 61, 88, 124, 137, 139, 146, 147, 164–165, 166, 170, 251, 280, 318, 319
Timing 72, 107, 213, 277
Times of importance 21 n, 132
Time-table 53, 75, 134, 153
Tone of voice 98, 132, 144, 312
Tongue shape 71, 72, 126, 152, 155, 345; **88 (Pl. 7); Pl. 46**
Town children 70, 299
Toys 23, 39, 134, 165, 315, 321
Training 265, 279, 291, 363
  for arena theatre 13, 126; college 338; in common sense 75; course 282–284; of the emotions 73–75; formal speech- 100; influence of 123; in listening 202; in loyalty and good manners 76; by noises 168; pre-leaving 157; results of in drama 125; in technique 127
Treasures 30, 32, 33, 34, 37, 38, 39, 48, 106, 125, 133, 134, 136, 165, 174, 315, 319, 338
  definition of 23 n
Tribal dance 140
Trophies 290
Trust 12, 32 n, 52, 98, 106, 133, 141, 142, 185
Truth about children's theatre, 280; facing the 73; perception of 39, 65

U

Unbalanced character 107
Understanding 19, 22, 52, 66, 79, 106, 118, 126, 141, 142, 163, 166, 167, 344

V

Value 21, 22, 37 n, 73, 74, 85, 174
  of child drama 105–122; child 132, 161, 321; social and moral 158
Violence 74, 214, 235, 342
Violent, action 121; emotions 106; outbursts 331; scenes 322; stories 325; themes 315
Vitality 56, 126, 232
Vocabulary 12, 66, 70, 75, 95, 101, 164
Voice 98, 99, 199
Vowels 93, 137, 165, 166, 341

W

Walking 21, 24, 25, 30, 42, 47, 134
Watching 273, 288
  learning by 59, 238; effect of 250
Weapons (imagined) 80, 85, 124, 153, 236, 327, 361
Wendy House 309
West Country Children's Theatre Company 256, 268, 269
Wisdom 80, 92, 107, 142, 314
Wit 55, 75, 170, 216
Women's Institutes 358
Woodwork 238
Words 45, 56, 74, 94, 95, 99, 118, 219, 237, 280, 344
  and action 13, 39–42; attack on 156, 165; choice of 333; factor against dramatic play 44; flow of 169; grew out of sound 93; imaginary, descriptive and musical 95; meaning of 133; through music 63; musical approach to 171; not pleasing 146; play without 142; stimulated by music 348; understood 126; use of children's own 145
Work 42, 45
  attitude to 115; sudden change of 69; as play 23, 109, 299
Work of art 19, 66, 224
Writing 81, 107
  play 65–66; a play 307; stories 147
Written play 66, 81, 216, 347

Y

Young Vic Company 268
Youth 52, 83, 116
Youth clubs 123–127, 152, 156–159, 288–264, 292, 350, 352, 358

Z

Zigzag, in play and pictures 50

INDEX OF NAMES

Adler 23

Bantock, Sir Granville 62
Bell, Clive 68
Biggar, Dr. Jean 26
Browne, E. Martin 62
Burns, Dr. C. L. C. 121
Burt, Prof. Sir Cyril 119, 120, 154 n

Chancerel, M. 90
Cizek, Prof. 108, 297, 357
Clarke, Egerton 75

Edmunds, Dr. Christopher 227
Eliot, T. S. 103, 362
English, John 92

Fernald, John 72 n
Fogerty, Elsie 27
Freud, S. 118
Froebel 109
Fry, Margery 120

Gibran, Kahlil 83
Gill, Eric 19
Gray, Terence 90, 348
Gwynne, M. B. 112

Hardwicke, Sir Cedric 311 n
Haskell, Arnold 156
Helpmann, Robert 314
Higham, M. B. 85

I-Kher-Nefert 84–85, 174

Jenkins, Warren 272 n
Jung, C. 26

Kraemer, W. P. 117–118, 121–122

Langdon, E. M. 33, 119
Littlewood, S. R. 270

MacCalman, Prof. 119
Marshall, Norman 91
Miller, Paul Edouard 89

Newton, Robert G. 90
Nicoll, Prof. Allardyce 92
Nunn, Sir Percy 109

O'Shaughnessy, Arthur 103

Parsons, Charles S. 311 n

Rapaport, Barbara 108
Read, Sir Herbert 122
Richardson, Marion 108
Rushforth, Dr. Winifred 21 n
Russell, Bertrand 109–111

Sayers, Dorothy 91, 214
Spengler, Sir Oswald 50
Stanislavsky, C. 26, 89
Stern, William 26

Travers, Prof. Morris W. 120

Viola, Dr. W. 26, 50, 108, 357

Way, Brian 7, 256
Wilde, Oscar 232
Wilder, Thornton 91
Wilenski, R. H. 19
Williams, Dr. G. Scott 120